Certified Information Systems Auditor® (CISA®) Cert Guide

Michael Gregg

Rob Johnson

800 East 96th Street
Indianapolis, Indiana 46240 USA

Certified Information Systems Auditor® (CISA®) Cert Guide

ISBN-13: 978-0-7897-5844-6

ISBN-10: 0-7897-5844-X

Library of Congress Control Number: 2017950730

Printed in the United States of America

1   17

Trademarks

Warning and Disclaimer

Special Sales

For information about buying this title in bulk quantities, or for special sales opportunities (which may include electronic versions; custom cover designs; and content particular to your business, training goals, marketing focus, or branding interests), please contact our corporate sales department at corpsales@pearsoned.com or (800) 382-3419.

For government sales inquiries, please contact governmentsales@pearsoned.com.

For questions about sales outside the U.S., please contact intlcs@pearson.com.

Editor-in-Chief
Mark Taub

Product Line Manager
Brett Bartow

Acquisitions Editor
Michelle Newcomb

Development Editor
Ellie C. Bru

Managing Editor
Sandra Schroder

Project Editor
Mandie Frank

Copy Editor
Kitty Wilson

Indexer
Ken Johnson

Proofreader
The Wordsmithery LLC

Technical Editor
Chris Crayton

Publishing Coordinator
Vanessa Evans

Designer
Chuti Prasertsith

Compositor
Tricia Bronkella

Contents at a Glance

Table of Contents

About the Authors

Michael Gregg (CISSP, SSCP, CISA, MCSE, MCT, CTT+, A+, N+, Security+, CCNA, CASP, CISA, CISM, CEH, CHFI, and GSEC) works for a Houston, Texas–based IT security consulting firm.

Michael is responsible for working with organizations to develop cost-effective and innovative technology solutions to security issues and for evaluating the security of emerging technologies. He has more than 20 years of experience in the IT field and holds two associate's degrees, a bachelor's degree, and a master's degree. In addition to co-authoring the first, second, and third editions of *Security Administrator Street Smarts*, Michael has written or co-authored 15 other books, including *The Network Security Test Lab: A Step-by-Step Guide* (Wiley, 2015); *CompTIA Security+ Rapid Review* (Microsoft, 2013); *Certified Ethical Hacker Cert Guide* (Pearson, 2017); and *CISSP Exam Cram* (Que, 2016).

Michael has been quoted in newspapers such as the *New York Times* and featured on various television and radio shows, including NPR, ABC, CBS, Fox News, CNN, and others, discussing cybersecurity and ethical hacking. He has created more than a dozen IT security training classes, and he has created and performed video instruction on many security topics, such as cybersecurity, CISSP, CASP, Security+, and others.

When not consulting, teaching, or writing, Michael enjoys 1960s muscle cars and has a slot in his garage for a new project car.

Rob Johnson (CISSP, CISA, CISM, CGEIT, and CRISC) is experienced in information risk, IT audit, privacy, and security management. He has a diverse background that includes hands-on operational experience as well as providing strategic risk assessment and support to leadership and board-level audiences.

Rob currently serves as a senior vice president and technology executive with global teams and responsibilities at Bank of America. He has held various technology and executive positions throughout his career, including chief information security officer for a global insurance company, head of IT audit for a major domestic bank, chief information security officer for a large midwestern bank, chief cybersecurity architect and product owner for a major software house where he led deployments across 15 countries, and senior partner at a consulting firm.

Rob is well known across a number of industry groups. He is a published author and frequent speaker at conferences. Rob has served on a number of ISACA global committees; for example, he was formerly the chair of the ISACA Education Committee and a member of the ISACA Assurance Committee to name a few. In addition, Rob was one of the 12 members of the prestigious ISACA COBIT 5 Task Force, which led to the creation of the COBIT 5 global standard.

Rob holds a Bachelor of Science Degree in Interdisciplinary Studies from the University of Houston. He lives a quiet life, where he enjoys his children, watches his amazing son Donald win chess tournaments, and spends time with his wonderful wife, Lin.

Dedication

In memory of Debbie Dahlin, who served as a technical editor for several of my books and fought a year-long battle against cancer. Cancer does not have a face until it's someone you know.—M.G.

To my extraordinary father, who always gives of himself to others and taught us the importance of how to live a simple life through family and country and to give of one's self.—R.J.

Acknowledgments

I would like to offer a big thank-you to Christine for her help and understanding during the long hours that a book project entails. I also want to thank my parents. A special thanks to the people of Pearson IT Certification, who helped make this project a reality.—Michael Gregg

I would like to thank Ellie Bru for her professional support in making this book happen and her keen ability to keep up with my never-ending travel schedule. She has the rare ability to track me down anywhere in the world to keep my edits on course. Thank you! I also thank Michelle and the team at Pearson IT Certification for the opportunity to make this book possible and the belief in its important contribution.—Rob Johnson

About the Technical Reviewer

Chris Crayton (MCSE) is an author, technical consultant, and trainer. He has worked as a computer technology and networking instructor, information security director, network administrator, network engineer, and PC specialist. Chris has authored several print and online books on PC repair, CompTIA A+, CompTIA Security+, and Microsoft Windows. He has also served as technical editor and content contributor on numerous technical titles for several leading publishing companies. He holds numerous industry certifications, has been recognized with many professional teaching awards, and has served as a state-level SkillsUSA competition judge.

We Want to Hear from You!

As the reader of this book, *you* are our most important critic and commentator. We value your opinion and want to know what we're doing right, what we could do better, what areas you'd like to see us publish in, and any other words of wisdom you're willing to pass our way.

We welcome your comments. You can email or write to let us know what you did or didn't like about this book—as well as what we can do to make our books better.

Please note that we cannot help you with technical problems related to the topic of this book.

When you write, please be sure to include this book's title and author as well as your name and email address. We will carefully review your comments and share them with the author and editors who worked on the book.

Email: feedback@pearsonitcertification.com

Mail: Pearson IT Certification
            ATTN: Reader Feedback
            800 East 96th Street
            Indianapolis, IN 46240 USA

Reader Services

Register your copy of *Certified Information Systems Auditor (CISA) Cert Guide* at www.pearsonitcertification.com for convenient access to downloads, updates, and corrections as they become available. To start the registration process, go to www.pearsonitcertification.com/register and log in or create an account*. Enter the product ISBN 9780789758446 and click Submit. When the process is complete, you will find any available bonus content under Registered Products.

*Be sure to check the box that you would like to hear from us to receive exclusive discounts on future editions of this product.

Introduction

The ISACA CISA exam has become the leading ethical hacking certification available today. CISA is recognized by both employers and the industry as providing candidates with a solid foundation of auditing and technical network assessment review. The CISA exam covers a broad range of IT auditing concepts to prepare candidates for roles in both audit and non-audit capacities, including IT risk management, IT compliance, and IT controls analysis.

This book offers you a one-stop shop for what you need to know to pass the CISA exam. To pass the exam, you do not have to take a class in addition to reading this book. However, depending on your personal study habits or learning style, you might benefit from buying this book *and* taking a class.

Cert Guides are meticulously crafted to give you the best possible learning experience for the particular characteristics of the technology covered and the certification exam. The instructional design implemented in the Cert Guides reflects the nature of the CISA certification exam. The Cert Guides provide you with the factual knowledge base you need for the exams and then take it to the next level with exercises and exam questions that require you to engage in the analytic thinking needed to pass the CISA exam.

ISACA recommends that a candidate for this exam have a minimum of 5 years of experience in audit and IT security. In addition, ISACA requires that candidates have that experience within the 10-year period preceding the application date for certification or within 5 years.

This book's goal is to prepare you for the CISA exam, and it reflects the vital and evolving responsibilities of IT auditors. It provides basics to get you started in the world of IT audit and prepare you for the exam. Those wanting to become experts in this field should be prepared for additional reading, training, and practical experience.

Goals and Methods

The most important and somewhat obvious goal of this book is to help you pass the CISA exam. In fact, if the primary objective of this book was different, the book's title would be misleading; however, the methods used in this book to help you pass the CISA exam are designed to also make you much more knowledgeable about how IT auditors do their job. This book and the accompanying online practice exams together have more than enough questions to help you prepare for the exam.

One key methodology used in this book is to help you discover the exam topics and tools that you need to review in more depth. The CISA exam will expect you to understand not only IT auditing concepts but common frameworks such as COBIT. This book does not try to help you pass the exam by memorization alone but helps you truly learn and understand the topics and know when specific approaches should be used. This book will help you pass the CISA exam by using the following methods:

- Helping you discover which test topics you still need to master

- Providing explanations and information to fill in your knowledge gaps

- Supplying exercises and scenarios that enhance your ability to recall and deduce the answers to test questions

- Providing practice exercises on the topics and the testing process via test questions online

Who Should Read This Book?

This book is not designed to be a general IT book or a book that teaches financial audits. This book looks specifically at how IT auditors assess networks, examine controls, and test defenses to determine their adequacy. Overall, this book is written with one goal in mind: to help you pass the exam.

So, why should you want to pass the CISA exam? Because it's one of the leading IT audit certifications. It is also featured as part of DoDD 8140, and having the certification might mean a raise, a promotion, or other recognition. It's also a chance to enhance your resume and to demonstrate that you are serious about continuing the learning process and are not content to rest on your laurels.

Strategies for Exam Preparation

Although this book is designed to prepare you to take and pass the CISA certification exam, there are no guarantees. Read this book, work through the questions and exercises, and when you feel confident, take the practice exams provided online. Your results should tell you whether you are ready for the real thing.

When taking the actual certification exam, make sure that you answer all the questions before your time limit expires. Do not spend too much time on any one question. If you are unsure about the answer to a question, answer it as best you can and then mark it for review.

Remember that the primary objective is not to pass the exam but to understand the material. When you understand the material, passing the exam should be simple.

Knowledge is similar to a pyramid in that to build upward, you need a solid foundation. This book and the CISA certification are designed to ensure that you have that solid foundation.

Regardless of the strategy you use or the background you have, the book is designed to help you get to the point where you can pass the exam in the least amount of time possible. Several book features will help you gain the confidence you need to be convinced that you know some material already and to help you know what topics you need to study more.

How This Book Is Organized

Although this book could be read cover to cover, it is designed to be flexible and allow you to easily move between chapters and sections of chapters to cover just the material that you need to work with further. Chapter 1, "The CISA Certification," provides an overview of the CISA certification and reviews some basics about exam preparation. Chapters 2 through 9 are the core chapters. If you intend to read them all, the order in the book is an excellent sequence to use.

The core chapters, Chapters 2 through 9, cover the following topics:

- **Chapter 2, "The Information Systems Audit":** This chapter discusses basic audit techniques and the skills that are required of an auditor. This chapter reviews guidance documents and auditing standards.

- **Chapter 3, "The Role of IT Governance":** This chapter discusses the basic ideas behind governance and steering committees. The chapter reviews management and control frameworks and process optimization.

- **Chapter 4, "Maintain Critical Services":** This chapter covers issues related to business continuity and disaster recovery. Maintaining critical services requires an understanding of criticality and maximum tolerable downtime.

- **Chapter 5, "Information Systems Acquisition and Development":** This chapter examines IT acquisition and the decision to build or buy. Project management and application development methodologies are discussed. Emerging technologies such as cloud computing are also covered.

- **Chapter 6, "Auditing and Understanding System Controls":** This chapter covers auditing and business controls.

- **Chapter 7, "System Maintenance and Service Management":** This chapter covers the basics of system maintenance and service management, including service management frameworks and networking infrastructure.

- **Chapter 8, "Protection of Assets":** This chapter examines the controls used to protect assets. These controls can be administrative, physical, or technical. The concept is to layer controls to provide reasonable assurance.

- **Chapter 9, "Asset Threats, Response, and Management":** This chapter discusses incident management and the response to threats from both insiders and outsiders.

How to Use This Book

This book uses several key methodologies to help you discover the exam topics on which you need more review, to help you fully understand and remember those details, and to help you prove to yourself that you have retained your knowledge of those topics. Therefore, this book does not try to help you pass the exams only by memorization but by truly learning and understanding the topics.

The book includes many features that provide different ways to study so you can be ready for the exam. If you understand a topic when you read it but do not study it any further, you probably will not be ready to pass the exam with confidence. The following features in this book give you tools that help you determine what you know, review what you know, better learn what you don't know, and be well prepared for the exam:

- **"Do I Know This Already?" quizzes:** Each chapter begins with a quiz that helps you determine the amount of time you need to spend studying that chapter.

- **Foundation Topics:** This section provides the core content of each chapter. In it you learn about the protocols, concepts, and configuration for the topics in the chapter.

- **Exam Preparation Tasks:** This section lists a series of study activities that should be done after reading the Foundation Topics section. Each chapter includes the activities that make the most sense for studying the topics in that chapter. This section includes the following activities:

  - **Key Topics Review:** The Key Topic icon appears next to the most important items in the Foundation Topics section of the chapter. The Key Topics Review activity lists the key topics from the chapter and their page numbers. Although the contents of the entire chapter could be on the exam, you should definitely know the information listed in each key topic. Review these topics carefully.

  - **Definition of Key Terms:** Although certification exams might be unlikely to ask you to define terms, the CISA exam requires you to learn and know a lot of terminology. This section lists some of the most important terms from the chapter and asks you to write a short definition and compare your answer to the Glossary.

- **Memory Tables:** Like most other certification guides from Pearson IT Certification, this book purposefully organizes information into tables and lists for easier study and review. Rereading these tables can be very useful before the exam. However, it is easy to skim over the tables without paying attention to every detail, especially when you remember having seen the table's contents when reading the chapter.

  Instead of simply reading the tables in the various chapters, you can use Appendix B, "Memory Tables," and Appendix C, "Memory Tables Answer Key," as another review tool. Appendix B lists partially completed versions of many of the tables from the book. You can open Appendix B (a PDF on the companion website page that comes with this book) and print the appendix. For review, attempt to complete the tables.

  Appendix C, also a PDF located on the companion website page, lists the completed tables so you can check yourself. You can also just refer to the tables as printed in the book.

- **Exercises:** At the end of each chapter are sample exercises that list a series of tasks for you to practice to apply the lessons from the chapter in a real-world setting.

- **Review Questions:** These questions help you confirm that you understand the content just covered.

- **Answers and Explanations:** We provide the answer to each of the Review Questions, as well as explanations about why each possible answer is correct or incorrect.

- **Suggested Readings and Resources:** Each chapter provides a list of links to further information on topics related to the chapter you've just read.

Companion Website

To access the book's companion website, simply follow these steps:

1. Register your book by going to PearsonITCertification.com/register and entering the ISBN 9780789758446.

2. Respond to the challenge questions.

3. Go to your account page and select the **Registered Products** tab.

4. Click on the **Access Bonus Content** link under the product listing.

Pearson Test Prep Practice Test Software

This book comes complete with the Pearson Test Prep practice test software, containing two full exams. These practice tests are available to you either online or as an offline Windows application. To access the practice exams that were developed with this book, please see the instructions in the card inserted in the sleeve in the back of the book. This card includes a unique access code that enables you to activate your exams in the Pearson Test Prep software.

Accessing the Pearson Test Prep Software Online

The online version of this software can be used on any device that has a browser and connectivity to the Internet, including desktop machines, tablets, and smartphones. To start using your practice exams online, simply follow these steps:

Step 1. Go to www.PearsonTestPrep.com.

Step 2. Select Pearson IT Certification as your product group.

Step 3. Enter your email/password for your account. If you don't have an account on PearsonITCertification.com or CiscoPress.com, you need to establish one by going to PearsonITCertification.com/join.

Step 4. In the My Products tab, click the **Activate New Product** button.

Step 5. Enter the access code printed on the insert card in the back of your book to activate your product.

Step 6. The product will now be listed in your My Products page. Click the **Exams** button to launch the exam settings screen and start your exam.

Accessing the Pearson Test Prep Software Offline

If you wish to study offline, you can download and install the Windows version of the Pearson Test Prep software. There is a download link for this software on the book's companion website, or you can just enter this link in your browser: www.pearsonitcertification.com/content/downloads/pcpt/engine.zip.

To access the book's companion website and the software, simply follow these steps:

Step 1. Register your book by going to PearsonITCertification.com/register and entering the ISBN **9780789758446**.

Step 2. Correctly answer the challenge questions.

Step 3. Go to your account page and select the **Registered Products** tab.

Step 4.   Click the **Access Bonus Content** link under the product listing.

Step 5.   Click the **Install Pearson Test Prep Desktop Version** link under the Practice Exams section of the page to download the software.

Step 6.   When the software finishes downloading, unzip all the files on your computer.

Step 7.   Double-click the application file to start the installation and follow the onscreen instructions to complete the registration.

Step 8.   When the installation is complete, launch the application and click the **Activate Exam** button on the My Products tab.

Step 9.   Click the **Activate a Product** button in the Activate Product Wizard.

Step 10.   Enter the unique access code found on the card in in the back of your book and click the **Activate** button.

Step 11.   Click **Next** and then click **Finish** to download the exam data to your application.

Step 12.   You can now start using the practice exams by selecting the product and clicking the **Open Exam** button to open the exam settings screen.

NOTE   The offline and online versions will sync together, so saved exams and grade results recorded on one version will be available to you on the other as well.

Customizing Your Exams

When you are in the exam settings screen, you can choose to take exams in one of three modes:

- **Study Mode:** Study Mode allows you to fully customize your exams and review answers as you are taking the exam. This is typically the mode you use first, to assess your knowledge and identify information gaps.

- **Practice Exam Mode:** Practice Exam Mode locks certain customization options and presents a realistic exam experience. Use this mode when you are preparing to test your exam readiness.

- **Flash Card Mode:** Flash Card Mode strips out the answers and presents you with only the question stem. This mode is great for late-stage preparation, when you really want to challenge yourself to provide answers without the benefit of seeing multiple choice options. This mode will not provide the detailed score reports that the other two modes will, so it should not be used if you are trying to identify knowledge gaps.

In addition to using these three modes, you can select the source of your questions. You can choose to take exams that cover all the chapters, or you can narrow your selection to just a single chapter or the chapters in specific parts of the book. All chapters are selected by default. If you want to narrow your focus to individual chapters, simply deselect all the chapters then select only those on which you wish to focus in the Objectives area.

You can also select the exam banks on which to focus. Each exam bank comes complete with a full exam of questions that cover topics in every chapter. The two exams printed in the book are available to you, along with two additional exams of unique questions. You can have the test engine serve up exams from all four banks or just from one individual bank by selecting the desired banks in the exam bank area.

There are several other customizations you can make to your exam from the exam settings screen, such as the time allowed for the exam, the number of questions served up, whether to randomize questions and answers, whether to show the number of correct answers for multiple-answer questions, or whether to serve up only specific types of questions. You can also create custom test banks by selecting only questions that you have marked or questions for which you have added notes.

Updating Your Exams

If you are using the online version of the Pearson Test Prep software, you should always have access to the latest version of the software as well as the exam data. If you are using the Windows desktop version, every time you launch the software, it will check to see if there are any updates to your exam data and automatically download any changes that have been made since the last time you used the software. You must be connected to the Internet at the time you launch the software.

Sometimes, due to many factors, the exam data may not fully download when you activate your exam. If you find that figures or exhibits are missing, you may need to manually update your exams.

To update a particular exam you have already activated and downloaded, simply select the **Tools** tab and click the **Update Products** button. Again, this is only an issue with the desktop Windows application.

If you wish to check for updates to the Pearson Test Prep exam engine software, Windows desktop version, simply select the **Tools** tab and click the **Update Application** button to ensure that you are running the latest version of the software engine.

Premium Edition eBook and Practice Tests

This book includes an exclusive offer for 70 percent off the Premium Edition eBook and Practice Tests edition of this title. See the coupon code included with the cardboard sleeve for information on how to purchase the Premium Edition.

End-of-Chapter Review Tools

Chapters 1 through 9 each have several features in the "Exam Preparation Tasks" and "Review Questions" sections at the end of the chapter. You might have already worked through these in each chapter. However, you might also find it helpful to use these tools again as you make your final preparations for the exam.

CHAPTER 1

The CISA Certification

This chapter will help you understand the Certified Information Systems Auditor (CISA) exam. This chapter covers the fundamentals of the CISA exam—including the intent, requirements, knowledge domains covered, types of questions you will encounter, scoring, test results, and more. The chapter explains the difference between the CISA exam and CISA certification. Understanding these fundamentals will help you better appreciate the complexity and scope of knowledge expected. It will also prepare you to navigate the exam.

Exam Intent

It is important that you understand the target audience and how the CISA exam has evolved over time. The CISA exam was established in 1978 by the Information Systems Audit and Control Association (ISACA). At the time of this writing, more than 129,000 individuals have obtained CISA certification worldwide, and more than 31,000 of them are audit directors, managers, consultants, or auditors. In North America, more than 33,000 individuals have CISA certification.

To understand the popularity of CISA certification, you need to understand the exam's intent. The key mission of the CISA exam, as stated by ISACA, is as follows:

To develop and maintain a testing instrument that can be used to evaluate an individual's competency in conducting information systems audits.

This mission statement only begins to scratch the surface of the intent of the CISA exam. Consider how much the business world and technology have evolved in recent years. Globalization, fueled by the Internet, has in many ways broken down national barriers. Technology has evolved at lightning speeds—beyond the capability of the current laws to keep pace. Core issues related to personal privacy, electronic surveillance, and corporate ethics continue to challenge how personal rights are perceived in this digital age.

No doubt we have all been recipients of the benefits of this digital and technology explosion. Just consider what today's life would be like without the ability to instantly connect through smartphones or how narrow our perception of the world would be without the Internet.

As businesses and governments continue to innovate through technology, they challenge the boundaries between personal and professional life. It often seems that every aspect of a person's life has been digitized somewhere by someone—from health records and school records to personal emails and photos. The advent of social media has made it increasingly difficult for us to control our own personal data or to maintain privacy.

As a result, businesses, governments, and individuals are on a constantly evolving journey, dealing with how to realize the benefits that technology provides while figuring out how to navigate the risks. On this journey, events and technology innovation continually redefine what is considered acceptable. Think about major cyber-security breaches in which millions of customer credit card accounts or health care records are stolen. Or consider the evolution of autonomous vehicles: Driverless cars are more and more making life-and-death decisions on behalf of passengers and pedestrians.

Top leadership in any organization needs the assurance that the organization is doing everything possible to follow a common set of accepted rules and principles. In this way, top leadership can be assured that they are managing these technology risks in an acceptable manner.

Why the CISA Certification Is So Important

The CISA exam codifies a core set of commonly accepted technology rules and principles. CISA certification ensures that individuals have the competency to provide leadership with the assurance that their organization complies with these industry norms.

Why is this assurance to top leadership so important to an organization? In addition to just being the right thing to do, in many cases, it's the law. Top leaders of an organization can be personally liable for failure to put in place digital safeguards to protect customers and shareholders from technology risks.

When the U.S. Congress passed the Sarbanes-Oxley Act of 2002, it wanted to restore the confidence of investors by improving the reliability of financial reporting and strengthening the control environment, such as information systems controls. The law calls out specific obligations for officers of a company, such as the principal executive (often called the *chief executive officer*) and financial officer (often called the *chief financial officer*), who must certify compliance with the law and ensure that the related control environment is in place and working. If this certification is found to be materially flawed or fraudulent, the officers can be held personally accountable and subject to heavy fines and potentially even prison time.

Senior executives need to know whether their organization is compliant with the Sarbanes-Oxley Act, but this can be a daunting task, especially in a large organization where operations and technical knowledge are siloed. Senior executives, therefore, need to have competent individuals to build, maintain, and audit their technology. We have looked briefly at a single law and a single company. Now take this one example and multiply by thousands of laws, rules, and regulations across thousands of companies in hundreds of industries. You can quickly see the need for a core set of commonly accepted rules and principles. The CISA exam addresses this important need, and that's why it continues to gain popularity.

CISA: The Gold Standard

The CISA certification's growth in popularity has made it the gold standard in the industry for many professionals. The certification is often seen as being key to advancement in information systems auditing and a growing number of other information systems roles.

To quickly get a sense of its importance, you can search any major job board, such as Indeed.com or Monster.com, for "CISA." The results will reveal its popularity in the thousands of listings that note the CISA certification as a job requirement.

Over the years, the intent of CISA certification has moved well beyond the systems audit community. The individuals accountable for building, implementing, and maintaining technology controls have just as much need to understand the core set of commonly accepted rules and principles—and top leadership expect them to. The population of the individuals taking the CISA exam today is diverse and includes many disciplines, including the following:

- Auditing
- Compliance
- Control
- Information security/cybersecurity
- Legal function
- Operations/information technology risk

In seeking to take the CISA exam, you are taking a major step forward into becoming part of this growing community of information systems control professionals!

Exam Requirements

Simply passing the CISA exam does not mean you are CISA certified. Remember that the CISA certification is intended to ensure that you are competent in your discipline related to the core set of commonly accepted rules and principles in information systems.

Think of it this way: If you passed the written driver's license test without having spent much or any time behind the wheel, would you be competent to drive? Of course not. You also need driving experience under the watchful eye of an experienced driver. Once you pass the physical road test, in addition to the written test, you can obtain a driver's license.

The CISA certification takes a similar approach, requiring a combination of passing a knowledge test and also demonstrating competence through actual work experience. To obtain CISA certification, you must meet four key requirements:

- Pass the CISA exam

- Demonstrate five years of professional work experience, which will be verified through your employer

- Agree to adhere to the ISACA rules related to the ISACA Code of Professional Ethics, standards, and continuing education

- Submit an application for CISA certification

CISA Exam Windows

In years past, the CISA exam was offered just three days per year. Starting in 2017, ISACA opened up three two-month CISA exam windows for taking the exam each year, and you now can take the exam in any available exam window.

The schedule is published on the ISACA website (www.isaca.org). The three exam windows can change from year to year but will typically align to the following schedule:

- May 1–June 30

- August 1–September 30

- November 1–December 31

The exam is administered by a professional testing company called PSI. To find the PSI locations for taking the exam, see the ISACA website (www.isaca.org/examlocations). Exam locations can fill up quickly, so it's important to register at least a month before you plan to take the exam. In addition, each exam location services multiple certifications. It's not unusual for a testing room to be filled with individuals taking tests for other certifications.

Scheduling to Take the Exam

The CISA exam is open to everyone, and scheduling to take the CISA examination is a straightforward process. All you need to start is to set up an account with ISACA through its website (www.isaca.org). Once you set up an account, you can schedule to take the CISA exam by clicking on My Certifications and then Exam Schedule. It is similar to shopping online in that you pick the product (in this case the CISA exam) and then pay for it during checkout.

After you register and pay, ISACA sends you an email confirmation. Several weeks prior to the scheduled test date, you should receive an admission ticket for the exam by email.

On exam day you must bring a government-issued picture ID. Without proper identification that exactly matches the admission ticket, you will not be allowed to take the exam. If you have any question on the forms of acceptable identification, you should call the testing center directly. Generally, the testing centers accept the following forms of identification:

- Driver's license

- Non-driver state ID card

- Passport or passport card

- Military ID

- Permanent resident card (green card)

NOTE Be sure to arrive at the testing location early and well rested. If you are late, you may not be allowed to take the exam.

Check the weather forecast! Severe weather can close a testing center, in which case your exam will be rescheduled at no cost. You can contact the PSI test center or check the PSI website for closures due to weather.

Deadline to Apply for the CISA Certification

Once you pass the CISA exam, the results are good for five years. This means that if you don't apply for CISA certification within five years of passing the CISA exam, you will be required to retake the exam.

The requirement to have five years of professional work experience often creates anxiety for individuals who are new in the technology field. The good news is that ISACA has a waiver program that allows individuals to substitute up to three of the five years of work experience. At the time of this writing, the waiver program generally allows the following substitutions for work experience:

- One year's credit for either one year of information systems experience or one year of non-IS auditing
- One year's credit for a two-year associate's degree
- Two years' credit for a four-year bachelor's degree
- One year's credit for a master's degree
- Two years' credit for Chartered Institute of Management Accountants (CIMA) full certification
- Two years' credit for member status from the Association of Chartered Certified Accountants (ACCA)
- One year's credit for every two years as a full-time university instructor in a related field (for example, computer science, accounting, information systems auditing)

You can mix and match these credits but cannot substitute for more than three of the five years of work experience.

NOTE   All work experience—including the substitutions listed here—must be within the past 10 years of the date of the application.

The best source of information on what ISACA will accept as credit for work experience is the CISA certification application form. The instructions on how to fill out the form detail the credits that are available, the restrictions, and how they can be combined. Be sure to download the correct form aligned with the year you passed the exam to identify any changes to the waiver program.

A CISA candidate has the option to specify in which language the CISA exam will be taken. At the time of this writing, the CISA exam can be taken in English, Chinese Simplified, Chinese Traditional, French, German, Hebrew, Italian, Japanese, Korean, Spanish, and Turkish. Not all languages may be offered at the same time, so it's important that you check on the preferred language at the time and location you wish to take the exam.

For the purpose of planning, there are three key points to remember:

- Passing the CISA exam does not mean you are CISA certified.

- You must demonstrate five years of work experience and apply for the CISA certification within five years of passing the CISA exam.

- You can get up to three years' work experience credit through the ISACA waiver program.

ISACA Agreements

As part of the CISA application, you must sign off on three agreements. You must agree to the following:

- To conduct yourself honestly and ethically and abide by the Code of Professional Ethics (see www.isaca.org/ethics for details)

- To abide by the information systems standards, as adopted by ISACA (see www.isaca.org/standards for details)

- To maintain your competency through continuing professional education (CPE) (see www.isaca.org/cisacpepolicy for details)

These three agreements are part of the CISA application form, and ISACA takes them very seriously. Violations are rarely found, but when a clear violation is identified, the penalty may include revocation of CISA certification.

You should read ISACA's information on ethics, information systems standards, and the CISA CPE policy prior to the taking the CISA exam. While much of the content of these agreements will not be on the exam as specific questions, reading these agreements will help you put yourself in the right mindset for the exam. Reading these agreements will help you immerse yourself in the language of and thinking behind the exam questions. (Any content-specific items that will be on the exam are covered in this book.)

What do we mean by having the right mindset for the exam? We will not go through these three agreements in detail, but consider the ethics document as an example. I have found the ethics document to be rich in content. It is short and easy to read, and it outlines core principles you need to follow as a professional and sets the bar on how you should think about the challenges presented to you.

The following is an example of a statement from ISACA's Code of Professional Ethics:

Members and ISACA certification holders shall…perform their duties with objectivity, due diligence and professional care, in accordance with professional standards.

What do *objectivity* and *due diligence* mean? The meaning depends on the context. Suppose you are assessing a specific technology or solution, and a senior executive and decision maker had a bias for one of the solutions well before the assessment started. We all have some bias to some extent, but if the executive's bias was preventing the team from looking at all the options honestly and openly, there would be a lack of objectivity and due diligence. We as professionals are obligated to have the objectivity to perform the proper level of due diligence. This often means we need to answer hard questions and elevate concerns to appropriate leadership, regardless of the consequences.

We'll get into these topics more later in the book. For now, the takeaway is that preparing for the exam is not just about facts but also about mindset.

CISA Exam Domains

The CISA exam is divided into five job practice areas, or domains. (ISACA has used both the terms *job practice area* and *job domain*, and the two terms mean the same thing in the context of the CISA exam.) The CISA exam domains serve as the basis for the exam and the requirements to earn the certification. The exam domains consist of task and knowledge statements representing the work performed in information systems audit, assurance, and control.

These are the five domains:

- **Domain 1: The Process of Auditing Information Systems:** This domain and its exam section cover how IT audit services are provided in accordance with audit standards, including planning and conducting an audit and reporting findings. The exam section goes into detail related to tasks used to develop and implement a risk-based audit strategy.

- **Domain 2: Governance and Management of IT:** This domain and its exam section cover how information technology is governed and managed. You need to know the different parts of an organization and how risk is governed and managed across the organization.

- **Domain 3: Information Systems Acquisition, Development and Implementation:** This domain and its exam section cover best practices for the acquisition, development, testing, and implementation of information systems to meet the organization's needs and strategic objectives.

- **Domain 4: Information Systems Operations, Maintenance and Service Management:** This domain and its exam section cover the information systems back-office operations, from the organization structure that supports it to the infrastructure and network technology it rides on. This exam section goes into detail related to tasks which provide assurance that the processes supporting information systems operations, maintenance, and service management meet the organization's needs.

- **Domain 5: Protection of Information Assets:** This domain and its exam section cover information security and cybersecurity disciplines, including how to provide assurance that the organization's security policies, standards, procedures, and controls are working properly. In addition, this domain involves ensuring the confidentiality, integrity, and availability of data assets. This domain speaks to both logical and physical security risks, as well as evolving technologies such as mobile computing.

NOTE Don't be thrown off by all the *audit* references in the training material available for the CISA exam. Look beyond these references and focus on the content.

In the early days, the CISA exam was primarily focused on information security auditors because ISACA was formed through the audit community, which saw a need for an information systems specialist audit discipline.

The information security auditor community regards CISA certification as its gold standard. Consequently, the information security audit community influences the exam and supporting material.

Table 1-1 describes the different exam domains in more detail and provides the percentage of the exam related to each domain.

Table 1-1 CISA Exam Domain Breakdown

Job Practice Area	Key Topics	Percentage of Exam
Domain 1: The Process of Auditing Information Systems	Management of the IS audit function	21%
	ISACA IT audit and assurance standards and guidelines	
	Risk analysis	
	Internal controls	
	Performing an information systems audit	
	Control self-assessment	
	How information systems audits have evolved	

Job Practice Area	Key Topics	Percentage of Exam
Domain 2: Governance and Management of IT	Corporate and IT governance	16%
	Technology monitoring	
	Assurance for board and senior management, maturity and process improvement models, IT investment and allocation practices, policies and procedures	
	Risk management	
	Information organization structure	
	Information organization responsibilities	
	Business continuity planning and auditing	
Domain 3: Information Systems Acquisition, Development and Implementation	Business realization	18%
	Project management	
	Application development	
	Acquisition and maintenance	
	Alternative forms of software project organization and development	
	Infrastructure development and acquisition	
	System development tools	
	Application controls	
	Application auditing	
Domain 4: Information Systems Operations, Maintenance and Service Management	Information systems operations	20%
	Information systems hardware	
	Information systems architecture	
	Information systems software	
	Information systems networks	
	Information systems infrastructure	
	Auditing infrastructure and operations	
	Disaster recovery planning	
Domain 5: Protection of Information Assets	Information security organization	25%
	Information security management	
	Logical access	
	Network infrastructure	
	Auditing information security management framework	
	Environmental controls	
	Physical access controls	
	Mobile computing	

Don't be concerned at this point if many of the terms in Table 1-1 are unfamiliar. Use the table as a reference guide as you work through the subsequent chapters to understand the alignment of the chapters' material to the exam domains. When you are finished with the rest of the book, return to this table to ensure that you have a solid understanding of each of these topic areas.

Question Format and Grading

The CISA exam consists of 150 multiple-choice questions with four possible answers each. (The number of questions was reduced from 200 to 150 in 2016.) You are allowed four hours to complete the exam.

One of the most significant changes for the CISA exam in 2017 is the shift from a paper-and-pencil system to computer-based testing (CBT). Not all testing locations have CBT capability, and where that is the case, the old paper-and-pencil system is still used. However, the CBT system is such a marked improvement that there is a significant push for all locations to adopt this technology.

CAUTION   CBT has many advantages, but the technology is not forgiving! Once you submit your answers, the test is done.

Be careful and review the questions you've already answered if you have the time. Just remember that once you submit the answers, the test is over.

If you are unfamiliar with CBT, arrive early and ask for a walkthrough. All testing locations will take the time to ensure that you are familiar with the CBT technology before you start the test.

Exam Grading

The CISA exam is graded on a scale from 200 to 800, with 450 being a passing score. ISACA sees a score of 450 or higher as demonstrating consistent understanding and knowledge of the material.

ISACA uses a scaling factor in scoring the exam. (It is not simply calculated as a percentage of the total number of questions correctly answered.) ISACA uses this scaling to normalize scores across a large population of test takers. That is, scores are reported on a scale, and the scale can be adjusted. Such scaling adjustments are almost always made so that an individual is not penalized for an outlier question or two. The scale eliminates the noise so the true competency of an individual's knowledge of the subject material can be understood. Suppose, for example, that a new question is introduced and the vast majority of test takers answer incorrectly. ISACA has the capability through this scaling process to throw out the question without penalizing individuals.

> **TIP** You don't need to fully understand how the grading works. The ISACA grading has evolved over many years and does not affect how you need to study for the exam. The best advice is to put your energy into exam preparation instead of focusing on the grade. If you put the work into preparation, the grade will take care of itself.

Exam Questions

The exam questions are often described as application based, which means the questions tend to be situational. This is not an exam you can pass simply by memorizing facts and figures. You must read each question carefully and apply the context of the situation to the answer. Consequently, is it important that you understand the concepts in this book and master when and how core exam material knowledge is applied.

> **NOTE** Reading the CISA exam question for context hints will greatly improve your chance of selecting the right answer.
>
> Look for hints in key words and phrases such as *most likely* or *best option*. While all the answers may be possible, such hint words can help you narrow the choices.

Let's consider a sample test question from the self-assessment on ISACA's website for CISA exam preparation:

1. Which control is the BEST way to ensure that the data in a file has not been changed during transmission?

   a. Reasonableness check

   b. Parity bits

   c. Hash values

   d. Check digits

While you may rationalize that all the answers can be applied in some context, the hint word is important. The hint word here is *BEST*, so which of these acceptable methods provides the most assurance that data has not been changed during transmission?

To illustrate this point, let's examine possible answers to the question, with a focus on finding the *BEST* way to determine if data was changed:

a. Reasonableness check—Used to approximate what data values are expected

b. Parity bits—Used to identify data errors

c. Hash values—Used to verify the integrity of data

d. Check digits—Used to verify data input

All these items listed in the answers could be indicators of potential data tampering. But remember that the hint word is *BEST*. So if you could have only one of these controls, which one, in the context of the question, would you choose? Answer C is correct because hash values focus on data integrity, which is defined based on the assurance of data accuracy.

Understanding the exam question language, format, and context takes some practice. As you move through this book, you will become more familiar with how to answer the exam questions. This book is designed to help you quickly assess questions, identify hint words, and understand context. As you master these skills, you will find that narrowing down to the correct answer is much easier.

Getting Exam Results and Retests

Official CISA exam results are mailed approximately five weeks after you take the exam. After working for months to prepare for the exam, waiting so long may be frustrating.

The good news is that with the adoption of CBT technology, many testing centers provide an unofficial score the same day. Be sure to ask on the day of the exam how to obtain your unofficial score. In fact, some CBT systems display your raw unofficial score when you submit your answers to end the testing session. So be sure to read the screen carefully after submitting your answers.

Unfortunately, if you are at a location that only offers paper-and-pencil testing, you will have to wait longer for your scores. However, ISACA recognizes this frustration and is continuously working to improve the process. You can also opt in for email notification during registration, and you will receive an email indicating passing or failure before the official results are mailed.

Scores also become available through the ISACA website. Look in your profile at the My ISACA > My Certifications page on the ISACA website.

The official exam results show your scores for all the domains. While the scale grading may be hard to understand, the domain scores help you identify areas of strength and weakness. The domain breakdown is particularly useful if you do not pass the exam the first time as it will help you determine for which domains you should put in the most exam prep effort.

To retake the CISA exam, you simply register for the exam again and pay the appropriate exam fee. The one restriction is that you are not allowed to take the exam twice within the same testing window. For example, if you failed the exam in May (during the May–June testing window), the soonest you can retake the exam is August (during the August–September testing window). In other words, you can't fail the exam in May and retake the exam in June as that would be the same testing window.

Maintaining CISA Certification

Once you have obtained your CISA certification, you must pay an annual fee and keep your knowledge current through continuing professional education (CPE). The CPE policy at the ISACA website details the educational requirements to maintain certification (see www.isaca.org/cisacpepolicy).

The following are the highlights of the CPE policy:

- Attain and report an annual minimum of 20 CPE hours
- Annually report the CPE hours you have earned
- Attain a minimum of 120 CPE hours for a three-year reporting period

Reporting CPE Hours Earned

You can pay the annual maintenance fee and report your CPE hours through the ISACA website (My ISACA > My Certifications). You can easily see if any fees are owed or CPE hours are missing (see Figure 1-1).

The ISACA website has greatly improved in recent years. From the My Certifications page, you can manage all your ISACA certifications, pay fees, and report CPE hours.

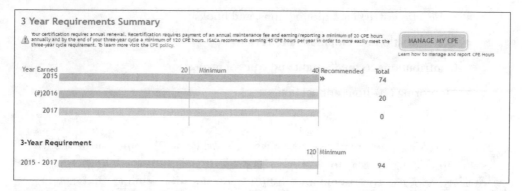

Figure 1-1 ISACA Credit Tracking

All certifications are assigned a three-year cycle. Figure 1-1 is an actual screen shot from the My Certifications page. This page quickly shows your progress in maintaining your CISA certification. In this example, the certification is on a three-year cycle starting in 2015 and ending in 2017. This means that by the end of 2017, the individual must have earned 120 CPE hours, and at least 20 of them must have been earned within each of the three years 2015, 2016, and 2017.

As Figure 1-1 illustrates, assuming that the current year is 2017, the individual has met the ISACA CPE requirements by earning 94 CPE hours during 2015 and 2016 and meeting the minimum threshold of 20 CPE hours per year. To complete the CPE requirements, this person must complete a minimum of 26 (120 – 94 = 26) CPE hours in 2017. Also note in Figure 1-1 that this person has a warning message which says that to maintain the CISA certification, the individual needs to also pay the annual renewal fee.

Earning CPE Hours

Earning 120 CPE hours may seem daunting. The best advice is to plan and spread the hours as evenly as possible over the three-year cycle, which means aiming for at least 40 hours of CPE credits per year.

There are many ways to earn CPE hours. Consider the following list from the CPE policy guide, for example:

- ISACA professional education activities and meetings
- Non-ISACA professional education activities and meetings
- Self-study courses
- Vendor sales/marketing presentations (10-hour annual limit)
- Teaching/lecturing/presenting

- Publication of articles, monographs, and books
- Exam question development and review
- Contributions to the IS audit and control profession
- Mentoring (10-hour annual limitation)

NOTE   ISACA has more than 200 local chapters worldwide. Becoming involved with a local chapter is a great way to network with professionals and earn CPE hours. Many ISACA local chapters hold low-cost (or free) education seminars and meetings for which you can earn CPE hours.

In addition, remember to register your CPE hours promptly and retain evidence of participation (such as a certificate of attendance) in case ISACA challenges the CPE hours. It's much easier to remember the details and hours spent immediately after an event than to scramble at the end of each year.

Top 10 Tips and Tricks

The following is a quick, high-level review of a number of tips and tricks that will help you prepare for the CISA exam and get ready for exam day:

- **Tip 1:** Read through this book at least twice. Become familiar with the language of and mindset behind the material.

- **Tip 2:** Focus on the context of the question. Ask what key problem each question is trying to solve. That may mean rereading a question several times. A single word or a phrase and hint words can change the context and lead to a different meaning. Understand why one answer is more suitable than the others.

  Even as you focus carefully on each question, keep in mind that it is a timed test. Taking a disciplined approach to reading the questions will help you build a natural rhythm in taking the exam.

- **Tip 3:** Arrive at least 30 minutes early. Assume that there will be delays and be flexible. Don't be afraid to ask questions about the facilities and CBT options.

- **Tip 4:** Look for additional prep material judiciously. There is a lot of material on the market and available for free. Much of it is outdated. You can get prepared more quickly with a few well-constructed sources that you have reviewed multiple times than with massive amounts of verbose conflicting sources.

- **Tip 5:** The CISA Review Questions, Answers & Explanations (QAE) Manual from ISACA is an excellent prep guide supplement. The manual contains in-depth questions, answers, and well-constructed explanations.

- **Tip 6:** Take your time to prepare. Everyone learns at a unique pace and starts with a unique set of knowledge and skills. You are not likely to pass the CISA exam through last-minute cramming sessions.

  A typical CISA prep schedule may be two to four months or longer, depending on the amount of time and knowledge you have.

- **Tip 7:** The week before the exam, focus on sample tests. Be sure to work on the mindset and rhythm mentioned in Tip 2.

- **Tip 8:** Reach out to the local ISACA chapter. Often these chapters have CISA study groups and mentors to help you understand the material and get you motivated!

- **Tip 9:** Don't burn out before the test even begins. Relax the day before you take the exam and take the day off on exam day so your body and mind are fresh.

- **Tip 10:** Bring a brown bag lunch and a snack such as a protein bar to the testing center just in case it doesn't have vending machines. Each testing center is different, and you may end up in an exam center that offers only a drinking fountain and a rest room.

Chapter Summary

This chapter examines the fundamentals of the CISA exam. It discusses the history and intent of the exam, including why CISA certification is so important.

The chapter also discusses the difference between the CISA exam and CISA certification. It explains the requirements and deadlines for applying for CISA certification and how to maintain the certification once achieved.

The chapter explores the five domains of the CISA exam. It shows how each domain is weighed and gives you a look at the question format.

Finally, one of the most important takeaways from the chapter is the importance of having the right mindset going into the exam. The chapter discusses how to break down an exam question and look for context and hint words. The chapter provides a list of 10 tips and tricks to get ready for exam day.

Attaining CISA certification distinguishes you as being highly qualified to work in information systems auditing, control, or security. Passing the CISA exam is not easy. But the rewards in personal growth and professional recognition are substantial. The likelihood of passing the CISA exam is higher if you have deep background knowledge in information systems. Regardless of where you are on the learning curve, a CISA preparation plan is a must. Even for seasoned professionals, having a solid plan for preparing to take the CISA exam is essential.

Subsequent chapters focus on the CISA exam content and the knowledge needed to answer exam questions.

Define Key Terms

Define the following key terms from this chapter and check your answers against the glossary:

audit function, CISA certification, CISA exam domains, CISA exam windows, Code of Professional Ethics, compliance function, computer-based testing (CBT), continuing professional education (CPE), control function, CPE hours, domains, information security/cybersecurity, information systems standards, job practice areas, legal function, mindset, My Certifications (ISACA website), operations/information technology risk, waiver program

Suggested Readings and Resources

- **CISA self-assessment:** www.isaca.org/certification/cisa-certified-information-systems-auditor/prepare-for-the-exam/pages/cisaselfassessment.aspx?id=100002

- **Job Practice Areas 2017:** www.isaca.org/certification/cism-certified-information-security-manager/job-practice-areas/pages/default.aspx

- **Prepare for the CISA Exam – Documents:** www.isaca.org/Certification/CISA-Certified-Information-Systems-Auditor/Prepare-for-the-Exam/Documents/Forms/AllItems.aspx

The following exam domain is partially covered in this chapter:

Domain 1—The Process of Auditing Information Systems

This chapter covers the following topics:

- **Skills and Knowledge Required to Be an IS Auditor:** This section provides an overview of certifications and work-related skills needed in the field.

- **Knowledge of Ethical Standards:** This section provides an overview of the ISACA Code of Professional Ethics.

- **ISACA Standards, Procedures, Guidelines, and Baselines:** This section gives you a foundational understanding of standards, procedures, guidelines, and baselines. In addition, this section covers major laws, rules, regulations, and international standards.

- **Risk Assessment Concepts:** This section provides an overview of how to define, assess, manage, and mitigate various types of risks.

- **Auditing and the Use of Internal Controls:** This section defines and reviews common types of internal controls an auditor will encounter.

- **The Auditing Life Cycle:** This section examines the stages of the audit process, including planning, examination, reporting and following up.

- **The Control Self-Assessment Process:** This section defines the attributes of a self-assessment process and explains its importance in the audit process.

- **Continuous Monitoring:** This section explains why continuous monitoring is important and describes its benefits.

- **Quality Assurance:** This section reviews QA attributes that help businesses prevent costly mistakes or defects and control risks.

- **The Challenges of Audits:** This section describes the types of audit opinions that are typically issued by an auditor and the challenges related to issuing an audit opinion.

CHAPTER 2

The Information Systems Audit

Most organizations, no matter their size, have a heavy reliance on information technology to stay ahead of their competition. Information systems drive revenue and often reflect the organization's image on the Internet. Information systems (IS) auditing ensures that an organization's data is confidentially stored, that data integrity is maintained, and that information systems are available when needed. The audit process is therefore an excellent place to start your preparation for the CISA exam.

Many foundational concepts of the audit process are leveraged across the CISA exam. This chapter helps you prepare for the exam by covering the ISACA objectives, which include understanding the role and importance of auditing standards, guidelines, and best practices. When you complete this chapter, you will be able to do the following:

- Understand the skills needed to be an IS auditor
- Explain what an IS audit is
- Explain how an IS audit is managed and performed
- Define risks and how to analyze them
- Describe internal controls
- Understand how control assessments are performed
- Understand how an audit report is written and issued
- Explain the end-to-end audit process and understand the challenges

"Do I Know This Already?" Quiz

The "Do I Know This Already?" quiz allows you to assess whether you should read this entire chapter thoroughly or jump to the "Exam Preparation Tasks" section. If you are in doubt about your answers to these questions or your own assessment of your knowledge of the topics, read the entire chapter. Table 2-1 lists the major headings in this chapter and their corresponding "Do I Know

This Already?" quiz questions. You can find the answers in Appendix A, "Answers to the 'Do I Know This Already?' Quizzes and Review Questions."

Table 2-1 "Do I Know This Already?" Section-to-Question Mapping

Foundation Topics Section	Questions Covered in This Section
Skills and Knowledge Required to Be an IS Auditor	1
Knowledge of Ethical Standards	2
ISACA Standards, Procedures, Guidelines, and Baselines	3
Risk Assessment Concepts	4
Auditing and the Use of Internal Controls	5
The Auditing Life Cycle	6
The Control Self-Assessment Process	7
Continuous Monitoring	8
Quality Assurance	9
The Challenges of Audits	10

CAUTION The goal of self-assessment is to gauge your mastery of the topics in this chapter. If you do not know the answer to a question or are only partially sure of the answer, you should mark that question as incorrect for purposes of the self-assessment. Giving yourself credit for an answer you correctly guess skews your self-assessment results and might provide you with a false sense of security.

1. Which of the following is an important work-related soft skill an auditor needs?

   a. Knowledge of laws, rules, and regulations

   b. Ability to code

   c. Careful attention to detail when completing work tasks

   d. Knowledge of project management tools

2. To whom is the ISACA Code of Professional Ethics applied?

   a. Auditors

   b. Clients

   c. Stakeholders

   d. Sponsors

3. Which of the following are mandatory actions, explicitly stated rules, or controls that are designed to support and conform to a policy?

   a. Baselines

   b. Standards

   c. Procedures

   d. Guidelines

4. Which of the following is a risk that naturally occurs because of the nature of the business before controls are applied?

   a. Control risk

   b. Detection risk

   c. Inherent risk

   d. Residual risk

5. Which of the following control categories is designed to reduce the impact of a threat and attempts to minimize the impact of a problem?

   a. Detective

   b. Corrective

   c. Preventive

   d. Selective

6. At which step in the auditing life cycle does an auditor identify interviewees, identify processes to be tested and verified, and obtain documents such as policies, procedures, and standards?

   a. Evaluation of results

   b. Audit scope

   c. Audit objective

   d. Data gathering

7. Which of the following is not true of the control self-assessment process?

   a. It tends to raise the level of control, which allows risk to be detected sooner and, consequently, reduces cost.

   b. It empowers employees and gives them responsibility.

   c. It decreases awareness of staff and employees of internal controls and their objectives.

   d. It involves employees and raises their level of awareness.

8. Which of the following is a precondition that should be present before an organization can adopt continuous auditing?

    a. The information system must have a manually operated secondary control system.

    b. The system must have acceptable prebuilt characteristics that are solely considered over cost and technical skill.

    c. The auditor does not need to be proficient in the system and information technology but can be trained later.

    d. The information system must be reliable, have existing primary controls, and collect data on the system.

9. When reviewing quality assurance, the goal is to improve which two key attributes?

    a. Intent and design

    b. Quality and adherence

    c. Intent and adherence

    d. Compliance and design

10. Of the following audit opinion categories, which one is rendered when appropriate testing and obtained evidence exist to cite instances of control weaknesses but the opinion cannot conclude that the control weakness is pervasive?

    a. Disclaimer

    b. Adverse opinion

    c. Unqualified opinion

    d. Qualified opinion

Foundation Topics

Skills and Knowledge Required to Be an IS Auditor

The knowledge statement questions on the CISA exam cover hard skills such as how to plan an audit. The task statement questions on the exam, in combination with situational context, test a candidate on the soft skills an auditor needs, such as how to communicate audit examination results.

NOTE   When a situational CISA exam question is presented for which you are unsure of the answer, remember to put yourself in the mindset of an auditor. The ISACA Code of Professional Ethics and both this book's and ISACA's practice exams can help you develop that mindset. For example, think of an auditor like an insurance policy for management who works in partnership with the business to expose risk to the company. The ISACA Code of Professional Ethics is reviewed in detail later in this chapter and is available at www.isaca.org/certification/code-of-professional-ethics/pages/default.aspx.

Work-Related Skills

An auditor has a successful career when he or she has an ever-improving set of skills that are applied consistently, relentlessly, and professionally, along with excellent interpersonal soft skills. It is said that a good auditor needs to be knowledgeable about the business, efficient, capable of exposing risk, able to deliver a tough message, and still welcome to go out for a beer afterward.

Table 2-2 lists some of the important work-related soft and hard skills an auditor needs.

Table 2-2   Important Work-Related Auditor Skills

Skill Type	Skill
Soft	Honest and ethical
Hard	Technically competent, having the skills and knowledge necessary to perform the auditor's work
Soft	Ability to pay careful attention to detail when completing work tasks

Skill Type	Skill
Hard	Excellent verbal and written communication skills
Hard	Analytical thinking skills and ability to analyze information through sound logical thinking
Soft	Excellent interpersonal skills, displaying a good nature and the ability to stay focused and calm
Soft	Ability to create and maintain professional relationships and develop allies
Soft	Willingness to lead, take charge, and offer opinions
Soft	Strong active listening and ability to understand other points of view
Hard	Good project management and organizational skills
Hard	Critical thinking and the ability to use logic and reasoning techniques to identify weaknesses and develop solutions to problems

Many new auditors are surprised at the number of soft skills listed in Table 2-2. While not an exhaustive list, it illustrates the skills that typically separate good auditors from bad auditors.

Knowledge of Ethical Standards

The ISACA Code of Professional Ethics involves more than conducting an audit and goes beyond legal requirements; it defines principles and values that govern acceptable behavior. As an auditor, you must be above question at all times. You must treat clients honestly and fairly, and your actions must reflect positively on yourself, your company, and your profession.

> **NOTE**   The word *client* in this context means the leadership of the area you are auditing. If you are auditing within a company, then you have internal clients for the audit services you are providing.

Answers to the "Do I Know This Already?" Quiz:

1. C; 2. A; 3. B; 4. C; 5. B; 6. D; 7. C; 8. D; 9. B; 10. D

To help guide auditors in this defined level of conduct, ISACA has developed the following Code of Professional Ethics:

Members and ISACA certification holders shall:

1. Support the implementation of, and encourage compliance with, appropriate standards and procedures for the effective governance and management of enterprise information systems and technology, including: audit, control, security and risk management.

2. Perform their duties with objectivity, due diligence and professional care, in accordance with professional standards.

3. Serve in the interest of stakeholders in a lawful manner, while maintaining high standards of conduct and character, and not discrediting their profession or the Association.

4. Maintain the privacy and confidentiality of information obtained in the course of their activities unless disclosure is required by legal authority. Such information shall not be used for personal benefit or released to inappropriate parties.

5. Maintain competency in their respective fields and agree to undertake only those activities they can reasonably expect to complete with the necessary skills, knowledge and competence.

6. Inform appropriate parties of the results of work performed including the disclosure of all significant facts known to them that, if not disclosed, may distort the reporting of the results.

7. Support the professional education of stakeholders in enhancing their understanding of the governance and management of enterprise information systems and technology, including: audit, control, security and risk management.

Failure to comply with this Code of Professional Ethics can result in an investigation into a member's or certification holder's conduct and, ultimately, in disciplinary measures.

NOTE   The ISACA Code of Professional Ethics will be on the exam in the form of situational questions and phrased as choices on how to meet an auditor's obligation. CISA candidates are not expected to memorize the exact wording of the ISACA Code of Professional Ethics, but they are expected to understand its goals and how it should be applied and used.

Let's consider one major historical event that illustrates the importance of ethical standards. Enron was founded in 1985, and at its peak in 2000, it was one of America's largest energy companies. By 2001 Enron was taking on massive liabilities and incurring massive losses. To keep its stock price up and hide the losses form the public, it used highly questionable offshore transactions and creative bookkeeping methods. Arthur Andersen was one of the five largest accounting firms in the United States at the time. It had a reputation for high standards and quality. Arthur Andersen oversaw, audited, and signed off on Enron's financials and accounts. By December 2001, Enron declared bankruptcy. By August 2002, Arthur Andersen had closed its doors.

Let's look at the events involving the Arthur Andersen auditors at Enron from the point of view of the ISACA Code of Professional Ethics. Knowing that the accounting practices were at the time questionable and not consistent with industry norms, what was the auditors' obligation? They could have refused to sign off on the company's books. But that might have caused the accounting firm to be fired and lose millions of dollars in accounting fees. What they chose to do was to sign off, put their firm's reputation behind Enron, and, worse yet, when the regulators began investigating, they destroyed some of their Enron audit documents. Like Enron, they faced criminal charges and ended up having to close their doors.

What was Arthur Andersen auditors' obligation? Let's break down the third point in the statements in the ISACA Code of Professional Ethics:

- **Serve in the interest of stakeholders...:** Stakeholders include the Enron shareholders, the pensions dependent on the Enron stock, and the Enron employees, to name a few. None were well served by the auditors' decision.

- **...in a lawful manner...:** We can assume that even if the auditors thought the accounting practices were questionable rather than illegal, it was clear that their intent was not to be honest.

- **...while maintaining high standards of conduct and character, and not discrediting their profession or the Association:** At the time, Arthur Andersen auditors not only hurt their firm but called into question the professionalism of the industry. Fortunately, Arthur Andersen closing its doors helps demonstrate that such conduct is unacceptable to the industry and not the norm.

CISA exam questions will raise a number of situational questions related to the Code of Professional Ethics. A CISA candidate is not expected to recite each word in the code of ethics. However, a candidate needs to understand the importance of conduct during an audit and of conveying the results honestly and transparently.

ISACA Standards, Procedures, Guidelines, and Baselines

The CISA exam questions expect a candidate to understand the difference between a standard, a procedure, a guideline, and a baseline. A CISA candidate is expected not only to know the definitions but also in what situations they should be applied.

There are a number of definitions in the industry for these four terms. Given that this is an ISACA-created exam, ISACA's COBIT 5 use of the terms can be found in Table 2-3. (COBIT 5 is discussed later in this chapter.)

Table 2-3   Description of Standards, Procedures, Guidelines, and Baselines

Title	Description
Standards	Mandatory actions, explicit rules, or controls that are designed to support and conform to a policy. A standard should make a policy more meaningful and effective by including accepted specifications for hardware, software, or behavior. Standards should always point to the policy to which they relate.
Procedures	Written steps to execute policies through specific, prescribed actions; this is the *how* in relation to a policy. Procedures tend to be more detailed than policies. They identify the method and state, in a series of steps, exactly how to accomplish an intended task, achieve a desired business or functional outcome, and execute a policy.
Guidelines	An outline for a statement of conduct. This is an additional (optional) document in support of policies, standards, and procedures and provides general guidance on what to do in particular circumstances. Guidelines are not requirements to be met but are strongly recommended.
Baselines	Platform-specific rules that are accepted across the industry as providing the most effective approach to a specific implementation.

NOTE   The CISA exam requires more than memorization. When you encounter a term, first read it to understand its definition and then try to understand when it would be used. Looking at definitions is a starting point that can help you form a compare-and-contrast perspective that helps understand not only the term but also its utility. For example, don't just read the definitions of a *standards* and *procedures* in Table 2-3. Consider how you would explain the difference and in which situation would one be a better choice over the other.

Let's look at an example to gain a deeper understanding. Say that you have this question on an exam: "If you bought a car, which term would best describe the fact that, on average, you should change the oil every 5,000 miles?" Your answer choices are standard, procedure, guideline, and baseline. Here's how you could logically break down the question to pick the best choice:

- **Baseline:** A baseline could be the right answer if there were more details about the car, such as the type of car, age of the car, driving habits, and so on. A salesperson driving a car 120,000 miles per year will change the oil far more often than a telecommuter driving 5,000 miles per year. A generic statement about cars would not be considered platform specific.

- **Procedure:** A procedure is a set of steps to follow. This definition is not a fit, given the question.

- **Standard:** A standard could be the right answer if the question said the car is under a lease, and the lease agreement requires changing the oil every 5,000 miles. In the lease situation, the changing of the oil is mandatory, which would make standard a good answer. A giveaway that a standard does not apply, is the use of the hint word *should*, which conveys that there are options. It's generally accepted that standards that use the word *should* are poorly written because standards are mandatory.

- **Guideline:** The term *guideline* is the correct answer because a guideline provides a general rule. If you didn't have any other specific information, then changing your car's oil every 5,000 miles would make sense. If you were to gain more information, you could adjust the frequency of oil change. For example, some of the newer (and more expensive) synthetic oils last longer, and thus you can drive 10,000 miles between oil changes.

While it's unlikely that you will find a car-related question on the CISA exam, you should expect to break down questions just as is done here. You will likely be able to throw away one or two answers very quickly. The difference between a right answer and a wrong answer can often be found in the context and the hint words provided.

Standards and guidelines are the cornerstone of the audit profession. Standards articulate what must be followed, and they are typically technology platform agnostic. In comparison, a guideline is more of a *use case* for a standard. A guideline explains how to comply with a standard. It's important to understand that the ISACA standards and guidelines are issued across multiple industries and across multiple countries. One size does not fit all! Guidelines are optional, intended to give organizations examples of successful implementation of ISACA standards.

Now we've talked about the terms *standard*, *procedure*, *guideline*, and *baseline* broadly as well as in the context of ISACA publications. Is there a difference between these two uses? Yes, an organization will have standards, procedures, guidelines, and baselines. Will an organization's standards be the same as the ISACA audit and assurance standards? No. An organization typically selects the standards that best meet its needs. ISACA's audit and assurance standards are one source. A manufacturing company may place heavy reliance on International Organization for Standardization (ISO) standards, a credit card merchant will place heavy reliance on Payment Card Industry Data Security Standards (PCI DSS), and so forth.

The terms *procedure* and *baseline* can be confusing. A *procedure* usually is a series of steps to achieve a specific outcome—for example, the particular steps in a company that you have to take to obtain a logon account for a new employee. A *baseline* is platform specific on a set of accepted rules—for example, setting a workstation's Windows 10 platform to time out after 15 minutes. The line between a baseline and a procedure can be blurry. The workstation Windows 10 platform baseline may not only state that a 15-minute timeout is required but may also show the steps and a screenshot for how to make the setting. In that case, it is still a baseline, not a procedure. For the ISACA exam, remember that if a document is platform specific to implement a specific rule, you can treat it as a baseline. If the document is purely procedural steps with a focus on a specific outcome (such as a deliverable), you can treat it as a procedure.

ISACA publishes documents periodically. The best source of the current list of documents is the ISACA website (see "Suggested Readings and Resources," at the end of this chapter).

At the time of this writing, ISACA had published 17 standards:

- Audit Charter
- Organizational Independence
- Professional Independence
- Reasonable Expectation
- Due Professional Care
- Proficiency
- Assertions
- Criteria
- Engagement Planning
- Risk Assessment in Planning
- Performance and Supervision
- Materiality
- Evidence
- Using the Work of Other Experts

- Irregularity and Illegal Acts
- Reporting
- Follow-up Activities

ISACA has also published 18 guidelines:

- Audit Charter
- Organizational Independence
- Professional Independence
- Reasonable Expectation
- Due Professional Care
- Proficiency
- Assertions
- Criteria
- Engagement Planning
- Risk Assessment in Planning
- Performance and Supervision
- Materiality
- Evidence
- Using the Work of Other Experts
- Irregularity and Illegal Acts
- Audit Sampling
- Reporting
- Follow-up Activities

NOTE A good way to prepare for the exam is to read as many ISACA standards and guidelines as possible. Do not memorize them but focus on their intent. These documents include references to situations on how to apply the job practice across domain areas. Learning how to apply knowledge to tasks will be helpful during the exam.

Knowledge of Regulatory Standards

An organization must work within a framework of laws and regulations, which may dictate how data is processed, handled, stored, and destroyed. Businesses are increasingly being tasked with processing a growing amount of electronic information. If they fail to handle this information properly and with due care, they could be subject to legal fines or loss of public confidence, and the top executive may even run the risk of jail time. Companies can be held liable if personal data is disclosed to an unauthorized person.

For example, the European Union (EU) Privacy Shield law prohibits the transfer of personal data to countries that do not meet the EU standard for privacy protection. Companies that fail to meet these standards can face legal recourse, suffer a loss of public confidence, or even be blocked from doing business in the EU.

The following list of regulatory standards and links to websites, while not exhaustive, is a good representation of important U.S. regulatory expectations:

- **U.S. Health Insurance Portability and Accountability Act (HIPAA):** U.S. standards on management of health care data (www.hhs.gov/hipaa/for-professionals/privacy/laws-regulations/index.html)

- **Sarbanes-Oxley Act (SOX):** U.S. financial and accounting disclosure and accountability for public companies (www.soxlaw.com)

- **Basel III:** Risk management in banking (www.bis.org/bcbs/basel3.htm)

- **Payment Card Industry (PCI) standards:** Handling and processing of credit cards (www.pcisecuritystandards.org/pdfs/pcissc_overview.pdf)

- **U.S. Federal Information Security Management Act (FISMA):** Security standards for U.S. government systems (www.gsa.gov/portal/content/150159)

- **Committee of Sponsoring Organizations of the Treadway Commission (COSO):** A series of frameworks to help identify factors that lead to fraudulent financial reporting (www.coso.org/Pages/default.aspx)

- **U.S. Supervisory Controls and Data Acquisition (SCADA):** Enhanced security for automated control systems such as those found in the power plants or oil and gas industry (www.dhs.gov/sites/default/files/publications/csd-nist-guidetosupervisoryanddataccquisition-scadaandindustrialcontrolsystemssecurity-2007.pdf)

- **U.S. Fair and Accurate Credit Transaction ACT of 2003 (FACTA):** Legislation to reduce fraud and identity theft (www.ftc.gov/enforcement/statutes/fair-accurate-credit-transactions-act-2003)

Some regulatory guidelines are not truly laws. For example, PCI is not a law but was developed by the major credit card companies (Visa, MasterCard, American Express, Discover, and JCB) and is referenced in regulatory guidelines such as the *FFIEC Handbook* for best practices for banks. Whether a regulation calls out a framework as best practices or is written into the law makes little practical difference. The regulator knocking on your door has an expectation of compliance or a very clearly articulated and well-managed reason compliance was not possible. Consideration for regulatory requirements is a high priority when planning and scoping an audit.

NOTE ISACA does not expect CISA candidates to know the specifics of each law, rule, or regulation. Candidates are expected to understand the steps used to audit compliance with the regulations.

Guidance Documents

While regulatory guidance is important, it's typically not comprehensive. A challenge with regulatory guidance is that it's often too late! Many laws are written in response to an event such as, in the case of information systems, a major breach. Enacting laws takes a long time because of public debate, hearings, pressure from special interests, and so on.

Industry norms emerge from the combination of industry guidance documents and regulation guidance. These industry guidance documents align to major regulatory requirements and often are more detailed and published more often. This is particularly important when a new threat in cybersecurity is identified.

The CISA exam will not require detailed knowledge of each industry guidance. A CISA candidate needs to understand what industry guidance is and most importantly the benefits of effectively adopting industry guidance, which include the following:

- Demonstrating to customers compliance with industry best practices

- Demonstrating the ability to adopt lessons learned across the globe

- Ensuring that organizations' products and services meet quality and environmental stewardship

- Proving through audits that an organization's systems operate according to accepted norms, as defined by industry standards

- Ensuring that products and services are produced with acceptable consistency

- Reacting quickly to emerging events related to technology defects and breaches

Notice that the benefits depend on effectively adopting the industry guidance. An important role of an auditor is verifying compliance. Some industry standards have certification programs in which an external examiner audits the organization and certifies the organization's compliance with specific industry guidance. These external examiners are similar to a health inspectors, who ensure that a restaurant meets health codes. If an organization passes, it obtains a certification of compliance, which may give it a business advantage or provide evidence to a regulator that it is operating within industry norms.

The following list of industry guidance, while not exhaustive, is a good sampling of important U.S. industry expectations:

- **Control Objectives for Information and Related Technologies (COBIT):** COBIT was first published in 1996 as one of the first definitive guides for IS auditors. COBIT has evolved into a globally accepted framework, providing an end-to-end business view of the governance of enterprise IT. COBIT 5 is the latest version and is considered a framework that embodies global thought guidance for information systems audit, assurance, and control functions.

- **International Organization for Standardization (ISO):** Since 1987 the ISO has created a series of international standards that define and structure a company's management systems. These standards are rigorous, and obtaining certification is not easy. While they cover multiple industries, they often are referred to in manufacturing. The standards cover design, manufacturing, production, purchasing, quality control, packaging, handling, storage, shipping, and customer service.

- **National Institute of Standards and Technology (NIST) standards:** NIST, a unit of the U.S. Commerce Department, issues a number of technology-related standards. Most notably, in 2014 the U.S. government issued a NIST Cybersecurity Framework. Initially this framework only applied to U.S. government systems, but today the NIST Cybersecurity Framework has been widely adopted by banking and other industries.

- **Federal Information Processing Standards (FIPS):** FIPS is a set of U.S. government standards that describe document processing, encryption algorithms, and related information technology standards for use in nonmilitary U.S. government agencies. Government vendors and contractors who work for government agencies must comply with FIPS.

Auditing Compliance with Regulatory Standards

The growing dependence on automated IT systems to store and transmit data has driven the creation of many compliance rules and regulations. An auditor's role is to evaluate the design and operation of internal controls.

Most organizations want to do the right thing and are interested in proper controls. They might be overwhelmed by the day-to-day demands of business. However, it is very important for auditors to verify their compliance.

The process of verifying regulatory compliance is highly structured and detailed. The results may have to be presented to a regulator to demonstrate due care. Most organizations must comply with many different laws and legal requirements, and this has an impact on an audit. An organization must be aware of these laws and regulations and must have evidence that the organization's controls demonstrate compliance. The following is a step-by-step high-level procedure for verifying regulatory compliance:

1. Based on the industry and jurisdiction locale in which the organization operates, keep an inventory of laws, rules, and regulations that the organization must adhere to.

> **TIP**   Many organizations have a compliance or legal department that maintains the inventory. In addition, trade organizations or industry groups may share inventories.

2. Review the specific laws and regulations with which the organization must be compliant.

3. Determine whether the organization's policies and procedures and controls reflect these laws and regulations.

4. Determine whether identified standards and procedures adhere to regulatory requirements.

5. Determine whether the employees are adhering to specified standards and procedures or whether discrepancies exist.

Knowledge of Business Processes

Knowledge of the business and related processes is needed throughout an audit, from planning, examination, and reporting through follow-up. This business knowledge provides the filter and context by which an audit assesses and identifies issues.

Although you might not think of scuba diving when discussing auditing, the two are actually similar. They both follow standards and guidelines. No one who has ever gone diving would consider jumping into the ocean without checking the oxygen tank or performing other basic safety checks. Auditing is similar, in that you cannot just show up at a site and announce that you are there to perform an audit. Auditing requires a specific set of skills and knowledge. For example, an auditor must know when to perform a compliance test or a substantive test and must understand the differences between them.

Compliance tests are used to verify conformity, whereas *substantive tests* verify the integrity of claims. What does it mean to *verify conformity*? It means that an audit verifies that the proper controls are in place to ensure compliance to a specific standard. The compliance test, in essence, makes sure the control is in place. What does the *integrity of claims* mean? It means the controls are actually working. So compliance tests ensure that controls are in place, and substantive tests ensure that controls are working.

Let's consider a home inspection company example. Say that a government program provides first-time home buyers a deeply discounted mortgage rate but requires a home inspection. Consider the following questions and answers:

1. What type of audit is it if the auditor assesses that the closing process control of the mortgage includes a home inspection?

   Answer: Compliance test. The test tells us whether the closing process control is compliant with the intent of the government program.

2. What type of audit is it if the auditor assesses that the home inspectors are qualified and their inspections are highly accurate?

   Answer: Substantive test. The test tells us whether the closing process control is working effectively.

Types of Audits

A key step in audit planning is to select the type of audit to perform. This decision will help drive the scope and determine which audit area will take the lead. There are three basic types of audits:

- **Financial:** A *financial audit* is an audit of financial statements and processes. An IS auditor is typically not involved in a purely financial audit.

- **Integrated:** When a financial audit's scope includes the underlying technology, such as application and network infrastructure, the IS auditor joins the assessment. This type of audit, which covers non-technology (such as financial) controls and technology controls is referred to as an *integrated audit*. One of the major advantages of an integrated audit is that the business is only audited once rather than twice (for example, for financials and for technology).

■ **Operational:** An *operational audit* assesses how well the business operations are managed. This includes reviewing the organization's policies, key processes, controls, and operating environment. An example of an operations IS audit is an assessment of data center operations.

The various audits together are typically referred to as an *audit program*. Each audit program has a specific objective, scope, and predetermined methodology. An enterprise's information systems can be audited in many different ways, and each audit program can be customized—for example, a cybersecurity audit versus a data center operations audit versus a compliance audit for a specific regulation. Collectively, the audit programs represent the scope of risk covered by the auditors.

A *compliance audit* is a comprehensive review of an organization's adherence to regulatory guidelines. IS auditors are playing an increased role in compliance audits today. One reason is that handling, notification, storage, and processing information has emerged as a central theme in many regulations. For instance, the Sarbanes-Oxley Act requirements designate that an entity must utilize an IT control framework (such as COBIT) as a foundation for IT systems and processes. Health care providers that store or transmit electronic health (e-health) records, such as personal health information (PHI), are subject to HIPAA requirements.

An audit program should be defined so that the scope of audit objectives and the scope of procedures are clear. The scope and type of testing that occurs may vary depending on how the understanding of risk has changed since the last audit. Testing and evaluation of system controls require an auditor to fully understand proper test procedures, which can include the following:

■ Sampling of a population

■ Auditing through observation

■ Reviewing documentation

■ Documenting systems and processes by means of flowcharting

■ Examining log files and data records

■ Using specialized software packages to examine system parameter files

Risk Assessment Concepts

You might think that defining risk is fairly straightforward, but virtually every framework changes the definition just enough to introduce more questions and confusion. COBIT 5 defines *risk* as "the combination of the probability of an event and its consequence." This means if you know how likely it is that an event will occur and you know what the impact is if it occurs, then you can understand the risk.

Understanding risk is one of the most important steps in audit planning. The goal should be to plan an audit that assesses the greatest amount of the risk controllable by the organization.

> **NOTE**   As you prepare for the CISA exam, you may see multiple documents with slightly differing or conflicting definitions of *risk*. This is not unusual, even within ISACA's own documents. COBIT 5 was a major release for ISACA that normalized many definitions and is a good source to reconcile differing definitions for the CISA exam.

Auditors typically focus on the risks that have the highest impact on an organization. Table 2-4 describes the three main risks that are called out by COBIT 5.

Table 2-4   Key Risk Types

Item	Attributes
Inherent risk	The risk that naturally occurs because of the nature of the business before controls are applied
Control risk	The risk that internal controls will not prevent a material error
Detection risk	The risk that misstatements or possibly material errors have occurred and were not detected

Let's explore each of these risks and the natural variations. The CISA exam will include questions to determine whether you can understand the differences between the risk types. A term you may see on the exam is *material*, which is generally defined as an item of significance that has a real impact on the organization. For example, a traffic accident that delays your arrival at work may or may not be material. If your late arrival causes you to lose a million-dollar contract because the client gets tired of waiting, then it most likely is material. Arriving at the office late and finding that the offer is gone is not material. Understanding of these risks helps you judge whether something is material:

- **Inherent risk:** *Inherent risk* is often described as the risk that exists if no controls have been deployed. Given the nature of a business, what is its susceptibility to making a material error if there are no internal controls? For example, given the nature of driving, would having no speed limits be an inherent risk? Yes!

- **Control risk:** *Control risk* is often described as a control that is deployed but not working as expected. For example, assume that your car has an airbag only in the steering column. A driver-side collision occurs, and the airbag fails to deploy. There is a risk that the airbag has a defect and also a risk that the design of the airbag is flawed.

- **Detection and audit risk:** *Detection risk* is often described as a defect in a control going undetected. An *audit risk* is a type of detection risk in which an auditor fails to find a material error or defect in a control. Detection risks can also result from an internal failure of a business, such as an inadequate quality assurance program. Detection control risk is often realized when volumes are high. For example, reviewing security logs is an important control. The volume of logs could increase the likelihood that an event is missed and increase the detection risk.

- **Residual risk:** The *residual risk* is the risk that remains after controls are applied to the inherent risk. This risk is not included in Table 2-4 because it's not directly referenced in COBIT. Nonetheless, it is a common term in the industry and an important concept for the CISA exam. Residual risk in essence is inherent risk minus controls. For example, the inherent risk may be high for driving with no speed limit signs, but that risk becomes greatly reduced when speed limit signs are posted. The risk is further reduced when police presence is visible. It's an important concept that residual risk is reduced by layering controls against the inherent risk.

The assessment of what is material is left to the professional judgment of the auditor. This includes both *quantitative* analysis and *qualitative* judgment, based on the understanding of the business and the potential for errors and omissions.

The concept of *quantitative* analysis involves coming to an objective conclusion based on a series of measurements. The following are some measurements that may be taken related to risk:

- Identifying populations (for example, information assets)

- Valuing the assets (for example, cost to recover)

- Identifying the risks to the assets

- Identifying the likelihood of the risk being realized

- Identifying the cost to the organization of the risk being realized

- Identifying the cost to mitigate the risk

A quantitative analysis based on these measurements may conclude that the cost to mitigate such a risk is too high. For example, say that the measurements captured indicate that a particular risk is predicted to occur is every three years, the cost to remediate is $100,000 per year, and the recovery cost is $50,000 per event. The quantitative analysis may show that it's not worth the cost to mitigate.

A qualitative judgment looks at the broad understanding of the business and asks the question, what might go wrong? A qualitative judgment can override a quantitative analysis. In that case, be sure to clearly document the rationale. For example, you may be entering a new market and, given the uncertainty and concerns over how the regulators will react, you err on side of caution and remediate the potential risk.

When quantitative analysis is not available, then qualitative judgment is used. Be careful to avoid overreliance on judgment versus analysis. Often a hybrid approach is used, where both methods are applied. When both are applied, the quantitative analysis can be used to validate the qualitative judgment.

Risk Management

Risk management is the practice of identifying risks, assessing them, making a judgment of disposition, and monitoring. Many organizations, especially those that operate in regulated industries, have formal risk management programs.

Risk management follows a defined process that includes the following steps:

1. Implement a formal risk management program.

2. Identify assets.

3. Identify threats.

4. Perform risk analysis.

5. Disposition of risk.

6. Monitor.

A risk management program often falls under the corporate governance function, such as the chief risk officer. It should be a formal program that is supported by senior leadership. The risk-management team needs support and funding from senior management and should be led by someone with strong project-management skills.

Organizations must identify assets and understand their value to the business. For example, Coca-Cola places value on the original formula for Coke and must protect it. Assets include people, processes, and technology. It is important not to define assets too narrowly. Any asset that is bought or built has value. Depending on the size of the organization, a material threshold should be used. For example, a $5,000 copier/fax machine is not material to a billion-dollar corporation. But if that asset sits in the chairman's office, the asset becomes much more valuable. Getting the balance right so an inventory can be quickly obtained is the purpose of setting a materiality threshold.

The identification of threats should be part of both an ongoing refresh of the threat inventory and a threat assessment of each business area at least annually. It should include an exercise that includes senior management.

Risk analysis is performed using both quantitative and qualitative methods. Regardless of the method used, the idea is to rank threats in some order to determine what requires immediate action. Some threats might have the potential for great impact but very little risk. Other threats might present a high level of risk but have very little impact. The idea is for the team to identify high-impact, high-risk concerns and focus on those items. For example, a company based in Galveston, Texas, would most likely consider a hurricane a high-risk, high-impact item. The island has no point of land that is more than 14 feet above sea level, and the Gulf of Mexico is a prime area for strong storms. This same approach should be used during audits to ensure that audit time is spent on areas with the highest risks.

The disposition of risk has changed over the years. For example, immediately following the financial meltdown in 2008, regulators were at times driving for high rates of risk remediation, regardless of cost. As risks across the financial industry were demonstrated to be more balanced with the threats, there was some easing on the push for massive remediation efforts.

NOTE   Remember that there is a difference between a threat and a risk. A *threat* is something that can happen to create a negative impact, such as a malware attack. A *risk* is the outcome of the threat, such as the online shopping website being shut down. The CISA exam expects candidates to understand the difference between threats and risks.

After identifying high-risk, high-impact concerns, the risk-management team can move on to the risk mitigation or risk disposition phase. Risk can be disposed of in the following ways:

- **Avoiding risk (also referred to as *risk avoidance*):** Avoiding risk can seem like a simple alternative: You simply don't perform the activity that allows the risk to be present. In reality, many activities cannot be avoided. Even when they can be, an opportunity cost might be involved so that avoiding the risk involves missing the opportunity for profit.

- **Reducing risk (also referred to as *risk reduction*):** Reducing risk is one of the most common methods of dealing with risk. Examples include installing a firewall and implementing a new internal accounting control.

- **Accepting risk (also referred to as *risk acceptance*)**—Risk acceptance means that the organization knows about a risk and makes a conscious decision to accept it. Accepting risk means that the company is retaining the potential costs that are associated with the risk. For example, a business might be considering building an e-commerce website but has determined that it will face an added risk. However, along with the risk is the potential to increase revenue, so the company accepts the risk.

- **Transferring risk (also referred to as *risk transference*):** Transferring risk means placing the risk in someone else's hands. A good example of risk transference is insurance. Although there are benefits to risk transference, there are also some drawbacks. Chief among them is that insurance is an ongoing expense. In addition, it is time-consuming and costly to document and settle relatively small losses. Finally, even small payouts by the insurance company can have an adverse effect on future insurance costs.

The monitoring of the portfolio of risks is important. You can think of monitoring as a type of change management. Any time a change is made to systems or the operating environment, a reassessment should be performed to see how the changes affect a potential risk. Risk analysis is a powerful tool in the hands of an auditor because it can help identify risks and threats. It also aids the auditor in examining existing controls to determine their effectiveness and helps the auditor focus his or her efforts on a high-risk, high-impact area.

Auditing and the Use of Internal Controls

An organization deploys controls to comply with internal policies, meet regulatory expectation, and reduce the level of risk to a tolerable threshold. All business involves risk. Anyone who gets in a car in the morning to go to work takes a risk of a traffic accident. The question is one of risk and reward. As long the reward outweighs the risk, a business can generally be successful. The key is to deploy the right type of controls to reduce risk to an acceptable level, which is sometimes referred to as a *risk tolerance*.

Management might give an auditor a general control objective to review during the audit, but the primary goal is to verify the confidentiality, integrity, and availability (CIA) of information resources. Assuring compliance is also important. Compliance reviews are an integral part of any IT auditor job. Audited systems must meet regulatory and legal requirements while assuring compliance. An auditor can test compliance in several ways, as discussed in this section.

How much substantive testing is required depends on the level of internal controls and the amount of confidence the auditor has in the operation of the internal control structure. IS audits that examine systems with a large number of internal controls that have high confidence lower the number of required substantive tests.

Management uses internal controls to exercise authority and effectively manage the organization. Controls typically start with high-level policy and apply to all areas of the company. IS auditors are interested in IS controls because they are used to verify that systems are maintained in a controlled state. IS controls should protect the integrity, reliability, and accuracy of information and data. Properly implemented IS control objectives should guarantee efficiency and effectiveness, protect the organization against outages, and provide for an effective incident response. As stated earlier, these controls filter down the organizational structure by means of policy and procedure. These procedures can be divided into two categories: general control procedures and IS control procedures.

General control procedures are established by management to provide a reasonable amount of assurance that specific objectives will be achieved. To illustrate, Table 2-5 describes a sampling of general control procedures and IS control procedures.

Table 2-5   Control Procedures

General Control Procedures	Examples of Information System Control Procedures
Internal accounting controls used to safeguard financial records	Procedures that provide reasonable assurance for the control of database administration cannot impact financial statements.
Operational controls that are focused on recovery of day-to-day activities	Business continuity planning (BCP) and disaster-recovery procedures that provide reasonable assurance that the organization is secure against disasters. (BCP covers all critical areas of the organization and is not exclusively an IS control.)
Administrative controls designed for corporate compliance	System-development methodologies and change-control procedures implemented to protect the organization and maintain compliance.
Procedures that safeguard access and use of organizational resources	Procedures that provide reasonable assurance for the control of access to data and programs.
Logical security policies designed to support proper transactions	Procedures that provide reasonable assurance for the control and management of data-processing operations.
Logical security policies designed to support transactional audit trails	Procedures that provide reasonable assurance for the control of networks and communications.
Security policies that address the physical control of data centers	Physical access control procedures that provide assurance for the organization's safety.

Controls can be preventive, detective, or corrective. Table 2-6 describes these controls in more detail. Regardless of how well controls are designed, they can provide only reasonable assurance. Using the three types of controls in conjunction with each other creates a system of checks and balances, which helps provide a greater level of assurance and ensures that processes operate in a controlled manner. Keep in mind that no system is perfect, and controls will always be subject to error due to breakdowns or system overrides or even employees or outsiders.

Table 2-6   Control Categories

Class	Function	Example
Preventive	Prevents problems before they occur	Access control software that uses passwords, tokens, and/or biometrics
Detective	Senses and detects problems as they occur	Security logs
Corrective	Reduces the impact of threats and minimizes the impact of problems	Backup power supplies

The key difference between preventive, detective, and corrective controls is in how a threat is handled. A preventive control stops a threat immediately. A detective control identifies a threat after the fact. A corrective control tries to remediate risk of a threat after the fact.

The Auditing Life Cycle

It's important to view an audit from many perspectives, given the variety of CISA exam questions that can be thrown your way. An audit can be defined as a planned, independent, and documented assessment to determine whether agreed-upon requirements and standards of operations are being met. Basically, it is a review of an operation and its activities. An IS audit deals specifically with the technology used for information processing. An auditor is responsible for reporting the facts and providing an independent review of the technology and manual systems. As an auditor, you are in a position of *fiduciary* responsibility, which means you hold a position of special trust and confidence.

Audit Methodology

The purpose of an IS audit is to evaluate controls against predetermined control objectives. For example, an operational control objective might be used to ensure that funds accepted on the company's e-commerce website are properly posted in the company's bank account. However, in an IS audit, the objective might be expanded to make sure that dollar amounts are entered correctly into the e-commerce website and that they match the posted prices of the items being sold.

An *audit methodology* is a documented approach for performing an audit in a consistent and repeatable manner. The audit methodology is designed to meet audit objectives by defining the following:

- A statement of work
- A statement of scope
- A statement of audit objectives

The methodology should be approved by management and thoroughly documented so that it provides a highly repeatable process. The audit methodology is an important educational tool for avoiding surprises during an audit. All audit employees must be trained and must have knowledge of the methodology.

The Auditing Life Cycle Steps

Using a structured and repeatable methodology fosters the establishment of boundaries and builds confidence in the audit process. The steps of the audit process are described in greater detail here:

1. **Audit subject:** Identify which areas are to be audited, based on risk.

2. **Audit objective:** Define why the audit is occurring. For example, the objective of an audit might be to ensure that access to private information, such as Social Security numbers, is controlled.

3. **Audit scope:** Identify which specific functions or systems are to be examined.

4. **Pre-audit planning:** Identify what skills are needed for the audit, how many auditors are required, and what other resources are needed. Necessary policies or procedures should be identified, as should the plans of the audit. The plans should identify what controls will be verified and tested.

5. **Data gathering:** Identify interviewees, identify processes to be tested and verified, and obtain documents such as policies, procedures, and standards. Develop procedures to test controls.

6. **Evaluation of test results:** Results will be organization specific. The objective is to review the results.

7. **Communication with management:** Document preliminary results and communicate them to management.

TIP Pose initial auditor's observations as questions—for example, "We observed *X*. Can you help us understand how this should be handled and why?" Based on feedback and additional evidence, a determination can be made about whether the observation is truly an issue to be reported on the audit report.

8. **Preparation of audit report:** Ensure that the audit report is the culmination of the audit process and might include the identification of follow-up items.

Chain of Custody and Evidence Handling

Chain of custody is an important issue that cannot be overlooked during an audit—especially one that may be litigated. To show chain of custody, an auditor must be able to account for who had access to the collected data, ensure that the access to the information was controlled, and show that it has been protected from tampering. For example, say that a server was breached, and there is a log file of the user accounts that were logged into a server at the time of the breach. That log file could be captured and preserved by being written to write-once media. The write-once media could indicate when the log file was captured and ensure that evidence cannot be altered. In addition, the evidence would need to be locked up so that from the point when the evidence was captured to the point it is used in court, there is proof that the evidence could not have be altered. This is generally considered maintaining the chain of custody.

Evidence handling refers to the auditor handling any information obtained during the audit. Evidence can be obtained from interviews, work papers, direct observation, internal documentation, compliance testing, and/or substantive testing. All evidence is not created equal; some evidence has more value and provides a higher level of confidence than other forms. Evidence the auditor obtains should be sufficient, usable, reliable, and relevant, and it should achieve audit objectives effectively. This is sometimes referred to as the SURRE rule:

Sufficient

Usable

Reliable

Relevant

Effective

CISA candidates should be aware of ISACA standards for auditing and should understand how evidence can be used to support any findings. The ISACA website is available at www.isaca.org and provides both standards and guidelines related to evidence handling:

- IS Audit and Assurance Standard 1205 on Evidence
- IS Audit and Assurance Guideline 2205 on Evidence

Table 2-7 lists some basic questions to answer in determining the reliability of evidence.

Table 2-7   Evidence Reliability

Question	Description
Is the provider of the evidence independent?	Evidence from inside sources is not considered as reliable as evidence obtained from outside sources.
Is the evidence provider qualified?	The person providing the evidence has to have his or her qualifications reviewed to validate his or her credibility.
How objective is the evidence?	Some evidence requires considerable judgment; other evidence (such as dollar amounts) is easy to evaluate.
When is the evidence available?	Backups, the write process, and updates can affect when and how long evidence is available.

Auditors should observe auditees in the performance of their duties to assist in gathering evidence and understanding how procedures, job roles, and documentation match actual duties. Auditors should perform the following:

- Observe employee activity
- Examine and review procedures and processes
- Verify employee security awareness training and knowledge
- Examine reporting relationships to verify segregation of duties

Automated Work Papers

An important part of auditing methodology is documentation. Findings, activities, and tests should be documented in work papers (WPs), which can be either hard copy or electronic documents. However, because they are created and stored, they must be properly dated, labeled, and detailed; clear; and self-contained. ISACA IS auditing standards and guidelines detail specifications that pertain to WPs. WPs are subject to review by regulators.

Auditors are aware of the importance of the control of WPs; these same controls must be provided for automated WPs. Controls that protect the confidentiality, integrity, and availability of electronic WPs should be applied at the same level as their paper-based counterparts. Some items to consider include the following:

- Encryption to provide confidentiality

- Backups to provide availability

- Audit trails and controls

- Access controls to maintain authorized access

NOTE Remember that accountability for maintaining confidentiality of paper, electronic, and sensitive client information rests with an auditor. Sensitive information should always be protected.

CAATs

Audit teams in recent years have moved to simplify and automate the auditing process. Although auditors have used word processors and spreadsheet programs for quite some time, audit teams are moving to more advanced methods for automating WPs. Computer-assisted audit techniques (CAATs) are one example of this. CAATs are software audit tools used for statistical sampling and data analysis.

An area of particular interest to auditors is sampling using software. What do you do when you cannot test an entire population or a complete batch? You use sampling—which is the process of selecting items from a population of interest. The practice of sampling can give the auditor generalized results for the population as a whole. There are two basic types of audit sampling:

- **Statistical sampling:** This type of sampling is based on probability. Every item in the population has a known chance of selection. The prominent feature of statistical sampling is its capability to measure risk and the use of quantitative assessment. An auditor quantitatively determines the sample size and confidence level.

- **Nonstatistical sampling:** This type of sampling involves using auditor judgment to select the sample size and determine which items to select. Nonstatistical sampling is also known as *judgmental sampling*.

Each sampling type, statistical and nonstatistical, has two subgroups of sampling techniques:

- **Variable sampling:** Variable sampling is used primarily for substantive testing. It measures characteristics of the sample population, such as dollar amounts or other units of measurement.

- **Attribute sampling:** Attribute sampling is used primarily for compliance testing. It records deviations by measuring the rate of occurrence that a sample has a certain attribute. Attribute sampling can be further divided into three subcategories:

  - **Frequency estimating sampling:** Answers the question "How many?"

  - **Stop-and-go sampling:** Used when it is believed that few errors exist

  - **Discovery sampling:** Used to discover fraud or irregularities

NOTE   When sampling is required, the most appropriate method is to pull samples by using an automated tool.

Sampling is not the only way to ensure compliance. Ongoing monitoring might be required. One ongoing monitoring method is to use *embedded audit modules*. Embedded modules are designed to be an integral part of an application and are designed to identify and report specific transactions or other information, based on predetermined criteria. Identification of reportable items occurs as part of real-time processing. Reporting can be performed by means of real-time processing or online processing, or it can use store-and-forward methods. *Parallel simulation* is another test technique that examines real results that are compared to those generated by the auditor. *Integrated test facilities* (*ITFs*) use data that represents fake entities, such as products, items, or departments. ITF is processed on actual production systems.

Audit Closing

After interviewing employees, reviewing documentation, performing testing, and making personal observations, an auditor is ready to compile the information and provide findings. These findings should be recorded in the audit opinion. The audit opinion is part of the auditor's report and should include the following components:

- Name of the organization being audited

- Auditor's Name, date, and signature

- Statement of audit objectives

- Audit scope

- Any limitations of scope

- Audience

- Standards used in the audit

- Details of the findings

- Conclusions, reservations, and qualifications

- Suggestions for corrective actions

- Other significant events

CAUTION   Auditors should always attempt to follow written procedures. If procedures are not followed, the auditor must keep documentation on why procedures were not followed and what the findings were.

Report Writing

After the closing session, typically an auditor has all the information needed to write the audit report. The auditor should be clear and unambiguous about which issues should be in the report and the reasoning. The audit report language should be equally clear and supported by the evidence obtained.

An audit report is designed to provide information needed persuade to the audience where corrective action is needed and why. An audit report with no major issues is valuable! Such an audit report confirms that the controls in place are working effectively, which means management can spend limited resources elsewhere.

When issues are raised, a well-written audit report is a call to action for leadership to not only improve control defects but potentially address why it took an auditor to find the control defect.

When writing an audit report, consider this sampling of best practices:

- **Timely manner:** An audit report issued months after an audit is completed may no longer represent the current state of controls.

- **Report classification:** Be clear on the intended recipients and any restrictions on handling.

- **Key message:** Keep the report centered on the final opinion and key supporting evidence; keep the focus on the results and not on how those results were obtained.

- **Scope clarity:** Be sure the reader knows immediately the scope of the audit and any qualifications, such as the results being limited to compliance tests versus substantive tests.

- **Severity of issues:** A good audit report tells the reader the severity of the issues and opinion in the context of the risk; the audit report tells a risk story and should be compelling.

- **Tech jargon:** Avoid unnecessary technical language. Effective audit reports use simple language to convey powerful ideas.

- **Leverage WPs:** Keep details in the work papers.

The Control Self-Assessment Process

In an ideal world, any control defect should be identified and remediated through the risk management program. One step closer to an ideal state is to identify and remediate control defects through the control self-assessment process, which is when the business participates in a formal self-assessment.

Although the traditional approach to auditing has proven itself over the years, it does have some problems, primarily because responsibility for the audit is placed on the auditors. Managers and employees might feel that it is an auditor's job to find and report problems. Using a *control self-assessment* (*CSA*) is an attempt to overcome the shortcomings of the traditional approach. According to ISACA, the CSA methodology is designed to provide assurance to stakeholders, customers, and employees that internal controls have been designed to minimize risks.

CSAs are used to verify the reliability of internal controls. Unlike in traditional auditing, some of the control monitoring responsibilities are shifted to functional areas of the business. Because the functional areas are directly involved and play an important role in the design of the controls that protect critical assets, employees tend to be motivated. CSAs also tend to raise the level of control, which allows risk to be detected sooner and, consequently, reduces cost.

Table 2-8 outlines the differences between traditional auditing and the CSA approach.

Table 2-8   CSA Versus Traditional Auditing

CSA	Traditional Auditing
Empowers employees and gives them responsibility	Places responsibility on the auditing staff and management
Offers a method for continuous improvement	Limited by policies and rules and does not involve functional area management or give them as much control
Involves employees and raises their level of awareness	Offers little employee participation
Involves staff and employees and makes them the first line of control	Decreased awareness of staff and employees of internal controls and their objectives

You might be thinking that CSA appears to be a cure for all auditing problems, but it does have drawbacks. Some individuals have a misconception that CSAs can replace audits. This is not correct. CSA was not designed to replace the audit function; it was designed to enhance the audit function. Some employees might also offer objections because a CSA program places an additional workload on employees. The key to making a CSA program work is to identify what processes are the most important to the department under examination.

Interviews, meetings with appropriate business unit employees, and questionnaires are some of the methods used to identify key processes. COBIT 5 under the Monitor and Evaluation Section documents the CSA control objectives (referred to as COBIT 5 ME2.4) and provides related material for CSA.

Continuous Monitoring

Both the speed of transactions and the volume of accompanying data have exploded in recent years. Changes in technology result in quicker transactions, and the need for instant information has grown.

Continuous monitoring can help meet the demand. Continuous monitoring allows an auditor to program certain control tests. It can alert an auditor to a potential threat or control breakdown. Continuous monitoring is not itself an audit. When a potential threat or control breakdown is detected through continuous monitoring, further examination through an audit is typically required. This is akin to a doctor finding an abnormality in an X-ray and wanting to run further tests to understand more.

Continuous monitoring works well for automated processes that capture, manipulate, store, and disseminate data. Research produced by the American Institute of Certified Public Accountants and the Chartered Professional Accountants of Canada found that six preconditions should be present before an organization can adopt continuous auditing:

- The system must have acceptable characteristics. Cost and factors such as technical skill must be considered.

- The information system must be reliable, have existing primary controls, and collect data on the system.

- The information system must have a highly automated secondary control system.

- The auditor must be proficient in the system and information technology.

- The audit process must offer a reliable method for obtaining the audit procedure results.

- Verifiable controls of the audit reporting process must exist.

There are challenges in implementing a continuous monitoring program. It is important to allocate the appropriate amount of time and effort for the development of a continuous auditing environment. Auditors need to acquire the skills for this program to meet the demands of the changing audit environment.

Quality Assurance

The core concept of quality assurance (QA) is to improve two key attributes: quality and adherence. In both cases, you need to measure the QA results with a yardstick. In other words, QA needs a definition of quality and adherence. The QA process tests transactions against the quality and adherence yardsticks. Deviations are typically reported to the business for remediation.

At a minimum, adherence should mean adherence to the organization's standards. Consequently, adherence expectations should be well defined and easier than quality to measure. When regulatory obligations are baked into an organization's standards, adherence to the standards results in adherence to regulatory obligations.

If quality expectations are baked into standards, adherence to those standards can drive improvement in quality. If they are not defined in standards, then separate testing is needed through the QA program.

Defects identified and corrected through a QA program are generally not considered an audit issue. This is because the QA process is a control specifically designed to catch and remediate defects. As long as the defect rate stays at acceptable levels, the QA process is working as it is designed to work.

An auditor's interest in the QA process should be to perform testing of the controls to ensure that the program is well designed and effective. The QA process is audited as any other process, starting with understanding the intent and overall design. The QA process would most likely result in an operational audit that includes both compliance and substantive testing.

The Challenges of Audits

Most auditors realize early in their careers that auditing can be challenging and is not a popularity contest. It's important to keep in mind that an auditor's presence disrupts the normal operations of the business and can make staff feel uncomfortable. Individuals may take an audit personally and consider it a grading of their work. Some individuals may perceive a negative outcome of an audit to reflect their competency and to have a negative impact on their career.

Many of these fears are unwarranted. An auditor must nevertheless overcome any unwarranted perceptions and demonstrate confidence. A smart, experienced auditor doesn't waste people's time and makes a point to ask relevant questions. The better the auditor knows the business and can ask insightful and deep questions, the more likely it is that the business will have confidence in the audit.

An audit is successful when the business recognizes that the auditor has no agenda beyond finding risk exposures that allowed the business to potentially avoid business disruptions or losses. This perception of value is not always shared by a control owner who has a defect identified through an audit. The reactions can range from reluctant admission to lukewarm denial to borderline threats of complaints about the auditor to management. Police officers are not often thanked for issuing speeding tickets, but those tickets inevitably save some lives!

Communicating Results

The best way to avoid surprises is to *communicate frequently* to the stakeholders of an audit. A common pitfall is waiting until the end of an audit to communicate any major issue. It's highly effective to communicate interim observations to the control owner, who can provide supplemental evidence if necessary.

When examination concludes, an auditor needs to be clear and concise about the type of opinion that will be reported. An auditor looks at the controls, the findings, and the supporting evidence in the context of all the material respects of the design and operational control procedures tested. The auditor then forms an opinion, in one of four possible categories, illustrated in Table 2-9.

Table 2-9   Audit Opinion Categories

Opinion Category	Description
Unqualified opinion	Testing and obtained evidence are complete and persuasive.
Qualified opinion	Appropriate testing and obtained evidence exist that cite instances of control weaknesses but the opinion cannot conclude that the control weakness is pervasive.
Adverse opinion	Multiple significant deficiencies add up to a material and pervasive weakness.
Disclaimer	An auditor cannot obtain appropriate evidence on which to base an opinion.

These opinions can be applied to either an entire audit report or a specific finding. For example, say that you have 10 findings, of which 9 are unqualified in that the evidence and testing obtained are clear and persuasive. Now assume the tenth issue is qualified because the test results are just not clear in terms of the extent to which the control weakness exists. At this point, an auditor has a few choices, depending on the nature of the issues found. The auditor could drop the tenth issue from the report and issue the entire report as an unqualified opinion. Alternatively, the auditor could issue the report as qualified and clearly state that the tenth issue indicates a concern that may not be fully understood.

Many organizations determine an audit report opinion based on the scope, number, and severity of risks found. These audit rating labels can vary greatly. For example, a simple rating scheme for audit reports could be *unrated*, *satisfactory*, and *unsatisfactory*, based on the following mapping to opinion categories:

- **Unrated report:** Some findings disclaimed

- **Satisfactory report:** A low volume of qualified or unqualified findings

- **Unsatisfactory:** Any adverse opinion

NOTE   ISACA expects CISA candidates to understand audit opinion categories and how they are applied.

Negotiation and the Art of Handling Conflicts

Negotiations start when an auditor starts communicating to stakeholders observations or findings. An auditor can expect disagreements. The key obligation of an auditor is to ensure that any observation or finding is fact based and fair and that the conclusion is reasonable, given the obtained evidence. Reaching consensus may not always be possible.

When stakeholders want to challenge and negotiate, their arguments typically fall within three possible areas of disagreement:

1. **The finding itself:** Are the facts accurate and complete?

2. **The severity of the finding:** Is the risk well calculated?

3. **The process by which the finding was identified:** Was the testing fair and unbiased?

It's important for an auditor to review the facts and evidence from the client perspective for gaps or inconsistencies. An audit that is well prepared with facts and a well-documented audit program can be very persuasive.

Conflict can be handled by staying calm and letting the audit process and results speak for themselves. When you have a sound audit process, your observations (that is, findings) will be strong. As a result, many conflicts and negotiations focus on the severity and the aggregated risk as the point of disagreement.

The best way to negotiate and cut down the disagreements is to make an audit report relevant to the business. Relevance is critical for stakeholder satisfaction. Focus the interim discussions on each individual finding to ensure that it is factual. As the audit begins to wind down, the negotiation focus will shift to the severity. The overall audit report rating is typically reserved for discussion with senior leaders. Discussing the overall rating with key stakeholders (such as the control owner) will help drive awareness and provide an opportunity for senior leaders to negotiate any concerns with the report's wording.

Any audit report rating is typically not open to negotiation. Once the facts have been verified, an auditor must issue an independent opinion. Independence is not only the concern of the auditor but also of senior management, who need an independent view of their control environment.

Chapter Summary

This chapter discusses the foundational items needed to understand the IS audit process. The goal of this chapter is to provide you with basic knowledge to help you master the IS audit job practice domain area of the CISA exam. The exam ensures that individuals have the competency to be successful auditors, and this includes having a strong understanding of ISACA IS auditing standards and guidelines.

This chapter discusses the auditor's valuable position in the organization and the need for the auditor to abide by legal and ethical standards, including the ISACA Code of Professional Ethics.

This chapter discusses the fact that auditors must also be able to evaluate and understand risks. Organizations have limited resources, so it's important to identify areas of high risk and focus auditing efforts there. An effective auditor focuses on those areas and uses effective communication skills to facilitate and negotiate positive improvements to reduce material risks.

The next chapter builds on what you have learned in this chapter and focuses on the role of IT governance, with an emphasis on management routines.

Exam Preparation Tasks

As mentioned in the section "How to Use This Book" in the Introduction, you have a couple choices for exam preparation: the exercises here; Chapter 10, "Final Preparation;" and the exam simulation questions on the book's companion web page (www.informit.com/title/9780789758446).

Review All the Key Topics

Review the most important topics in this chapter, noted with the Key Topic icon in the outer margin of the page. Table 9-7 lists these key topics and the page number on which each is found.

Table 2-10   Key Topics in Chapter 2

Key Topic Element	Description	Page Number
Table 2-2	Important work-related skills	27
Table 2-3	Description of standards, procedures, guidelines, and baselines	31
List	ISACA standards for IS auditing and assurance	33
Step List	Procedure for verifying regulatory compliance	38
Table 2-4	Key risk types	41
Step List	Risk management process	43
Table 2-5	Control procedures	46
Table 2-6	Control categories	47
Table 2-7	Evidence reliability	50

Key Topic Element	Description	Page Number
Table 2-8	Control self-assessment (CSA) attributes	55
Table 2-9	Audit opinion category descriptions	58

Complete Tables from Memory

Print a copy of Appendix B, "Memory Tables" (found on the companion web page), or at least the section for this chapter, and complete the tables from memory. Appendix C, "Memory Tables Answer Key," also on the companion web page, includes completed tables you can use to check your work.

Define Key Terms

Define the following key terms from this chapter and check your answers against the glossary:

baselines, chain of custody, Code of Professional Ethics, compliance test, computer-assisted audit techniques (CAATs), continuous monitoring, control risk, control self-assessment (CSA), detection risk, fiduciary, financial audit, guidelines, inherent risk, integrated audit, knowledge statements, material, nonstatistical sampling, operational audit, procedures, risk acceptance, risk avoidance, risk reduction, risk transference, standards, statistical sampling, substantive test, task statements

Exercises

2.1 Network Inventory

Estimated time: 15 minutes

This chapter introduces some of the aspects of the IS audit process, including risk. As you might remember, the risk assessment process consists of the following steps:

1. Implement a formal risk management program.

2. Identify assets.

3. Identify threats.

4. Perform risk analysis.

5. Disposition of risk.

6. Monitor.

This exercise introduces you to one way to perform the second step of the risk process, identifying assets. Although ISACA does not test knowledge on the use of any type of applications, this exercise is designed to provide a deeper understanding of the material.

This exercise looks at an automated inventory tool used to audit systems and software.

1. Download Network Inventory from https://emcosoftware.com/download. Network Inventory generates hardware and software information for Microsoft networks and also verifies software license information.

2. Execute the setup program as shown in Figure 2-1. Accept the license agreement and all default installation settings.

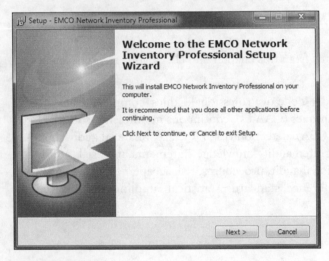

Figure 2-1   Network Inventory Professional Setup

3. When the program launches, choose Enumerate LAN to have the program scan the local network and identify available systems (see Figure 2-2). Allow the program several minutes to finish its enumeration.

4. When the enumeration has finished, from the Machine Management window, under Installed Applications, highlight your local computer. The Data field to the right then lists all applications discovered on the local computer, as shown in Figure 2-3.

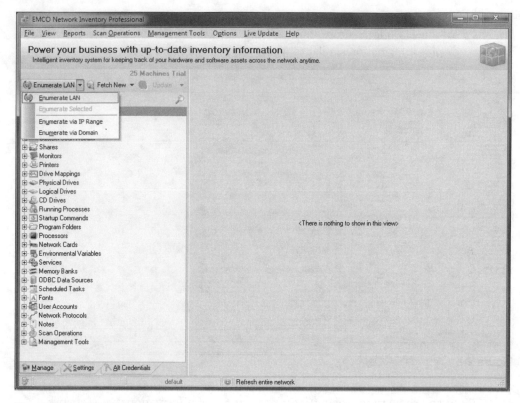

Figure 2-2 LAN Enumeration

Figure 2-3 Installed Applications

5. The program provides an easy way to quickly see all programs that have been installed. To learn more about any one application, simply double-click it to display information similar to what is shown in Figure 2-4.

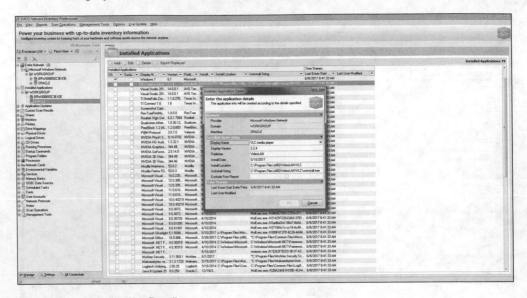

Figure 2-4   Application Details

6. Spend some time looking at the other types of information that Network Inventory can provide to an auditor. In the Machine Management window, examine some of the other types of information the program can provide, such as processes, hotfixes, scheduled tasks, and user accounts.

Review Questions

1. Which of the following best describes a baseline document?

   a. A PCI industry standard requiring a 15-minute session timeout

   b. Installation step recommendations from the vendor for an Active Directory server

   c. A network topography diagram of the Active Directory forest

   d. Security configuration settings for an Active Directory server

2. Which audit opinion best describes a finding that failed a compliance test in 3 of 1,300 locations?

   a. Unqualified

   b. Qualified

   c. Adverse

   d. Disclaimer

3. Which of the following best describes integrated auditing?

   a. Integrated auditing places internal control in the hands of management and reduces the time between the audit and the time of reporting.

   b. Integrated auditing combines the operational audit function, the financial audit function, and the IS audit function.

   c. Integrated auditing combines the operational audit function and the IS audit function.

   d. Integrated auditing combines the financial audit function and the IS audit function.

4. Which storage of evidence would best preserve the chain of custody of evidence obtained during an audit?

   a. Locked department safe behind card access doors

   b. Offsite location, such as home, out of reach by anyone at work

   c. Archival at a third-party offsite facility

   d. Locked cabinet on the department floor with only one key, in the possession of the auditor

5. Which of the following best describes risk that can be caused by the failure of internal controls and can result in a material error?

   a. Residual risk

   b. Inherent risk

   c. Detection risk

   d. Control risk

6. Which of the following is not one of the best techniques for gathering evidence during an audit?

    a. Attend board meetings

    b. Examine and review actual procedures and processes

    c. Verify employee security awareness training and knowledge

    d. Examine reporting relationships to verify segregation of duties

7. Which of the following is not an advantage of control self-assessment (CSA)?

    a. CSA helps provide early detection of risks.

    b. CSA is an audit function replacement.

    c. CSA reduces control costs.

    d. CSA provides increased levels of assurance.

8. If an auditor cannot obtain the material needed to complete an audit, what type of opinion should the auditor issue?

    a. Unqualified opinion

    b. Qualified opinion

    c. Adverse opinion

    d. Disclaimer

9. Which of the following is the best example of general control procedures?

    a. Internal accounting controls used to safeguard financial records

    b. Business continuity and disaster-recovery procedures that provide reasonable assurance that the organization is secure against disasters

    c. Procedures that provide reasonable assurance for the control of access to data and programs

    d. Procedures that provide reasonable assurance and have been developed to control and manage data-processing operations

10. Which of the following describes a significant level of risk that the organization is unwilling to accept?

    a. Detection risk

    b. Material risk

    c. Business risk

    d. Irregularities

11. Which of the following is the most accurate description of a substantive test in which the data represents fake entities such as products, items, or departments?

    a. Parallel tests

    b. Integrated test facility

    c. Embedded audit module

    d. Test data

12. You need to review an organization's balance sheet for material transactions. Which of the following would be the best sampling technique?

    a. Attribute sampling

    b. Frequency estimating sampling

    c. Stop-and-go sampling

    d. Variable sampling

13. Which of the following best describes types of questions that might be on the CISA exam related to how to implement specific risk types discussed in this chapter?

    a. Task statements

    b. Operational audits

    c. Knowledge statements

    d. Integrated audits

14. Which of the following is not a benefit of CSA?

    a. Provides early detection of risks

    b. Reduces potential audit costs

    c. Increases employee awareness of internal controls

    d. Can be used to avoid a regulator audit

15. Which of the following should have priority on the planning and scoping of an IS audit?

    a. Company standards

    b. Organization's master plan

    c. Regulatory requirements

    d. Industry best practices

Suggested Readings and Resources

- **ISACA IS audit and assurance standards:** www.isaca.org/Knowledge-Center/ITAF-IS-Assurance-Audit-/IS-Audit-and-Assurance/Pages/Standards-for-IT-Audit-and-Assurance.aspx

- **ISACA IS audit and assurance guidelines:** www.isaca.org/Knowledge-Center/ITAF-IS-Assurance-Audit-/IS-Audit-and-Assurance/Pages/IT-Audit-and-Assurance-Guidelines.aspx

- **IS audit basics:** www.isaca.org/Journal/archives/2017/Volume-2/Pages/risk-based-audit-planning-for-beginners.aspx

- **COBIT:** www.isaca.org/cobit/pages/default.aspx

- **Auditing Standard 15—Audit evidence:** https://pcaobus.org/Standards/Auditing/pages/auditing_standard_15.aspx

- **Auditor's responsibility for fraud detection:** www.claconnect.com/resources/articles/are-financial-auditors-responsible-for-detecting-internal-fraud

- **NIST Cybersecurity Framework:** www.nist.gov/news-events/news/2017/01/nist-releases-update-cybersecurity-framework

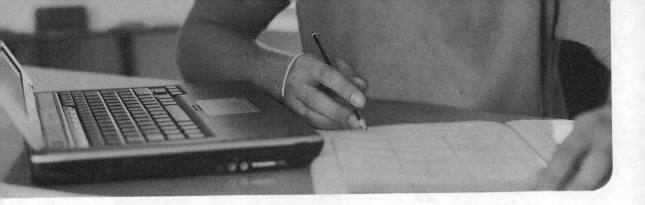

The following exam domain is partially covered in this chapter:

Domain 2—Governance and Management of IT

This chapter covers the following topics:

- **The IT Steering Committee:** This section defines the role and importance of the IT steering committee in corporate governance.

- **Corporate Structure:** This section defines the most common types of corporate structures in business today.

- **IT Governance Frameworks:** This section explains common IT governance frameworks and their roles in governance.

- **Enterprise Risk Management:** This section details common techniques for enterprise risk management.

- **Policy Development:** This section provides an overview of policy development approaches and related implementation strategies.

- **Management Practices of Employees:** This section describes common policies and controls related to how people are hired, promoted, retained, and terminated.

- **Performance Management:** This section reviews methods to measure performance to ensure that the organization's goals are consistently being met in an effective and efficient manner.

- **Management and Control Frameworks:** This section reviews how a control framework categorizes and aligns an organization's internal controls to identify and manage risk in the most optimal manner.

- **Maturity Models:** This section reviews the basics of maturity models and how maturity levels are measured against controls and processes.

- **Management's Role in Compliance:** This section defines management's role in driving adoption of policies to ensure compliance.

- **Process Optimization Techniques:** This section describes various techniques and methods to optimize processes.

- **Management of IT Suppliers:** This section reviews key controls related to the support and management of an IT supplier, IT vendor, or IT third-party provider.

CHAPTER 3

The Role of IT Governance

IT governance is a subset of corporate governance that focuses on the belief that the managers, directors, and others in charge of an organization must establish key roles and responsibilities to control IT risks. Management must implement rules and policies to control the IT infrastructure and develop practices to distribute responsibilities. Not only does this prevent a single person or department from shouldering responsibility, it also sets up a framework of control.

IT governance is established by creating an IT strategy committee, developing policies and procedures, defining job roles, executing good HR practices, and performing risk assessments and periodic audits. This chapter discusses each of these topics.

This chapter discusses IT governance, which involves control, including items that are strategic in nature. Senior management and the IT steering committee help provide the long-term vision so that control can be implemented on a more tactical level.

"Do I Know This Already?" Quiz

The "Do I Know This Already?" quiz allows you to assess whether you should read this entire chapter thoroughly or jump to the "Exam Preparation Tasks" section. If you are in doubt about your answers to these questions or your own assessment of your knowledge of the topics, read the entire chapter. Table 3-1 lists the major headings in this chapter and their corresponding "Do I Know This Already?" quiz questions. You can find the answers in Appendix A, "Answers to the 'Do I Know This Already?' Quizzes and Review Questions."

Table 3-1 "Do I Know This Already?" Section-to-Question Mapping

Foundation Topics Section	Questions
The IT Steering Committee	1
Corporate Structure	2
IT Governance Frameworks	3
Enterprise Risk Management	4

Foundation Topics Section	Questions
Policy Development	5
Management Practices of Employees	6
Performance Management	7
Management and Control Frameworks	8
Maturity Models	9
Management's Role in Compliance	10
Process Optimization Techniques	11
Management of IT Suppliers	12

CAUTION   The goal of self-assessment is to gauge your mastery of the topics in this chapter. If you do not know the answer to a question or are only partially sure of the answer, you should mark that question as incorrect for purposes of the self-assessment. Giving yourself credit for an answer you correctly guess skews your self-assessment results and might provide you with a false sense of security.

1. Which of the following is not a typical IT steering committee group or member?

    a. Business management

    b. Chief technology officer

    c. Human resources

    d. Chief information officer

2. Which of the following is a funding strategy related to paying for an information system's services and requires individual departments to directly be charged for the specific services they use?

    a. Shared cost

    b. Guarantor cost

    c. Chargeback

    d. Sponsor pays

3. Which of the following IT governance frameworks is best suited to define the quality, control, and reliability of information systems by establishing IT governance and management structure and objectives?

   a. ITIL

   b. COBIT

   c. COSO

   d. All the above

4. Which role is typically not aligned to the Three Lines of Defense model?

   a. End user

   b. Business unit leadership

   c. Risk and compliance teams

   d. Auditor

5. Which category would be the best fit to classify data-related IT process documentation in a simple data classification model?

   a. Public

   b. Business confidential

   c. Customer confidential

   d. Proprietary

6. Which of the following control(s) should be used during the hiring process?

   a. Confidentiality agreements

   b. Non-compete agreements

   c. Background check

   d. All the above

7. Which of the following key performance terms refers to how well a process is performing?

   a. Balanced scorecard

   b. Target value

   c. Key performance indicator

   d. Key goal indicator

8. Consider the following list of management and control framework examples. Which of them provides guidance on how to assess and improve the ability to prevent, detect, and respond to cyberattacks?

   a. COBIT

   b. COSO

   c. NIST CSF

   d. ISO

9. Which of the following capability maturity model levels best fits an ad hoc process with no documentation?

   a. Initial

   b. Repeatable

   c. Defined

   d. Optimized

10. Which of the following laws requires accurate financial and accounting disclosure for U.S. public companies?

    a. U.S. Federal Information Security Management Act (FISMA)

    b. U.S. Fair and Accurate Credit Transaction ACT of 2003 (FACTA)

    c. U.S. Health Insurance Portability and Accountability Act (HIPAA)

    d. Sarbanes-Oxley Act (SOX)

11. During which stage of the Plan-Do-Check-Act (PDCA) approach does the auditor measure actual process outcome against objectives?

    a. Plan

    b. Do

    c. Check

    d. Act

12. Which location would not be best suited for third-party outsourcing?

    a. Corporate HQ functions

    b. Data center functions

    c. Help desk functions

    d. Payroll processing functions

Foundation Topics

The IT Steering Committee

An IT steering committee, which also may be referred to as an IT strategy committee, is tasked with ensuring that the IT department's goals are properly aligned with the goals of the business. This is accomplished by using the committee as a conduit to move information and objectives back and forth between senior business management and IT management.

The exact makeup of the IT steering committee will vary by organization based on size, industry, regulatory mandates, and leadership strength. In general, the IT steering committee needs to be made up of senior leaders from IT, corporate functions, and lines of business. The following are typical IT steering committee members:

- **Business management**: The committee is managed by the chief executive officer (CEO) or by another person who is appointed, such as the chief information officer (CIO).

- **IT management**: IT management is represented by the CIO or a CIO representative.

- **Legal**: The legal group is represented by an executive from the legal department.

- **Finance**: A representative from finance is needed to provide financial guidance.

- **Marketing**: A representative from marketing should also be on the committee.

- **Sales**: A senior manager for sales should be on the committee to make sure the organization has the technology needed to convert shoppers into buyers.

- **Quality control**: Quality control ensures that consumers view products and services favorably and that products meet required standards. Therefore, quality control should be represented on the committee.

- **Research and development (R&D)**: Because R&D focuses on developing new products, this department should be represented on the committee. IT must meet the needs of new product development.

- **Human resources (HR)**: Managing employees is as complex as the technology needed to be successful. HR should be represented on the committee.

Notice that the IT steering committee does not typically consist of technologists such as the chief technology officer (CTO) because this is primarily viewed as a business committee. The chief information officer (CIO) typically is a member and acts as the bridge between the IT steering committee and the technology department. The IT steering meeting provides an opportunity for exchange of views where the business communicates its business goals and IT discusses how it can align and enable the business' goals through the use of technology. Often this includes IT leadership educating the business on the limits and risks of technology.

Once an understanding is reached between the business and IT leadership on goals, the CTO and other technologies engage in implementation planning. Although membership might vary, the goal of the committee should be consistent. In additional to goal setting, the committee is responsible for reviewing major IT projects, budgets, and plans.

The duties and responsibilities of the IT steering committee should be defined in a formal charter. If an organization lacks a charter or doesn't have a steering committee, this should be a clear warning that IT and the business may not be closely aligned. Although the charter gives the committee the power to provide strategic guidance, it should not be involved in the day-to-day activities of the IT department. Evidence that indicates otherwise should alert auditors that the committee has strayed from its charter or that the charter is not clear on the committee's responsibilities. A steering committee is just one of three items needed to build a framework of success. The other two are performance measurement and risk management.

The IT steering committee is a good place to start understanding the separation between governance and management. Senior management's role in the IT steering committee process is at a strategic level, not a tactical one. Consider eBay, for example. Although eBay's senior management is very concerned about merchandise being listed for the duration of an auction and about bidding and closing occurring seamlessly, they should have little concern about the operating system and platform. As long as the technology can meet the stated business goal and budget constraints, the choice of Windows, Linux, or UNIX should be left up to the IT department. Senior management's goal is to ensure that goals are aligned, IT is tasked with meeting those business needs, and the auditor is responsible for ensuring that controls are present and operating effectively.

Answers to the "Do I Know This Already?" Quiz:

1. B; 2. C; 3. B; 4. A; 5. D; 6. D; 7. C; 8. C; 9. A; 10. D; 11. C; 12. A

Corporate Structure

Senior management must select a strategy to determine who will pay for the information systems services. Funding is an important topic because departments must have adequate funds to operate. Each funding option has advantages and disadvantages. These are the three most common funding options:

- **Shared cost**: With this method, all departments in the organization share the cost. The advantage of this method is that it is relatively easy to implement and for accounting to handle. Its disadvantage is that some departments might feel that they are paying for something they do not use.

- **Chargeback**: With this method, individual departments are directly charged for the services they use. This is a type of pay-as-you-go system. Proponents of this system believe that it shifts costs to the users of services. Those opposing the chargeback system believe that it is not so clear-cut. For example, what if your city of 1,000 people decided to divide electrical bills evenly so that everyone pays the same? Many might complain, as not everyone uses the same amount of electricity. Opponents of the chargeback system make the same argument, as end users don't consume IT resources evenly.

- **Sponsor pays**: With this method, project sponsors pay all costs. Therefore, if sales asks for a new system to be implemented, sales is responsible for paying the bills. Although this gives the sponsor more control over the project, it might lead to the feeling that some departments are getting a free ride, which can cause conflicts.

IT Governance Frameworks

IT governance frameworks offer blueprints for achieving the key organizational objectives set by the IT steering committee, including meeting compliance and cybersecurity expectations. These frameworks represent best practices as techniques and approaches that have been proven to provide consistent desired outcomes. IT governance best practices require the organization to meet specific goals:

- **Align the goals of IT to the goals of the organization:** Both must be focused on and working for the common goal.

- **Establish accountability:** Accountability requires that individuals be held responsible for their actions. Accountability can be seen as a pyramid of responsibility that starts with the lowest level of employees and builds up to top management.

- **Define supporting policies and processes:** It is important to establish the rules of the road and expected behavior.

Not all IT governance frameworks are created equal. Each IT governance framework was designed to meet a specific industry or regulatory guidance need. While many frameworks overlap to some degree, they are also often complementary, building on the strengths and weaknesses of others. Because of this natural synergy, many organizations adopt multiple governance frameworks. Let's examine this synergy by examining COBIT and ITIL.

COBIT

Control Objectives for Information and Related Technologies (COBIT) is used to ensure quality, control, and reliability of information systems by establishing IT governance and management structure and objectives. COBIT promotes goals alignment, better collaboration, and agility, and as a result, it reduces IT risks.

COBIT essentially defines *what* is needed to achieve the organization's goals and defines the high-level organizational structure and control requirements needed to reduce IT risks.

COBIT 5 is the newest version of COBIT, released in 2012. It outlines five core governance principles:

1. Meeting stakeholder needs
2. Covering the enterprise end to end
3. Applying a single integrated framework
4. Enabling a holistic approach
5. Separating governance from management

COBIT 5 describes these principles in terms of enabler requirements that support an enterprise in meeting stakeholder needs related to the use of IT assets and resources across the enterprise. There is a significant emphasis on governance, responsibilities, and accountability. COBIT requires management to understand and manage the business risk.

There are two types of processes in COBIT 5: governance processes (evaluate, direct, and monitor) and management processes (plan, build, run, and monitor). COBIT 5 is a broad framework that can be applied to any industry to organizations of all sizes.

ITIL

Information Technology Infrastructure Library (ITIL) is a series of documents that define how to execute IT service management (ITSM) processes. In a nutshell,

ITSM is the alignment of enterprise IT services and information systems against the IT steering committee goals and broad organizational principles such as those set by COBIT. ITSM defines how to deliver value to the business and customer, and how to manage the underlying technology.

ITIL essentially defines *how* to achieve the organization's goals and defines the low-level organizational structure and process requirements needed to reduce IT risks.

ITIL provides a set of interrelated best practices that provide detailed guidance for developing, delivering, and managing enterprise IT services. There are five stages in the ITIL service life cycle:

1. Service strategy

2. Service design

3. Service transition

4. Service operation

5. Continual service improvement

COBIT Versus ITIL

Broadly speaking COBIT provides the "what" on governance objectives that must be achieved, and ITIL provides the detail on "how" to achieve the objectives. This is, of course, an oversimplification, but understanding this *what* and *how* distinction is what you need for the CISA exam—especially regarding COBIT-related questions on the exam.

Think of COBIT as defining the coaching staff for an NFL team. In this analogy, COBIT would define the need for an offensive coordinator and a defensive coordinator. COBIT would define their roles and accountabilities, what type of records they should keep, how often the player health should be checked, and so on. What's missing? The plays—the specific drill routines and much more. Whereas COBIT talks about the running of the team, ITIL talks about all the details of how to win each game.

The NFL team analogy illustrates the synergy between the frameworks; without both a well-run team and effective execution on the field, the team cannot win games.

Governance frameworks can and do overlap. Typically, they overlap in how they define certain functions or placement of those functions within an organization. For example, ITIL calls out IT risk management as a unique topic and chooses to integrate the practice across its services. COBIT calls out both IT risk management as a topic with separate and unique process requirements for its management. While accommodation may be needed so they coexist, in the end they are complementary. In fact, ITIL provides detailed advice on how to carry out several COBIT processes. Change management is an example where ITIL can define a structure and a process to achieve COBIT control objectives.

Ultimately, IT governance frameworks are often adjusted to accommodate the organizational, industry, and technology environment in which they are to be implemented. These accommodations make each IT governance framework implementation unique.

While auditors may have a firm grasp on any framework at an academic level, they need to understand the accommodations made before they can effectively audit the environment. Here is a high-level list of what an auditor needs to consider as part of an IT governance framework audit:

- Familiarize yourself with the implemented frameworks.

- Understand the business goals and objectives from the IT steering committee.

- Focus on the strengths and weaknesses of each of the applicable frameworks to ensure coverage of goals and business objectives.

- Ensure that accommodations between frameworks have not resulted in conflicting definition or redundant processes.

- Ensure that measurement systems are complementary.

NOTE   ISACA does not expect CISA candidates to know the specifics of each IT governance framework. Candidates should, however, understand the importance of the frameworks and how they generally create the foundation for governance within an organization.

Enterprise Risk Management

The goal of enterprise risk management (ERM) is to provide key stakeholders with a substantiated and consistent opinion of risk across the enterprise. ERM provides leadership with confidence that both individual risk events and the enterprise's aggregated risk are being effectively managed.

The first step in the risk management process is to identify and classify the organization's assets. Information and systems must be assessed to determine their worth. When asset identification and valuation are complete, the organization can start the risk-identification process to identify potential risks and threats to the organization's assets.

A risk management team is tasked with identifying these threats. The team can then examine the impact of the identified threats. This process can be based on real monetary amounts or a reasonable estimate based on experience.

Chapter 2, "The Information Systems Audit," discusses types of threats and how to manage the associated risks. It covers recognizing different types of risk: inherent, control, detection, and residual. Chapter 2 also discusses the fact that, after identifying high-risk, high-impact concerns, the risk management team can move on to the risk mitigation or risk disposition phase. Risk can be disposed of in the following ways:

- Avoiding risk
- Reducing risk
- Accepting risk
- Transferring risk

The same tools and methods discussed in Chapter 2 also apply to ERM. The difference is that ERM applies these tools to the entire end-to-end population of risk. For example, consider weather forecasting. Every day we can use tools to measure the weather. But there is also value in looking at the pattern of weather for the month, year, decade, and century. ERM is the processes that take the aggregate view of risk.

The Risk Management Team

The risk management team is tasked with identifying and analyzing risks. Its members should be assembled from across the company and most likely will include managers, IT employees, auditors, programmers, and security professionals. Having a cross-section of employees from across the company ensures that the team can address the many threats it must examine.

Teams of specialists may be formed to address emerging or high-profile risks. These teams are not created in a void but are developed within a risk management program with a purpose. For example, a program might be developed to look at ways to decrease insurance costs, reduce attacks against the company's website, or verify compliance with privacy laws.

After the purpose of the team is established, the team can be assigned responsibility for developing, modifying, and/or implementing a more comprehensive risk management program. This is a huge responsibility because it requires not only identification of risk but also implementation of the team's recommendations.

Asset Identification

At the center of most ERM processes is a comprehensive list of assets. Asset identification is the task of identifying all the organization's assets, which can be both tangible and intangible. The following assets are commonly examined:

- Hardware
- Software
- Employees
- Services
- Reputation
- Documentation

When looking at an asset, the team must first think about the replacement cost of the item before assigning its value. The team should consider the value brought by an asset more than just the cost to create or purchase it. These considerations are key:

- What did the asset cost to acquire or create?
- What is the liability if the asset is compromised?
- What is the production cost if the asset is made unavailable?
- What is the value of the asset to competitors and foreign governments?
- How critical is the asset, and how would its loss affect the company?

NOTE   Asset valuation is an onerous task that requires a lot of expertise and work. For the CISA exam, keep the focus on understanding the key ERM processes.

Threat Identification

The risk management team can gather input from a range of sources to help identify threats. These individuals or sources should be consulted or considered to help identify current and emerging threats:

- Business owners and senior managers
- Legal counsel
- HR representatives

- IS auditors

- Network administrators

- Security administrators

- Operations

- Facility records

- Government records and watchdog groups, such as CERT

A *threat* is any circumstance or event that has the potential to negatively impact an asset by means of unauthorized access, destruction, disclosure, or modification. Identifying all potential threats is a huge responsibility. A somewhat easier approach is to categorize the common types of threats:

- Physical threat/theft

- Human error

- Application error/buffer overflow

- Equipment malfunction

- Environmental hazards

- Malicious software/covert channels

A threat coupled with a vulnerability can lead to a loss. *Vulnerabilities* are flaws or weaknesses in security systems, software, or procedures. An example of a vulnerability is human error. This vulnerability might lead an improperly trained help desk employee to unknowingly give a password to a potential hacker, resulting in a loss. Examples of losses or impacts include the following:

- Financial loss

- Loss of reputation

- Danger or injury to staff, clients, or customers

- Loss of business opportunity

- Breach of confidence or violation of law

Losses can be immediate or delayed. A delayed loss is not immediate; it has a negative effect on the organization after some period of time—in a few days, months, or years. For example, an organization could have its website hacked and thus suffer an immediate loss. No e-commerce transactions occur, technical support has to be brought in to rebuild the web server, and normal processing halts. All these are immediate losses. Later, when the local news channel reports that the company was hacked and that personal information was lost, the company loses the goodwill of its customers. Some might remember this event for years to come and choose to use a competitor. This is a delayed loss.

Thus far, we have discussed building a risk management team that has the support of senior management, identifying tangible and nontangible assets, and performing threat identification.

Quantitative Risk Assessment

Performing a quantitative risk assessment involves quantifying all elements of the process, including asset value, impact, threat frequency, safeguard effectiveness, safeguard costs, uncertainty, and probability. This involves six basic steps:

1. Determine the asset value (AV) for each information asset.

2. Identify threats to the asset.

3. Determine the exposure factor (EF) for each information asset in relation to each threat.

4. Calculate the single loss expectancy (SLE).

5. Calculate the annualized rate of occurrence (ARO).

6. Calculate the annualized loss expectancy (ALE).

The advantage of a quantitative risk assessment is that it assigns monetary values, which are easy for management to work with and understand. However, a disadvantage of a quantitative risk assessment is that it is also based on monetary amounts. Consider that it's difficult, if not impossible, to assign monetary values to all elements. Therefore, some qualitative measures must be applied to quantitative elements. Even then, this is a huge responsibility; therefore, a quantitative assessment is usually performed with the help of automated software tools.

If asset values have been determined as previously discussed and threats have been identified, the next steps in the process for quantitative risk assessment are as follows:

1. **Determine the exposure factor:** This is a subjective potential percentage of loss to a specific asset if a specific threat is realized. This is usually in the form of a percentage, similar to how weather reports predict the likelihood of rainy conditions.

2. **Calculate the single loss expectancy (SLE):** The SLE value is a monetary figure that represents the organization's loss from a single loss or the loss of this particular information asset. SLE is calculated as follows:

   Single loss expectancy = Asset value × Exposure factor

   Items to consider when calculating SLE include the physical destruction or theft of assets, loss of data, theft of information, and threats that might delay processing.

3. **Assign a value for the annualized rate of occurrence (ARO):** The ARO represents the estimated frequency at which a given threat is expected to occur. Simply stated, how many times is this expected to happen in one year?

4. **Assign a value for the annualized loss expectancy (ALE):** The ALE is an annual expected financial loss to an organization's information asset because of a particular threat occurring within that same calendar year. ALE is calculated as follows:

   Annualized loss expectancy (ALE) =

   Single loss expectancy (SLE) × Annualized rate of occurrence (ARO)

   The ALE is typically the value that senior management needs to assess to prioritize resources and determine what threats should receive the most attention.

5. **Analyze the risk to the organization:** The final step is to evaluate the data and decide whether to accept, reduce, or transfer the risk.

Much of the process of quantitative risk assessment is built on determining the exposure factor and the annualized loss expectancy, which rely heavily on probability and expectancy. When looking at events such as storms or other natural phenomena, it can be difficult to predict their actual behavior. Yet over time, a trend can be established. These events can be considered stochastic. A *stochastic* event is based on random behavior because the occurrence of individual events cannot be predicted, yet measuring the distribution of all observations usually follows a predictable pattern. In the end, however, quantitative risk management faces challenges when estimating risk, and it must therefore rely on some elements of the qualitative approach.

Another item that is sometimes overlooked in quantitative risk assessment is the total cost of a loss. The team should review these items as it's assessing costs:

- Lost productivity
- Cost of repair

- Value of the damaged equipment or lost data

- Cost to replace the equipment or reload the data

When these costs are accumulated and specific threats are determined, the true picture of annualized loss expectancy can be assessed. Now the team can build a complete picture of the organization's risks. Table 3-2 shows sample results.

Table 3-2   Sample Assessment Results

Asset	Risk	Asset Value	EF	SLE	Annualized Frequency	ALE
Customer database	Loss of consumer data due to lack of a backup	$126,000	78.06%	$93,355	.25	$24,588
E-commerce website	Hacked	$35,500	35.50%	$12,603	.45	$5,671
Domain controller	Power supply failure	$18,000	27.27%	$4,907	.25	$1,227

Although automated tools are available to minimize the effort of the manual process, these programs should not become a crutch to prevent businesses from using common sense or practicing due diligence. Care should also be taken when examining high-impact events, even for the probability. Many of us witnessed the 100-year storm that would supposedly never occur in our lifetime and that hit the Gulf coast and severely damaged the city of New Orleans. Organizations must be realistic when examining such potential events and must openly discuss how such a situation should be dealt with. Just because an event is rated as a one-in-100-year probability does not mean that it can't happen again next year.

Qualitative Risk Assessment

Maybe you're thinking that there has to be another way to perform the assessment. If so, you're right. A qualitative assessment is scenario driven and does not attempt to assign monetary values to components of the risk analysis. A qualitative assessment ranks the seriousness of threats and sensitivity of assets by grade or class, such as low, medium, or high. You can see an example of this in NIST 800-26, a document that uses confidentiality, integrity, and availability as categories for a loss. It then rates each loss according to a scale of low, medium, or high. Table 3-3 shows an example of how this process is performed. A rating of low, medium, or high is subjective. In this example, the following categories are defined:

- **Low**: Minor inconvenience; can be tolerated for a short period of time but will not result in financial loss

- **Medium**: Can result in damage to the organization, cost a moderate amount of money to repair, and result in negative publicity

- **High**: Will result in a loss of goodwill between the company and a client or an employee; may result in a large legal action or fine; and may cause the company to significantly lose revenue or earnings

Table 3-3   Performing a Qualitative Assessment

Asset	Loss of Confidentiality	Loss of Integrity	Loss of Availability
Customer credit card and billing information	High	High	Medium
Production documentation	Medium	Medium	Low
Advertising and marketing literature	Low	Low	Low
HR (employee) records	High	High	Medium

The downside of performing a qualitative assessment is that you are not working with monetary values; therefore, this type of assessment lacks the rigor that accounting teams and management typically prefer.

Other types of qualitative assessment techniques include these:

- **The Delphi technique**: This group assessment process allows individuals to contribute anonymous opinions.

- **Facilitated Risk Assessment Process (FRAP)**: This subjective process obtains results by asking a series of questions. It places each risk into one of 26 categories. FRAP is designed to be completed in a matter of hours, making it a quick process to perform.

NOTE   When it is not possible to calculate specific items quantitatively, qualitative methods can be used. This is known as semi-quantitative analysis.

The Three Lines of Defense Model

Internal control functions are an essential part of the ERM model. It works with the idea that no process is expected to be perfect. Over time, technology wears out, processes become prone to errors, and the rotation of personnel introduces unskilled workers. Whatever the cause, over time, process defects begin to be introduced into products or services.

Without a cohesive and coordinated approach to managing risk, the number of defects and problems can increase. The Three Lines of Defense model is one method to continually assess the environment to ensure that people, process, and technology are meeting the organization's goals. The Three Lines of Defense model provides a simple and effective way to ensure that risk is identified and reported to leadership. This model works for all industries and organizations of all sizes.

The Three Lines of Defense model identifies the key roles and responsibilities for managing risk in layers. The idea is that while one or two layers may miss a material risk, it is highly unlikely that all three layers would miss identifying a major risk. The roles and responsibilities in this model are as follows:

- **Business unit leadership:** These business leaders have primary and ultimate accountability to ensure that appropriate management and internal controls are in place to manage risk. Key responsibilities include the following:

  - Day-to-day risk management of defects and process problems

  - Following policies and risk management process

  - Promptly remediating and reporting risk

- **Risk and compliance teams:** These teams vary from one organization to another and generally advise and verify that management and internal controls are working as designed. Compliance and operational risk teams are typical examples of this internal control function. Key responsibilities include the following:

  - Advising and educating management on required controls and emerging risks

  - Managing key ERM processes

  - Testing to ensure that management and internal controls are working

  - Reporting to senior leadership on enterprise aggregated risk

- **Auditor:** An auditor provides the risk governance committees and senior management with comprehensive assurance that risk is being appropriately managed across the enterprise. Key responsibilities include the following:

  - Reviewing the first and second lines of defense

  - Providing an independent opinion to senior leadership and the board of directors on the state of risk in the enterprise

  - Promptly remediating and reporting risk

The CISA exam expects a candidate to have a deep understanding of the auditor's role. A key fact is understanding the auditor's independence in the reporting structure. Audit teams generally report directly to a board of directors audit committee. In addition, for publicly traded companies, the head of the internal audit department (sometimes referred to as the *General Auditor*) is required to meet with the full board of directors several times each year.

Because the audit department reports directly to the board of directors, auditors' opinions are considered the highest level of independence and objectivity in the organization. This high level of independence is not available in the second line of defense. Because the first and second lines of defense are subject to management oversight (including annual performance reviews), they cannot be considered completely independent.

Auditors play a big role in the success of an organization. Auditors must be independent of management and have the authority to cross departmental boundaries. Auditors must also have the proper skills. If in-house individuals do not have the skills required to lead an audit, an external independent third-party auditor should be hired. This situation requires careful attention. It's natural to develop relationships with those we work with. Internal auditors interact extensively with their clients. This can lead to problems because the level of closeness between management and internal auditors might affect the results of an audit.

Finally, both external and internal auditors can burn out as a result of staleness and repetition, and they may thus start to lose attention to detail, which is very important.

An auditor is expected to be free to provide guidance and recommendations to senior management. The objective of providing recommendations is to improve quality and effectiveness. The first step of this process is to review the following:

- **Learn the organization:** Know the company's goals and objectives. Start by reviewing the mission statement.

- **Review the IT strategic plan:** Strategic plans provide details for the next three to five years.

- **Analyze organizational charts:** Become familiar with the roles and responsibilities of individuals in the company.

- **Study job descriptions:** Job descriptions detail the level of responsibility and accountability for employees' actions.

- **Evaluate existing policies and procedures:** These documents detail the approved activities of employees.

NOTE   Expect the exam to include questions on how the audit process should start. This includes reviewing the organization's IT strategic plan and understanding the organization's goals and objectives.

Policy Development

Policies are more than words on paper or data stored electronically. Policies reflect how management views risk. Policies reflect how much risk the business is willing to tolerate and reflect how leadership wants the business to run.

For example, for a pizza shop that sells 12-inch hand-tossed pizzas, if the pizzas turn out to be between 11.5 inches and 12.5 inches, that may be well within the tolerance set by policy. However, for an airplane engine manufacturer, the parts design tolerance must be within 1 to 5 microns. These examples show the need to establish tolerance and the amount of risk that management is willing to accept.

Always remember that policies reflect leadership perception of priorities. An auditor has two main roles related to policies: (1) ensure that a policy is complete and reasonable, given industry norms, and (2) identify any misalignment between stated policies and actual practice.

An auditor can learn a great deal about an organization by simply reviewing the strategic plan and examining the company's policies. These documents reflect management's view of the company. Some might even say that policies are only as good as the management team that created them. Policies should exist to cover almost every aspect of organizational control because companies have legal and business requirements to achieve organizational goals.

Management is responsible for dividing the company into smaller subgroups so that control can be managed effectively. Policies will dictate how activities occur in each of the functional areas. One of the first steps in an audit is for the auditor to examine these critical documents. Any finding an auditor makes should be referenced back to the policy. This allows the auditor to specify how to rectify identified problems according to management views on risk.

Policies don't last forever. Like most other things in life, they need to be reviewed periodically to make sure they stay current. Technology becomes obsolete, new technology becomes affordable, and business processes change. Although it's sometimes easy to see that low-level procedures need to be updated, this also applies to high-level policies.

We defined *standards*, *procedures*, *guidelines*, and *baselines* in Chapter 2. In this chapter, we discuss the broad policy environment and how each artifact is developed, including the terms defined in Chapter 2.

Policy

The term *policy* can be misleading; it can mean the policy environment, which includes standards, procedures, guidelines, and baselines. Or the term can refer to a specific document, which typically reflects a broad strategic view of risk taken by the highest levels of the organization.

For the purpose of this chapter, we use the term *policy* to reflect the policy environment. In this context, not all policies are created in the same way. The policy process can be driven from the top or from the bottom of the organization.

Top-down policy development means that policies are pushed down from the top of the company. The advantage of a top-down policy development approach is that it ensures that policy is aligned with the strategy of the company. It lacks speed, however, and may not reflect a complete understanding of how detailed processes actually work. This lack of understanding of detail could lead to confusion and unrealistic expectations. It's a time-consuming process that requires a substantial amount of time to implement.

A second approach is bottom-up policy development. *Bottom-up policy development* addresses the concerns of operational employees because it starts with their input and concerns and builds on known risk. This is faster than a top-down approach but has a huge disadvantage in that it risks lack of senior management support.

NOTE   CISA exam candidates must know that a risk assessment typically drives bottom-up policy development more than top-down policy development.

No matter what the development type, policies are designed to address specific concerns, including the following:

- **Regulatory:** Regulatory policies ensure that the organization's standards are in accordance with local, state, and federal laws. Industries that frequently use these documents include health care, public utilities, refining, and the federal government.

- **Advisory:** Advisory policies ensure that all employees know the consequences of certain behaviors and actions. An example of an advisory policy is one covering acceptable use of the Internet. This policy, called an acceptable use policy (AUP), might state how employees can use the Internet during the course of business; violating the policy could lead to disciplinary action or dismissal.

- **Informative:** Informative policies are designed not for strict enforcement but for teaching. Their goal is to inform employees and/or customers. An example of an informative policy is a return policy on goods purchased on the business's website.

Policy, Standards, Procedures, and Baselines

The relationship between policy, standards, procedures, and baselines can be confusing. The easiest way to understand the difference is to understand each document's intent and the level at which it reduces risk. Table 3-4 shows the relationships of these documents.

Table 3-4 Documentation/Level of Control

Level/Intent	Policy	Standard	Procedure	Baselines
Strategic	✓			
Tactical		✓		
Operational			✓	✓

Let's discuss *policy* as a strategic document. A policy document outlines broad and strategic goals. A policy document is typically approved by a board of directors–level committee. The policy document outlines accountabilities and broad risk tolerance statements in the form of a business document. For example, a policy document may authorize the chief information security officer (CISO) to be accountable for setting and enforcing information and cybersecurity standards and procedures across the enterprise. The intent can ensure that the CISO has the authority to stop a cybersecurity attack, which may include taking some business systems offline. The policy may also outline the business's priority for IT, such as stating opening up of operations in Europe is a strategic goal and holding the CIO accountable to ensure that appropriate technology is in place to control the cross-border movement of data.

Standards, in contrast to policy, describe how control should be deployed to achieve the policy and IT steering committee goals. Standards are much more specific than policies. A standard reflects industry-accepted norms and specifications for hardware, software, or human behavior. Standards should always point to the policies to which they relate. Standards are often technology agnostic. For example, a standard may say that "database administrators must use dual-factor authentication." In this case, the standard does not specify which technology would be used to satisfy this requirement.

A *procedure* is an operational document that lays out specific steps or processes required to meet the requirements within the standards. Procedures also identify roles and accountabilities. To extend our dual-factor authentication example, procedures might say that to obtain a hardware token, an individual must request the device from a specific internal website and then get the device activated by the individual's manager.

During an audit, an auditor must review all relevant procedures and map them to employee behavior through direct observation or interview. Misalignment can mean that there are no existing procedures, that procedures don't map well to existing practices, or employees have not had the proper or adequate training on the procedures they are tasked with following.

Baselines procedures are operational documents that define the minimum configuration settings to achieve the standards requirements and support the procedure steps. This is the absolute minimum level that a system, network, or device must adhere to. To extend our dual-factor authentication example, a baseline may describe how to configure a Windows OS and Oracle database to accept only the approved hardware tokens for authentication. The Windows OS and Oracle database configuration setting for dual-factor authentication would be quite different, and thus two separate baselines would be created.

NOTE The CISA exam may include questions on dual-factor authentication. Dual-factor authentication requires not only an ID and password but also something only the individual has, such as a hard token that generates a unique key every few minutes. In this example, the individual would need both physical possession of the hard token to obtain the key and also knowledge of the ID and password. Then access is granted.

Auditing Policies, Standards, Procedures, and Baselines

An audit of policies documentation can improve the quality of the control environment. Audits can verify that documents are being used in the way that management has authorized and intended them to be used. An audit can also help verify that policies are up-to-date and are adhered to. Per ISACA, the following items should be examined:

- Risk management documents, especially the identification and inventory of risks

- Human resources documents

- Quality assurance procedures

- Process and operation manuals

- Change management documentation

- IT forecasts and budgets

- Security policies and procedures

- Organizational charts and functional diagrams

- Job details and descriptions

- Steering committee reports

Documents that deal with external entities (sometimes referred to as *third parties*) should also be reviewed. A company might have contracts with vendors or suppliers for an array of products and services. How vendors are chosen, how the bidding process functions, what factors are used to determine the best bid, and what process is used to verify contract completion should all be reviewed. During the review process with policies, procedures, and documentation, any of the following might indicate potential problems:

- Lack of guidance on what policies are to be followed

- Excessive costs

- Budget overruns

- Late projects

- A large number of aborted projects

- Unsupported hardware changes or unauthorized purchases

- Lack of documentation

- Out-of-date documentation

- Employees unaware of or not knowledgeable about documentation

Policies related to external entities (that is, third parties) is a complicated topic and often a point of interest for regulators. The reason the topic can get complicated is that an organization is ultimately accountable for how an external entity conducts business on its behalf. Yet often the organization has no direct control over how the external entity operates—no direct control but ultimately accountable for someone else's actions. Confusing, right? For example, assume that a company makes loans and, in the process, collects all kinds of personal and private information. The organization then hires an external entity (typically referred to as a *vendor*) to obtain a credit report on each applicant and sort the results by credit scores and demographics by region. Now let's assume that there is a data breach of the external entity's computer, and someone steals all your customers' personal information.

Let's examine who may be legally accountable for a breach at the external entity or vendor site, given our example. As an auditor, you would be expected to sort through the complexities and determine internal accountabilities—that is, what went wrong and why. An auditor does not determine legal accountability but can determine whether the actions taken by the organization meet the requirements and rules set by the regulators. Only the courts and a judge can determine legal accountability. In this example, here are a few assessment areas that may be of interest to an auditor:

- **The quality of the vendor:** How were the vendor selection and the vendor's capability assessed by the organization? Did the vendor have the resources to properly protect the organization's data? An organization should never select a vendor exclusively based on cost.

- **Expectations on the vendor:** Were expectations clearly conveyed to the vendor through contract, policies, standards, and so on? How were those expectations monitored by the organization? An organization has an obligation to monitor whether vendors are living up to their expectations. This may include onsite inspections of the vendor's facilities.

- **Expectations on the organization:** Did the organizational policies and controls contribute to the vendor's breach? Let's assume that to obtain credit scores and determine demographics, the vendor needed a tax ID, name, and ZIP Code. Let's also assume that the organization passes all the personal information obtained during the loan application process, such as address, salary information, mother's maiden name, and so on. While the organization did not contribute to the failure to protect the customer's information effectively, the organization did contribute to the impact of the breach by sending too much personal information to the vendor. In other words, an organization should send to the vendor only the information needed to perform the contracted service. The unnecessary exposure of customer information to a vendor can create legal accountability in the form of fines for the organization.

This is an important concept related to business accountability and drives many organizations' policies related to external entities such as vendors. Regulators are consistent in requiring that once an organization collects personal information, it has an obligation to ensure that it is properly handled—including by third-party vendors.

> **NOTE** The CISA exam will not include details on what documents are within the scope of an audit. You are expected to understand the types of documents in policies and their purpose.

Data Classification

Every piece of data has its own value to an organization and unique legal handling requirements. Most organizations have huge data stores. It's not practical or cost-effective to examine how to handle every individual piece of data. Data classification is used to simplify the data handling rules by categorizing data into distinct classes. Then each data class (or data classification) can be subject to common rules for how the data should be treated.

Most organizations prefer to use three to five data classifications. This way, handling rules and controls can be simplified and standardized. In addition, the smaller the number of data classifications, the easier it is to train personnel. Data and information assets are classified with respect to the risk of unauthorized disclosure, such as lost, stolen, and inadvertently disclosed. A simple data classification scheme is illustrated in Table 3-5.

Table 3-5 Simple Data Classification Scheme

Class	Description
Public	Information released to the public
	Examples: press release, Dow Jones stock price
Proprietary	Information related to processes and methods that are necessary for staff to perform their work and day-today communication within the business
	Examples: emails, meeting minutes
Business confidential	Information critical to the business that provides a significant competitive advantage, such as trade secrets
	Example: secret recipe for Coca-Cola
Customer confidential	Information related to the customers of the business
	Examples: tax ID information, health records

A data classification process typically separates information into distinct classes, which are then aligned to various standards, procedures, and baselines. It is also important to align these policies with regulatory requirements. For example, the Health Insurance Portability and Accountability Act (HIPAA), a U.S. law designed to provide privacy standards to protect patients' medical records, requires that patient information be stored securely. Electronic health records could be classified as customer confidential, and the hospital standards could require such data to be stored in encrypted form.

NOTE The CISA exam may have questions related to PII and PHI. It is important to understand these terms. PII is short for *personal identifiable information*. PHI is short for *protected health information*.

PII identifies a person as a specific individual. A Social Security number is PII; a ZIP Code is not because it cannot alone identify you as a unique individual. Various privacy laws require PII to be protected.

PHI relates to personal health records, such as those kept in your doctor's office. HIPAA requires that PHI be protected.

From time to time, information must be destroyed. To facilitate the destruction of data, an organization could classify data into different groupings. For example, emails could be classified as a group of data that must be deleted after 90 days. Such a policy allows an organization to consistently purge obsolete data against a consistent set of classification rules.

Given the explosion of data collected in recent years, data classification has become increasingly important to managing the dizzying volume of information. Keep in mind the cost of classifying data. Data that is more valuable requires more controls. The more controls applied to data, the higher the cost to securely collect, store, and manage the data.

The first step to take before classifying any information is to define the levels of classification and what controls should be applied to each classification. Consider the overall costs of the controls, based on the volume and value of data.

Once classifications are defined, an organization faces the costs of inventorying existing data against the classification types and of implementing the supporting controls. Automation can help. For example, data loss prevention (DLP) technology can help automate the protection of data such as blocking any attempt to email documents labeled "business confidential." Automation can be used to manage data leakage and generate reports that support these policies. In addition, automation can support records retention schedules by identifying the types of data specified and their location, allowing for proper archiving or destruction to occur.

DLP systems can also be incorporated in baseline and configuration settings that block the transfer of data onto a USB drive. Another action could result in the system encrypting the sensitive data in such a way that only authorized users can decrypt it. The key point is that data classification is a powerful tool that can support the policies of an organization.

An audit of data classification processes is important to gain an accurate view of the nature of the data, including how data is valued and types of risks perceived by leadership if that data was compromised.

An audit can start with the existing metadata information, as well as the details of where and how the information has been stored, to give the richest possible view of the content. It's important for an audit to sample data based on the metadata definitions and standards. For example, a payroll clerk might, out of convenience, create a spreadsheet to balance a department budget. If that spreadsheet is stored on the clerk's laptop, it may be more susceptible to a data breach, which may violate the organization's security standards.

NOTE   The CISA exam expects you understand the term *metadata*, which means "data about data." Metadata describes the type of data contained in a file. Think of metadata as the file layout. For example, metadata can answer the question "Does the file contain credit card information, or is it a file of medical records?" Metadata describes the fields in the file, such as the length of a credit card number field or the length of the insurance number field. The important point is that metadata does not contain the actual file content, such as credit card or insurance numbers. Metadata only contains information about how such fields are stored.

Security Policy

One specific type of policy is the organization's *security policy*, which dictates management's commitment to the use, operation, and security of information systems and assets. It specifies the role security plays in the organization. The security policy should be driven by business objectives and should meet all applicable laws and regulations. The security policy should also act as a basis to integrate security into all business functions. It serves as a high-level guide to developing lower-level documentation, such as procedures. The security policy must be balanced in the sense that all organizations are looking for ways to implement adequate security without hindering productivity. The issue also arises that the cost of security cannot be greater than the value of the asset.

An auditor must look closely at security policies during the audit process and should review them to get a better idea of how specific access controls should function. Often security requirements are added to many different types of policies. For example, an auditor should examine policies that have been developed for disaster recovery and business continuity. Some questions to consider are what kind of hardware and software backup are used; whether the software backup media is stored offsite; and, if so, what kind of security the offsite location has and what type of access is available. These are just a few security-related items an auditor needs to review.

NOTE   CISA exam candidates should be aware that direct observation is one way to identify problems. For example, if a policy specifies a lockout policy, yet direct observation reveals that no lockout policy has been implemented, an auditor can then interview the employees to find out why. Is it a technical limitation, a failure to implement a baseline on that specific platform, or something else?

It's fairly common to see the *principle of least privilege* in security policies. The idea is that you can improve security by limiting access to just the functions that are consistent with the individual's job function. That way, if an account is compromised, the amount of harm that can be performed is contained or limited to that job's role.

The concept is simple, but the implementation quickly becomes challenging as the size of an organization grows. Assume that an organization has thousands or hundreds of thousands of accounts. The idea of going through each account one at a time and customizing security may not be practical. Grouping the accounts into roles and assigning access permissions by roles is much simpler. The challenge is that two users may be almost identical except in terms of a few functions that are different. What do you do? Create two roles with lots of duplication? Put both users in the same role, knowing they may have slightly more access than they need?

Many organizations adopt the principle of least privilege but make compromises to balance the need to reduce access to the least amount practically possible. In other words, least privilege is a concept, not a hard rule.

Most security policies make a distinction between privileged and non-privileged accounts. Think of *privileged accounts* as administrative accounts and accounts with higher risk privileges, such as the ability to transfer money. The privileged accounts are sometimes referred to as *superusers*, or users with the "keys to the kingdom;" if these accounts are compromised, the risk of significant impact to the organization rises. Think of *non-privileged accounts* as standard users whose access is limited under least privilege to a single job function and typically a specific set of transactions. If these accounts are compromised, the risk of significant impact to the organization is reduced compared with a privileged account.

Management Practices of Employees

Employee management practices deal with the policies and procedures that detail how people are hired, promoted, retained, and terminated. Employees can have a huge impact on the security of a company. Insiders have greater access and opportunity for misuse than outsiders typically do. Insiders can pose a malicious, accidental, or intentional threat to security. Although there is no way to predict future events, employee risks can be reduced by implementing and following good basic human resources (HR) practices.

Everyone wants to get the right person for the job, but good HR practices require more than just matching a resume to an open position. Depending on the position to be filled, company officials need to perform due diligence in verifying that they have matched the right person to the right job. For example, Kevin might be the best security expert around, but if it is discovered that he served a 10-year sentence for extortion and racketeering, his chances of being hired by an interested company will be slim. Some basic common controls should be used during the hiring practice:

- Background checks
- Educational checks
- Reference checks
- Confidentiality agreements
- Non-compete agreements
- Conflict-of-interest agreements

Hiring practices should be performed with due diligence. References can be checked, education verified, military records reviewed, and even drug tests performed, if necessary. When an employee is hired, he brings not only his skills but also his background, history, attitude, and behavior.

Once hired, employees should be provided with an employee handbook detailing the employee code of conduct, acceptable use of company assets, and employee responsibilities to the company. Per ISACA, the handbook should address the following issues:

- Use of social media while at work
- Use of company-owned devices (assets and technology)

- Employee package of benefits
- Paid holiday and vacation policy
- Work schedule and overtime policy
- Moonlighting and outside employment
- Employee evaluations
- Disaster response and emergency procedures
- Disciplinary action process for noncompliance

Hiring is just the first step in good employee management. Employees can follow policies only if they understand them. Auditors should verify that HR has a written, well-defined performance evaluation process. Performance assessments should occur on a predetermined schedule and should be based on known goals and results. A fair and objective process should be used. Pay raises and bonuses should be based strictly on performance.

Training is another area that falls under the responsibility of HR and the business unit. Employees might not know proper policies and procedures if they are not informed and trained. Training increases effectiveness and efficiency. When a new process or technology is introduced in the organization, employees should be trained for proper operation. Training is also beneficial because it increases morale; it makes people feel better, so they strive to do a better job. Training categories include those for technical, personnel management, project management, and security needs.

NOTE   The CISA exam may include a question on security awareness training. The content of the training will not be on the exam. A CISA candidate is expected to understand and be able to define this type of training.

Training can range from lunchtime programs to learning programs, multiday events, or degree programs. Common training methods include the following:

- In-house training
- Classroom training
- Vendor training
- On-the-job training
- Apprenticeship programs

- Degree programs
- Continuing education programs

Forced Vacations, Rotation of Assignments, and Dual Control

It may sound odd, but forcing employees to take vacations is an important control. A required vacation is not something that is done strictly for the health or benefit of the employee. Required vacations also enable the company to ensure that someone else does the regular employee's job tasks for at least a week. This control helps verify that improper or illegal acts have not been occurring. It also makes it harder for an employee to hide any misuse.

Required vacations are just one of the employee controls that can be used. Another control is *rotation of assignment*, which allows more than one person to perform a specific task. This not only helps ensure a backup if an employee is unavailable but also can reduce fraud or misuse by preventing an individual from having too much control over an area.

One other closely related control worth mentioning is dual control. *Dual control* requires two individuals to provide input or approval before a transaction or an activity can take place. In banking, moving large sums of money is often under dual control. For example, sending a large wire transfer from one account to another typically requires the manager and supervisor to sign off on the transaction. This prevents a manager from wiring herself a large sum of money and disappearing.

Separation Events

An employee termination is often referred to as a *separation event*. The term *termination* has a bit of rough tone and does not fully describe why the employee is leaving; therefore, separation event has become a common term. A separation event could be for any reason, such as the employee finding a better job or being dismissed. HR typically manages the separation procedures, which should include a checklist to verify that the employee has returned all equipment that has been in his possession, including remote access tokens, keys, ID cards, cell phones, pagers, credit cards, laptops, and software.

A separation event may not be voluntary, and there needs to be a process to handle the situation properly. The applicable policy must cover issues such as escorting the employee out of the facility, exit interviews, review of non-disclosure agreements (NDAs), and suspension of network access.

NOTE   It's important to understand that a background check may be performed multiple times.

Imagine that your company has an employee who has had a little too much fun on a Friday night and gets arrested for a DWI or DUI. Luckily, the employee has enough cash to make bail and is back home before sunrise on Saturday morning. He believes that it's a brand-new day, time to start fresh again. No one will ever find out, right? Wrong! Well, maybe.

Today, companies such as Verified Person offer continuous employment checks to companies that subscribe to their services. Not only can the HR department use these services to check an individual's background before being hired, but they can continue to monitor employees throughout their employment. In other words, an employee's criminal and civil history can be monitored 24 hours a day, 7 days a week.

Roles and Responsibilities

Individuals can hold any number of roles or responsibilities within an organization. The responsibilities each employee has and to whom he or she reports should be noted. An auditor's first option for determining this information should be an organizational chart. After obtaining and reviewing the organizational chart, the auditor should spend some time reviewing each employee's area to see how the job description matches actual activities. The areas to focus attention on include these:

- Help desk
- End-user support manager
- Quality assurance manager
- Data manager
- Rank-and-file employees
- Systems development manager
- Software development manager

NOTE   When thinking about exam questions about roles and responsibilities, keep in mind the context of the question and hint words such as *new employee, transferred roles, least privilege*, and so on.

For example, an area of interest for an auditor may be an individual transferring between departments. Has the previous role's access been revoked?

Most organizations have clearly defined controls that specify what each job role is responsible for. An auditor should be concerned with these common roles in the IS structure:

- **Data-entry employees:** Although most data-entry activities are now outsourced, in the not-too-distant past, these activities were performed in-house at an information processing facility (IPF). A full-time data-entry person was assigned the task of entering all data. Barcodes, scanning, and web entry forms have also reduced the demand for these services. If this role is still used, key verification is one of the primary means of control.

- **Systems administrators:** This employee is responsible for the operation and maintenance of the LAN and associated components, such as midrange or mainframe systems. Although small organizations might have only one systems administrator, larger organizations have many.

- **Quality assurance employees:** Employees in a quality assurance role can fill one of two roles: quality assurance or quality control. Quality assurance employees make sure programs and documentation adhere to standards; quality control employees perform tests at various stages of product development to make sure products are free of defects.

- **Database administrators:** This employee is responsible for the organization's data and maintains the data structure. The database administrator has control over all the data; therefore, detective controls and supervision of duties must be observed closely. This is usually a role filled by a senior information systems employee because these employees have control over the physical data definition, implementing data definition controls, and defining and initiating backup and recovery.

- **Systems analysts:** These employees are involved in the system development life cycle (SDLC) process. They are responsible for determining the needs of users and developing requirements and specifications for the design of needed software programs.

- **Network administrators:** These employees are responsible for the maintenance and configuration of network equipment, such as routers, switches, firewalls, wireless access points, and so on.

- **Security architects:** These employees examine the security infrastructure of the organization's network.

Segregation of Duties (SoD)

Job titles can be confusing, and different organizations sometimes use different titles for various positions. It helps when the title matches the actual job duties the employee performs. Some roles and functions are just not compatible. For an auditor, concern over such incompatibility focuses on the risks these roles represent when combined. Segregation of duties, or separation of duties, usually falls into four areas of control:

- **Authorization:** Verifying cash, approving purchases, and approving changes

- **Custody:** Accessing cash, merchandise, or inventories

- **Record keeping:** Preparing receipts, maintaining records, and posting payments

- **Reconciliation:** Comparing monetary amounts, counts, reports, and payroll summaries

An individual having excessive access privileges beyond those needed for his or her role may lead to malicious, negligent, or accidental misuse of access. The more dangerous combinations of access that could cause the greatest harm are sometimes referred to as *toxic combinations*. Table 3-6 lists some of the duties (that is, toxic combinations) that should not be combined because they can result in control weaknesses.

Table 3-6   Separation of Duties

First Job Role	Combined (Yes/No)	Second Job Role
Systems analyst	No	Security administrator
Application programmer	Yes	Systems analyst
Help desk	No	Network administrator
Data entry	Yes	Quality assurance
Computer operator	No	Systems programmer
Database administrator	Yes	Systems analyst
Systems administrator	No	Database administrator
Security administrator	No	Application programmer
Systems programmer	No	Security administrator

NOTE CISA exam candidates must understand generally which job duties should not be combined. Examples include security administrator/programmer and database administrator/network administrator. The CISA exam will have questions related to segregation of duties (SoD).

Compensating Controls

Because of the problems that can occur when certain tasks are combined, separation of duties is required to provide accountability and control. When it cannot be used, compensating controls should be considered. In small organizations, it may be very difficult to adequately separate job tasks. In these instances, one or more of the following compensating controls should be considered:

- **Job rotation:** The concept is to not have one person in one position for too long a period of time. This prevents a single employee from having too much control.

- **Audit trail:** Although audit trails are popular after security breaches, they should be examined more frequently. Audit trails enable an auditor to determine what actions specific individuals performed; they provide accountability.

- **Reconciliation:** This is a specific type of audit in which records are compared to make sure they balance. Although it is primarily used in financial audits, reconciliation can also be used for computer batch processing and other areas in which totals should be compared.

- **Exception report:** This type of report notes errors or exceptions. Exception reports should be made available to managers and supervisors so that they can track errors and other problems.

- **Transaction log:** This type of report tracks transactions and the time of occurrence. Managers should use transaction reports to track specific activities.

- **Supervisor review:** Supervisor reviews can be performed through observation or inquiry, or they can be done remotely, using software tools and applications.

Key Employee Controls

Table 3-7 reviews the key employee controls discussed in this section.

Table 3-7   Key Employee Controls

Terms	Control Usage	Attributes
Background checks	Hiring practice	Helps match the right person to the right job
Required vacations	Uncovers misuse	Serves as a detective control to uncover employee malfeasance
Rotation of assignment	Prevents excessive control	Rotates employees to new areas
Dual control	Limits control	Aids in separation of duties
Non-disclosure agreement (NDA)	Aids in confidentiality	Helps prevent disclosure of sensitive information
Security training	Improves performance	Improves performance and gives employees information on how to handle certain situations
Segregation of duties (SoD)	Reduces the risk of error and fraud	Reduces the risk of human error or fraud by requiring that higher-risk transactions be performed by two or more people

Performance Management

Measuring performance is important to ensure that the organization's goals are consistently being met in an effective and efficient manner. You take measurements to see if you're headed in the right direction through quantitative analysis. This may seem obvious, but organizations have for years had difficulty selecting and understanding what to measure and how to measure an organization's performance.

Let's consider a few examples of what IT performance management should measure. Does measuring the number of technology changes implemented over the past month seem important? Or does measuring the number of business service requests seem more appropriate? These measurements certainly have value, but they do not tell leadership whether the services are effective, cost-efficient, or aligned to strategic goals.

When we think about performance management, we need to think broader than the processes we run. Let's consider the following perspectives:

- **The customer perspective:** Includes the importance the company places on meeting customer needs. Even if financial indicators are good, poor customer ratings will eventually lead to financial decline.

- **Internal operations:** Includes the metrics managers use to measure how well the organization is performing and how closely its products meet customer needs.

- **Innovation and learning:** Includes corporate culture and its attitudes toward learning, growth, and training.

- **Financial evaluation:** Includes timely and accurate financial data. Typically focuses on profit and market share.

We put these broader perspectives into performance management, which helps us understand not only *what we produce* but also *what we consume* to produce our products and services. The pitfall of performance management measurements is taking the easy way out and only measuring quantitative waypoints that are readily available, such as the number of widgets produced, cost, speed, and quality. These readily available metrics have operational value but by themselves do not tell management if they are headed in the right direction.

When we add the broader perspective just discussed, we force performance management to align measurements to business objectives. For example, rather than just measuring speed to delivery in the abstract, you might measure customer satisfaction. Measuring customers who are highly satisfied with the product or service will tell you if the speed and quality are meeting their expectation. Conversely, customers who are less satisfied will have an issue with quality, the speed of delivery, and/or cost.

> **NOTE**   A CISA exam candidate is expected to know how to define *performance management*. In addition, expect exam questions related to performance measurement terms (including KPI and KGI, which are discussed below) and be prepared to compare and contrast them.

Key Performance Terms

Table 3-8 reviews key performance measurement terms and usage that we discuss in this section.

Table 3-8   Key Performance Measurement Terms and Examples

Term	Definition	Example
Metric	A unit of measurement	Four malware events per year
Unit	Scale against which a unit is measured	Number of outages caused by malware
Target value	Business goal	One per year

Term	Definition	Example
Threshold	A minimum or maximum limit that indicates an unacceptable defect	One per quarter
Key performance indicator (KPI)	Defines how well a process is performing	95% detection
Key goal indicator (KGI)	Defines how well a process is performing against a stated goal	–400%
Balanced scorecard (BSC)	A scorecard that brings together in one view key measurements such as metrics, target values, and key indicators	Daily dashboard

Let's explore each of the terms in Table 3-8 in the context of the malware example mentioned in the table. Say that management is trying to understand the effectiveness of the malware controls. The key to preventing operational disruptions is the capability to detect and cleanse malware. Knowing that cleansing is automated based on detection, management chooses the rate at which it can detect malware as its KPI. A high detection rate means less malware can cause disruptions. Knowing the level of redundancy in the processes, assume that management is comfortable that they can successfully manage one malware event per quarter. This threshold (typically referred to as a *risk threshold*) may indicate for the business the level at which unacceptable disruptions occur for products or services.

Sounds like a lot of moving parts? Yes. Performance management is all about what needs to be accomplished, the business goals, and key measurements. Once a goal is set, it's a matter of comparing actual measurements against targets. In our example, the risk threshold is to have no more than one malware event per quarter, and given that the total number of malware events was four for the year, that threshold was achieved. Then why is the KGI a –400 percent? While the risk threshold was achieved, the business target value goal was to have only one malware event per year. The KGI is a broader indication of the business goal to be achieved. There is a close relationship between KPI and KGI: as the KPI changes, so does the KGI. In our example, if the malware detection rate is raised (as represented by the KPI), then we would expect to see a business goal being achieved, as represented by the KGI.

A steering committee needs to measure performance and align business strategy with IT objectives. A steering committee can be flooded with metrics. Selecting the metrics that are most insightful and can foster consensus among different organizational departments and groups to take action is essential in promoting healthy change. This is where a balanced scorecard (BSC) comes in. The information gathered using the balanced scorecard should be passed down the organizational structure to supervisors, teams, and employees. Managers can use the information to align employees' performance plans with organizational goals.

There is no set format for a balanced scorecard. The measurements should reflect business goals and targets compared to actual performance. There should be a direct or implied relationship between the measurements. That is, as one performance measure changes, related indicators should also change, as in the example that increased malware detection capability will have a positive effect on achieving a business goal.

Management and Control Frameworks

A control framework categorizes and aligns an organization's internal controls to identify and manage risk in the most optimal manner. A control framework is based on industry best practices to provide management with an effective tool to establish processes that create business value and minimize risk.

An organization will adopt multiple management and control frameworks, based on the risk being controlled. For example, an enterprise architecture framework is adopted to control the risks related to software and system deployments. A security framework is adopted to control risks related to information and cybersecurity, and a quality management framework is adopted to ensure that products and services are maintained within acceptable risk thresholds.

Think of management and control frameworks as *best practices rules* for unique disciplines in an organization. A larger organization with more diverse disciplines will have a greater number of frameworks adopted. This concept of organizational disciplines is important and explains many of the origins of the frameworks. This is especially true for the information systems disciplines. A finance department will have very different risks and challenges than an information security department. Both are important disciplines, and both have industry groups and associations promoting industry best practices. These industry groups and associations eventually create what we know as management and control frameworks. Table 3-8 reviews commonly adopted frameworks.

Table 3-9 Common Management and Control Frameworks

Framework	Definition
Committee of Sponsoring Organizations of the Treadway Commission (COSO)	COSO is a commonly used framework for running an efficient and well-controlled financial environment.

Framework	Definition
Control Objectives for Information and Related Technologies (COBIT)	The Information Systems Audit and Control Association (ISACA), an international industry association, has published COBIT, which is used to ensure quality, control, and reliability of information systems by establishing IT governance and management structure and objectives. COBIT promotes goals alignment, better collaboration, and agility, and as a result, it reduces IT risks.
ISO	International Organization for Standardization (ISO), an international industry group, creates requirements, specifications, and guidelines across many information system disciplines. The following example illustrates several key ISO publications:
	ISO 9001 series focuses on quality management
	ISO 14001 series focuses on environmental systems
	ISO 27000 series focuses on information security
NIST Cybersecurity Framework (CSF)	The National Institute of Standards and Technology (NIST), a unit of the U.S. Commerce Department, published the CSF, which provides guidance on how to assess and improve the ability to prevent, detect, and respond to cyberattacks. The framework is mandatory for many non-defense U.S. government agencies and has been adopted by the private sector.

Table 3-9 is not an exhaustive list of management and control frameworks but is intended to illustrate the diverse disciplines and highlight common frameworks an IS auditor will encounter.

Enterprise Architecture

Enterprise architecture is a good example of multiple frameworks coming together to define a discipline within an organization. Let's consider information security governance focuses on the availability of services, integrity of information, and protection of data confidentiality. Information security governance has become a much more important activity in the past decade. The growing number of Internet businesses and services has accelerated this trend. The Internet and global connectivity extend a company's network far beyond its traditional border. This places new demands on information security and its governance. Attacks can originate from not just inside the organization but from anywhere in the world. Failure to adequately address this important concern can have serious consequences.

One way to enhance security and governance is to implement components of the NIST framework as requirements in an *enterprise architecture* (*EA*) plan. Such a plan organizes and documents a company's IT assets to enhance planning, management, and expansion. The primary purpose of using EA is to ensure that business strategy and IT investments are aligned. The benefit of EA is that it provides traceability that extends from the highest level of business strategy down to the fundamental technology. EA has grown since John Zachman, the originator of the Framework for Enterprise Architecture, first developed it in the 1980s; companies such as Intel, BP, and the U.S. government now use this methodology.

Federal law requires government agencies to set up EA and a structure for its governance. This process is guided by the Federal Enterprise Architecture Framework (FEAF) reference model, which is designed to use six models:

- **Performance reference model (PRM):** A framework used to measure performance of major IT investments

- **Business reference model (BRM):** A framework used to provide an organized, hierarchical model for day-to-day business operations

- **Infrastructure reference model (IRM):** A framework used to classify service components with respect to how technology supports the business through hardware, hosting, data centers, cloud, and virtualization

- **Application reference model (ARM):** A framework used to categorize the standards, specifications, and applications that support and enable the delivery of service components and capabilities

- **Data reference model (DRM):** A framework used to provide a standard means by which data may be described, categorized, and shared

- **Security reference model (SRM):** A framework used to provide a standard means to describe information security and cybersecurity controls and how to adjust the risk and protect individuals' privacy

Management is tasked with the guidance and control of the organization; managers are the individuals who are responsible for the organization. Although companies are heavily dependent on technology, a large part of management's duties still involves people, processes, and related technology. People are key to making a company successful. Therefore, a large portion of management's duties depends on people skills, including interaction with staff and with those outside the traditional organizational boundaries.

Outsourcing might not be a term that some people like, but it's a fact of life that companies depend on an array of components and services from around the world. For example, consider Dell Computer. Dell might be based in Round Rock, Texas, but its distribution hub is in Memphis, Tennessee; Dell assembles PCs in Malaysia and has customer support in India. Many other parts come from the far corners of the globe. The controls that a company places on its employees and contracts, as well as its agreements with business partners and suppliers, must be examined and reviewed. The next several sections focus on good management practices. More outsourcing examples are discussed later in this chapter, in the section "Management of IT Suppliers."

Change Management

Change is inevitable, especially when dealing with technology, whose evolution is relentlessly fast paced. When it comes to meeting management and customer expectations, the stakes are high. Get it right, and you are a hero! Have enough failed deployments or system outages, and you may be looking for a new job.

Technologists and IS auditors are tasked with ensuring that all changes are documented, accounted for, and controlled. Companies should have a well-structured process for change requests (CRs). The following steps provide a generic overview of the change management process:

1. Request a change.

2. Approve the request.

3. Document the proposed change.

4. Test the proposed change.

5. Implement the change.

CRs are typically examined by a subject matter expert (SME) before being implemented. CRs must also be assessed to ensure that no change poses a risk for the organization. If an application or code is being examined for a potential change, other issues must be addressed, including how the new code will move from the coding to a production environment and how the code will be tested, as well as an examination of user training. Change management ensures that proper governance and control are maintained.

Quality Management

Quality management is an ongoing effort to provide information systems–related services that meet or exceed customer expectations. It's a philosophy to improve quality and strive for continuous improvement. An auditor should be knowledgeable in these areas:

- Hardware and software requisitioning

- Software development

- Information systems operations

- Human resources management

- Security

Why are so many quality management controls and change management methods needed? Most companies move data among multiple business groups, divisions, and IT systems. Auditors must verify the controls and attest to their accuracy. ISO 9001 is one quality management standard that is receiving widespread support and attention. ISO 9001 describes how production processes are to be managed and reviewed. It is not a standard of quality but covers how well a system or process is documented. Companies that want to obtain an ISO 9001 certification must perform a gap analysis to determine what areas need improvement. The ISO 9001 consists of six procedure documents that specify the following:

- Control of documents

- Control of records

- Control of nonconforming product

- Corrective action

- Preventive action

- Internal audits

NOTE The ISO 9001 certification requires an organization to perform a gap analysis, which allows the company to identify shortcomings that must be addressed to obtain certification.

Many companies view ISO 9001 certification as a competitive advantage, providing their customers the comfort that they are following industry best practices to produce the highest-quality products possible.

Being ISO certified means that the organization has the capability to provide products that meet specific requirements; this includes the process of continual improvement. Being ISO certified can also have a direct bearing on an IS audit because it places strong controls on documented procedures.

Another ISO document that an auditor should be aware of is ISO 27000 series, which is considered a code of practice for information security. These documents are written for individuals who are responsible for initiating, implementing, or maintaining information security management systems. Its goal is to help protect confidentiality, integrity, and availability, and it includes the following:

- Risk assessment and treatment

- Security policy

- Organization of information security

- Asset management

- Human resources security

- Physical and environmental security

- Communications and operations management

- Access control

- Information systems acquisition, development, and maintenance

- Information security incident management

- Business continuity management

- Compliance

For more information on the ISO, see www.iso.org/isoiec-27001-information-security.html and www.iso.org/iso-9001-quality-management.html.

A final control framework worth mentioning is the Committee of Sponsoring Organizations of the Treadway Commission (COSO), which was designed to improve the quality of financial reporting. The COSO framework sets specifications for the following:

- Defining internal control

- Categories of objectives

- Components and principles of internal control

- Requirements for financial control effectiveness

The COSO framework is a series of documents that illustrates approaches and examples of how principles are applied in preparing financial statements. These components constitute a viable framework for describing and analyzing an organization's internal control system in a way that conforms to financial regulations. The framework considers changes in business and operating environments and demonstrates how a variety of entities should operate, including public, private, not-for-profit, and government organizations. COSO framework definitions and principles include the following core areas:

- Control Environment

- Risk Assessment

- Control Activities

- Information & Communications

- Monitoring Activities

For more information on COSO, visit www.coso.org/Pages/default.aspx.

The underlying premise of all these management and control frameworks is that an organization exists to provide value for its stakeholders. All organizations face uncertainty, and the challenge for management is to determine how much uncertainty to accept as it strives to grow its services to its customers and drive stakeholder value. Uncertainty presents both risk and opportunity. Effective management of risk can bolster confidence or enhance value. Management and control frameworks can maximize value when management sets strategy and objectives to strike an optimal balance between delivery, growth, and risks. Effective management and control frameworks will achieve the following:

- Align strategy and risk appetite

- Implement effective processes to enable risk response decisions

- Reduce operational surprises and losses

Maturity Models

Another means of quality management is the *capability maturity model* (*CMM*), designed to improve any process. As processes mature, the quality of their products and services become more consistent and reliable.

There are many CMMs on the market, focused on different industries and addressing different risks. Most CMMs align to five maturity levels, as described in Table 3-10.

Table 3-10 Capability Maturity Model Levels

Maturity Level	Name	Description
1	Initial	This is an ad hoc process with no assurance of repeatability.
2	Repeatable	Change control and quality assurance are in place and controlled by management, although a formal process is not defined.
3	Defined	Defined processes and procedures are in place and used. Qualitative process improvement is in place.

Maturity Level	Name	Description
4	Managed	Quantitative data is collected and analyzed. A process improvement program is used.
5	Optimized	Continuous process improvement is in place and has been budgeted for.

Carnegie Mellon University provided one of the first major CMM models adopted by the industry in 1990. In 2006 Carnegie Mellon University released a major upgrade, referred to as the *capability maturity model integration* (*CMMI*) model. The COBIT 5 Capability Maturity Model references the same five maturity levels and is based on the ISO/IEC 15504 Capability Determination Model.

A CMM is an activity-based model. It focuses on the completion of a process and does not care about the desired result and, hence, does not motivate the organization to make the necessary changes. In contrast, CMMI is a result-oriented model based on key performance areas and, therefore, represents best practice for a given knowledge area. The idea is that establishing and continually improving knowledge areas will help organizations decrease costs and improve quality and speed of delivery. The core CMMI bodies of knowledge are illustrated in Figure 3-1.

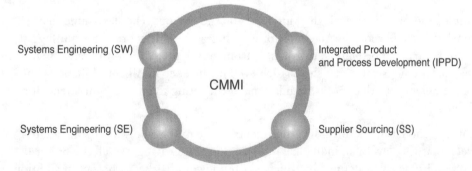

CMMI Bodies of Knowledge

Systems Engineering (SW)

Integrated Product and Process Development (IPPD)

CMMI

Systems Engineering (SE)

Supplier Sourcing (SS)

Figure 3-1   CMMI Bodies of Knowledge

The COBIT 5 CMM is outcome based. The difference between COBIT 5 CMM and CMMI is that COBIT 5 is applied broadly against five domains that include 37 processes, covering all aspects of managing and delivering technology solutions, from the board level to the developer. These are the five COBIT 5 domains:

- Evaluate, Direct and Monitor (EDM)
- Align, Plan and Organize (APO)

- Build, Acquire and Implement (BAI)

- Deliver, Service and Support (DSS)

- Monitor, Evaluate and Assess (MEA)

While both CMMI and COBIT 5 CMM are outcomes based, CMMI can be viewed as more industry and specific process focused. The CMMI knowledge areas tend to be more prescriptive and detailed. In contrast, COBIT 5 CMM has broader application across multiple industries and aligns to specific control objectives across 37 well-defined processes.

NOTE   CISA exam candidates are expected to understand the five levels of a maturity model and to be able to apply them to varying situations. The CISA exam will not require memorization of each prescriptive requirement for each level within CMMI or the COBIT 5 framework.

Implementing a Maturity Model

Implementation of a maturity model is fairly straightforward. Depending on the maturity model framework selected (such as CMMI or COBIT 5 CMM), the framework defines each maturity level in the context of specific artifacts.

Think about maturity levels the same way you think about school. Assume that your local school requires Algebra I for eighth grade and Algebra II for ninth grade. An individual will be eligible to graduate from eighth grade to ninth grade only when she demonstrates that she has achieved proficiency in Algebra I. In addition, the proficiency in Algebra I is foundational for meeting the next requirements for Algebra II.

Maturity models work much like the algebra graduation analogy. To graduate between maturity levels, an individual must demonstrate having met all the prescriptive requirements, as defined by whichever framework has been chosen. In addition, each subsequent layer will build on the previous layer as the maturity level increases. We can illustrate this point with a simplified example related to project management process maturity requirements:

- Level 2 requires the following:

  - Establish cost estimates.

  - Establish a plan.

  - Obtain approval.

- Level 3 requires the following:

    - Coordinate and collaborate with stakeholders.

    - Establish a back out plan.

The project management process maturity requirements shown here illustrate the set of simplified requirements needed to graduate from Level 2 to Level 3 maturity. This is not to suggest that the project would not be successful at maturity Level 2. As maturity level rises, risk is taken out of the process. In this case, two risks would be eliminated in moving from maturity Level 2 to Level 3. The first risk is reduced by formally engaging the stakeholders in the development and deployment of the project. The second risk is reduced by ensuring that a formal backout plan is established in the event that the project does not function as expected. Neither of these risks may occur at Level 2. Nonetheless, having a formal plan to deal with both instances will increase the projected likelihood of success.

Achieving maturity Level 5 is generally accepted as applying a higher level of automation to reducing defects and driving consistency. Should all organizations strive for maturity Level 5? No. Each progressive maturity level comes at a cost. Applying maturity Level 5 to every process would be cost-prohibitive, and the introduction of automation can make simple tasks more complex. For example, updating a monthly price table may be ideal for humans, while scanning for malware requires a high degree of automation.

The determination of what maturity level is required is driven by balancing risk, cost, industry best practices, and what's needed to achieve regulatory compliance. An IS auditor needs to ensure that an appropriate set of tools and criteria have been used within management's risk decision process.

Management's Role in Compliance

In Chapter 2, the section "Knowledge of Regulatory Standards" reviews many of the key laws, rules, and regulations. It also discusses how regulators have set expectations on handling of data, including credit card data, as defined in the Payment Card Industry (PCI) standards. Let's now consider management's role in compliance with these regulations, which were also introduced in Chapter 2:

- **U.S. Health Insurance Portability and Accountability Act (HIPAA):** U.S. standards on management of health care data

- **Sarbanes-Oxley Act (SOX):** U.S. financial and accounting disclosure and accountability for public companies

- **Payment Card Industry (PCI) standards:** Handling and processing of credit cards

- **U.S. Federal Information Security Management Act (FISMA):** Security standards for U.S. government systems

- **U.S. Fair and Accurate Credit Transaction Act of 2003 (FACTA):** Legislation to reduce fraud and identity theft

You should see two themes emerging from these regulations related to the importance of protecting privacy and maintaining effective information security controls. Laws are often enacted after a major event or data breach. After such an event that broadly impacts markets or millions of customers, lawmakers often feel pressure to do something to ensure that such events do not reoccur. That something often takes the form of passing new laws or regulations. Laws and regulations have the benefit of being mandatory, which is a strong motivator for the market to move in a certain direction. The inherent weakness of laws and regulations is that they take a long time to enact and often are not put into place until well after the initial event occurred. Consequently, laws and regulations are typically considered *lagging indicators* of risk.

Management and control frameworks created by industry groups and associations are much better *leading indicators* of risk. These frameworks have the benefit of direct support and updates from industry leaders. In addition, industry framework updates are released on a much shorter timeline than laws and regulations. The inherent weakness of these frameworks is that they are optional and not enforceable in the same way as laws and regulations. The scope and level of adoption of industry frameworks are dependent on leadership's commitment, regulatory inquiries, and peer pressure. Consequently, organizations will comply with both regulations and industry frameworks to control technology risks. Industries that are highly regulated generally tend to have more formal adoption programs related to industry frameworks and regulatory mandates.

Management must demonstrate and evidence compliance. It's not enough to have trained teams of employees and published standards. An IS auditor looks for evidence that an organization complies with key requirements and controls risk consistently. Regulators want to see a culture of managing risk effectively through regulatory compliance. Organizations that tend to do well during an audit or a regulatory exam have the following in place to support evidence of compliance:

- **Organizational functions dedicated to compliance:** Management must demonstrate that teams understand regulatory expectations and continually review internal controls for compliance

    Examples: Compliance, operational risk, and audit functions

- **Risk culture:** Management must promote a risk culture. More than publishing standards, management must establish a *tone at the top*—a term that refers to actions taken by leadership to visibility demonstrate active support for the compliance program.

  Examples: Leadership placing risk discussion as a priority on agendas and management reaction to noncompliance events

- **Risk strategy:** An organization needs to have a well-articulated risk strategy.

  Examples: Policies, standards, and processes to control risk and ensure compliance

- **Risk registry and risk assessments:** An organization needs to have continuous risk assessments and a repository that tracks risks from identification, to remediation, to acceptance. This includes the organization's ability to evaluate and communicate internal control deficiencies in a timely manner to the parties responsible for taking corrective action, including senior management and the board of directors, as appropriate.

  Examples: Audits, risk examination, remediation tracking

Process Optimization Techniques

Regardless of your role as an information systems audit, assurance, and control professional, you are expected to understand basic process optimization techniques. The concept behind process optimization is the ability to apply a systematic technique that reduces the following:

- Variances and inconsistencies

- Risks to the process operations

- Complexity

- Costs

The job competencies covered in the CISA exam apply equally well to an IS auditor who must assess the quality of the processes deployed and the quality of any management optimization efforts that are under way. The CISA exam treats the topic as a foundational topic required for understanding the importance, needs, and general methods applied to optimizing processes. This section provides two examples of process optimization techniques, referred to as the Taguchi and PDCA optimization methods.

NOTE   A good preparation for the exam is to read more examples related to process optimization on the Internet.

Do *not* memorize the descriptions of Taguchi and PDCA in the next few pages. Focus your review on how the break down of the process and the types of cost, complexity, and risks reduced. An exam candidate is not expected to know the specifics of each process optimization technique.

Taguchi

The Taguchi method was developed by Genichi Taguchi to improve the quality of manufacturing in Japan after World War II. The Japanese manufacturers were struggling with very limited resources and poor equipment. Genichi Taguchi developed his technique to optimize manufacturing processes to reduce costs, eliminate waste, and utilize resources for their maximum value. The Taguchi method is a statistical approach to optimizing how a process is designed and improving the quality of each of its components.

Since its introduction, the Taguchi method has been adopted and adjusted to work across industries beyond manufacturing. All processes are affected by outside influences, which Genichi Taguchi refers to as *noise*. The Taguchi method offers a systematic way of identifying the noise sources that have the greatest effects on product variability. The idea is that if you can reduce or eliminate this noise, you can produce products (and services) in an optimized and consistent manner.

While the Taguchi method can be used to improve existing processes, most engineers believe that the greatest value lies in applying the method when creating new processes. They believe that the best way to improve process quality is to design it into the process.

We will not go into the math or statistical formulas associated with the Taguchi method. While interesting, that level of detail will not be on the CISA exam and thus is beyond the scope of this text. (If you would like more information, you can find a number of studies related to the method on the Internet by entering "Taguchi method case study" as a key word search.)

The key concept to the Taguchi method is what's termed an *experiment*. It's an iterative process in that the following stages can be repeated over time:

$$\text{Build} \rightarrow \text{Test} \rightarrow \text{Fix}$$

Basically, each iteration of the test after the build is an experiment to measure the level of noise. As you pass through iterations and use statistical methods to measure the noise and outcome, you can determine the level of optimization being achieved.

The Taguchi principles and methods are a unique quality and process improvement technique. Optimized processes tend to produce consistent quality outcomes and be more insensitive to noise and variations in the environment. The Taguchi method to quality engineering places emphasis on minimizing variation as the main means of improving quality. The Taguchi approach is illustrated in the following iteration steps:

1. Identify the main function and unintended outcomes.

2. Identify the noise factors and testing condition.

3. Identify key quality characteristics.

4. Identify the objective method of measuring optimization.

5. Conduct the experiment.

6. Examine the data; predict optimum control levels and adjust.

7. Conduct the verification experiment.

This is a very useful method because it is statistically accurate. The outcome of the process becomes consistent and predictable, with low levels of variance. The Taguchi method gives you a quantitative way of measuring outcome quality. In addition, you can measure when optimization efforts result in no tangible effort or, worse, a negative effect. These experiments and measurements collectively improve management's understanding of the process and avoid wasted efforts that do not significantly improve quality.

PDCA

Whereas the Taguchi method is a quantitative approach that can be time-consuming, is expensive to execute, and requires a team that is well trained and experienced, the Plan-Do-Check-Act (PDCA) approach is more qualitative and, though less rigorous than the Taguchi method, can also be of value. The PDCA cycle is an iterative four-step problem-solving model that promotes continuous improvement.

The PDCA model dates back to 1939, when Walter A. Shewhart, an American physicist, engineer, and statistician, first published the concept that constant evaluation of management practices is key to the evolution of effective processes and a successful enterprise. Since its first introduction, the concept has been widely adopted across different industries as a means of achieving continuous process improvement.

The basic PDCA iterative four-step process is as follows (see Table 3-11):

Table 3-11   Basic Four-Step PDCA Model

Step Number	Step Name	Description
1	Plan	Establish process objectives.
2	Do	Implement the process.
3	Check	Measure actual process outcomes against objectives.
4	Act/adjust	Adjust the process to close the gap between actual and planned objectives.

- **Plan:** The *plan* step establishes formal control objectives, projects outcomes, and defines the processes needed to achieve the objectives and outcomes. The output from the expectations created in the plan step will become part of the development cycle for the check step. Pilot and prototype testing are encouraged in the PDCA model.

  As an IS auditor or control partner assessing the process, you would either obtain these details from existing process documentation or reverse engineer to obtain them.

- **Do:** The *do* step involves implementing the plan and executing the process. Data is then collected on the outcome, including data on the quality of the product and services produced. Data should be collected on each key requirement specified in the plan step.

- **Check:** During the *check* step, the outcome from the do step is assessed. This assessment is sometimes referred as the *PDCA study*. The assessment compares the actual results collected in the do step against the predicted results in the plan step. Variances can be positive or negative. Positive variance means more value is obtained. Negative variance means less value than expected is obtained. Negative variance typically requires some level of corrective action.

- **Act/adjust:** The *act/adjust* step takes as input the results from the check step and applies corrective action. During the act/adjust step, root causes are determined. Over time, trends are tracked and feedback is considered in the plan step so future processes can benefit. This iterative process establishes continuous improvement. Each pass through a PDCA iteration incrementally improves the process. The goal is to ensure that quality is both initially and continuously achieved.

Taguchi Versus PDCA

The Taguchi and PDCA methods share many common techniques. They are both iterative and incrementally improve quality over time. But quantitative and qualitative techniques are fundamentally as different as night and day. Both methods have utility and value when applied under the right circumstances.

The Taguchi quantitative approach is far more precise in the identification and statistical certainty of its outcome. Its high cost and complexity make it better suited for expensive and more critical processes. PDCA places a high reliance on qualitative judgment, and it's far more reliant on the expertise of the assessor. Its comparable lower cost and agility makes it ideal for lower-cost, low-volume processes, such as back-office IT support processes.

Management of IT Suppliers

As discussed earlier in this chapter, in the section "Enterprise Architecture," when an organization uses an external service provided to deliver IT solutions on its behalf, the practice is called *IT outsourcing*. The external service provided is called an *IT supplier*, *IT vendor*, or *IT third-party provider*, though often *IT* is dropped, and terms are shortened to *supplier*, *vendor*, or *third party*. The services provided by an IT supplier can include any IT function, such as hosting applications in the cloud, providing external data storage, or processing transactions on behalf of the organization.

Outsourced IT services can improve your organization's focus. It is neither practical nor possible to be a jack of all trades. Outsourcing lets management focus on core competencies and competitive advantage while suppliers focus on being the best at their business. Suppliers also have the advantage of scale when an organization outsources information technology to a supplier that specializes in a particular area and can spread costs across multiple customers.

An organization must effectively manage the relationship and services it provides—whether on its own or through third parties—and balance the benefits and risk of handing control to an external supplier.

Third-Party Outsourcing

Outsourced IT functions can occur at a wide range of locations, including the following:

- **Onsite:** Employees and contractors work at the company's facility.
- **Offsite:** Staff and contractors work at a remote location.
- **Offshore:** Staff and contractors work in a separate geographic region.

Organizations should go through a sourcing strategy to determine what information systems tasks must be done by employees. Commodity services that do not offer a competitive advantage are often targeted for IT outsourcing. That has the benefit of allowing an organization to focus internal IT resources on the services that provide maximum value. Commodity services that are often outsourced include the following:

- Data entry
- Application/web hosting
- Help desk
- Payroll processing
- Check processing
- Credit card processing

One key to the outsourcing decision is determining whether a task is part of the organization's *core competency* or *proficiency* that defines who the organization is. This is a fundamental set of skills or knowledge that gives the company a unique advantage. Outsourcing a core competency could put the company at risk because of the over reliance on the vendor. For example, if the core competencies were moved to a vendor who later went out of business then the company could lose that unique market advantage. Additionally, the company should analyze whether the tasks being considered for outsourcing can be duplicated at another location and whether they can be performed for the same or less cost.

Information security should also play a role in the outsourcing decision because some tasks take on a much greater risk if performed by others outside the organization. Any decisions should pass a thorough business process review. For example, does data entry report a large number of errors, is the help desk backlogged, or is application development more than three months behind schedule? Some of the most common outsourced tasks are data entry and processing. When a task is outsourced, accuracy can be retained by implementing a *key verification* process to ensure that the process was done correctly. For example, the company's data entry department might key in information just as the outsourcing partner does in India. After both data sets are entered, they can be compared to verify that the information was entered correctly. Any keystroke that does not match flags an alert so that a data-entry supervisor can examine and verify it.

Third-Party Audits

When the decision is made to outsource, management must be aware that it will lose some level of visibility when the process is no longer done in-house. Outsourcing partners face the same risks, threats, and vulnerabilities as the client, but they might not be as apparent to the client. Because of this loss of control, every outsourcing agreement should contain a *right-to-audit* clause. Without a right-to-audit statement, the client would be forced to negotiate every type of audit or review of the outsourcing partner's operation. These negotiations can be time-consuming and very costly. Therefore, a right-to-audit clause is one of the most powerful mechanisms a company can insist upon before an agreement is signed.

From a supplier's viewpoint, having large numbers of customers auditing processes and facilities can be disruptive and can impact costs. Many suppliers recognize the need to provide their customers' management with evidence that their processes are following industry best practices. Suppliers often hire external audit firms to perform what is called SSAE 16 assessments.

The SSAE 16 is an industry-accepted assessment of a supplier's general control environment. It allows a supplier to be audited once, and the reports can be provided to multiple customers. Customers' management can accept an audit in its entirety or call on its right-to-audit statement to focus on specific areas not covered by the SSAE 16 assessment.

NOTE   The Statement on Standards for Attestation Engagements (SSAE) No. 16, "Reporting on Controls at a Service Organization," was issued by the Auditing Standards Board of the American Institute of Certified Public Accountants (AICPA) in April 2010. The SSAE 16 replaced SAS 70 as the standard for reporting on external IT service providers.

While SSAE 16 is the current industry standard, it will soon be replaced by SSAE 18, which was formally approved for use effective May 2017. The transition between SSAE 16 and SSAE 18 is expected to take a year for many organizations.

Contract Management

An important control within a supplier's contract is the service level agreement (SLA). The supplier's SLA outlines management's expectations of the supplier, such as the timeliness and quality expected in the supplier's services.

With a time-sensitive process, implementing an SLA is one way to obtain a guarantee of the level of service from the supplier. The SLA should specify the uptime, response time, and maximum outage time to which the parties are agreeing.

Think of contracts as the early stages of establishing a relationship with an IT supplier. Both parties in negotiation convey their expectations and commitments. There is a difference between having committed outcomes and trying your best to achieve an outcome. If an organization's transaction must be completed within a specific time, the supplier should add that SLA to the contract. Once contract terms have been agreed upon, the parameters of the relationship have been set.

An important benefit of effective contract management is clarity. The terms of a contract often become what is measured and managed. For example, an outsourced call center may require that 99 percent of calls be answered within so many rings of the phone. That term in the contract can be used as a measurement point to monitor the vendor's performance.

A good contract anticipates disputes between management and the supplier and negotiates terms of mutual benefit. This concept of mutual benefit is important. When contract terms for the supplier are not cost-effective, the supplier may cut corners and may fail to deliver the quality and speed needed. Having healthy suppliers benefits the organization and the industry.

Performance Monitoring

Once the contract terms are in place, the supplier's performance must be monitored. Performance is typically monitored against specific terms set in the contract.

The key in performance monitoring of suppliers is to identify the risks that management wants to control. Not every term of a contract will be monitored. Management needs to focus on key risks to the business.

The organization is ultimately accountable for the performance of a supplier. It needs to view the supplier as an extension of the organization. The supplier will have access to the organization's data and product. As a result, the quality of the organization's products and services is often tied to a supplier's performance. Think of it this way: if management chose not to outsource and produced an IT service internally, would they check on the quality? If the answer is yes, then most likely management needs to also check on the supplier's quality.

Most risks can be avoided altogether if management creates a team that is dedicated to monitoring supplier performance and performing effective relationship management. Such a specialized team can establish a performance monitoring program based on controlling risks related the following themes:

- **Speed:** The SLA terms are typically used to monitor the speed of delivery by the supplier.

- **Quality:** Management should consider monitoring both the quality of the product or services being delivered by the supplier and the quality of the supplier's staff. The contract should include terms related to the qualifications of the supplier team working on the IT solutions (for example, background checks, technical expertise).

- **Cost:** Billing from the supplier should be monitored against contract terms. Outsourcing IT services often provides financial benefits that should be managed as well. A *change order* typically involves asking a supplier to vary the normal process. Costs associated with change orders need to be carefully monitored to ensure that a supplier does not overcharge and erode the cost benefits projected.

Relationship Management

Management can overcome many outsourcing difficulties simply through good communication with the supplier. This ongoing relationship builds trust and creates a partnership that helps manage risks consistently. Not every situation can be anticipated or codified in the contract.

When unexpected situations arise, you need two reasonable entities to come together to solve the problem to the mutual satisfaction of both parties. At the core of this process should be a well-established relationship. Relationship management takes time and effort. The benefits are obvious when it's done well. On the other hand, the outcome can be devastating when the supplier relationship is poor or when the supplier does the minimum to stay within prescriptive terms of the contract. For example, say that you have a supplier providing partial hosting services. Let's assume that your own data center has a significant power disruption that is estimated to last 24 hours. Management would ideally like to shift additional processing to the supplier hosting facility. However, the supplier is at nearly full capacity, and the additional hosting is beyond the terms of the agreement. Sounds like an unsolvable problem, and management simply needs to take the hit on being out of business for 24 hours. When a supplier perceives the relationship with the client as long-term and profitable, however, it will go to great lengths to preserve the relationship. This may include contacting other customers and determining the feasibility of freeing capacity for the next 24 hours so the supplier can support additional hosting services. Now let's reverse the example and assume that the supplier is moving between data center facilities, and the supplier will not be able to meet the contract's SLA during that period of time. In this case, management can plan for the SLA disruption and reduce any associated risks.

The point is that effective relationship management with suppliers can bridge the interests of both entities and balance rewards and risks. It can also protect both parties from unexpected situations and ensure that risks are effectively managed. Here's are some key takeaways:

- **Treat suppliers as an extension of your organization's accountability:** Maintain a close relationship with each supplier.

- **Expect the unexpected:** Not all situations can be anticipated or covered in a contract.

- **Anticipate problems:** Manage the supplier relationship for the long term and to mutual benefit.

- **Review core services at least annually:** Even if a contract has not expired, the terms should be reviewed periodically.

- **Monitor performance:** Monitor performance against key terms in the contract.

Chapter Summary

This chapter discusses IT governance, which starts with senior management and extends down through the organization. This chapter reviews how management creates the organizational constructs and related processes necessary to achieve the organization's strategy and goals. Technology plays an important role in supporting the company and helping it reach its goals.

Other requirements are policies, procedures, and standards. These documents not only provide a high-level view of the mission and direction of the company but also guide employees in their day-to-day activities. Auditors play an important role in independently verifying that governance is working as expected. Auditors are tasked with reviewing an organization's documents, standards, and policies to determine how closely they map to employee activities. This chapter discusses a variety of tools an organization may use, such as maturity models, optimization techniques, and third-party performance management.

Regardless of your role in an organization, it's important to understand how governance and related layers of controls work.

Exam Preparation Tasks

As mentioned in the section "How to Use This Book" in the Introduction, you have a couple choices for exam preparation: the exercises here; Chapter 10, "Final Preparation;" and the exam simulation questions on the book's companion web page (www.informit.com/title/9780789758446).

Review All the Key Topics

Review the most important topics in this chapter, noted with the Key Topic icon in the outer margin of the page. Table 3-12 lists these key topics and the page number on which each is found.

Table 3-12 Key Topics in Chapter 3

Key Topic Element	Description	Page Number
List	IT steering committee membership	75
List	Five stages in the ITIL service Life cycle	79
Table 3-2	Sample assessment results	86
Table 3-3	Performing a qualitative assessment	87
Table 3-4	Documentation/level of control	92
Table 3-5	Simple data classification scheme	96
Table 3-6	Separation of duties	105
Table 3-7	Key employee controls	107
Table 3-8	Key performance terms and examples	108
Table 3-9	Common management and control frameworks	110
Table 3-10	Capability maturity model levels	116
Figure 3-1	CMMI bodies of knowledge	117
List	The Taguchi method	123
Table 3-11	Basic four-step PDCA model	124

Complete Tables from Memory

Print a copy of Appendix B, "Memory Tables" (found on the companion web page), or at least the section for this chapter, and complete the tables from memory. Appendix C, "Memory Tables Answer Key," also on the companion web page, includes completed tables you can use to check your work.

Key Terms

Define the following key terms from this chapter and check your answers against the glossary:

balanced scorecard (BSC), baseline, capability maturity model (CMM), Control Objectives for Information and Related Technologies (COBIT), data classification, enterprise architecture (EA), enterprise risk management (ERM), guidelines, Information Technology Infrastructure Library (ITIL), IT steering committee, key performance indicator (KPI), lagging indicator, leading indicator, metadata, outsourcing, Plan-Do-Check-Act (PDCA), policy, principle of least privilege, procedures, qualitative risk assessment, quality assurance (QA), right-to-audit clause, risk acceptance, quantitative risk assessment, risk avoidance, risk reduction, risk transference, rotation of assignment, segregation of duties (SoD), standards, stochastic, Taguchi model, threat, three lines of defense, vulnerability

Exercises

3.1 Determining the steps for quantitative risk assessment

Estimated time: 5 minutes

You have read in this chapter about the importance of risk assessment. Inventorying assets, determining the risks to those assets, and evaluating countermeasure options are all part of good IT governance.

In this exercise, you examine the proper order for quantitative risk assessment.

1. Place the following quantitative risk analysis steps and calculations in the proper sequential order, from 1 (first step) to 6:

   _____ Determine the annual rate of occurrence (likelihood of occurrence).

   _____ Identify threats to the asset.

   _____ Determine the asset value (AV).

   _____ Calculate the annualized loss expectancy for each asset.

   _____ Calculate the single loss expectancy.

   _____ Identify the exposure factor for each asset in relation to the threat.

2. Compare your results to the answers here:

   1. Determine the asset value (AV).

   2. Identify threats to the asset.

   3. Identify the exposure factor for each asset in relation to the threat.

   4. Calculate the single loss expectancy.

   5. Determine the annual rate of occurrence (likelihood of occurrence).

   6. Calculate the annualized loss expectancy for each asset.

Review Questions

1. Which of the following is a control document that describes a software improvement process characterized by five levels, where each level describes a higher level of maturity?

    a. ISO 17799

    b. CMM

    c. COSO

    d. COBIT

2. Which of the following roles is a role whose duties should not be fulfilled by a network administrator?

    a. Quality assurance

    b. Systems administrator

    c. Application programmer

    d. Systems analyst

3. You are auditing a credit card payment system. The best assurance that information is entered correctly is by using which of the following?

    a. Audit trails

    b. Separation of data entry and computer operator duties

    c. Key verification

    d. Supervisory review

4. You are reviewing unfamiliar malware event records. Which of the following would be the best source of information to start your review about the file?

    a. Trending charts based on the event records

    b. Metadata information

    c. Security access information

    d. Executive summary on malware event

5. Look at the following common policy characteristics. The attribute most closely associated with a bottom-up policy development is that it _____.

    a. aligns policy with strategy

    b. is a very slow process

    c. does not address concerns of employees

    d. involves risk assessment

6. Which of the following best describes a balanced scorecard?

    a. Used for benchmarking a preferred level of service

    b. Used to measure the effectiveness of IT services by customers and clients

    c. Used to verify that the organization's strategy and IT services match

    d. Used to measure the evaluation of help desk employees

7. Your organization is considering using a new ISP for time-sensitive transactions. From an audit perspective, what would be the most important item to review?

    a. The service level agreement

    b. The physical security of the ISP site

    c. References from other clients of the ISP

    d. Background checks of the ISP's employees

8. Separation of duties is one way to limit fraud and misuse. Consider the following explanation: "This control allows employees access to cash or valuables." Of the four separation of duties controls, which one most closely matches this?

    a. Authorization

    b. Custody

    c. Record keeping

    d. Reconciliation

9. Which of the following combinations of two job roles can be combined to create the least amount of risk or opportunity for malicious acts? ·

    a. Systems analyst and quality assurance

    b. Computer operator and systems programmer

    c. Security administrator and application programmer

    d. Database administrator and systems analyst

10. You have been asked to perform a new audit assignment. Your first task is to review the organization's strategic plan. What is the first item that should be reviewed in the plan?

    a. Documentation that details the existing infrastructure

    b. Previous and planned budgets

    c. Organizational charts

    d. The business plan

Suggested Readings and Resources

- **COSO guidelines:** www.coso.org

- **COBIT framework:** www.isaca.org/cobit/

- **IT governance:** http://en.wikipedia.org/wiki/
  Information_technology_governance

- **Risk-based audit best practices:** www.journalofaccountancy.com/
  issues/2009/dec/20091789.html

The following exam domain is partially covered in this chapter:

Domain 4—Information Systems Operations, Maintenance and Service Management

This chapter covers the following topics:

- **Threats to Business Operations:** Businesses face many threats and must have the proper controls and countermeasures to deal with them.

- **The Business Continuity Planning (BCP) Process:** One of the key activities of business continuity is the measurement of the performance of the program. Good governance presumes analysis of ongoing business processes to ensure that they are fulfilling company objectives.

- **Recovery Strategies:** Many different recovery strategies exist to deal with potential outages. An organization must choose the right one to ensure that critical activities can continue.

CHAPTER 4

Maintaining Critical Services

"Do I Know This Already?" Quiz

The "Do I Know This Already?" quiz allows you to assess whether you should read this entire chapter thoroughly or jump to the "Exam Preparation Tasks" section. If you are in doubt about your answers to these questions or your own assessment of your knowledge of the topics, read the entire chapter. Table 4-1 lists the major headings in this chapter and their corresponding "Do I Know This Already?" quiz questions. You can find the answers at the bottom of the page following the quiz and in Appendix A, "Answers to the 'Do I Know This Already?' Quizzes and Review Questions."

Table 4-1   "Do I Know This Already?" Section-to-Question Mapping

Foundation Topics Section	Questions Covered in This Section
Threats to Business Operations	1, 10
The Business Continuity Planning (BCP) Process	2–5
Recovery Strategies	6–9

CAUTION   The goal of self-assessment is to gauge your mastery of the topics in this chapter. If you do not know the answer to a question or are only partially sure of the answer, you should mark that question as incorrect for purposes of the self-assessment. Giving yourself credit for an answer you correctly guess skews your self-assessment results and might provide you with a false sense of security.

1. Which of the following is the highest level of incident classification?

    a. Major

    b. Minor

    c. Defined

    d. Crisis

2. From an audit perspective, what best defines how current the data must be or how much data an organization can afford to lose?

   a. RTO

   b. RPO

   c. MTD

   d. WRT

3. Which of the following specifies the maximum elapsed time to recover an application at an alternate site?

   a. RTO

   b. RPO

   c. MTD

   d. WRT

4. Which of the following defines the maximum amount of time the organization can provide services at the alternate site? This value can be determined by items such as contractual values.

   a. SDO

   b. SLA

   c. MTD

   d. WRT

5. Which of the following activities are specifically required for critical processes and produce revenue?

   a. Core processing

   b. Non-discretionary processes

   c. Maximum acceptable outage

   d. Supporting processes

6. Which version of RAID offers no fault tolerance?

   a. RAID 0

   b. RAID 1

   c. RAID 10

   d. RAID 15

7. This tape-rotation scheme is named after a mathematical puzzle.

   a. Grandfather, Father, Son

   b. Complex

   c. Simple

   d. Tower of Hanoi

8. This recovery option is sometimes referred to as a gentleman's agreement.

   a. Hot site

   b. Redundant site

   c. Reciprocal

   d. Grandfather, father, son

9. Which of the following would be used to describe a non-repairable item that has reached end of life?

   a. MTTR

   b. MTTF

   c. MTBF

   d. SLA

10. Which of the following is the lowest level of incident classification?

   a. Major

   b. Minor

   c. Negligible

   d. Crisis

Foundation Topics

Threats to Business Operations

There is no shortage of events that can endanger business operations. Such events can come from inside or outside the organization and are typically categorized as either human-caused, technical, or natural threats, as shown in Figure 4-1. Natural threats are high on the list. In 2016, events such as Hurricane Matthew in the Caribbean, earthquakes in Ecuador, and catastrophic flooding in China topped the list. Such events highlight the need to be adequately prepared. Companies tend to seriously underestimate how long it would take to restore operations. In 2017, many companies were hit with ransomware because of flaws in their backup and offsite storage programs; other companies suffered because they had no workstation recovery plans for end users.

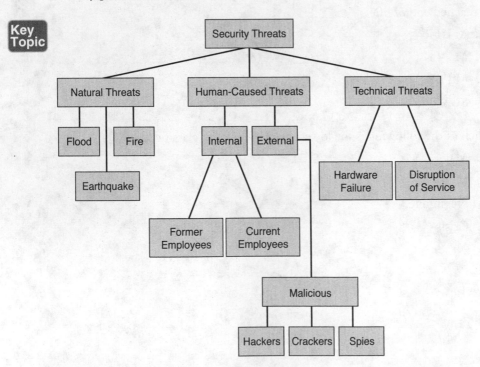

Figure 4-1   Sources of Security Threats

Answers to the "Do I Know This Already?" Quiz:

1. D; 2. B; 3. A; 4. C; 5. A; 6. A; 7. D; 8. C; 9. B; 10. C

A company may not always update its plans as the company grows, changes, or modifies existing processes, even though the results of poor planning can be disastrous for the company. Some estimates indicate that only a small percentage of businesses are required by regulation to have a disaster recovery plan. Disaster recovery must compete for limited funds. Companies might be lulled into thinking that these funds might be better spent on more immediate needs. Some businesses might simply underestimate the risk and hope that adverse events don't happen to them. Disaster recovery planning requires a shift of thinking from reactive to proactive.

Many of us would prefer not to plan for disasters. Many see it as an unpleasant exercise or would just prefer to ignore it. Sadly, we all must deal with disasters and incidents. They are dynamic by nature. For example, mainframes face a different set of threats than distributed systems, just as users connected to free wireless networks face a different set of threats than those connected to wired networks inside an organization. This means that management must be dynamic and must be able to change with time. Regardless of the source of a threat, each one has the potential to cause an incident. Incident management and disaster recovery are closely related. Incidents might or might not cause disruptions to normal operations. From the perspective of an auditor, a review of incident management should be performed to determine whether problems and incidents are prevented, detected, analyzed, reported, and resolved in a timely manner. This means the auditor should review existing incident response plans. The auditor also plays a critical role after an incident in that there should be a review of what worked and what did not so the plan can be optimized to be better prepared for the next incident.

An organization needs to have a way to measure incidents and quantify their damage. Table 4-2 lists the incident classification per ISACA. An auditor should have knowledge of problem and incident management practices.

Table 4-2   Incident Classification

Level	Description
Crisis	A crisis is considered a major problem. It is of sufficient impact that it adversely affects the organization's ability to continue business functions.
Major	A major incident is of sufficient strength to negatively impact one or more departments, or it might even affect external clients.
Minor	Although these events are noticeable, they cause little or no damage.
Negligible	These detectable events cause no damage or have no longer-term effect.

NOTE   Disruptive incients such as a crisis or major or minor events should be tracked and analyzed so that corrective actions can be taken to prevent these events from occurring in the future.

The Business Continuity Planning (BCP) Process

The BCP process can be described as the process of creating systems of prevention and recovery to deal with potential threats to a company. One of the best sources of information about the BCP process is the Disaster Recovery Institute International (DRII), which you can find online at www.drii.org. The process that DRII defines for BCP is much broader in scope than the ISACA process. DRII breaks down the disaster recovery process into 10 domains:

- Project initiation and management
- Risk evaluation and control
- Business impact analysis
- Developing business continuity management strategies
- Emergency response and operations
- Developing and implementing business continuity plans
- Awareness and training programs
- Exercising and maintaining business continuity plans
- Crisis communications
- Coordination with external agencies

The BCP process as defined by ISACA has a much narrower scope and focuses on the following seven steps, each of which is discussed in greater detail in the following sections:

1. Project management and initiation
2. Business impact analysis
3. Development and recovery strategy
4. Final plan design and implementation
5. Training and awareness
6. Implementation and testing
7. Monitoring and maintenance

NOTE   The auditors role in the business continuity process is to evaluate resilience and to determine whether the BCP process is controlled effectively and continue to support the organization's objectives.

Project Management and Initiation

Before the BCP process can begin, management must be on board. Management is ultimately responsible and must be actively involved in the process. Management sets the budget, determines the team leader, and gets the process started. The BCP team leader determines who will be on the BCP team. The team's responsibilities include the following:

- Identifying regulatory and legal requirements

- Identifying all possible threats and risks

- Estimating the possibilities of these threats and their loss potential and ranking them based on the likelihood of the event occurring

- Performing a business impact analysis (BIA)

- Outlining which departments, systems, and processes must be up and running first

- Developing procedures and steps in resuming business after a disaster

- Assigning tasks to individuals that they should perform during a crisis situation

- Documenting, communicating with employees, and performing training and drills

One of the first steps the team is tasked with is meeting with senior management. The purpose of this meeting is to define goals and objectives, discuss a project schedule, and discuss the overall goals of the BCP process. This should give everyone present some idea of the scope of the final BCP policy.

It's important for everyone involved to understand that the BCP is the most important *corrective control* the organization will have an opportunity to shape. Although the BCP process is primarily corrective, it also has the following elements:

- **Preventive:** Controls to identify critical assets and develop ways to prevent outages

- **Detective:** Controls to alert the organization quickly in case of outages or problems

- **Corrective:** Controls to return to normal operations as quickly as possible

Business Impact Analysis

Chance and uncertainty are part of the world we live in. We cannot predict what tomorrow will bring or whether a disaster will occur—but this doesn't mean we cannot plan for it. As an example, the city of Galveston, Texas, is in an area prone to hurricanes. Just because the possibility of a hurricane in winter in Galveston is extremely low doesn't mean that planning can't take place to reduce the potential negative impact of such an event actually occurring. This is what BIA is about. Its purpose is to think through all possible disasters that could take place, assess the risk, quantify the impact, determine the loss, and develop a plan to deal with the incidents that seem most likely to occur.

As a result, BIA should present a clear picture of what is needed to continue operations if a disaster occurs. The individuals responsible for BIA must look at the organization from many different angles and use information from a variety of inputs. For BIA to be successful, the BIA team must know what the key business processes are. This is something that businesses may already know but don't recognize it as such. As an example, a computer company that places a priority on selling computers over the service and repair of computers has determined the key activity. It's the selling of the product. As such, this activity needs to have controls in place to continue in the face of negative events. Questions the team must ask when determining critical processes might include the following:

- **Does the process support health and safety?** Items such as the loss of an air traffic control system at a major airport or the loss of power in a hospital operating room could be devastating to those involved and result in loss of life.

- **Does the loss of the process have a negative impact on income?** For example, a company such as eBay would find the loss of Internet connectivity devastating, whereas a small nonprofit organization might be able to live without connectivity for days.

- **Does the loss of the process violate legal or statutory requirements?** For example, a coal-powered electrical power plant might be using scrubbers to clean the air before emissions are released. Loss of these scrubbers might lead to a violation of federal law and result in huge regulatory fines.

- **How does the loss of the process affect users?** Returning to the example of the coal-powered electrical power plant, it is easy to see how problems with the steam-generation process would shut down power generation and leave many residential and business customers without power. This loss of power in the Alaskan winter or in the Houston summer would have a large impact.

As you might be starting to realize, performing BIA is no easy task. It requires not only knowledge of business processes but also a thorough understanding of the organization. This includes IT resources and individual business units, as well as the interrelationships between these pieces. This task requires the support of senior management and the cooperation of IT personnel, business unit managers, and end users. The general steps of BIA are as follows:

1. Determine data-gathering techniques.

2. Gather business impact analysis data.

3. Identify critical business functions and resources.

4. Verify completeness of data.

5. Establish recovery time for operations.

6. Define recovery alternatives and costs.

TIP   For the CISA exam, you should understand that many BIA programs look no further than the traditional network. It is important that BIA also look at systems and information that might normally be overlooked, such as information stored on end-user systems that are not backed up and laptops used by the sales force or management.

BIA typically includes both quantitative and qualitative components:

- *Quantitative analysis* deals with numbers and dollar amounts. It involves attempting to assign a monetary value to the elements of risk assessment and to place dollar amounts on the potential impact, including both loss of income and expenses. Quantitative impacts can include all associated costs, including these:

  - Lost productivity

  - Delayed or canceled orders

  - Cost of repair

  - Value of the damaged equipment or lost data

  - Cost of rental equipment

  - Cost of emergency services

  - Cost to replace the equipment or reload data

- *Qualitative assessment* is scenario driven and does not involve assigning dollar values to components of the risk analysis. A qualitative assessment ranks the seriousness of impacts into grades or classes, such as low, medium, and high. These are usually associated with items to which no dollar amount can be easily assigned:

  - **Low:** Minor inconvenience; customers might not notice.

  - **Medium:** Some loss of service; might result in negative press or cause customers to lose some confidence in the organization.

  - **High:** Will result in loss of goodwill between the company and a client or an employee; negative press also reduces the outlook for future products and services.

Although different approaches for calculating loss exist, one of the most popular methods of acquiring data is using a questionnaire. A team may develop a questionnaire for senior management and end users and might hand it out or use it during an interview process. This form might include items such as the recovery point objective (RPO), the recovery time objective (RTO), or even the mean time to recover (MTTR). Figure 4-2 provides an example of a typical BIA questionnaire.

The questionnaire can even be used in a round-table setting. This method of performing information gathering requires the BIA team to bring the required key individuals into a meeting and discuss as a group what impact specific types of disruptions would have on the organization. Auditors play a key role because they might be asked to contribute information such as past transaction volumes or the impact to the business of specific systems becoming unavailable.

NOTE   The BIA must typically determine criticality, downtime estimates, and resource requirements. Criticality can be determined by performing risk calculations such as annualized loss and its impact. Downtime estimates can be evaluated by examining the RTO. Determining the resource requirements requires an analysis of the inputs and outputs of systems. As an example, a generator is needed for backup, yet fuel is needed as a resource to keep the generator running.

Key Business Processes

Identify and describe the **_key_** business processes of the unit/division. For each process, identify its **_Recovery Time Objective (RTO)_**. **RTO** is defined as how quickly the process must be restored following a disaster. The Recovery Time Objective is an estimate of how long the process can be unavailable. Also identify a **_Recovery Point Objective (RPO)_** for each process. **RPO** is the determination of how much data loss, in terms of time, is tolerable before a process is significantly impacted. If the process can be performed manually, please use Attachment A to explain. Use multiple pages if needed.

Key Business Process	Recovery Time Objective	Recovery Point Objective	Can This Be Performed Manually? For How Long?	Computer Systems/Applications Required to Perform This Process

Figure 4-2   BIA Questionnaire

Criticality Analysis

How do you classify systems and resources according to their value or order of importance? You determine the estimated loss in the event of a disruption and calculate the likelihood that the disruption will occur. The quantitative method for this process involves three steps:

1. **Estimate potential losses (SLE):** This step involves determining the single loss expectancy (SLE), which is calculated as follows:

   Single loss expectancy = Asset value × Exposure factor

   Items to consider when calculating the SLE include the physical destruction of human-caused events, the loss of data, and threats that might cause a delay or disruption in processing. The exposure factor is the measure or percentage of damage that a realized threat would have on a specific asset.

2. **Conduct a threat analysis (ARO):** The purpose of a threat analysis is to determine the likelihood that an unwanted event will happen. The goal is to estimate the annual rate of occurrence (ARO). Simply stated, how many times is this event expected to happen in one year?

3. **Determine annual loss expectancy (ALE):** This third and final step of the quantitative assessment seeks to combine the potential loss and rate/year to determine the magnitude of the risk. This is expressed as annual loss expectancy (ALE). ALE is calculated as follows:

Annualized loss expectancy (ALE) =

Single loss expectancy (SLE) × Annualized rate of occurrence (ARO)

For example, suppose that the potential loss due to a hurricane on a business based in Tampa, Florida, is $1 million. An examination of previous weather patterns and historical trends reveals that there has been an average of one hurricane of serious magnitude to hit the city every 10 years, which translates to 1/10, or 0.1% per year. This means the assessed risk that the organization will face a serious disruption is $100,000 (= $1 million × 0.1) per year. That value is the annualized loss expectancy and, on average, is the amount per year that the disruption will cost the organization. Placing dollar amounts on such risks can aid senior management in determining what processes are most important and should be brought online first. Qualitatively, these items might be categorized not by dollar amount but by a risk-ranking scale. According to ISACA, the scale shown in Table 4-3 is used to classify systems according to their importance to the organization.

Table 4-3   System Classification

Classification	Description
Critical	These extremely important functions cannot be performed with duplicate systems or processes. These functions are extremely intolerant to disruptions, and any disruption is very costly.
Vital	Although these functions are important, they can be performed by a backup manual process—but not for a long period of time. These systems can tolerate disruptions for typically five days or less.
Sensitive	Although these tasks are important, they can be performed manually at a reasonable cost. However, this is inconvenient and requires additional resources or staffing.
Noncritical	These services are not critical and can be interrupted. They can be restored later with little or no negative effects.

After addressing all these questions, the BCP team can start to develop recommendations and look at some potential recovery strategies. The BCP team should report these findings to senior management as a prioritized list of key business resources and the order in which restoration should be processed. The report should also offer potential recovery scenarios. Many times it will be the network operations center

(NOC) or help desk that fist hears of a problem via end users. It's important to have processes that tie these reports back to BCP teams so that potential problems can be addressed quickly.

Before presenting the report to senior management, however, the team should distribute it to the various department heads. These individuals were interviewed, and the plan affects them and their departments; therefore, they should be given the opportunity to review it and note any discrepancies. The BIA information must be correct and accurate because all future decisions will be based on those findings.

NOTE   Interdependencies can make criticality analysis very complex. For example, you might have two assets that on their own are noncritical but in certain contexts or situations become critical!

Development and Recovery Strategy

At this point, the team has completed both the project initiation and BIA. Now it must determine the most cost-effective recovery mechanisms to be implemented based on the critical processes and threats determined during the BIA. An effective recovery strategy should apply preventive, detective, and corrective controls to meet the following objectives:

- Remove identified threats.
- Reduce the likelihood of identified risks.
- Reduce the impact of identified risks.

The recovery strategies should specify the best way to recover systems and processes in case of interruption. Operations can be interrupted in several different ways:

- **Data interruptions:** Caused by the loss of data. Solutions to data interruptions include backup, offsite storage, and remote journaling.
- **Operational interruptions:** Caused by the loss of equipment. Solutions to this type of interruption include hot sites, redundant equipment, and redundant array of independent disks (RAID).
- **Facility and supply interruptions:** Caused by interruptions due to fire, loss of inventory, transportation problems, HVAC problems, and telecommunications. Solutions to this type of interruption include redundant communication and transporting systems.

- **Business interruptions:** Caused by interruptions due to loss of human resources, strikes, critical equipment, supplies, and office space. Solutions to this
type of interruption include redundant sites, alternate locations, and temporary staff.

The selection of a recovery strategy is based on several factors, including cost, criticality of the systems or process, and the time required to recover. To determine the
best recovery strategy, follow these steps:

1. Document all costs for each possible alternative.

2. Obtain cost estimates for any outside services that might be needed.

3. Develop written agreements with the chosen vendor for such services.

4. Evaluate what resumption strategies are possible if there is a complete loss of
   the facility.

5. Document your findings and report your chosen recovery strategies to management for feedback and approval.

Normally, any IT system that runs a mission-critical application needs a recovery
strategy. There are many to choose from; the appropriate choice is based on the
impact to the organization of the loss of the system or process. Recovery strategies
include the following:

- Continuous processing

- Standby processing

- Standby database shadowing

- Remote data journaling

- Electronic vaulting

- Mobile site

- Hot site

- Warm site

- Cold site

- Reciprocal agreements

All of these options are discussed later in the chapter, in the section "Recovery
Strategies." To get a better idea of how each of these options compares to the
cost of implementation, take a moment to review Figure 4-3. At this point, it is

important to realize that there must be a balance between the level of service needed and the recovery method.

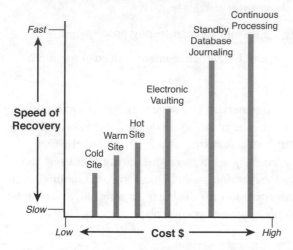

Figure 4-3 Recovery Options and Costs

TIP Exam candidates should understand that recovery strategies should be based on the disruptive cost versus the recovery costs. Finding a balance between the two enables recovery to occur at the minimized cost.

Final Plan Design and Implementation

In the final plan design and implementation phase, the team prepares and documents a detailed plan for recovering critical business systems. This plan should be based on information gathered during the project initiation, the BIA, and the recovery strategies phase. The plan should be a guide for implementation. The plan should address factors and variables such as these:

- Selecting critical functions and priorities for restoration

- Determining support systems that critical functions need

- Estimating potential disasters and calculating the minimum resources needed to recover from the catastrophe

- Determining the procedures for declaring a disaster and under what circumstances this will occur

- Identifying individuals responsible for each function in the plan

- Choosing recovery strategies and determining what systems and equipment will be needed to accomplish the recovery

- Determining who will manage the restoration and testing process

- Calculating what type of funding and fiscal management is needed to accomplish these goals

The plan should be written in easy-to-understand language that uses common terminology that everyone will understand. The plan should detail how the organization will interface with external groups such as customers, shareholders, the media, and community, region, and state emergency services groups during a disaster. Important teams should be formed so that training can be performed. The final step of the phase is to combine all this information into the business continuity plan and then interface it with the organization's other emergency plans.

> **NOTE**   Copies of the business continuity plan should be kept both onsite and offsite.

Training and Awareness

The goal of training and awareness is to make sure all employees know what to do in case of an emergency. Studies have shown that training improves response time and helps employees be better prepared. Employees need to know where to call or how to maintain contact with the organization if a disaster occurs. Therefore, the organization should design and develop training programs to make sure each employee knows what to do and how to do it. Training can include a range of specific programs, such as CPR, fire drills, crisis management, and emergency procedures. Employees assigned to specific tasks should be trained to carry out needed procedures. Cross-training of team members should occur, if possible, so that team members are familiar with a variety of recovery roles and responsibilities. Some people might not be able to lead under the pressure of crisis command; others might not be able to report to work. Table 4-4 describes some of the key groups involved in the BCP process and their responsibilities.

Table 4-4   BCP Process Responsibilities

Person or Department	Responsibility
Senior management	Project initiation, ultimate responsibility, overall approval and support
Middle management or business unit managers	Identification and prioritization of critical systems
BCP committee and team members	Planning, day-to-day management, implementation, and testing of the plan
Functional business units	Plan implementation, incorporation, and testing
IT audit	Business continuity plan review, test results evaluation, offsite storage facilities, alternate processing contracts, and insurance coverage

TIP   For the CISA exam you should know that the number-one priority of any business continuity plan or disaster recovery plan is to protect the safety of employees.

Implementation and Testing

During the implementation and testing phase, the BCP team ensures that the previously agreed-upon steps are implemented. No demonstrated recovery exists until a plan has been tested. Before examining the ways in which the testing can occur, look at some of the teams that are involved in the process:

- **Incident response team:** Team developed as a central clearinghouse for all incidents.

- **Emergency response team:** The first responders for the organization. They are tasked with evacuating personnel and saving lives.

- **Emergency management team:** Executives and line managers who are financially and legally responsible. They must also handle the media and public relations.

- **Damage assessment team:** The estimators. They must determine the damage and estimate the recovery time.

- **Salvage team:** Those responsible for reconstructing damaged facilities. This includes cleaning up, recovering assets, creating documentation for insurance filings or legal actions, and restoring paper documents and electronic media.

- **Communications team:** Those responsible for installing communications (data, voice, phone, fax, radio) at the recovery site.

- **Security team:** Those who manage the security of the organization during a time of crisis. They must maintain order after a disaster.

- **Emergency operations team:** Individuals who reside at the alternative site and manage systems operations. They are primarily operators and supervisors who are familiar with system operations.

- **Transportation team:** Those responsible for notifying employees that a disaster has occurred. They are also in charge of providing transportation, scheduling, and lodging for those who will be needed at the alternative site.

- **Coordination team:** Those tasked with managing operations at different remote sites and coordinating the recovery efforts.

- **Finance team:** Individuals who provide budgetary control for recovery and accurate accounting of costs.

- **Administrative support team:** Individuals who provide administrative support and also handle payroll functions and accounting.

- **Supplies team:** Individuals who coordinate with key vendors to maintain needed supplies.

- **Relocation team:** Those in charge of managing the process of moving from the alternative site to the restored original location.

- **Recovery test team:** Individuals deployed to test the business continuity plan/ disaster recovery plan and determine their effectiveness.

Did you notice that the last team listed is the recovery test team? This team consists of individuals who test the business continuity plan; this should be done at least once a year. Without testing, there is no guarantee that the plan will work. Testing helps bring theoretical plans into reality. To build confidence, the BCP team should start with easier parts of the plan and build to more complex items. The initial tests should focus on items that support core processing and should be scheduled during a time that causes minimal disruption to normal business operations. Tests should be observed by an auditor who can witness the process and record accurate test times. Having an auditor is not the only requirement: Key individuals who would be responsible in a real disaster must play a role in the testing process. Testing methods vary among organizations and range from simple to complex. Regardless of the method or types of testing performed, the idea is to learn from the practice and improve the process each time a problem is discovered. As a CISA exam candidate, you should be aware of the three different types of BCP testing, as defined by the ISACA:

- Paper tests
- Preparedness tests
- Full operation tests

The following sections describe these basic testing methods.

TIP ISACA defines three types of BCP tests: paper tests, preparedness tests, and full operation tests.

Paper Tests

The most basic method of BCP testing is the *paper test*. Although it is not considered a replacement for a full interruption or parallel test, it is a good start. A paper test is an exercise that can be performed by sending copies of the plan to different department managers and business unit managers for review. Each of these individuals can review the plan to make sure nothing has been overlooked and that everything that is being asked of them is possible.

A paper test can also be performed by having the members of the team come together and discuss the business continuity plan. This is sometimes known as *walk-through testing*. The plans are laid out across the table so that attendees have a chance to see how an actual emergency would be handled. By reviewing the plan in this way, some errors or problems should become apparent. With either method—sending the plan around or meeting to review the plan—the next step is usually a preparedness test.

Preparedness Tests

A *preparedness test* is a simulation in which team members go through an exercise that reenacts an actual outage or disaster. This type of test is typically used to test a portion of the plan. The preparedness test consumes time and money because it is an actual test that measures the team's response to situations that might someday occur. This type of testing provides a means of incrementally improving the plan.

TIP   During preparedness tests, team leaders might want to use the term *exercise* because the term *test* denotes passing or failing, which can add pressure on team members and can be detrimental to the goals of continual improvement. For example, during one disaster recovery test, the backup media was to be returned from the off-site location to the primary site. When the truck arrived with the media, it was discovered that the tapes had not been properly secured, and they were scattered around the bed of the truck. Even though the test could not continue, it was not a failure because it uncovered a weakness in the existing procedure.

Full Operation Tests

The *full operation test* is as close to an actual service disruption as you can get. The team should have performed paper tests and preparedness tests before attempting this level of interruption. This test is the most detailed, time-consuming, and thorough of all the tests discussed. A full interruption test mimics a real disaster, and all steps are performed to start up backup operations. It involves all the individuals who would be involved in a real emergency, including internal and external organizations. Goals of a full operation test include the following:

- Verifying the business continuity plan
- Evaluating the level of preparedness of the personnel involved
- Measuring the capability of the backup site to operate as planned
- Assessing the ability to retrieve vital records and information
- Evaluating the functionality of equipment
- Measuring overall preparedness for an actual disaster

TIP   The disaster recovery and continuity plan should be tested at least once yearly. Environments change; each time the plan is tested, more improvements might be uncovered.

Monitoring and Maintenance

When the testing process is complete, individuals tend to feel that their job is done. If someone is not made responsible for this process, the best plans in the world can start to become outdated in six months or less. Don't be surprised to find out that no one really wants to take on the task of documenting procedures and processes. The responsibility of performing periodic tests and maintaining the plan should be assigned to a specific person. While you might normally think of change-management practices being used to determine whether changes made to systems and applications are adequately controlled and documented, these same techniques should be used to address issues that might affect the business continuity plan.

A few additional items must be done to finish the business continuity plan. The primary remaining item is to put controls in place to maintain the current level of business continuity and disaster recovery. This is best accomplished by implementing change-management procedures. If changes to the approved plans are required, you will then have a documented structured way to accomplish this. A centralized command and control structure will ease this burden. Life is not static, and the organization's business continuity plans shouldn't be either.

Understanding BCP Metrics

Reviewing the results of the information obtained is the next step of the BIA process. During this step, the BIA team should ask questions such as these:

- **Are the systems identified critical?** All departments like to think of themselves as critical, but that is usually not the case. Some departments can be offline longer than others.

- **What is the required recovery time for critical resources?** If the resource is critical, costs will mount the longer the resource is offline. Depending on the service and the time of interruption, these times will vary.

All this information might seem a little overwhelming; however, it is needed because at the core of the BIA are two critical items:

- **Recovery point objective (RPO):** The RPO defines how current the data must be or how much data an organization can afford to lose. The greater the RPO, the more tolerant the process is to interruption.

- **Recovery time objective (RTO):** The RTO specifies the maximum elapsed time to recover an application at an alternate site. The greater the RTO, the longer the process can take to be restored.

The lower the time requirements are, the higher the cost will be to reduce loss or restore the system as quickly as possible. For example, most banks have a very low RPO because they cannot afford to lose any processed information. Think of the recovery strategy calculations as being designed to meet the required recovery time frames: Maximum tolerable downtime (MTD) = RTO + Work recovery time

(WRT). (The WRT is the remainder of the MTD used to restore all business operations.) Figure 4-4 presents an overview of how RPO and RTO are related.

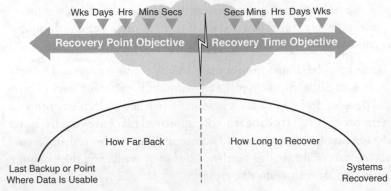

Figure 4-4   RPO and RTO

NOTE   The RTO specifies the maximum elapsed time to recover an application at an alternate site. The greater the RTO, the longer the process can take to be restored.

These items must be considered in addition to RTO and RPO:

- **Maximum acceptable outage:** This value is the time that systems can be offline before causing damage. This value is required in creating RTOs and is also known as maximum tolerable downtime (MTD).

- **Work recovery time (WRT):** The WRT is the time it takes to get critical business functions back up and running once the systems are restored.

- **Service delivery objective (SDO):** This defines the level of service provided by alternate processes while primary processing is offline. This value should be determined by examining the minimum business need.

- **Maximum tolerable outages:** This is the maximum amount of time the organization can provide services at the alternate site. This value can be determined using contractual values.

- **Core processes:** These activities are specifically required for critical processes and produce revenue.

- **Supporting processes:** These activities are required to support the minimum services needed to generate revenue.

- **Discretionary processes:** These include all other processes that are not part of the core or supporting processes and that are not required for any critical processes or functions.

Recovery Strategies

Recovery alternatives are the choices an organization has for restoring critical systems and the data in those systems. Recovery strategies can include the following:

- Alternate processing sites

- Hardware recovery

- Software and data recovery

- Backup and restoration

- Telecommunications recovery

The goal is to create a recovery strategy that balances the cost of downtime, the criticality of the system, and the likelihood of occurrence. As an example, if you have an RTO of less than 12 hours and the resource you are trying to recover is a mainframe computer, a cold-site facility would never work—because you can't buy a mainframe, install it, and get the cold site up and running in less than 12 hours. Therefore, although cost is important, so are criticality and the time to recover. The total outage time that the organization can endure is referred to as *maximum tolerable downtime* (MTD). Table 4-5 shows some MTDs used by many organizations.

Table 4-5   Required Recovery Times

Item	Required Recovery Time
Critical	Minutes to hours
Urgent	24 hours
Important	72 hours
Normal	7 days
Nonessential	30 days

Alternate Processing Sites

For disasters that have the potential to affect the primary facility, plans must be made for a backup process or an alternate site. Some organizations might opt for a *redundant processing site*. Redundant sites are equipped and configured just like the primary site. They are owned by the organization, and their cost is high. After all, the company must spend a large amount of funds to build and equip a complete, duplicate site. Although the cost might seem high, it must be noted that organizations that choose this option have done so because they have a very short (if any) RPO. A loss of services for even a very short period of time would cost the organization millions. The organization also might be subjected to regulations that require it to maintain redundant processing. Before choosing a location for a redundant site, it must be verified that the site is not subject to the same types of disasters as the primary site. Regular testing is also important to verify that the redundant site still meets the organization's needs and that it can handle the workload to meet minimum processing requirements.

Alternate Processing Options

Mobile sites are another alternate processing alternative. Mobile sites are usually tractor-trailer rigs that have been converted into data-processing centers. They contain all the necessary equipment and can be transported to a business location quickly. They can be chained together to provide space for data processing and can provide communication capabilities. Used by the military and large insurance agencies, mobile sites are a good choice in areas where no recovery facilities exist.

Another type of recovery alternative is *subscription services*, such as hot sites, warm sites, and cold sites.

A *hot site* facility is ready to go. It is fully configured and equipped with the same system as the production network. It can be made operational within just a few hours. A hot site merely needs staff, data files, and procedural documentation. Hot sites are a high-cost recovery option, but they can be justified when a short recovery time is required. Because a hot site is typically a subscription-based service, a range of fees is associated with it, including a monthly cost, subscription fees, testing costs, and usage or activation fees. Contracts for hot sites need to be closely examined; some might charge extremely high activation fees to prevent users from utilizing the facility for anything less than a true disaster.

Regardless of what fees are involved, the hot site needs to be periodically tested. Tests should evaluate processing abilities as well as security. The physical security of a hot site should be at the same level or greater than the physical security at the primary site. Finally, it is important to remember that the hot site is intended for short-term use only. With a subscriber service, other companies might be competing for the same resource. The organization should have a plan to recover primary services quickly or move to a secondary location.

NOTE   Hot sites should not be externally identifiable to decrease the risk of sabotage and other potential disruptions.

For a slightly less expensive alternative, an organization can choose a *warm site*. A warm site has data equipment and cables and is partially configured. It could be made operational in anywhere from a few hours to a few days. The assumption with a warm site is that computer equipment and software can be procured in case of a disaster. Although the warm site might have some computer equipment installed, it typically has lower processing power than the equipment at the primary site. The costs associated with a warm site are slightly lower than those of a hot site. The warm site is the most popular subscription alternative.

For organizations that are looking for a cheaper alternative and that have determined that they can tolerate a longer outage, a *cold site* might be the right choice. A cold site is basically an empty room with only rudimentary electrical, power, and computing capability. It might have a raised floor and some racks, but it is nowhere near ready for use. It might take several weeks to a month to get the site operational. A common misconception with cold sites is that the organization will be able to get the required equipment after a disaster. This might not be true with large disasters. For example, with Hurricanes Katrina, Sandy, and Irma, vendors sold out of equipment and could not meet demand. It is possible that backorders could push out the operation dates of a cold site to much longer than planned. Cold sites offer the least of the three subscription services discussed. Table 4-6 shows some examples of functions and their recovery times.

TIP   For the exam, you should understand that cold sites are a good choice for the recovery of noncritical services.

Table 4-6   Examples of Functions and Recovery Times

Process	Recovery Time	Recovery Strategy
Database	15 minutes to 1 hour	Database shadowing at a redundant site
Applications	12–24 hours	Hot site
Help desk	24–48 hours	Hot site
Purchasing	24–48 hours	Hot site
Payroll	1–3 days	Redundant site

Process	Recovery Time	Recovery Strategy
Asset inventory	5–7 days	Warm site
Nonessential services	30 days	Cold site
Emergency services (for example, for companies that need to set up operations quickly in areas that have been hit by disasters, such as insurance companies, governmental agencies, military, and so on)	Hours to a few days	Mobile site

With reciprocal agreements, two organizations pledge assistance to one another in the event of a disaster. These agreements are carried out by sharing space, computer facilities, and technology resources. On paper, this appears to be a cost-effective solution because the primary advantage is its low cost. However, reciprocal agreements have drawbacks and are infrequently used. The parties to such an agreement must trust each other to aid in the event of a disaster. However, the nonvictim might be hesitant to follow through if such a disaster occurs, based on concerns such as the realization that the damaged party might want to remain on location for a long period of time or that the victim company's presence will degrade the helping company's network services. Even concerns about the loss of competitive advantage can drive this hesitation. The issue of confidentiality also arises: The damaged organization is placed in a vulnerable position and must entrust the other party with confidential information. Finally, if the parties to the agreement are near each other, there is always the danger that disaster could strike both parties and thereby render the agreement useless. The legal departments of both firms need to look closely at such an agreement. ISACA recommends that organizations considering reciprocal agreements address the following concerns before entering into them:

- What amount of time will be available at the host computer site?
- Will the host site's employees be available for help?
- What specific facilities and equipment will be available?
- How long can emergency operations continue at the host site?
- How frequently can tests be scheduled at the host site?
- What type of physical security is available at the host site?
- What type of logical security is available at the host site?
- Is advance notice required for using the site? If so, how much?
- Are there any blocks of time or dates when the facility is not available?

NOTE   Although reciprocal agreements are not usually appropriate for organizations with large databases, some organizations, such as small banks, have been known to sign reciprocal agreements for the use of a shared hot site.

When reviewing alternative processing options, subscribers should look closely at any agreements and at the actual facility to make sure it meets the needs of the organization. One common problem is oversubscription. If situations such as Hurricane Harvey occur, there could be more organizations demanding a subscription service than the vendor can supply. The subscription agreement might also dictate when the organization may inhabit the facility. Thus, even though an organization might be in the path of a deadly storm, it might not be able to move into the facility yet because the area has not been declared a disaster area. Procedures and documentation should also be kept at the offsite location, and backups must be available. It's important to note that backup media should be kept in an area that is not subject to the same type of natural disaster as the primary site. For example, if the primary site is in a hurricane zone, the backup needs to be somewhere less prone to those conditions. If backup media is at another location, agreements should be in place to ensure that the media will be moved to the alternate site so it is available for the recovery process. A final item is that organizations must also have prior financial arrangements to procure needed equipment, software, and supplies during a disaster. This might include emergency credit lines, credit cards, or agreements with hardware and software vendors.

Hardware Recovery

Recovery alternatives are just one of the items that must be considered to cope with a disaster. Hardware recovery is another. Remember that an effective recovery strategy involves more than just corrective measures; it is also about prevention. Hardware failures are some of the most common disruptions that can occur. It is therefore important to examine ways to minimize the likelihood of occurrence and to reduce the effect if it does occur. This process can be enhanced by making well-informed decisions when buying equipment. At purchase time, you should know three important items associated with the reliability:

- **Mean time between failures (MTBF):** The MTBF calculates the expected lifetime of a device that can be repaired. A higher MTBF means the equipment should last longer.

- **Mean time to failure (MTTF):** The MTTF calculates the expected lifetime of a one-time-use item that is typically not repaired.

- **Mean time to repair (MTTR):** The MTTR estimates how long it would take to repair the equipment and get it back into use. For MTTR, lower numbers mean the equipment takes less time to repair and can be returned to service sooner.

For critical equipment, an organization might consider some form of service level management. This is simply an agreement between an IT service provider and a customer. The most common example is a *service level agreement* (*SLA*), which is a contract with a hardware vendor that provides a certain level of protection. For a fee, the vendor agrees to repair or replace the equipment within the contracted time.

Fault tolerance can be used at the server level or the drive level. At the server level is *clustering*, technology that groups several servers together yet allows them to be viewed logically as a single server. Users see the cluster as one unit, although it is actually many. The advantage is that if one server in the cluster fails, the remaining active servers will pick up the load and continue operation.

Redundant Array of Independent Disks

Fault tolerance on the drive level is achieved primarily with *redundant array of independent disks (RAID)*, which is used for hardware fault tolerance and/or performance improvements and is achieved by breaking up the data and writing it to multiple disks. RAID has humble beginnings that date back to the 1980s at the University of California. To applications and other devices, RAID appears as a single drive. Most RAID systems have *hot-swappable disks*, which means the drives can be removed or added while the computer systems are running. If a RAID system uses parity and is fault tolerant, the parity date is used to rebuild the newly replaced drive. Another RAID technique is *striping*, which means the data is divided and written over several drives. Although write performance remains almost constant, read performance drastically increases. According to ISACA, these are the most common levels of RAID used today:

- RAID 0
- RAID 3
- RAID 5

RAID level descriptions are as follows:

- **RAID 0: Striped disk array without fault tolerance:** Provides data striping and improves performance but provides no redundancy.
- **RAID 1: Mirroring and duplexing:** Duplicates the information on one disk to another. It provides twice the read transaction rate of single disks and the same write transaction rate as single disks yet effectively cuts disk space in half.

- **RAID 2: Error-correcting coding:** Rarely used because of the extensive computing resources needed. It stripes data at the bit level instead of the block level.

- **RAID 3: Parallel transfer with parity:** Uses byte-level striping with a dedicated disk. Although it provides fault tolerance, it is rarely used.

- **RAID 4: Shared parity drive:** Similar to RAID 3 but provides block-level striping with a parity disk. If a data disk fails, the parity data is used to create a replacement disk. Its primary disadvantage is that the parity disk can create write bottlenecks.

- **RAID 5: Block interleaved distributed parity:** Provides data striping of both data and parity. Level 5 has good performance and fault tolerance. It is a popular implementation of RAID. It requires at least three drives.

- **RAID 6: Independent data disks with double parity:** Provides high fault tolerance with block-level striping and parity data distributed across all disks.

- **RAID 10: A stripe of mirrors:** Known to have very high reliability. It requires a minimum of four drives.

- **RAID 0+1: A mirror of stripes:** Not one of the original RAID levels. RAID 0+1 uses RAID 0 to stripe data and creates a RAID 1 mirror. It provides high data rates.

- **RAID 15:** Creates mirrors (RAID 1) and distributed parity (RAID 5). This is not one of the original RAID levels.

One final drive-level solution worth mentioning is *just a bunch of disks (JBOD)*. JBOD is similar to RAID 0 but offers few of the advantages. What it does offer is the capability to combine two or more disks of various sizes into one large partition. It also has an advantage over RAID 0: In case of drive failure, only the data on the affected drive is lost; the data on surviving drives remains readable. This means that JBOD has no fault tolerance. JBOD does not provide the performance benefits associated with RAID 0.

Software and Data Recovery

Because data processing is essential to most organizations, having the software and data needed to continue this operation is critical to the recovery process. The objectives are to back up critical software and data and be able to restore them quickly. Policy should dictate when backups are performed, where the media is stored, who has access to the media, and what its reuse or rotation policy is. Backup media can include tape reels, tape cartridges, removable hard drives, disks, and cassettes. The organization must determine how often backups should be performed and what type of backup should be performed. These operations will vary depending on the cost of the media, the speed of the restoration needed, and the time allocated for backups. Typically, the following four backup methods are used:

- **Full backup**: All data is backed up. No data files are skipped or bypassed. All items are copied to one tape, set of tapes, or backup medium. If restoration is needed, only one tape or set of tapes is needed. A full backup requires the most time and space on the storage medium but takes the least time to restore.

- **Differential backup**: A full backup is done typically once a week, and a daily differential backup is done only to those files that have changed since the last full backup. If you need to restore, you need the last full backup and the most recent differential backup. This method takes less time per backup but takes longer to restore because both the full and differential backups are needed.

- **Incremental backup**: This method backs up only those files that have been modified since the previous incremental backup. An incremental backup requires additional backup media because the last full backup, the last incremental backup, and any additional incremental backups are required to restore the media.

- **Continuous backup:** Some backup applications perform a *continuous backup* that keeps a database of backup information. These systems are useful because if a restoration is needed, the application can provide a full restore, a point-in-time restore, or a restore based on a selected list of files.

NOTE   Tape continues to be a viable option for backup. One current backup format is linear tape-open (LTO). LTO provides high-capacity storage, and in its latest iteration, LTO-6, it offers 2.5TB of storage per tape cartridge. If compression is used an enterprise can store up to 6.25TB of data on a single tape.

Although tape and optical systems still have significant market share for backup systems, hardware alternatives and cloud based options are making inroads. One of these technologies is massive array of inactive disks (MAID). MAID offers a hardware storage option for the storage of data and applications. It was designed to reduce the operational costs and improve long-term reliability of disk-based archives and backups. MAID is similar to RAID, except that it provides power management and advanced disk monitoring. The MAID system powers down inactive drives, reduces heat output, reduces electrical consumption, and increases the drive's life expectancy. This represents real progress over using hard disks to back up data. Storage area networks (SANs) are another alternative. SANs are designed as a subnetwork of high-speed, shared storage devices. Cloud backup is gaining in popularity as it offers several benefits. These value-added functions include geographical redundancy, advanced search, content management and automatic offsite storage.

Backup and Restoration

Where backup media are stored can have a big impact on how quickly data can be restored and brought back online. The media should be stored in more than one physical location to reduce the possibility of loss. A tape librarian should manage these remote sites by maintaining the site, controlling access, rotating media, and protecting this valuable asset. Unauthorized access to the media is a huge risk because it could impact the organization's ability to provide uninterrupted service. Encryption can help mitigate this risk. Transportation to and from the remote site is also an important concern. Consider the following important items:

- Secure transportation to and from the site must be maintained.

- Delivery vehicles must be bonded.

- Backup media must be handled, loaded, and unloaded in an appropriate way.

- Drivers must be trained on the proper procedures to pick up, handle, and deliver backup media.

- Access to the backup facility should be 24×7 in case of emergency.

Offsite storage should be contracted with a known firm that has control of the facility and is responsible for its maintenance. Physical and environmental controls should be equal to or better than those of the organization's facility. A letter of agreement should specify who has access to the media and who is authorized to drop off or pick up media. There should also be an agreement on response time that is to be met in times of disaster. *Onsite storage* should be maintained to ensure the capability to recover critical files quickly. Backup media should be secured and kept in an environmentally controlled facility that has physical control sufficient to protect such a critical asset. This area should be fireproof, with controlled access so that anyone depositing or removing media is logged. Although most backup media is rather robust, it will not last forever and will fail over time. This means that tape rotation is another important part of backup and restoration.

Backup media must be periodically tested. Backups will be of little use if they malfunction during a disaster. Common media-rotation strategies include the following:

- **Simple**: A simple backup rotation scheme is to use one tape for every day of the week and then repeat the next week. One tape can be for Mondays, one for Tuesdays, and so on. You would add a set of new tapes each month and then archive the monthly sets. After a predetermined number of months, you would put the oldest tapes back into use.

- **Grandfather-father-son**: This rotation method includes four tapes for weekly backups, one tape for monthly backups, and four tapes for daily backups. It is called *grandfather-father-son* because the scheme establishes a kind of hierarchy. Grandfathers are the one monthly backup, fathers are the four weekly backups, and sons are the four daily backups.

- **Tower of Hanoi:** This tape-rotation scheme is named after a mathematical puzzle. It involves using five sets of tapes, each set labeled A through E. Set A is used every other day; set B is used on the first non-A backup day and is used every fourth day; set C is used on the first non-A or non-B backup day and is used every eighth day; set D is used on the first non-A, non-B, or non-C day and is used every 16th day; and set E alternates with set D.

NOTE An organization's backups are a complete mirror of the organization's data. Although most backups are password protected, this really offers only limited protection. If attackers have possession of the backup media, they are not under any time constraints and have ample time to crack passwords and access the data. Encryption can offer an additional layer of protection and help protect the confidentiality of the data.

SANs are an alternative to traditional backup. SANs support disk mirroring, backup and restore, archival and retrieval of archived data, and data migration from one storage device to another. SANs can be implemented locally or can use storage at a redundant facility. Another option is a *virtual SAN (VSAN)*, a SAN that offers isolation among devices that are physically connected to the same SAN fabric. A VSAN is sometimes called *fabric virtualization*.

Traditionally, SANs used Small Computer System Interface (SCSI) for connectivity, but there are more current options in use today. One is iSCSI, which is a SAN standard used for connecting data storage facilities and allowing remote SCSI devices to communicate. Fiber Channel over Ethernet (FCoE) is another SAN interface standard. FCoE is similar to iSCSI; it can operate at speeds of 10Gbps and rides on top of the Ethernet protocol. While it is fast, it has a disadvantage in that it is nonroutable.

One important issue with SAN and backups is location redundancy. This is the concept that content should be accessible from more than one location. An extra measure of redundancy can be provided by means of a replication service so that data is available even if the main storage backup system fails.

Another important item is security of the backups. This is where secure storage management and replication are important. The idea is that systems must be designed to allow a company to manage and handle all corporate data in a secure manner, with a focus on the confidentiality, integrity, and availability of the information. The replication service allows for the data to be duplicated in real time so that additional fault tolerance is achieved.

When you need to make point-in-time backups, you can use SAN snapshots. SAN snapshot software is typically sold with a SAN solution and offers a way to bypass typical backup operations. The snapshot software has the ability to temporarily stop writing to physical disk and make a point-in-time backup copy.

If budget is an issue, an organization can opt for *electronic vaulting*, which involves transferring data by electronic means to a backup site, as opposed to physical shipment. With electronic vaulting, an organization contracts with a vaulting provider. The organization typically loads a software agent onto systems to be backed up, and the vaulting service accesses these systems and copies the selected files. Moving large amounts of data can slow WAN service.

Another backup alternative is *standby database shadowing*. A standby database is an exact duplicate of a database maintained on a remote server. In case of disaster, it is ready to go. Changes are applied from the primary database to the standby database to keep records synchronized.

As an alternative to traditional backup techniques, using cloud services for backup may offer a cost-saving alternative. These services should be carefully evaluated, as there are many concerns when using them. Cloud backups can be deployed in a variety of configurations—for example, as an on-premises private cloud or as an offsite public or private cloud.

Telecommunications Recovery

Telecommunications recovery should play a key role in recovery. After all, the telecommunications network is a critical asset and should be given a high priority for recovery. Although these communications networks can be susceptible to the same threats as data centers, they also face some unique threats. Protection methods include redundant WAN links and bandwidth on demand. Whatever the choice, the organization should verify capacity requirements and acceptable outage times. The following are the primary methods for telecommunications network protection:

- **Redundancy**: This involves exceeding what is required or needed. Redundancy can be added by providing extra capacity, providing multiple routes, using dynamic routing protocols, and using failover devices to allow for continued operations.

- **Diverse routing**: This is the practice of routing traffic through different cable facilities. Organizations can obtain both diverse routing and alternate routing, but the cost is not low. Most of these systems use facilities that are buried, and they usually emerge through the basement and can sometimes share space with other mechanical equipment. This adds risk. Many cities have aging infrastructures, which is another potential point of failure.

- **Alternate routing**: This is the ability to use another transmission line if the regular line is busy or unavailable. This can include using a dial-up connection in place of a dedicated connection, a cell phone instead of a land line, or microwave communication in place of a fiber connection.

- **Long-haul diversity**: This is the practice of having different long-distance communication carriers. This recovery facility option helps ensure that service is maintained; auditors should verify that it is present.

- **Last-mile protection**: This is a good choice for recovery facilities in that it provides a second local loop connection and can add to security even more if an alternate carrier is used.

- **Voice communication recovery:** Many organizations are highly dependent on voice communications. Some of these organizations have started making the switch to VoIP because of the cost savings. Some land lines should be maintained to provide recovery capability.

NOTE   Recovery strategies have historically focused on computing resources and data. Networks are susceptible to many of the same problems, but often they are not properly backed up. This can be a real problem because there is a heavy reliance on networks to deliver data when needed.

Verification of Disaster Recovery and Business Continuity Process Tasks

As an auditor, you will be tasked with understanding and evaluating business continuity/disaster recovery strategy. An auditor should review a plan and make sure it is current and up-to-date. The auditor should also examine last year's test to verify the results and look for any problem areas. The business continuity coordinator is responsible for maintaining previous tests. Upon examination, an auditor should confirm that a test met targeted goals or minimum standards. The auditor should also inspect the offsite storage facility and review its security, policies, and configuration. This should include a detailed inventory that includes checking data files, applications, system software, system documentation, operational documents, consumables, supplies, and a copy of the business continuity plan.

Contracts and alternative processing agreements should also be reviewed. Any off-site processing facilities should be audited, and the owners should have a reference check. All agreements should be made in writing. The offsite facility should meet the same security standards as the primary facility and should have environmental controls such as raised floors, HVAC controls, fire prevention and detection, filtered power, and uninterruptible power supplies (UPSs). A UPS allows a computer to keep running for at least a short time when the primary power source is lost.

If the location is a shared site, the rules that determine who has access and when they have access should be examined. Another area of concern is the business continuity plan itself. An auditor must make sure the plan is written in easy-to-understand language and that users have been trained. This can be confirmed by interviewing employees.

Finally, insurance should be reviewed. An auditor should examine the level and types of insurance the organization has purchased. Insurance can be obtained for each of the following items:

- IS equipment
- Data centers
- Software recovery
- Business interruption
- Documents, records, and important papers
- Errors and omissions
- Media transportation

Insurance is not without drawbacks, which include high premiums, delayed claim payouts, denied claims, and problems proving financial loss. Finally, most policies pay for only a percentage of actual loss and do not pay for lost income, increased operating expenses, or consequential loss.

The purpose of disaster recovery is to get a damaged organization restarted so that critical business functions can resume. When a disaster occurs, the process of progressing from the disaster back to normal operations includes the following:

- Crisis management
- Recovery
- Reconstitution
- Resumption

An auditor should be concerned with all laws, mandates, and policies that govern the organization in a disaster situation. As an example, federal and state government entities typically use a Continuity of Operations (COOP) site, which is designed to take on operational capabilities when the primary site is not functioning. The length of time the COOP site is active and the criteria used to determine when the COOP site is enabled depend on the business continuity and disaster recovery plans. An example of the Disaster Lifecycle is shown in Figure 4-5.

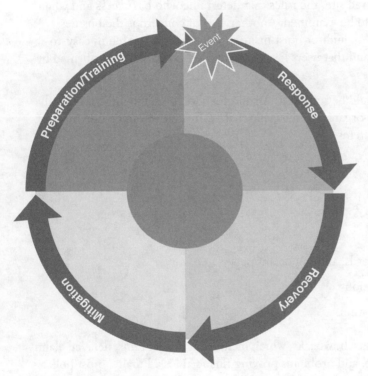

Figure 4-5   The Disaster Life Cycle

The Disaster Life Cycle

Both governmental and nongovernmental entities typically use a checklist to manage continuity of operations. Table 4-7 shows a sample disaster recovery checklist.

Table 4-7 Disaster Recovery Checklist

Time	Activity
When disaster occurs	Notify disaster recovery manager and recovery coordinator
Under 2 hours	Assess damage, notify senior management, and determine immediate course of action
Under 4 hours	Contact offsite facility, recover backups, and replace equipment as needed
Under 8 hours	Provide management with updated assessment and begin recovery at updated site
Under 36 hours	Reestablish full processing at alternative site and determine a timeline for return to the primary facility

NOTE An auditor should verify that the disaster recovery manager directs short-term recovery actions immediately following a disaster and has the approval and resources to do so.

Protection of life is a priority while working to mitigate damage. The areas impacted the most need attention first. Recovery from a disaster entails sending personnel to the recovery site. Individuals responsible for emergency management need to assess damage and perform triage. When employees and materials are at the recovery site, interim functions can resume operations. This might require installing software and hardware. Backup data or copies of configurations might need to be loaded, and systems might require setup.

When operations are moved from the alternative operations site back to the restored site, the efficiency of the new site must be tested. In other words, processes should be sequentially returned from least critical to most critical. In the event that a few glitches need to be worked out in the new facility, you can be confident that your most critical processes are still in full operation at the alternative site. When those processes are complete, normal operations can resume.

TIP When migrating from the backup site to the primary site, always move from least critical to most critical.

Chapter Summary

This chapter discusses the process of business continuity planning—preparing for the worst possible events that could happen to an organization. Many organizations give BCP a low priority for a host of reasons, including cost, inability to quantify some potential threats, and the belief that the organization can somehow escape these events.

The first step, initiation, requires that senior management establish business continuity as a priority. Developing and carrying out a successful business continuity plan takes much work and effort and should be done in a modular format. The business impact analysis is the next step. Although auditors are unlikely to be directly involved in this process, they can be of help here in providing data on the impact to the business if specific systems are unavailable. The goal of business impact analysis is to determine which processes need to happen first, second, third, and so on. Each step of the business continuity process builds on the last; the BCP team members must know the business and need to work with other departments and management to determine critical processes.

Recovery strategies must also be determined. For example, in case of loss of power, will a generator be used, or might the process continue at another location that has power? With these decisions made, a written plan must be developed that locks into policy whatever choices have been made. When the plan is implemented, the process is still not complete; the team must test the plan. During the test, an IS auditor should be present to observe the results. No demonstrated recovery exists until the plan has been tested. Common test methods include paper tests, preparedness tests, and full operation tests. To make sure these plans and procedures do not grow old or become obsolete, disaster recovery should become part of the decision-making process so that when changes are made, issues that may affect the policies can be updated. Business continuity and disaster recovery plans can also be added to job responsibilities and to yearly performance reviews.

Exam Preparation Tasks

As mentioned in the section "How to Use This Book" in the Introduction, you have a couple choices for exam preparation: the exercises here; Chapter 10, "Final Preparation;" and the exam simulation questions on the book's companion web page (www.informit.com/title/9780789758446).

Review All the Key Topics

Review the most important topics in this chapter, noted with the Key Topic icon in the outer margin of the page. Table 4-8 lists these key topics and the page number on which each is found.

Table 4-8   Key Topics in Chapter 4

Key Topic Element	Description	Page Number
Figure 4-1	Sources of security threats	140
Table 4-4	BCP process responsibilities	153
Figure 4-4	RPO and RTO	158
Section	Hardware recovery	163
List	The primary methods for network protection	169

Define Key Terms

Define the following key terms from this chapter and check your answers against the glossary:

business impact analysis, cold site, hot site, JBOD, massive array of inactive disks (MAID), paper test, protocol, recovery point objective (RPO), recovery testing, recovery time objective (RTO), redundant array of inexpensive disks (RAID), resilience, software, storage area network (SAN), telecommunications, transaction, uninterruptible power supply (UPS)

Exercises

4.1 Business Impact and Risk

Estimated time: 10 minutes

For this exercise, you need to walk through the profile and then answer the following questions.

Kerney, Cleveland, and Glass Law Firm

Driving concern: This law firm, located in the Washington, D.C., area has serviced a who's who of individuals inside and outside the Beltway. The firm recently suffered a major network outage after a key server failed, and it was determined that the backup media was corrupt. Management has existing business continuity plans but could not contact the person in charge of cloud backups during this late-night problem. They are now worried that the plans are not adequate.

Overview: The firm has two offices: one in the D.C. area and the other on the West Coast. The firm handles many confidential documents, often of high monetary value. The firm is always looking for ways to free up the partners from administrative tasks so that they can have more billable hours. Partners access their data from wireless LANs and remotely through a corporate VPN.

The two offices are connected by a T1 leased line. Each office has a connection to the Internet. The West Coast office connects to the Internet through the D.C. office. The wireless network supports Windows servers in the D.C. office. Partners also carry laptop computers that contain many confidential documents needed at client sites. The law firm has a bring-your-own-device (BYOD) policy and allows users to connect almost any device to the network. No encryption is used, and there is no insurance to protect against downtime or disruptions.

1. Which of the following items would you consider a priority if you were asked to audit the law firm's business continuity plan?

   ▪ Verify that the business continuity plan provides for the recovery of all systems? Yes/No

   ▪ Require that you or another auditor is present during a test of the business continuity plan? Yes/No

   ▪ Verify that the notification directory is being maintained and is current? Yes/No

   ▪ Verify that the IS department is responsible for declaring a disaster if such a situation occurred? Yes/No

   ▪ Suggest that the law firm increase its recovery time objective? Yes/No

   ▪ Determine the most critical finding?

2. Examine the list from Question 1 and compare your answers with the following:

   ▪ Verify that the business continuity plan provides for the recovery of all systems? Yes/No (Typically, only 50% of information is critical.)

   ▪ Require that you or another auditor is present during a test of the business continuity plan? Yes/No (The auditor should be present to make sure the test meets required targets.)

   ▪ Verify that the notification directory is being maintained and is current? Yes/No (Without a notification system, there is no easy way to contact employees or for them to check in case of disaster.)

- Verify that the IS department is responsible for declaring a disaster if such a situation occurred? Yes/No (Senior management should designate someone for that task.)

- Suggest that the law firm increase its recovery time objective? Yes/No (This would increase recovery time, not decrease it.)

- Determine the most critical finding? Lack of insurance/Loss of data (The most vital asset for an organization is its data.)

Review Questions

1. Which of the following should be the primary objective when using tape backup as a recovery strategy?

    a. That the RPO is high

    b. That the RPO is low

    c. That the RTO is low

    d. That fault tolerance is low

2. When performing an audit, which of the following is the best reason to use a hot site?

    a. It can be used for long-term processing.

    b. It is not a subscription service.

    c. There is no additional cost for using it or periodic testing.

    d. It is ready for service.

3. Which of the following is the greatest advantage of JBOD?

    a. In case of drive failure, only the data on the affected drive is lost.

    b. It is superior to disk mirroring.

    c. It offers greater performance gains than RAID.

    d. It offers greater fault tolerance than RAID.

4. Which of the following processes is most critical in terms of revenue generation?

    a. Discretionary

    b. Supporting

    c. Core

    d. Critical

5. As an auditor, how often would you say that a business continuity plan should be updated?

   a. Every five years

   b. Every year or as required

   c. Every six months

   d. Upon any change or modification

6. During an audit, you have been asked to review the disaster recovery and backup processes. When maintaining data backups at offsite locations, which of the following is the best way to control concern?

   a. The storage site should be as secure as the primary site.

   b. A suitable tape-rotation plan should be in use.

   c. That backup media should be tested regularly.

   d. That copies of current critical information should be kept offsite.

7. Which of the following is the most important purpose of BIA?

   a. Identifying countermeasures

   b. Prioritizing critical systems

   c. Developing recovery strategies

   d. Determining potential test strategies

8. Which of the following is not a valid BCP test type?

   a. Paper test

   b. Structured walk-through

   c. Full operation test

   d. Preparedness test

9. Which of the following is the practice of routing traffic through different cable facilities?

   a. Alternate routing

   b. Long-haul diversity

   c. Diverse routing

   d. Last-mile protection

10. When classifying critical systems, which category matches the following description: "These functions are important and can be performed by a backup manual process but not for a long period of time?"

    a. Vital

    b. Sensitive

    c. Critical

    d. Demand driven

Suggested Readings and Resources

- **The BIA process, according to NIST:** http://csrc.nist.gov/publications/ nistpubs/800-34-rev1/sp800-34-rev1_bia_template.docx

- **RPO and RTO explained:** www.bluelock.com/blog/ rpo-rto-pto-and-raas-disaster-recovery-explained/

- **BCP good practice guidelines:** www.drj.com/journal/fall-2013-volume- 26-issue-4/the-bcis-good-practice-guidelines.html

- **Cloud backup and storage:** www.informationweek.com/consumer/ online-backup-vs-cloud-storage/d/d-id/1107440

- **SLAs:** www.wired.com/insights/2011/12/ service-level-agreements-in-the-cloud-who-cares/

- **Business Impact Analysis:** http://ithandbook.ffiec.gov/it-booklets/business- continuity-planning/business-impact-analysis.aspx

- **Exploring Backup Alternatives:** http://searchdatabackup.techtarget.com/ feature/Modern-backup-alternatives

- **Auditing business continuity plans:** http://www.disaster-resource.com/ index.php?option=com_content&view=article&id=1701:how-to-audit- business-continuity-programs

The following exam domain is partially covered in this chapter:

Domain 3—Information Systems Acquisition, Development and Implementation

This chapter covers the following topics:

- **IT Acquisition and Project Management:** This section provides an overview of IT acquisition and project management control frameworks, practices, and tools.

- **Business Application Development:** Organizations run many applications, and an auditor must prioritize them and then test the ones that are critical to core business operations.

- **Information Systems Maintenance:** This section examines the process of modifying an information system via updates and patches to continually satisfy organizational and user requirements.

- **Outsourcing and Alternative System Development:** Many development methodologies exist, and each one uses a specific approach to development. Some of them may be better fits for an organization than others. An auditor should have a basic understanding of when and how each is used.

CHAPTER 5

Information Systems Acquisition and Development

This chapter covers practices related to ensuring that the acquisition, development, testing, and implementation of information systems meet the organization's strategies and objectives. CISA candidates need to understand project management, including initiating, planning, executing, controlling, and closing projects. Have you ever stopped to think about how much of an auditor's work revolves around project management? After all, projects are temporary endeavors, and each has a defined beginning, middle, and end. Each audit is unique and has different requirements and specifications.

Life cycle management requires that auditors understand the systems development life cycle (SDLC). Auditors can become deeply involved in the SDLC process. Auditors are responsible for helping ensure that sufficient controls are designed during this process and that these controls work as expected. Controls must be tested, and the overall design plan must be reviewed. Not all projects use the same development method. Today many alternative development methods—such as prototyping, rapid application development, and agile development—are used. An auditor must understand each of these in order to fulfill his job duties. After the rollout of new applications, an auditor's job is not done. Systems require maintenance, review of changes, and review and redesign of processes. Throughout the life cycle, auditors play a key role.

"Do I Know This Already?" Quiz

The "Do I Know This Already?" quiz allows you to assess whether you should read this entire chapter thoroughly or jump to the "Exam Preparation Tasks" section. If you are in doubt about your answers to these questions or your own assessment of your knowledge of the topics, read the entire chapter. Table 5-1 lists the major headings in this chapter and their corresponding "Do I Know This Already?" quiz questions. You can find the answers at the bottom of the page following the quiz and in Appendix A, "Answers to the 'Do I Know This Already?' Quizzes and Review Questions."

Table 5-1 "Do I Know This Already?" Section-to-Question Mapping

Foundation Topics Section	Questions Covered in This Section
IT Acquisition and Project Management	1–4
Business Application Development	5–7
Information Systems Maintenance	8
Outsourcing and Alternative System Development	9–10

CAUTION The goal of self-assessment is to gauge your mastery of the topics in this chapter. If you do not know the answer to a question or are only partially sure of the answer, you should mark that question as incorrect for purposes of the self-assessment. Giving yourself credit for an answer you correctly guess skews your self-assessment results and might provide you with a false sense of security.

1. Which of the following outlaws the manufacture, sale, or distribution of any equipment or device that can be used for code-cracking or illegally copying software?

   a. WTO

   b. CMM

   c. DMCA

   d. NIST

2. What project type is structured so that formal authority is held by the project manager, and the team may also have a dedicated project work area?

   a. Pure project

   b. Strong matrix

   c. Influence

   d. Balanced matrix

3. Which of the following is the first step in team development?

   a. Storming

   b. Forming

   c. Norming

   d. Performing

4. Which of the following is process oriented and shows what activities need to be completed in a hierarchical manner?

   a. Object breakdown structure

   b. Capability maturity model

   c. Work breakdown structure

   d. Critical path methodology

5. For which of the following development methodologies does progress flow from the top to the bottom through each phase?

   a. RAD

   b. Waterfall

   c. Extreme programming

   d. Scrum

6. Which of the following development methods is an iterative method that has repetitions that are referred to as sprints and typically last 30 days?

   A RAD

   b. Waterfall

   c. Extreme programming

   d. Scrum

7. For which of the following development methods do teams include business managers, programmers, and end users?

   a. RAD

   b. Waterfall

   c. Extreme programming

   d. Scrum

8. Which of the following is a client–server architecture in which presentation, application processing, and data management functions are physically separated?

   a. Virtualization

   b. Web

   c. Cloud

   d. N-tier

9. In virtualization, which of the following is a virtual machine manager that is installed as a software application on an existing operating system?

   a. Type 1

   b. Type 2

   c. Type 3

   d. Type 4

10. Which of the following is a cloud computing model and category of cloud computing services that provides a platform which allows customers to develop, run, and manage applications without the complexity of building and maintaining the infrastructure?

   a. PaaS

   b. IaaS

   c. MaaS

   d. SaaS

Foundation Topics

IT Acquisition and Project Management

IT acquisition and project management are two items that go well together. The acquisition of IT is by nature a temporary endeavor and as such falls under project management guidelines. Projects can be large or small, and they can involve hardware, software, or networks. A project can even be used to create a product or service.

IT Acquisition

IT acquisition involves the expenditure of funds for information technology. IT acquisition can be a single purchase or might involve multiple purchases over many years. One key decision that must be made is whether the organization will build or buy a solution. A business case should be made either way. The decision typically comes down to time, cost, and availability of a predesigned substitute.

Software Escrow Agreements

If the decision is made to make an IT acquisition, vendor management must be considered. What if the software developer goes bankrupt or is no longer in business? How is the organization supposed to maintain or update the needed code? These concerns can be addressed by a *software escrow* agreement, which allows an organization to maintain access to the source code of an application if the vendor goes bankrupt. Although the organization can modify the software for continued use, it can't steal the design or sell the code on the open market. A *software escrow* agreement protects you in case things go wrong and the vendor is no longer in business.

Software Licensing

Escrow is not the only IT acquisition issue to consider. Another concern is licensing. Intellectual property rights issues have always been hard to enforce. Just consider the uproar that Pirate Bay has caused over issues of intellectual property and the rights of individuals to share music and files. The software industry has long dealt with this issue. From the early days of computing, some individuals have been swapping, sharing, and illegally copying computer software. The unauthorized copying and sharing of software is considered software piracy, and it is illegal. Software piracy is big business, and accumulated loss to property owners is staggering. An auditor needs to review software licensing and usage. The cost of noncompliance can be huge.

Major software companies formed the Software Protection Association, which is one of the primary bodies that actively fight to enforce licensing agreements. Microsoft and others are also actively fighting to protect their property rights. The Software Alliance (BSA) and the Federation Against Software Theft are international groups targeting software piracy. These organizations target organizations of all sizes, from small, two-person companies to large, multinational organizations.

Software companies are also fighting back by making clear in their licenses what a user can and cannot do with the software. For example, Windows 10 requires users to accept all updates. License agreements can actually be distributed in several different ways, including the following:

- **Click-wrap license agreements:** Found in many software products, these agreements require you to click through and agree to terms to install the software product. These are often called *contracts of adhesion* because such contracts are a "take it or leave it" proposition.

- **Master license agreements:** These agreements are used by large companies that develop specific software solutions that specify how the customer can use the product.

- **Shrink-wrap license agreements:** These agreements were created when software started to be sold commercially and are named for the fact that breaking the shrink wrap signifies your acceptance of the license.

> **TIP**   CISA exam candidates should understand licensing agreements because failure to comply can be extremely costly to an organization.

Even with licensing and increased policing activities by organizations such as the BSA, improved technologies make it increasingly easy to pirate software, music, books, and other types of intellectual property. These factors and the need to obtain compliance with two World Trade Organization (WTO) treaties led to the passage in 1998 of the Digital Millennium Copyright Act (DMCA). Salient highlights include the following:

- The DMCA makes it a crime to bypass or circumvent antipiracy measures built into commercial software products.

Answers to the "Do I Know This Already?" Quiz:

1. C; 2. A; 3. B; 4. C; 5. B; 6. D; 7. C; 8. D; 9. B; 10. D

- The DMCA outlaws the manufacture, sale, or distribution of any equipment or device that can be used for code-cracking or illegally copying software.

- The DMCA provides exemptions from anti-circumvention provisions for libraries and educational institutions under certain circumstances; however, for those not covered by such exceptions, the act provides for penalties up to $1 million and 10 years in prison.

- The DMCA provides Internet service providers exceptions from copyright infringement liability to enable transmissions of information across the Internet.

Project Management

Projects are temporary endeavors. The purpose of project management, which is a one-time effort, is to meet a defined goal of creating a specific product, service, or result. When all the objectives are met, a project is terminated. Projects have unique attributes:

- A unique purpose
- A temporary nature
- A primary customer and/or sponsor
- Uncertainty

Projects are constrained in a number of ways that you need to understand:

- **Scope:** How much work is defined? What do the sponsor and the customer expect from this project?

- **Time:** How long is this project scheduled to run? Does it have a defined schedule? When does the product need to be launched, or when does the service need to be operational? Answering these questions will help determine how long the project will run.

- **Cost:** How much money is this project expected to cost? Has the sponsor approved it?

Many approaches and standards exist to meet this triple constraint. Regardless of which one or ones are used, an auditor must verify that business requirements are going to be met and that the project is being achieved in a cost-effective manner while managing potential risk. The most well known of these approaches and standards are the Project Management Body of Knowledge (PMBOK; IEEE Standard 1490), Prince2 (Projects in Controlled Environments), and standards from the Project Management Institute (PMI). Each of these is somewhat different, but they share common attributes. The following section looks at some of the common roles and responsibilities in project management activities.

Roles, Responsibility, and Structure of Project Management

An auditor should play an active part in the project management process and should know the various roles and responsibilities. It is important that an auditor conduct periodic reviews to determine whether a project is progressing in accordance with project plans. Auditors should understand who is responsible and be able to identify key stakeholders, including the following:

- **Senior management:** Managers who provide the necessary resources to complete a project.

- **Stakeholder:** A person, group, or business unit that has a share or an interest in the project activities.

- **Project steering committee or oversight board:** The group that is ultimately responsible for ensuring that the stakeholders' needs are met and overseeing the direction and scope of the project. The committee acts as project-oversight board.

- **Project sponsor:** A person who works with the project manager to ensure success and is responsible for allocating funding for the project.

- **Project manager:** A person who is responsible for day-to-day management of the project team.

- **Project team:** A person who is responsible for performing operational tasks within the project.

- **Quality assurance:** A person who is responsible for reviewing the activities of the project management team and ensuring that output meets quality standards. This role/group does not necessarily act as part of the project team as a whole. QA activities can be carried out by parties outside the project team, including auditors.

Projects must take on an organizational form or framework, which can be either loosely structured or very rigid. In the latter case, the program manager has complete authority over the group and is assigned to the group for the duration of the project. Table 5-2 shows the primary types of project organizational forms.

Table 5-2   Project Organizational Forms

Form	Description
Pure project	Formal authority is held by the project manager. The team may have a dedicated project work area.
Influence	The project manager has no real authority, and the functional manager remains in charge.
Weak matrix	The project manager has little or no authority and is part of the functional organization.
Balanced matrix	The project manager has some functional authority, and management duties are shared with functional managers.
Strong matrix	In this more expensive model, the project has members assigned for dedicated tasks. The advantage is that this offers a greater level of authority.

TIP   CISA exam candidates should understand the various organizational forms.

Project Culture and Objectives

Each team has a unique culture. Project managers can play a part in developing a healthy culture by holding a kick-off meeting that allows team members to get to know each other. The kick-off meeting also gives the project manager a forum in which to discuss the goals of the project and the tasks that need to be completed to meet the desired goal. The program manager might also want to use this time to perform some team-building activities, such as having the group develop a team name, establish a mission statement, or create a project logo.

As the team progresses, it typically goes through four stages:

1. Forming

2. Storming

3. Norming

4. Performing

Throughout these ups and downs, the team must stay clearly focused on the deliverables. Some deliverables are considered main objectives, and others are considered nonobjectives. The main objectives are directly linked to the success of the project; nonobjectives add value by clarifying and defining the main objectives. The project management process usually starts with the team working on an *object breakdown structure* (*OBS*), which defines each component of the project and the relationships of the components to each other. The OBS can help make sure the team doesn't leave anything out and that all requirements are clearly defined. Next, a *work breakdown structure (WBS)* can be developed. A WBS is process oriented and shows what activities need to be completed, in a hierarchical manner. It allows for easy identification of tasks that need to be completed. One advantage of a WBS is that tasks are defined as achievable work units. Figure 5-1 shows an example of a WBS.

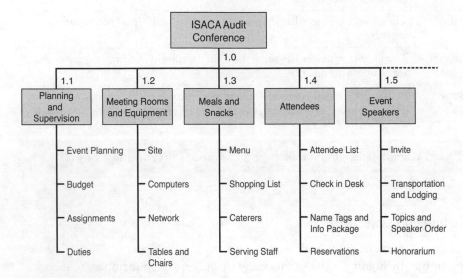

Figure 5-1 Work Breakdown Structure

TIP Developing a WBS is an important task at the start of the project management process because it involves identifying specific tasks and specifying what resources are needed for completion of each task.

Making the Business Case for Investment

There are two primary ways to make a case for business investment:

- **Business case analysis:** A business case analysis is the more in-depth of the two. A business case analysis should contain a description of the objectives, possible alternatives, the anticipated impact in terms of improvement or dollar savings of each option, as well as a cost–benefit assessment.

- **Feasibility study:** A feasibility study examines a variety of items such as demographic, geographic, and regulatory factors. A feasibility study usually offers a go/no go recommendation.

Both of these methods can help stakeholders determine if an investment should be made.

If an investment is recommended, some form of requirements analysis must be conducted. This is simply the process of determining user expectations for a new or modified product. If a product is software, this is usually referred to as the functional specification. The requirements analysis process should occur early in a project and requires the stakeholders, auditors, users, and others to meet and discuss the requirements for the proposed product or process. This can be challenging as all the customers and their interests are brought into the process of determining what is a must-have versus what is a nice-to-have.

Security requirements should be determined early in a project. It is much cheaper to build in security at the beginning of a project than to add it later. One way to think about the cost of security is to think of security in terms of quality. Having a product that is released and is immediately found to be vulnerable can have a real impact in tangible and intangible ways. Measuring cost accurately is not always easy. Some believe that the cost to correct security flaws at the requirements level is up to 100 times less than the cost to correct security flaws in fielded software. Auditors should be aware that the cost of not building in security up front is magnified by the expense of developing and releasing patches.

Return on Investment

Historically, return on investment (ROI) has been used to determine the profitability ratio. There are several ways to determine ROI, but the most frequently used method is to divide net profit by total assets. So, if your net profit is $10,000 and your total assets are $50,000, your ROI is .20, or 20 percent.

However, an auditor must also consider ROI in terms of the non-financial benefits of IT investments. Such benefits might include impacts on operations, increased sales, support for modern technology, mission performance, and improved customer satisfaction.

Before a project begins, stakeholders must make decisions based on the perceived value of the investment. Value is examined by looking at the relationship between the organization's costs and the expected benefits. The greater the benefits in relationship to cost, the greater the value of the IT project. Besides ROI, some other measures of profitability include the following:

- **Payback period:** The amount of time required for the benefits to pay back the cost of a project.

- **Net present value (NPV):** The value of future benefits restated in terms of to-day's money.

- **Total cost of ownership (TCO):** A financial estimate used to help determine the direct and indirect costs of a product or system.

- **Internal rate of return (IRR):** The benefits restated as an interest rate.

When a project is finished, an auditor should perform a gap analysis. This type of analysis involves comparing actual performance with potential or desired performance. In the long term, there is even more work as the longer an item has been released or available, the more vulnerable it becomes. An auditor needs to verify that proper vulnerability management is being performed.

> **NOTE** A gap analysis requires the comparison of actual performance with potential or desired performance.

Project Management Activities and Practices

Good project management practices can help ensure that the goals of a project are met. Project risk is a real concern. Project management faces three constraints:

- **Scope:** The scope of a project can be better defined by understanding the areas, activities, and human resources needed to complete the project. For example, software projects must define how big the applications will be. Will the project involve a few thousand lines of code or millions of lines of code?

- **Time:** Time can be better established by building a project timeline that lists each task and specifies a time frame for each.

- **Cost:** Cost can be determined by examining the lines of code, the number of people on the project team, and the time needed for each phase of the project.

The following sections discuss specific project management activities and items of concern.

Project Initiation

Project initiation is the first stage. Sometimes attention and effort are focused on the endpoint and final deliverable. Projects must be managed carefully during the initiation stage. At this point, a project sponsor seeks to obtain funding and approval for a project through a project initiation document (PID). The PID is used to obtain authorization for the project to begin. It justifies the project to management, clearly defines the scope of the project, documents all roles and responsibilities, and sets up and runs a project office environment.

Project Planning

Project planning is the part of project management that relates to schedules and estimation. A project manager must develop a realistic estimate of how much time a project will take and determine what tasks must be accomplished. Project planning involves not just time but also the identification and quantification of all required resources. Task management is not just about handing out tasks to each member of the team; it is about determining who is most capable of accomplishing each task. Program Evaluation and Review Technique (PERT) charts and Gantt charts, discussed later in this chapter, are two tools that help with this.

Project planning requires that the sequence of tasks be determined. Some tasks can be performed in any order, whereas others must flow in a specific order. For example, building a house requires the foundation to be laid before the walls can be built. Each of these tasks must have a time estimate performed; the project manager must determine how long each task will take. The resources needed will vary depending on the task. As in the previous example, a foundation requires concrete and rebar, while walls require wood and nails. The following sections look at some of the pieces of project planning.

Software Cost Estimation

Most of us put a lot of effort into cost estimation in our personal lives. When considering a new job offer, most people look closely at the cost of living in a different area, and when shopping for a car, most people check with several dealerships to find the best deal. The business world is constrained by similar budget factors. These components drive up the cost of software:

- **Source code language:** Using an obscure or unpopular language will most likely drive up costs.

- **Size of the application:** The size or complexity of an application has a bearing on its cost. As an example, the *level of security needed* will affect the complexity of a given application. This also has a direct correlation to the *scope* of a project.

- **Project time constraints:** If a project needs to be completed in one month versus the projected three months, this might mean that more overtime needs to be paid, along with fees for rushed services.

- **Computer and resource accessibility:** If resources are available only during certain times, the output of the project team will most likely be reduced.

- **Project team experience:** Every individual has a learning curve, and this means inexperienced team members cost extra.

- **Level of security needed:** A project that needs very high levels of security controls takes additional time and effort to develop.

One early cost model, developed by Barry Boehm, is known as the Constructive Cost Model (COCOMO). It was replaced by COCOMO II. This model considers "what if" calculations to determine how changes to human and other resources affect project cost. Figure 5-2 shows the COCOMO II model. (You can find a web version of the tool online at http://csse.usc.edu/tools/cocomoii.php, and you can also download it for use with standard spreadsheet applications such as Microsoft Excel.)

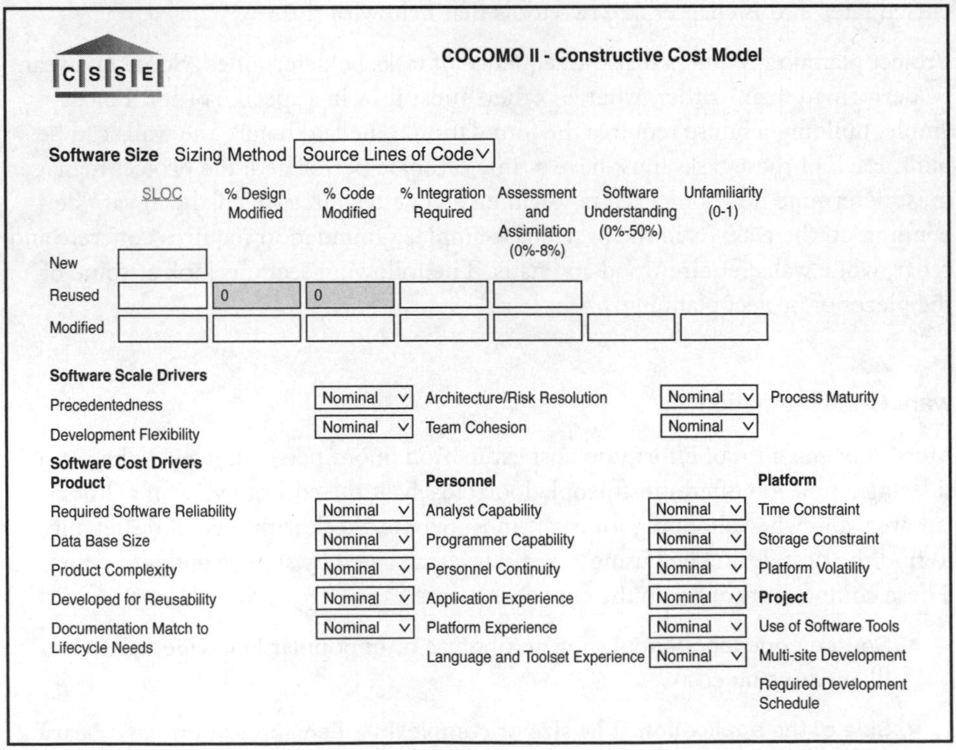

Figure 5-2   COCOMO II Software Estimation

When you have a reasonable idea of the software cost estimates, the next step is to examine methods to determine software size, in terms of lines of code.

Software Size Estimation

Originally, software sizing was done by counting *source lines of code* (*SLOC*). This method of software sizing was developed because early programs were written in FORTRAN and other line-oriented languages. To get an idea of how big programs can be, Linux 2.6 had about 5.7 million lines of code. With programs of such size, counts are usually done in *kilo lines of code* (*KLOC*). Both SLOC and KLOC determine cost solely on one factor—length of code—which does not work as well in modern development programs because additional factors affect overall costs, such as the complexity of the application/program being written. Considering that development packages can generate hundreds of lines of code from only a few mouse clicks demonstrates that this model is not as useful as in years past.

One modern way of estimating software size is to use *function point analysis* (*FPA*). FPA is a method that the ISO has approved as a standard to estimate the complexity of software. FPA can be used to budget application-development costs, estimate productivity after project completion, and determine annual maintenance costs. FPA is based on the number of inputs, outputs, interfaces, files, and queries. Figure 5-3 shows an overview of FPA.

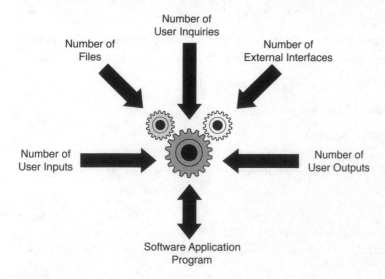

Figure 5-3   Function Point Analysis

Per ISACA, function points are first computed by completing a table, as demonstrated in Table 5-3. The purpose of the table is to determine whether the task is simple, average, or very complex. One way to determine this subjective weighting factor is to apply the Halstead Complexity Measures: the number of user inputs, number of user outputs, number of user inquiries, number of files, and number of external interfaces. Take a moment to review Table 5-3.

Table 5-3 Computing Metrics of Function Point Analysis

Measurement Parameter	Count	Simple	Weighing Factor Average	Complex	Results
Number of user inputs	X3	4		6	=____
Number of user outputs	X4	5		7	=____
Number of user inquiries	X3	4		6	=____
Number of files	X7	10		15	=____
Number of external interfaces	X5	7		10	=____
Total count:					

NOTE If an organization decides to use function point analysis, it must develop criteria for determining whether an entry is simple, average, or complex.

When a table like Table 5-3 is completed, the organization can run its computed totals through an algorithm to determine factors such as reliability, cost, and quality:

- Productivity = Function points / Person-month

- Quality = Defects / Function points

- Cost = $ / Function points

With these calculations completed, the project team can identify resources needed for each specific task.

TIP CISA exam candidates should know that when assessing the scope of an application-development project, function point analysis is one of the best techniques for estimating the scope and cost of the project.

Scheduling

With software size and cost determined, the project team can turn its attention to scheduling. Scheduling involves linking individual tasks. The relationship between these tasks is linked either by earliest start date or by latest expected finish date. Using a Gantt chart is one way to display these relationships.

The Gantt chart was developed in the early 1900s as a tool to schedule activities and monitor progress. A Gantt chart shows the start and finish dates of each element of a project, as well as the relationship between the activities, in a calendar-like format. Gantt charts are one of the primary tools used to communicate project schedule information. This type of chart uses a baseline to illustrate what will happen if a task is finished early or late.

Program Evaluation and Review Technique (PERT) is the preferred tool for estimating time when a degree of uncertainty exists. PERT uses a critical-path method, which applies a weighted average duration estimate.

PERT uses a three-point time estimate to develop best, worst, and most likely time estimates. The PERT weighted average is calculated as follows:

PERT weighted average = Optimistic time + 4 × Most likely time + Pessimistic time / 6

A PERT chart is used to depict this information. Each chart begins with the first task and branches out to a connecting line that contains three estimates:

- The most optimistic time in which the task will be completed

- The most likely time in which the task will be completed

- The worst-case scenario, or longest the task will take

Figure 5-4 shows an example of a PERT chart.

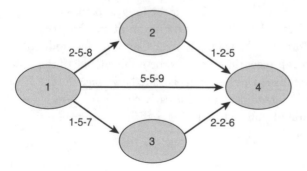

Figure 5-4   PERT Chart

TIP   Estimating the time and resources needed for application development is typically the most difficult part of the initial application-development activities.

For example, suppose that a project team has been assigned to design an online user-registration system for the organization and that one task is to develop the Java input screen the user will use to enter personal data. It might be reasonable to estimate that this task will take five workdays to complete. With PERT, the best and worst completion time estimates would also be factored in.

Critical Paths

In project management, anything can go wrong. Things can happen to affect the time, cost, or success of a project. That is why all project management techniques compute the critical path, or the sequence of tasks that must be completed on schedule for the project to be finished on time. We can expand on the house-building example we used earlier. Having a foundation is a task on the critical path; it must be completed before the walls and roof can be built. Exterior painting is not on the critical path and can be done at any time after the foundation, walls, and roof are completed.

Critical path methodology (*CPM*) determines what activities are critical and what the dependencies are between the various tasks. CPM involves the following tasks:

- Compiling a list of the tasks required to complete the project
- Determining the time that each task will take, from start to finish
- Examining the dependencies between the tasks

Critical tasks have little flexibility in completion time. The critical path can be determined by examining all possible tasks and identifying the longest path. Even if completed on time, this path indicates the shortest amount of time in which the project can be completed. CPM offers real advantages over Gantt, in that it identifies this minimum time. If the total project time needs to be reduced, one of the tasks on the critical path must be finished earlier. This is called *crashing*, and the project sponsor must be prepared to pay a premium for early completion—as a bonus or in overtime charges. The disadvantage to CPM is that the relationships of tasks are not as easily seen as with Gantt charts.

TIP   CISA exam candidates should understand that CPM is considered a project management planning and control technique.

Timebox Management

Timebox management is used in projects when time is the most critical aspect and software projects need to be delivered quickly. It is used to lock in specifications and prevent creep. For example, if given time, engineers might overengineer a system or decide to add more functionality or options. Although users might appreciate the added functionality, these items add time to the build phase and slow progress. Timeboxing counteracts this tendency by placing a very rigid time limit on the build of the system. When using timeboxing, the project time must never slip or be extended. If the project manager foresees time problems, he should consider taking corrective action, such as reducing the scope of the project or adding human or other resources.

Project Control and Execution

Project control requires the collection, measurement, and dissemination of information and project performance. The bulk of the budget will be spent during the execution of a project. It is entirely possible that project changes might be needed. If so, the changes to the project must be recorded. Changes typically result in additional funds, human resources, or time. An auditor must be aware of any changes and must examine how they could affect any existing controls and the overall project. An auditor must also be concerned with end-user training. When new software products are released to users, the users must be trained on how the application works, what type of authentication is required, and how overrides or dual controls work.

Project Closing

The last step in the project management process is to close the project. Projects are, after all, temporary endeavors. At the conclusion of a project, the project manager must transfer control to the appropriate individuals. The project closing includes the following tasks:

- Administrative closure

- Release of final product or service

- Update of organizational assets

At the close of a project, three items to consider are control implementation, benefits realization, and performance measurement. Surveys or postproject reviews might be performed. This is a chance to survey the project team and end users to gauge their satisfaction with the project and examine how things could have been done differently or what changes should be implemented next time. A postmortem review is similar but is usually held after the project has been in use for some time.

Business Application Development

Business application development is largely a product of the systems development life cycle (SDLC). New applications are typically created when new opportunities are discovered and when companies want to take advantage of new technology or use technology to solve an existing problem. Organizations use a structured approach for three reasons:

- To minimize risk
- To maximize return
- To establish controls to increase the likelihood that the software will meet user needs

As an auditor, you are not expected to be an expert programmer or understand the inner workings of a Java program. Instead, an auditor must know how to manage the development process so that adequate controls are developed and implemented. An auditor must be able to review information at each step of the process and provide input on the adequacy of controls being designed. Auditors are also responsible for reporting independently to management on the status of a project and the implementation of controls. Auditors might also become more deeply involved in a process based on their individual skills and abilities. Now let's look more closely at how the SDLC process works.

Systems-Development Methodology

The SDLC is designed to produce high-quality software in a structured way that minimizes risk. The traditional approach to SDLC is the waterfall model, illustrated in Figure 5-5. This model is closely allied with the project management life cycle model. The name of this model comes from the fact that progress flows from the top to the bottom, moving through each phase. W.W. Royce originally described the model as having seven phases. Some variations show it as having five or six phases. ISACA uses a modified model that has five primary phases plus a post-implementation phase.

As Figure 5-5 illustrates, the waterfall model starts with a feasibility study and progresses through implementation. The advantage of this model is that it is well known and extremely stable when requirements are not expected to change and the architecture is well known. Table 5-4 describes each phase of the SDLC.

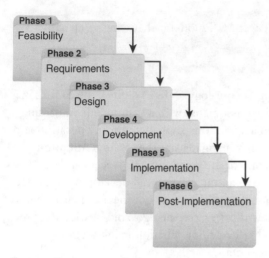

Figure 5-5 The Waterfall Model

Table 5-4 The NIST SDLC Process (NIST SP 800-34)

Waterfall Phase	Description
Initiation	Benefits and needs are determined at this phase of the SDLC.
Development / Acquisition	At this phase, the purpose of the project must be defined. The systems must be designed, developed, constructed, or purchased.
Implementation	The system is installed and end users are trained. At this point, the auditor must verify that all required controls that are in the design function as described.
Operation / Maintenance	The system or program perform the work for which it was designed. Patching and maintenance are important at this point.
Disposal	At this phase the system or program is retired and data is destroyed or archived in an approved method.

TIP At the conclusion of the preceding five steps, a formal review should occur to evaluate controls and the adequacy of the system. A cost–benefit analysis and review can be performed to determine the value of the project and to improve future projects.

TIP CISA exam candidates should understand that auditors must verify controls during the design phase of development.

TIP A primary characteristic of the classic waterfall model is that when each step ends, there is no turning back.

The National Institute of Standards and Technology (NIST) defines the SDLC in NIST SP 800-34 as "the scope of activities associated with a system, encompassing the system's initiation, development and acquisition, implementation, operation and maintenance, and ultimately its disposal that instigates another system initiation." Therefore, the goal of the SDLC is to control the development process and add security checks at each phase. The failure to adopt a structured development model increases risk and the likelihood that the final product may not meet the customer's needs. A good resource for further review is http://csrc.nist.gov/publications/nistbul/april2009_system-development-life-cycle.pdf. The following sections describe the phases of the SDLC in more detail.

Phase 1: Initiation phase

In the initiation phase of the NIST SDLC, the feasibility of the project is considered and a requirements analysis is performed. The cost of the project must be discussed, as well as the potential benefits that it will bring to the system's users. A payback analysis must be performed to determine how long the project will take to pay for itself. In other words, the payback analysis determines how much time will lapse before accrued benefits will overtake accrued and continuing costs. Figure 5-6 shows an example of this. If it is determined that the project will move forward, the team should develop a preliminary timeline. During the feasibility phase, everyone gets a chance to meet and understand the goals of the project.

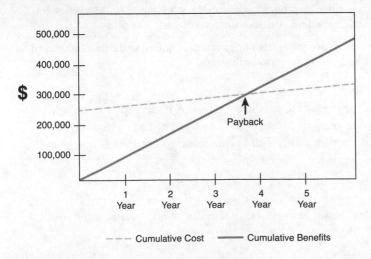

Figure 5-6 Charting the Payback Period

This is also the point at which users should be involved because they should have input into how the applications are designed. An *entity relationship diagram (ERD)* is often used to help map the requirements and define the relationship between elements. The basic components of an ERD are an entity and a relationship. An entity is very much like a database, in that it is a grouping of like data elements. An entity has specific attributes, which are called the entity's *primary key*. Entities are drawn as a rectangular box with an identifying name. Relationships describe how entities are related to each other and are defined as a diamond. ERDs can be used to help define a data dictionary. When a data dictionary is designed, the database schema can be developed. The database schema defines the database tables and fields, as well as the relationship between them. Figure 5-7 shows the basic design of an ERD. The completed ERD will be used in the design phase as the blueprint for the design.

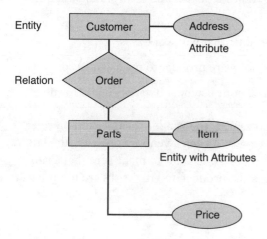

Figure 5-7   Entity Relationship Diagram

During the requirements phase, auditors must verify the requirements and determine whether adequate security controls are being defined. These controls should include the following mechanisms:

- **Preventive:** Preventive controls can include user authentication and data encryption.

- **Detective:** Detective controls can include embedded audit modules and audit trails.

- **Corrective:** Corrective controls can include fault-tolerance controls and data-integrity mechanisms.

TIP   You might be tested on the types of controls that need to be considered when designing new applications and systems.

TIP   You might be tested on the fact that user acceptance plans are usually developed during the requirements phase.

Before moving forward, a decision may be made to buy instead of build. With the option to buy, the project team should develop a request for proposal (RFP) to solicit bids from vendors. Vendor responses should be closely examined to find the vendor that best meets the project team's requirements. The team should ask questions such as these:

- Does the vendor have a software product that will work as is?

- Will the vendor have to modify the software product to meet our needs?

- Will the vendor have to create a new, nonexistent software product for us?

The reputation of the vendor is also important. Is the vendor reliable, and do references demonstrate past commitment to service? When a vendor is chosen, the last step is to negotiate and sign a contract. Auditors will want to make sure that a sufficient level of security will be designed into the product and that risks are minimized.

Phase 2: Development

During the development phase, users might not be involved, but the auditor is still working in an advisory role. The auditor must again check that security controls are still in the design and test documents. Test plans should detail how security controls will be tested. Tests should be performed to validate specific program units, subsystems, interfaces, and backup/recovery. Change-control procedures should be developed to prevent uncontrolled changes.

NOTE   *Scope creep* is the addition of products, features, or items to an original design so that more and more items are added on. This is sometimes referred to as the "kitchen sink syndrome." Scope creep is most likely to occur in the design phase. Little changes might not appear to have a big cost impact on a project, but they will have a cumulative effect and increase the length and cost of the project.

There are ways to decrease design and development time. *Reverse engineering* is one such technique. Reverse engineering converts executable code into a human-readable format and can be performed with tools such as IDA Pro. This is a somewhat controversial subject because, although reverse engineering has legitimate uses, a company could use it to disassemble another company's program. Most software licenses make this illegal. Reverse engineering is also sometimes used to bypass access-restriction mechanisms.

Programmers might use online programming facilities so that many programmers can access the code directly from their workstation. Although this typically increases productivity, it also increases risk because someone might gain unauthorized access to the program library. Programmers should strive to develop modules that have high cohesion and low coupling. *Cohesion* addresses the fact that a module is focused on a single task. *Coupling* is the degree of interconnection between modules. Low coupling means that a change to one module should not affect another. Figure 5-8 demonstrates this concept.

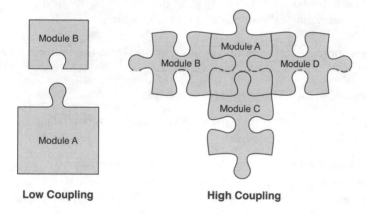

Figure 5-8   High and Low Coupling

NOTE   Programmers should strive to develop modules that have high cohesion and low coupling.

During development, auditors must verify that input and output controls, audit mechanisms, file-protection schemes, and a software version control system are being used. Examples of input controls include dollar counts, transaction counts, error detection, and correction. Examples of output controls include validity checking and control authorization. One way to manage and track changes to source code is by using a source control software package.

NOTE   A source control software package is used to secure source code and for version control. Examples of these products include Team Foundation Server (TFS) and Mercurial.

Testing these controls and the functionality of the program is an important part of this phase. Testing can be done by using one of the following testing methods:

- **Top down:** Top-down testing starts with a depth or breadth approach. Its advantage is that it gets programmers working with the program so that interface problems can be found sooner. It also allows for early testing of major functions.

- **Bottom up:** Bottom-up testing works up from the code to modules, programs, and systems. The advantage of bottom-up testing is that it can be started as soon as modules are complete; work does not have to wait until the entire system is finished. This approach also allows errors in modules to be discovered early. Most application testing follows the bottom-up approach.

Regardless of the chosen approach, test classifications are divided into the following categories:

- **Unit testing:** Examines an individual program or module.

- **Interface testing:** Examines hardware or software to evaluate how well data can be passed from one entity to another.

- **System testing:** Involves a series of tests that can include recovery testing, security testing, stress testing, volume testing, and performance testing. Although unit and interface testing focus on individual objects, the objective of system testing is to assess how well the system functions as a whole.

- **Final acceptance testing:** When the project staff is satisfied with all other tests, *final acceptance testing*, or user acceptance testing, must be performed. This occurs before the application is implemented into a production environment.

One big reason all this testing is performed is to verify the completeness, accuracy, validity, and authorization of transactions and data. Table 5-5 lists some other types of tests that are used for requirements verification.

Table 5-5   Testing Types

Test Type	Description
Alpha test	The first and earliest version of an application, followed by a beta version. Both are considered prereleases.
Pilot test	Used as an evaluation to verify functionality of the application.
White-box test	A type of test that verifies inner program logic. This testing is typically cost-prohibitive on a large application or system.
Black-box test	Integrity-based testing that looks at inputs and outputs. Black-box testing can be used to ensure the integrity of system interfaces.
Function test	A type of test that validates a program against a checklist of requirements.
Regression test	A type of test that verifies that changes in one part of the application did not affect any other parts in the same application or interfaces.
Parallel test	Parallel tests involve the use of two systems or applications at the same time. The purpose of this testing is to verify a new or changed system or application by feeding data into both and comparing the results.
Sociability test	A type of test which verifies that the system can operate in its targeted environment.

NOTE   Another name for beta testing is user acceptance testing (UAT). The idea of this type of testing is to put the software through a real-world test.

NOTE   One important item that must be verified during development is exception handling. When programs don't work as required or something must be done outside the normal process, close examination is needed. Exception handling is the act of replying to the occurrence of exceptions or anomalies or exceptional conditions that require special processing. This can change the normal flow of program execution.

Before coding can begin, programmers must decide what programming language they will use. To some extent, the organization will decide this. For example, if the company has used C++ for engineering projects for the past 5 years, it might make sense to do so for the current project. Programming has evolved through five generations of programming languages to this point:

- **First generation (1GL):** Machine language

- **Second generation (2GL):** Assembly language

- **Third generation (3GL):** High-level language

- **Fourth generation (4GL):** Very high-level language

- **Fifth generation (5GL):** Natural language

Figure 5-9 shows the five generations of languages and an example of each, with their syntax.

> **NOTE**   Organizations might have many individuals who are able to write code, but this does not mean they are *authorized* to do so. End-user computing (EUC) refers to systems in which nonprogrammers can create working applications. Such applications and the citizen programmers who create them can have a detrimental effect on security if not properly managed. No single user should ever have complete control over the development of an application program. There should always be checks and balances to prevent fraud and maintain control.

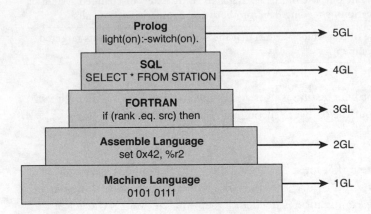

Figure 5-9   Programming Languages

Phase 3: Implementation

In the implementation phase, the application is prepared for release into its intended environment. Final user acceptance is performed, as are certification and accreditation. This is typically the final step in accepting the application and agreeing that it is ready for use. *Certification* is the technical review of the system or application. Certification testing might include an audit of security controls, a risk assessment, or a security evaluation. *Accreditation* is management's formal acceptance of a system or application. Typically, the results of the certification testing are compiled into a report, and management's acceptance of the report is used for accreditation. Management might request additional testing, ask questions about the certification report, or accept the results as is. Once the results are accepted, a formal acceptance statement is usually issued.

NOTE Data conversion tools may be used to migrate data from one system to another. Data conversion is simply conversion of computer data from one format to another.

NOTE You might be tested on the fact that final user acceptance testing is performed during the implementation phase.

The rollout of the application or system migration might be all at once or phased in over time. Changeover techniques, as shown in Figure 5-10, include the following:

- **Parallel operation:** Both the old and new systems are run at the same time. Results between the two systems can be compared. Fine-tuning can also be performed on the new system as needed. As confidence in the new system improves, the old system can be shut down. The primary disadvantage of this method is that both systems must be maintained for a period of time.

- **Direct changeover:** This method establishes a date at which users are forced to change over. The advantage of a direct, or hard, changeover is that it forces all users to change at once. However, this introduces a level of risk into the environment because things can go wrong.

- **Phased changeover:** If the system is large, a phased changeover might be possible. With this method, systems are upgraded one piece at a time.

- **Pilot changeover:** This method requires that an entire new system be used at one location.

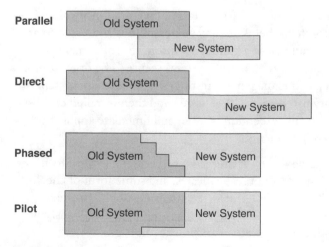

Figure 5-10   Changeover Techniques

Phase 4: Operation and Maintenance

In the operation and maintenance phase, it is time to roll out the application to the users. Some support functions need to be established. Items such as maintenance, support, and technical response must be addressed. Data conversion might also need to be considered. If an existing system is being replaced, data from the system might need to be migrated to the new one. Computer-aided software engineering (CASE) is used for program and data conversions.

NOTE Hopefully, some of the users have been involved throughout the process and can help in the training process. The training can include classroom training, online training, practice sessions, and user manuals.

Some may think that once an application is deployed that the work of an auditor is done, but that is far from the case. A large part of information systems maintenance involves keeping the code up to date. This means someone must be checking for vulnerabilities and patching known concerns. One source of information on this topic is the common vulnerabilities and exposures (CVE) database, a dictionary of identifiers and details of publicly known information security vulnerabilities. It can be viewed at https://cve.mitre.org.

Vulnerability assessment can be traced back to applications such as SATAN and SAINT. An auditor should review how vulnerability assessment and remediation are being handled. For example, Nessus might be used on a weekly basis, with vulnerabilities being labeled high, medium, or low. Items defined as high might require action within 24 hours of discovery, whereas items labeled low might not require action for up to 30 days.

Closely related to vulnerability assessment is patching and updates. Once vulnerabilities are found, patch management helps get any vulnerabilities addressed in an expedient manner to reduce overall risk of a system compromise. Patch management is key to keeping applications and operating systems secure. The organization should have a well-developed patch management testing and deployment system in place. The most recent security patches should be tested and then installed on host systems as soon as possible. The only exception is when an immediate application would interfere with business requirements.

Before a patch can be tested and deployed, it must first be verified. Typical forms of verification include digital signatures, digital certificates, and some form of checksum and/or integrity verification. This is a critical step that must be performed before testing and deployment to make sure the patch has not been maliciously or accidentally altered. Once testing is complete, deployment can begin.

Another post-implementation activity is a review of the overall success of the project. Actual costs versus projected costs should be reviewed to see how well cost estimating was done during the feasibility phase. ROI and payback analysis should be reviewed. A gap analysis can determine whether there is a gap between requirements that were and were not met. An independent group might conduct performance measurement, such as an audit. If this occurs, it should not be done by auditors who were involved in the SDLC process. Overall, post-implementation should answer the following questions:

- Is the system adequate?

- What is the true ROI?

- Were the chosen standards followed?

- Were good project management techniques used?

NOTE The release management step involves managing an application, maintaining traceability, and ensuring the version once the application has been released.

Phase 5: Disposal

Applications and systems don't last forever. At some point, systems must be decommissioned and disposed of. This step of the process is reached when an application or a system is no longer needed. Those involved in the disposal process must consider the disposition of the application. Should it be destroyed or archived, or does the information need to be migrated into a new system? Disk sanitization and destruction are also important to ensure confidentiality. This important step is sometimes overlooked. Table 5-6 outlines a sample policy for data disposal.

NOTE Disposal of an existing application might be required when the maintenance cost surpasses the benefits/returns from the application.

Table 5-6 Sample Media Destruction Policy

Media	Wipe Standard	Description
Rewritable magnetic media (hard drive, flash drive, and so on)	Drive wiping or degaussing	DOD 5220.22-M seven-pass drive wipe or electric degaussing
Optical media (CD-RW, DVD-RW, DVD+RW, CD-R, DVD-R, and so on)	Physical destruction	Physical destruction of the media by shredding or breaking

Tools and Methods for Software Development

Globalization has increased the pace of change and reduced the amount of time that organizations have to respond to changes. New systems must be brought online quickly. The SDLC is not the only development methodology used today. As an auditor, you must be knowledgeable about other development methods and have a basic understanding of their operations. Some popular models include the following:

- **Incremental development:** This method involves developing systems in stages so that development is performed one step at a time. A minimal working system might be deployed while subsequent releases build on functionality or scope.

- **Spiral development:** The spiral model was developed based on the experience of the waterfall model and the concept that software development is evolutionary. The spiral model begins by creating a series of prototypes to develop a solution. As the project continues, it spirals out, becoming more detailed. Each step passes through planning, requirements, risks, and development phases.

- **Prototyping:** The prototyping model reduces the time required to deploy applications. Prototyping involves using high-level code to quickly turn design requirements into application screens and reports that users can review. User feedback can be used to fine-tune the application and improve it. Top-down testing works well with prototyping. Although prototyping clarifies user requirements, it can result in overly optimistic project timelines. Also, when change happens quickly, it might not be properly documented, which is of concern for an auditor.

NOTE The advantage of prototyping is that it can provide great savings in development time and costs.

- **Rapid application development (RAD):** RAD uses an evolving prototype and requires heavy user involvement. According to ISACA, RAD requires well-trained development teams that use integrated power tools for modeling and prototyping. With the RAD model, strict limits are placed on development time. RAD has four unique stages: concept, functional design, development, and deployment.

TIP The CISA exam might test you on whether RAD uses prototyping as its core development tool.

These models share a common element: They each have a predictive life cycle. This means that when a project is laid out, costs are calculated, and a schedule is defined.

Another category of application development is called *agile software development*. With this development model, teams of programmers and business experts work closely together. Project requirements are developed using an *iterative* approach because the project is both mission driven and component based. The project manager is much more of a facilitator in these situations. Popular agile development models include the following:

- **Extreme programming (XP):** The XP development model requires that teams include business managers, programmers, and end users. These teams are responsible for developing usable applications in short periods of time. Issues with XP are that teams are responsible not only for coding but also for writing the tests used to verify the code. Lack of documentation is also a concern. XP does not scale well for large projects.

- **Scrum:** Scrum is an iterative development method in which repetitions are referred to as *sprints* and typically last 30 days. Scrum is typically used with object-oriented technology and requires strong leadership and a team meeting each day for a short time. The idea is for the project manager to give over more planning and directing tasks to the team. The project manager's main task is to work on removing any obstacles from the team's path.

NOTE Reengineering involves converting an existing business process. Reengineering means updating software by reusing as many of the components as possible instead of designing an entirely new system.

Information Systems Maintenance

When a system moves into production, the work is not yet done. Changes need to be made and must be done in a controlled manner. The integrity of the application and source code must be ensured. Most organizations use a change-control board that includes a senior manager as the chairperson and individuals from various organizational groups. The change-control board is responsible for developing a change-control process and also for approving changes.

Although the types of changes vary, change control follows a predictable process:

1. Request the change.

2. Approve the change request.

3. Document the change request.

4. Test the proposed change.

5. Present the results to the change-control board.

6. Implement the change, if approved.

7. Document the new configuration.

Documentation is key to a good change-control process. All system documents should be updated to indicate any changes that have been made to the system or environment. The system maintenance staff or department responsible for requesting the change should keep a copy of the change approval.

An auditor should ensure that backup copies of critical documents are created. These documents should be kept offsite in case of a disaster or other situation. The auditor should also watch for the possibility of unauthorized changes due to poor oversight or lack of proper security controls. Items to look for include the following:

- Changes are implemented directly by the software vendor, without internal control.

- Programmers place code in an application that has not been tested or validated.

- The changed source code has not been reviewed by the proper employee.

- No formal change process is in place.

- The change review board has not authorized the change.

- The programmer has access to both the object code and the production library.

Even if an auditor takes all these measures, a situation may still arise in which a change must bypass the change-control process. Emergency changes might have to be made because of situations that endanger production or halt a critical process. In such situations, it is important to maintain the integrity of the process. These changes should be followed up by procedures to ensure that standard controls are applied retroactively. If programmers are given special access or an increased level of control, the accounts and mechanisms they use should be closely monitored.

Outsourcing and Alternative System Development

Third-party outsourcing is the practice of handing over responsibility for an organization's information systems development and operations to an outside firm. There are many reasons a firm might decide to outsource. High on the list are typically cost and problems with internal IS performance. One common approach to outsourcing involves these steps:

1. Identify, select, and plan a system.

2. Conduct system analysis.

3. Develop a request for proposal.

4. Select a vendor.

Not all outsourcing relationships are the same. It is important to ensure that an organization's service levels and requisite controls are met. When reaching outsourcing agreements, certain stipulations may be applied. For example, does your company have employees, contractors, or business partners sign NDAs? Doing so is one way to help provide security for sensitive information and proprietary data. As an auditor, you should have a basic understanding of the following documents and how they are used with outsourcing partners:

- **Interconnection security agreement (ISA):** An ISA is a security document that details the requirements for establishing, operating, and maintaining an interconnection between systems or networks. An ISA typically details how specific systems and networks are connected and contains a drawing of the network topology.

- **Memorandum of understanding (MOU):** An MOU typically documents conditions and applied terms for outsourcing partner organizations that must share data and information resources. To be binding, the MOU must be signed by a representative from each organization that has the legal authority to sign. Such documents are typically secured, as they are considered confidential.

- **Operating level agreement (OLA):** An OLA works in conjunction with SLAs by supporting the SLA process. An OLA defines the responsibilities of each partner's internal support group. So, whereas an SLA may promise no more than five minutes of downtime, an OLA defines what group and resources are used to meet a specified goal.

- **Uptime agreement (UA):** A UA is one of the best-known types of SLAs; it details the agreed amount of uptime. For example, UAs can be used for network services such as a WAN link or equipment like servers. A UA may, for example, specify cloud server uptime of 99.9999999 percent (nine nines).

- **Business Partnership Security Agreement (BPA):** A BPA is a written agreement created by lawyers with the input from the partners that contains standard clauses related to security and cooperation. A BPA is an example of a legally binding document that is designed to provide safeguards and compel certain actions among business partners in relation to specific security-related activities.

TIP   CISA exam candidates should be able to define each of the types of agreements listed above.

NOTE   When dealing with business partners, auditors should review Statements on Standards for Attestation Engagements No. 16. SSAE 16 verifies controls and processes and requires a written assertion regarding the design and operating effectiveness of the controls being reviewed.

Cloud Computing

Cloud computing is a type of outsourcing that involves turning over the operation of a service to an outside entity. Depending on the cloud model being used, a varying amount of control is given to the cloud service provider. There are several cloud computing models, as shown in Figure 5-11:

- **Public cloud:** This cloud model is based on the concept that the service provider makes resources, such as applications and storage, available to the general public. An example is Dropbox.

- **Private cloud:** This cloud model is based on the concept that the cloud is owned and operated by a private entity.

- **Community cloud:** This cloud model can be used by several entities.

- **Hybrid cloud:** This cloud model can be a combination of any of the other cloud models.

TIP   The CISA exam might ask you about the different types of cloud models.

You can think of cloud computing as a type of computing that uses shared Internet computer resources and data to computers and other devices on demand. When a service is operated on premises, the entire process is under the organization's control. When cloud computing is used, the organization gives up a portion or all of this activity to the cloud provider. Basic cloud services include Infrastructure as a Service (IaaS), Platform as a Service (PaaS), and Software as a Service (SaaS), as shown in Table 5-7. Figure 5-12 provides an overview of the different cloud services.

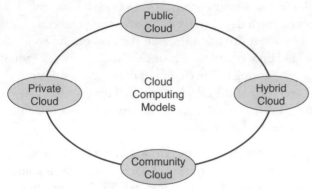

Figure 5-11   Cloud Models

Table 5-7   Cloud Services

Service	Description
Infrastructure as a Service	A form of cloud computing services that provides virtualized computing resources over the Internet.
Platform as a Service	A form of cloud computing services in which a platform allows customers to develop, run, and manage applications without the complexity of building and maintaining the infrastructure typically associated with it.
Software as a Service	A form of cloud computing services in which a third-party provider hosts applications and makes them available to customers over the Internet.

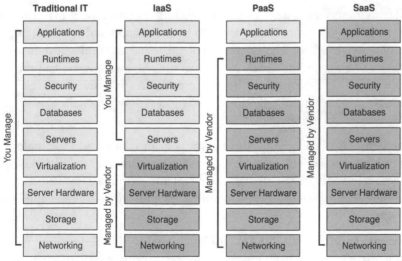

Figure 5-12   Cloud Computing Overview

There are many reasons organizations are increasingly moving to cloud-based services, including cost, portability, and a desire to focus on core competencies. Regardless of the reason, making the transition to the cloud requires careful contract negotiation. An auditor should understand that, historically, the network group has had complete control; however, moving to the cloud requires the organization to relinquish some control and oversight to the cloud provider. This transition requires networking professionals to move beyond their traditional packet-processing mindset in order to really grasp cloud computing.

Auditors should know that companies operating in the United States, Canada, or the European Union have many regulatory requirements by which they must abide, including ISO/IEC 27001, EU-U.S. Privacy Shield Framework, IT Infrastructure Library, and COBIT. It is important to have a framework for the contract that both parties can agree on, such as ISO 27001. The cloud provider must be able to meet these requirements and be willing to undergo certification, accreditation, and review. The cloud provider should also agree in writing to comply with an auditing standard, such as SSAE 16. With cloud computing, proving to auditors and assessors that compliance is being met is becoming more challenging and more difficult to demonstrate. Of the many regulations dealing with IT, few were written with cloud computing in mind. Auditors and assessors may not be familiar with cloud computing or with a given cloud service.

Cloud Threats

Organizations must consider a variety of potential threats before they move to a cloud model. To that end, a cloud provider should agree in writing to provide the level of security an organization requires.

Access control is an important issue. How will cloud authentication be managed? Insider attacks are an ongoing threat. Anyone who has been approved to access the cloud can be a potential problem. Here's an example: Say that an employee quits or is terminated, and then you find out he or she was the only person who had the password. Or, perhaps the employee was the one responsible for ensuring that the cloud provider gets paid. You need to know who has access, how he or she was screened, and how access is terminated.

Training is another issue of concern. Knowing how your provider trains its employees is an important item to review. Most attacks are both technical and social. The steps a provider takes to address social-engineering attacks stemming from email, malicious links, phone, and other methods should be included in its training and awareness program.

Auditors should also inquire about the standard being used to classify data and whether the provider supports it. Tokenization is a growing alternative to encryption and can help ensure compliance with regulatory requirements such as those under the Health Insurance Portability and Accountability Act (HIPAA), Payment Card Industry Data Security Standard (PCI-DSS), the Gramm–Leach–Bliley Act, and the EU data protection regulations.

Encryption should be reviewed. Will the original data leave the organization, or will it stay internal to satisfy compliance requirements? Will encryption be used while the data is at rest, in transit, or both? You will also want to know what type of encryption is being used. There are, for example, important differences between DES and AES. And make sure you understand who maintains the encryption keys before moving forward with a contract. Encryption should always be on the list of critical cloud security tips.

How long has the cloud provider been in business, and what is its track record? If it goes out of business, what happens to your data? Will your data be returned in its original format?

If a security incident occurs, what support will you receive from the cloud provider? While many providers promote their services as being unhackable, cloud-based services are an attractive target to hackers. Side channel, session riding, cross-site scripting, and distributed denial of service attacks are just some of the threats to data in the cloud.

While you may not know the physical location of your services, they are located somewhere. And all physical locations face threats from fire, storms, natural disasters, and loss of power. If any of these events occur, how will the cloud provider respond, and what guarantee of continued services does it promise?

Some reports indicate that in the next three years, more than four-fifths of all data center traffic will be based in the cloud. This means if you have not yet audited a cloud-based service, you most likely will do so soon.

Application-Development Approaches

Applications are written in programming languages. Programming languages can be low level so that the system easily understands the language; they also can be high level, enabling humans to easily understand them but requiring translation for the system. The programs used to turn high-level programs into object- or machine-readable code are known as *interpreters*, *compilers*, or *assemblers*. Most applications are compiled. The information also can be grouped for the development process in various ways, including the following:

- **Data-oriented system development (DOSD):** DOSD uses a process of focusing on software requirements. It helps eliminate problems with porting and conversion because the client uses the data in its predescribed format. Stock exchanges, airlines, and bus and other transit companies use DOSD.

- **Object-oriented systems development (OOSD):** OOSD uses a process of solution specifications and models, with items grouped as objects. OOSD is valued because it can model complex relationships, work with many data types, and meet the demands of a changing environment.

- **Component-based development (CBD):** CBD helps objects communicate with each other. The benefit of CBD is that it enables developers to buy pre-developed tested software from vendors that is ready to be used or integrated into an application. Microsoft's Component Object Model (COM), Common Object Request Broker Architecture (CORBA), and Enterprise JavaBeans (EJB) are examples of component models.

- **Web-based application development (WBAD):** WBAD uses a process to standardize code modules to allow for cross-platform operation and program integration. WBAD offers the use of application-development technologies such as Extensible Markup Language (XML). Its components include Simple Object Access Protocol (SOAP), Web Services Description Language (WSDL), and Universal Description, Discovery, and Integration (UDDI).

No matter what approach is used for development, to a large extent, success depends on how well the different groups work and communicate together. DevOps (development operations) seeks to address this need. DevOps, which represents a change in IT culture, emphasizes the collaboration and communication of software developers and information technology (IT) professionals while seeking to improve collaboration between operations and development teams. That is of huge importance because, as most auditors understand, the relationship is often adversarial. DevOps seeks to address this issue and plays a pivotal role in cloud computing, but its principles apply to on-premises deployments as well.

N-tier

The concept behind n-tier is to provide a model by which developers can create flexible and reusable applications. N-tier accomplishes this by separating an application into tiers, and developers acquire the option of modifying or adding a specific layer instead of reworking the entire application. Think of a tier as a physical structuring mechanism for the system infrastructure. A three-tier architecture is typically composed of a presentation tier, a domain logic tier, and a data storage tier. The most common implementation of n-tier is the three-tier approach.

With a three-tier application, the work is divided into three major parts, and each part is distributed to a different place or location in a network:

- **The workstation or presentation interface:** This tier is located on the local workstation and may contain data that is local or unique for the workstation.

It includes the coding that provides the graphical user interface (GUI) and application-specific entry forms or windows.

- **The business logic:** This tier is located on a local area network (LAN) server and acts as the server for client requests from workstations. The business logic unit determines what data is needed and acts as a client in relation to a third tier.

- **The database and programming related to managing it:** Located on a server, this third tier is the database and a program used to manage read/write access.

The primary advantage of the three-tier approach is that each of the three tiers can be developed concurrently by different programmers coding in different languages. One tier may have multiple layers. A layer can be thought of as a logical structuring mechanism for the elements that make up the software solution of one tier.

The most common implementation deployment model consists of the LAMP (Linux, Apache, MySQL, and PHP/Python/Perl) stack. This is possible because the programming for a tier can be changed or relocated without affecting the other tiers. Some readers may see the similarity to the three-tier model and the OSI model in that each layer is responsible for certain items. This approach also lowers development costs and makes it easier for an enterprise or software packager to continually evolve an application as the need arises.

Virtualization

Cloud computing is not the only game in town. Virtualization is also an option for development or deployment of an application. Virtualized computing makes use of a virtual machine (VM). A *virtual server* is a virtualized computer that executes programs like a physical machine. VMware and Hyper-V are two examples of hypervisors. A hypervisor is basically the combination of software and hardware that creates and runs a virtual machine. Virtual machines are a huge trend and can be used for development and system administration and production, as well as to reduce the number of physical devices needed.

One of the primary advantages of virtualized systems is server consolidation. Virtualization allows you to host many virtual machines on one physical server. Virtualization allows rapid deployment of new systems and offers the ability to test applications in a controlled environment. This reduces deployment time and makes better use of existing resources. Virtualization also helps with research and development. Virtual machine snapshots or checkpoints allow for easy image backup before changes are made and thus allow a means to quickly revert to the previous good image. This is very useful for all types of testing and production scenarios. Consider the fact that it's only a matter of time before a physical server fails or has a malfunction or even a hardware failure. In these situations, virtualization can be a huge advantage.

Even with all the advantages, there are some items an auditor should review when dealing with virtualized systems. Virtualization adds another layer of complexity, which can cause problems that may be difficult to troubleshoot. Vulnerabilities associated with a single physical server hosting multiple companies' virtual machines include the fact that there is comingling of data. Even if none of these items are an issue, there is still the concern that the platform might be misconfigured. Such events can have devastating consequences for all the virtual systems residing on a single platform. The following are also concerns:

- **Privilege escalation:** This type of exploit allows an attacker to move from one user account to another either vertically or horizontally.

- **Live VM migration:** During live migration, a threat agent might attempt to capture the data as it moves over the network.

- **Data remanence:** It is entirely possible that in multi-tenant environments where VMs get provisioned and deprovisioned, residual data from previous use could be exposed.

Virtualization systems fall into two categories: Type 1 and Type 2. Type 1 hypervisors reside directly on hardware. Type 2 hypervisors require an underlying OS. Examples of Type 2 systems include VirtualBox and VMware Workstation. Regardless of the type of VM being used, virtualized systems are an additional component that an auditor needs to consider.

Chapter Summary

This chapter covers the systems development life cycle and project management. These topics are important to an auditor from the standpoint of governance. An auditor has a leadership role throughout these processes. The goal of this chapter is to introduce auditors to the various steps, review the activity performed at each stage, and help auditors become familiar with the terms and concepts used in software development.

Exam Preparation Tasks

As mentioned in the section "How to Use This Book" in the Introduction, you have a couple choices for exam preparation: the exercises here; Chapter 10, "Final Preparation;" and the exam simulation questions on the book's companion web page (www.informit.com/title/9780789758446).

Review All the Key Topics

Review the most important topics in this chapter, noted with the Key Topic icon in the outer margin of the page. Table 5-8 lists these key topics and the page number on which each is found.

Table 5-8   Key Topics in Chapter 5

Key Topic Element	Description	Page Number
List	License agreements	186
Table 5-5	Testing types	207
List	Change control	213
Figure 5-11	Cloud models	217
Figure 5-12	Cloud computing overview and differences	217
Section	Cloud threats	218

Complete Tables from Memory

Print a copy of Appendix B, "Memory Tables" (found on the companion web page), or at least the section for this chapter, and complete the tables from memory. Appendix C, "Memory Tables Answer Key," also on the companion web page, includes completed tables you can use to check your work.

Define Key Terms

Define the following key terms from this chapter and check your answers against the glossary:

accreditation, agile, certification, critical path methodology (CPM), enterprise architecture (EA), entity relationship diagram (ERD), function point analysis (FPA), kilo lines of code (KLOC), object breakdown structure (OBS), prototyping, rapid application development (RAD), return on investment (ROI), reverse engineering, source lines of code (SLOC), systems development life cycle (SDLC), top-down testing, total cost of ownership (TCO), work breakdown structure (WBS)

Exercises

5.1 Project Management

Estimated time: 10 minutes

A new software update project has three items that have been determined to be in the critical path:

- The build process has a minimum of 30 days, a maximum of 70 days, and an average of 45 days.

- The testing process has a minimum of 12 days, a maximum of 20 days, and an average of 14 days.

- The deployment process has a minimum of 5 days, a maximum of 15 days, and an average of 7 days.

You have been asked to compute critical path times. Complete the PERT calculations in Table 5-9.

Table 5-9 Challenge Question

Item	Description	Critical Path Time
1	Build	
2	Test	
3	Deploy	
Total time		

Verify your answers by using Table 5-10.

Table 5-10   Challenge Answer

Item	Description	Critical Path Time
1	Build	**46 Days**
2	Test	**18 Days**
3	Deploy	**8 Days**
Total time		**72 Days**

5.2 Project Management

Estimated time: 10 minutes

Complete Table 5-11 and describe each one of these techniques.

Table 5-11   Application-Development Methods

Method	Description of Method
Incremental	
Waterfall	
Spiral	
Prototyping	
Rapid application development	
Extreme programming	
Scrum	

NOTE   Return to the section "Outsourcing and Alternative System Development" if you have trouble filling in this table.

Answers to Table 5-11

Application Method	Description of Method
Incremental	Breaks down a concept into components for development piece by piece
Waterfall	Historic method, one step at a time
Spiral	Uses four steps
Prototyping	Builds front-end screens or what the user would see first
Rapid application development	Designed to overcome problems with the waterfall model
Extreme programming	Designed to improve software quality and responsiveness to changing customer requirements
Scrum	An iterative and incremental agile software development framework

Review Questions

1. As an IS auditor, at which step of the SDLC would you want to verify that final user acceptance is performed?

    a. Design

    b. Development

    c. Implementation

    d. Requirements

2. When planning to add time constraints to a project, which of the following should be examined most closely?

    a. Budget

    b. Critical path

    c. Skills of the project team

    d. Tasks that require the most time

3. During the implementation review of SDLC, which of the following best describes activities that should be performed?

    a. Perform an ROI

    b. Design the audit trail

    c. Complete an entity relationship diagram

    d. Perform acceptance testing

4. Which of the following types of tests is used to verify that the proposed design will function in its intended environment?

    a. Regression testing

    b. Function testing

    c. Pilot testing

    d. Sociability testing

5. Which of the following development methods is known to not work well for large projects?

    a. Spiral model

    b. Rapid application development

    c. Scrum

    d. Extreme programming

6. Programming languages that most closely map to database management are found at what generational level?

    a. 2GL

    b. 3GL

    c. 4GL

    d. 5GL

7. Which of the following does the PERT weighted average consider?

    a. High cost, low cost, and best cost

    b. Average cost plus 5%

    c. Best time, worst time, and average time

    d. Average time plus 5%

8. As an IS auditor, which changeover process would you recommend if the requirements were that all users get up to speed in advance so that a defined changeover can be set to a fixed date?

    a. Pilot changeover

    b. Direct changeover

    c. Phased changeover

    d. Parallel changeover

9. Entity relationship diagrams are built using two essential components. What are they?

   a. Processes and attributes

   b. Processes and decision blocks

   c. Entities and relationships

   d. Nouns and adverbs

10. Which of the following development techniques uses short cycles, referred to as sprints, and is focused on object-oriented technology?

   a. Spiral model

   b. Rapid application development

   c. Scrum

   d. Extreme programming

11. Dropbox can best be described as which of the following types of cloud services?

   a. Public

   b. Private

   c. Community

   d. Hybrid

12. Which of the following is a growing alternative to encryption and can help ensure compliance with regulatory requirements in a cloud environment?

   a. Random numbers

   b. Tokenization

   c. Cookies

   d. User ID

13. VirtualBox is an example of which of the following?

   a. Type 1 hypervisor

   b. Type 2 hypervisor

   c. Type 3 hypervisor

   d. Type 4 hypervisor

14. Which of the following is the most common implementation of n-tier?

    a. Workstation and server

    b. LAMP stack

    c. Workstation and cloud

    d. Workstation, server, and database

15. As an IS auditor, which of the following reports would you review to verify that an outsourcing or business partner has had its control objectives and activities examined by an independent accounting and auditing firm?

    a. Privacy Shield

    b. COBIT

    c. ITIL

    d. SAS 70

Suggested Readings and Resources

- **Project management:** www.pmi.org/about/learn-about-pmi/what-is-project-management

- **Best programming languages to learn today:** https://usersnap.com/blog/programming-languages-2017/

- **The application audit process:** www.sans.org/reading-room/whitepapers/auditing/application-audit-process-guide-information-security-professionals-1534

- **IT audits of cloud and SaaS:** www.isaca.org/Journal/archives/2010/Volume-3/Pages/IT-Audits-of-Cloud-and-Saas.aspx/

- **Test steps for auditing virtualization:** https://esj.com/articles/2011/03/29/test-steps-auditing-virtualization.aspx

- **The role of an auditor in projects:** www.iia.nl/SiteFiles/Role__auditor_in_projects_Huibers_2013_AOM_article%20published%20in%20EDPACS.pdf

- **Overview of SSAE 16:** https://en.wikipedia.org/wiki/SSAE_16

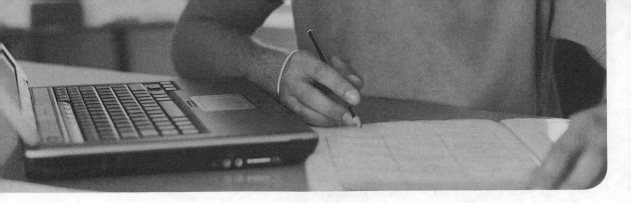

The following exam domains are partially covered in this chapter:

Domain 1—The Process of Auditing Information Systems

Domain 2—Governance and Management of IT

Domain 3—Information Systems Acquisition, Development and Implementation

This chapter covers the following topics:

- **Audit Universe and Application Auditing:** This section describes how an audit universe can be used to define the range of audit activities and auditable entities to be covered in an application audit.

- **Programmed and Manual Application Controls:** This section defines, compares, and contrasts the differences between programmed and manual controls.

- **Auditing Application Controls:** This section describes different types of application controls and techniques used when auditing applications.

- **Auditing Systems Development, Acquisition, and Maintenance:** This section describes the systems development life cycle and its phases.

- **Business Application Systems:** This section describes different types of business systems and why they are important.

CHAPTER 6

Auditing and Understanding System Controls

System controls and related application topics in this chapter apply to multiple domains of the CISA exam. This chapter examines elements in Domain 1, "The Process of Auditing Information Systems," that touch on creating a risk-based approach to application audits. It also explores the continuous auditing concepts covered in Domain 2, "Governance and Management of IT." Finally, this chapter explores elements of Domain 3, "Information Systems Acquisition, Development and Implementation," related to the definition and development of application controls.

To understand this convergence of domain elements, this chapter discusses application controls and how these controls can be audited to verify their functionality. This chapter also examines business application systems and looks at the risks such as those related to electronic funds transfer and electronic banking.

"Do I Know This Already?" Quiz

The "Do I Know This Already?" quiz allows you to assess whether you should read this entire chapter thoroughly or jump to the "Exam Preparation Tasks" section. If you are in doubt about your answers to these questions or your own assessment of your knowledge of the topics, read the entire chapter. Table 6-1 lists the major headings in this chapter and their corresponding "Do I Know This Already?" quiz questions. You can find the answers at the bottom of the page following the quiz and in Appendix A, "Answers to the 'Do I Know This Already?' Quizzes and Review Questions."

Table 6-1 "Do I Know This Already?" Section-to-Question Mapping

Foundation Topics Section	Questions
Audit Universe and Application Auditing	1, 6
Programmed and Manual Application Controls	2, 7
Auditing Application Controls	3, 8
Auditing Systems Development, Acquisition, and Maintenance	4, 9
Business Application Systems	5, 10

CAUTION The goal of self-assessment is to gauge your mastery of the topics in this chapter. If you do not know the answer to a question or are only partially sure of the answer, you should mark that question as incorrect for purposes of the self-assessment. Giving yourself credit for an answer you correctly guess skews your self-assessment results and might provide you with a false sense of security.

1. Which of the following is not a criterion typically considered when assessing risk during an IT audit?

   a. Core business

   b. Regulatory compliance

   c. Market risk

   d. Brand

2. The act of balancing debits, credits, and totals between two systems is what processing control technique?

   a. Manual recalculations

   b. Programming controls

   c. Reasonableness verification

   d. Reconciliation of file totals

3. Which part of the ACID test means to ensure that transactions are processed only if they meet system-defined integrity constraints?

   a. Atomicity

   b. Consistency

   c. Isolation

   d. Durability

4. In which stage of the audit controls and quality assurance checks does an auditor review how the system handles erroneous input and data?

   a. Software acquisition process

   b. Feasibility

   c. Design and development

   d. Requirements definition

5. Which of the following is a technology designed to facilitate the exchange of data between computer systems?

   a. ATM

   b. EDI

   c. EFT

   d. Application system

6. True or false: An audit universe is not required in the audit process planning stage.

   a. True

   b. False

7. Which of the following is not an example of data file control categories?

   a. System control parameters

   b. Static data

   c. Reconciliation totals

   d. Transaction files

8. What typical control should be observed to verify that run-to-run totals are reconciled on a timely basis?

   a. Separation of duties

   b. Report distribution

   c. Input authorization

   d. Balancing

9. In which stage of the audit controls and quality assurance checks does an auditor evaluate how the chosen solution meets the user's needs?

   a. Requirements definition

   b. Feasibility

   c. Design and development

   d. Software acquisition process

10. The data architecture needed to support a business intelligence solution includes which of the following components?

   a. Data presentation

   b. Data access

   c. Data mining

   d. All the above

Audit Universe and Application Auditing

An audit universe represents the range of audit activities and auditable entities to be covered. An audit universe is typically refreshed annually as part of the audit planning phase. An auditable entity is the part of a business that has sufficient risk to audit. For example, account receivables within the accounting department may be an auditable entity.

An audit universe is not required in the audit process planning stage. However, the audit universe concept is a useful tool for identifying focus areas for an application audit. It allows an individual to create a risk-based application audit approach by systematically breaking down the business environment into key functions and processes and then rating the risk of each.

Let's consider a few steps in a simple e-commerce transaction:

1. The customer must browse the merchant's online store.

2. The customer must complete an order form and pass on his or her personal information and credit card number.

3. The customer must review and approve the form.

4. The credit card information must be authorized through the bank's payment system.

5. The merchant must send a notice to the customer that the order was received and is being processed.

6. The bank must send payment to the merchant.

7. The order is shipped.

Even this high-level overview illustrates the level of complexity that an auditor must understand and the many controls related to the business. Each process is further broken down and can be highly complex. Issues such as when an order was processed, where the customer's data is stored, where the product is shipped from, and jurisdictional tax requirements are all relevant concerns. Without this knowledge, an auditor cannot verify that proper security measures have been implemented. Think of an audit universe as a means of organizing this business understanding.

Once key functions and processes are mapped, they must be ranked based on risk. There is no one method of risk ranking, but the common objective of risk ranking is to understand the impact that a system failure or security breach would have on the organization. Three criteria are typically considered when assessing the risk to functions and processes:

- **Core business:** Will the core business cease or be significantly disrupted (typically measured in loss of revenue)?

- **Regulatory compliance:** Will the business or officers be subject to significant legal liabilities, including fines and potential lawsuits?

- **Brand:** Will significant disruptions impact brand and market share?

Once the risk is ranked, the higher-risk entities are assessed. Such assessment generally includes a review of controls related to relevant applications, processes, and resources that collectively contribute to the achievement of the strategic objectives.

An audit universe can be used broadly to identify higher-risk functions and which parts of an organization carry significant risk. This chapter focuses on applications and related controls. From the high-risk functions and processes identified, you would then identify the underlying applications and controls to audit.

A risk-based audit plan would be developed through consultation with senior management and business planners. This audit universe approach also allows an audit to leverage the understanding of risk to identify key focus areas of the audit, such as controls related to the following:

- Supporting technologies

- Alignment with business and technology strategies

- Compliance with laws, rules, and regulations

- Effectiveness of organization support

Programmed and Manual Application Controls

This section discusses programmed (also referred to as *automated*) and manual application controls as they relate to input, output, and processed information. These controls can be either manually or automatically programmed:

- *Programmed*, or *automated*, *controls* include validation and edit checks, programmed logic functions, and controls.

- *Manual controls* are those that the staff manually verify, such as the review of reconciliation reports and exception reports.

Answers to the "Do I Know This Already?" Quiz:

1. C; 2. D; 3. B; 4. C; 5. B; 6. A; 7. C; 8. D; 9. B; 10. D

The purpose of automated and manual controls is to verify the following:

- The validity of data processed is ensured.

- The accuracy of data processed is ensured.

- The data is stored so that controls maintain the security of the data so that accuracy, validity, confidentiality, and integrity of the data are maintained.

- Processed data is valid and meets expectations.

Business Process Controls

Before controls can be examined, an auditor must understand the business strategy and the business process. The information gathered as part of the audit universe risk ranking should be leveraged as the starting point. This should include a review of the company's business plan. Next, the auditor should review in more detail the long-term and short-term business goals.

Long-term business goals are considered strategic and focus on activities planned for the next three to five years. *Short-term business goals* are tactical and address immediate concerns that are no more than 18 months into the future.

After reviewing this background information, examine process flowcharts and determine key applications and controls. Next, review application controls, data integrity controls, and controls for business systems. While not an exhaustive list, Table 6-2 provides examples of controls.

Table 6-2 Business Process Control Examples

Controls	Processing Controls
Input Controls	Input authorization and Batch Controls
Processing Controls	Processing, Validation, and Editing
Output Controls	Logging and Security signature

The following sections look at each of these categories of controls in more detail.

Input Controls

When reviewing input controls, an auditor must ensure that all transactions have been entered correctly. Whatever controls are used, they should be capable of checking that input is valid. This is important because in many automated systems, the output of one system is the input of another. Data should therefore be checked to verify the information from both the sending and receiving applications.

Controls can have either automated authorization or manual authorization. For example, consider the last time you were at your local discount store and, at checkout, an item did not ring up at the advertised sale price. Most likely, you had to wait for the clerk to signal a supervisor to advise of the error in the sale price. The supervisor then had to enter a second-level password to authorize the price change. This is a *manual authorization control*. Other types of authorization controls include these:

- Signatures on forms or documents approving a change.

- Password controls that are required to process a change.

- Client identification controls that allow only certain clients to authorize the change. (For example, the clerk at the store cannot authorize a price override, but the manager can do so by using a special access login.)

A *batch control* is another type of input control. Batch controls combine transactions into a group. The group then has a value assigned. The total of this transaction can be based on dollar amounts, total counts, total document numbers, or hash totals.

NOTE   The CISA exam will expect candidates to understand the difference between a batch total and a hashing control.

Total dollar amounts verify that each item totals up to the correct batched total amount. *Total item counts* verify the total counts match. For example, if 312 items were ordered, 312 items should have been processed and shipped. *Total document numbers* verify that the total number of documents in the batch equals the total number of documents processed. Documents could be invoices generated, orders, or any document count that is used to track accuracy. *Hash totals* are generated by choosing a selected number of fields in a series of transactions. These values are computed again later to see if the numbers match. An incorrect value indicates that something has been lost or entered incorrectly or that the transmission has been corrupted somehow. As an example of hashing, consider that the totaling of part numbers on an order normally provides no usable value, but the total can be compared to the shipping order to verify accuracy.

NOTE   Hash totals can be thought of as working similarly to the way that cryptographic hashing algorithms (such as MD5) work to verify integrity. In this case, a hash is taken on the entire document. Any alteration or change in the document will result in the hash being different between the sending and receiving points.

Batch controls must be combined with the proper follow-up procedures. For example, if rejected items are resubmitted, controls must be in place to detect this anomaly. In addition, procedures must be in place to follow up on any discrepancies found when batch controls are performed. Batch balancing is used to verify that a batch was processed correctly. It can be accomplished by comparing computer-generated batch quantities to manual batch counts. Control accounts can also be used. Control accounts write an initial batch value to a data file. After processing, the processed value is compared to the initially stored value. An example of this can be seen in *batch registers*, which allow for the manual recording of batch totals. These are saved and then compared to totals that are generated by the system. If they do not agree, a batch can be rejected.

Processing Controls

Processing controls are used to ensure the accuracy, completeness, and timeliness of data during online or batch processing. Controls should be in place to verify that data is processed only through authorized routines. Processing controls should be designed to detect problems and initiate corrective action. If procedures are in place to override these controls, their use should be logged. Individuals who have the ability to override these controls should not be the same ones responsible for reviewing the log. Edit controls can be used after the data has been entered into the system but before it has been processed. Edit controls can be considered a type of preventive control. Table 6-3 describes edit control examples.

Table 6-3   Processing Edit Control Examples

Validation Edit	Description
Sequence check	Sequence numbers ensure that all data falls within a given range. For example, checks are numbered sequentially. The day's first check that was issued had the number 120, and the day's last check was number 144. All checks issued that day should fall between those numbers, and none should be missing.
Limit check	Data to be processed should not exceed a predetermined limit. For example, the weekly sale item is limited to five per customer. Sales over that quantity should trigger an alert.
Range check	A range check ensures that the data is within a predetermined range. For example, a range check might verify that the data is after 01/01/2017 and before 01/01/2025.
Validity check	This type of check looks at the validity of data.
Reasonableness check	This check verifies the reasonableness of the data. For example, if an order is usually for no more than 20 items and the order is for 2,000 items, an alert should be generated.

Validation Edit	Description
Table look-ups	This check verifies that the data matches the data in a look-up table.
Existence check	An existence check verifies that all required data is entered.
Key verification	Key verification requires a second employee to re-enter the data. A match must occur before the data can be processed.
Check digit	A check digit verifies accuracy. A check digit is a sum of a value appended to the data.
Completeness check	This check ensures that all required data has been added and that no fields contain null values.
Duplicate check	This check ensures that a data item is not a duplicate. For example, before payment is made, accounts payable verifies that invoice number 833 for $1,612 has not already been paid.
Logical relationship check	This type of edit check verifies logic. If one condition is true, additional items must also be true. For example, in 2017, if the data shows that an applicant is old enough to vote, logic dictates that person must have been born before 1998.

NOTE   The CISA exam typically includes questions on preventive versus detective controls. Validation edit controls are applied before processing the transaction, and they are therefore considered preventive controls.

Now that you understand edit controls, let's turn our attention to processing controls used to ensure that the data remains unchanged until processed by an authorized process. Table 6-4 outlines the control techniques used to protect the integrity of the data.

Table 6-4   Processing Control Techniques

Processing Control	Description
Manual recalculations	Some transactions might be recalculated to ensure that processing is operating correctly.
Editing	A program instruction controls input or processing of data to verify its validity.
Run-to-run totals	Various stages of processing ensure the validity of data.
Programming controls	Software-based controls flag problems and initiate corrective action.
Reasonableness verification	This control ensures the reasonableness of data. For example, if someone tries to process a negative amount through a payment system, a reasonableness control should flag the result as invalid.

Processing Control	Description
Limit checks	This control sets bounds on what are reasonable amounts. For example, someone might attempt to order 55 flat-screen TVs.
Reconciliation of file totals	This refers to the act of balancing debits, credits, and totals between two systems. This control should be performed periodically to verify the accuracy and completeness of data.
Exception reports	This type of report should be generated when transactions appear to be incorrect.

NOTE The CISA exam typically includes both definition questions on the different controls and situation questions about which is the best control. For example, a customer has entered an order for 55 TVs in error instead of the intended 5 TVs to be ordered. Would a limit check or exception report be the more effective control? A limit check could catch this type of error because it sets a practical limit on what a typical customer would buy and can force an out-of-band order to be manually verified through customer service. Exception reports would only detect an error in the transaction itself, such as an invalid shipping address.

Data File Controls

Data files or database tables can be put into categories to better understand their content and purpose. There are many data category types. The following are four typical examples:

- *System control parameters* control values such as how much money can be transferred in a single transaction with approval.

- *Static data* refers to information that changes infrequently. An example of static data is a customer's name, address, and phone number. Because these values do not frequently change, an alteration should be controlled and should require authorization.

- *Balance data* refers to various values and totals that might be held temporarily during processing. These values should be strictly controlled; any manual alteration of these values should require authorization and should be logged.

- *Transaction files* deal with the transmission of information between two systems or applications. Transaction files should be managed with exception reports or validation checks.

Each data category can then have various controls applied, such as the following:

- **Before-and-after image reports:** By taking a snapshot of computer data before and after a transaction, you can determine what changes have been made to the data. There are applications that can apply snapshots automatically and send an alert when a file changes. These automated tools are useful for detecting changes to files outside normal change windows, such as changes to a security configuration file, which may be evidence of a breach.

- **Maintenance error reporting:** Procedures should be established to verify that any errors or exceptions are rectified and reconciled. The employee who generated a transaction should not have the authorization to clear an error with it.

- **Internal and external labeling:** Internal labeling ensures that proper data files are used and that all information is present. External labeling applies to removable media.

- **Data file security:** This control ensures that individuals who process data cannot bypass validity checks, clear logs, or alter stored data.

- **One-to-one checking:** Documents entered for processing should match processed totals.

- **Transaction logs:** Transactional information such as date, time, terminal, user ID, and so on should be recorded to create a usable audit trail.

- **Parity checking:** Data integrity should be verified in the event of a transmission error.

Output Controls

Output controls are designed to provide assurance with data that has completed processing. Output data must be delivered accurately and in a timely manner so that it is useful in the decision-making process. Output controls should be designed to ensure that data is distributed and stored in a secure manner. Sensitive data should have sufficient controls to monitor usage and control who has access to it. These controls will vary depending on whether the information is centrally stored or distributed to end-user workstations.

NOTE Auditors should be aware that one way to control distribution is to place controls on data that limit what information is to be printed and to whose printer it should be directed. For example, some reports might be configured so that they are printed only to the supervisor's printer. Software printing controls are another example of this. Products such as the Adobe Reader can be used to limit printing or embed password controls for viewing or printing.

Auditing Application Controls

Application software is the engine behind business transactions. Business transactions today are fast paced and are often measured in sub-second response time. To remain competitive, businesses must automate many customer transactions. This keeps costs controlled and enhances reliability—and it means increased use and integration of application software.

Two control terms are often used:

- **Application controls:** These controls are related to a specific individual process or application.

- **General controls:** These controls apply across all system components, processes, and data.

These systems might process payroll, manage inventory, or even invoice and bill customers. Most users see only the application interface, but what does the application really do? An auditor should be most concerned about the limits, controls, and rules that define how an application interacts with the organization's data.

Understanding the Application

One of the first questions an auditor should ask is "What does the application do?" How this question is answered will vary from organization to organization and from business to business. The audit universe and related risk ranking are important tools that help focus an auditor on higher-risk applications and transactions.

An auditor can start by asking for documentation. If an application was developed in-house, system development methodology documents might be available. These documents will provide the auditor with insight into what the user requirements were and what cost–benefit analysis was done to justify development of the application. Functional design specifications should also be reviewed. These specifications are a great resource because they detail how the application is designed and what it was developed to achieve. If the application has been in use for a while, program change documents that list any changes or updates also might exist. Checking outstanding bugs and issues in release notes documentation and software build information also can provide good information. After reviewing these documents, the auditor can develop an application flowchart to accomplish the following:

- Validate every input to the system against the applicable criteria

- Review logical access controls and authorization controls

- Evaluate exception handling and logging

- Examine data flow to find control weaknesses

With an understanding of the application and knowledge of how transactions flow through the application and related risks, the auditor can move to the next step: observation and testing.

Observation and Testing

A big part of an auditor's job is observation. Auditors are tasked with observing how users interact with an application. Auditors should also test the limits of the application, such as buffer overflows. Buffer overflows can occur when attackers try to stuff more than the total number of characters allowed in a field. The design specification might state that the application does not accept negative numbers, but is that actually the case? If you enter a negative number or a negative quantity in a field, will the application actually accept it? It shouldn't.

Even if the application were to accept an invalid input activity, reports should track the IP address and device name used to complete the entry. Logging should also track the date and time of activity. In addition, invalid entries should be logged so that violation reports can be created.

When working with applications, auditors should observe and test the items listed in Table 6-5.

Table 6-5 Observation and Testing

Observation or Test	Details
Separation of duties	Auditors should verify separation of duties, which provides control by limiting the ability of each employee. For example, one department might have the capability to issue checks but might be required to send the checks to a second department for signatures.
Input authorization	Auditors should review records to verify who is authorized to access applications. Supervisor override being used frequently might signal problems.
Balancing	Auditors should verify that run-to-run totals are reconciled in a timely manner.
Report distribution	Auditors should review report distribution logs to see who has access to view and print reports. Controls used to limit the distribution of reports should also be reviewed.
Error correction and control	Auditors should review past error corrections and verify that they are viewed and addressed in a timely manner.
Access control and authorization	Auditors should verify that access is limited to individuals who have a clearly demonstrated need. Testing can be performed to ensure that access controls are in place as specified.

Data Integrity Controls

Data integrity testing is performed to ensure the accuracy, completeness, consistency, and authorization of data. Integrity testing is considered a substitutive test. Data can be stored in files or in databases.

NOTE Data integrity testing is the best method of examining the accuracy, completeness, consistency, and authorization of data. Data integrity testing can be used to find failures in input and processing controls.

Data stored in databases has unique requirements because it differs from data stored or processed by an application. Database integrity testing can be performed using several methods. *Referential integrity* guarantees that all foreign keys reference existing primary keys.

NOTE If you are not familiar with the database terms *primary* and *secondary keys*, you should supplement your study with database concepts by searching for related white-papers on the Internet.

Controls in most databases should prevent the primary key from being deleted when it is linked to existing foreign keys. *Relational integrity* ensures that validation routines test data before it is entered into a database and that any modification can be detected. A third integrity control is *entity integrity*. For example, if the primary keys are names of banks, *entity integrity* ensures that each database transaction record contains a primary key. Without the capability to associate each primary key with a bank, entity integrity cannot be maintained, and the database is not intact.

Online data integrity has somewhat different concerns because online databases most likely are distributed or clustered for performance and fault tolerance. Online databases work in real time. This might mean that several databases must be updated simultaneously. These complexities mean that the *ACID test* should be applied:

- **Atomicity:** Ensures that the results are either all or nothing.

- **Consistency:** Ensures that transactions are processed only if they meet system-defined integrity constraints.

- **Isolation:** Ensures that each transaction is isolated from all others until complete.

- **Durability:** Ensures that when a transaction is processed, the transaction cannot be rolled back and is accurate.

Application System Testing

Application testing is a critical part of the audit process. Testing enables an auditor to evaluate a program, review its controls, and monitor the transaction process. The primary methods used for application testing are as follows:

- **Snapshots:** These are used to monitor and record the flow of data through an application. Although snapshots require in-depth knowledge about the application, they are useful in verifying logic.

- **Mapping:** Unlike snapshots, mapping verifies program logic that might not have been performed or tested. This is useful because it might detect undiscovered problems.

- **Tracing and tagging:** Tagging is used to mark selected transactions, which enables these tagged transactions to be monitored.

- **Using test data:** An auditor can use test data to verify program operation. This technique requires little knowledge of the environment and does not require the review of the source code.

- **Base case system evaluation:** This compressive test uses test data that was developed to thoroughly test the environment. This method is useful because it requires great effort and close cooperation among various internal groups.

- **Parallel operation:** Both old and new systems process data so that the results can be compared.

- **Integrated test facility:** This test method creates a fictitious entity in a database to process sample test transactions at the same time live input is being processed.

- **Parallel simulation:** Another useful audit tool uses computer programs to simulate program logic.

- **Transaction selection:** This method of testing uses audit software to determine what transactions should be processed.

NOTE   A number of these test techniques are invasive, which means the test can alter or disrupt normal transactions and reporting. To minimize production disruption, a number of these tests can be applied to the development environment rather than the production environment. In these cases, it is critical that the development environment have the same code set and properly mimic the production environment.

Continuous Online Auditing

Testing a system before rollout might provide a baseline of information, but it offers no ongoing feedback on the operation of the application. Continuous online auditing gives auditors the tools needed to perform ongoing monitoring. Continuous online auditing produces audit results either at real-time intervals or after a short period of time. This method actually can reduce costs because the need for conventional audits might be reduced or eliminated. In a conventional audit, the auditor has a limited amount of time to design tests and examine data. Continuous online auditing greatly increases the quantity and scope of data available to the auditor. With continuous auditing, the auditor can evaluate data on an ongoing schedule and alert management to problems as needed. Paperwork is reduced, and the auditor can electronically examine application data and report problems directly as needed.

Continuous online auditing also increases security. Consider a bank that allows online access to customer accounts and funds. Although such systems are convenient for users, they present an additional risk for the bank. Continuous online auditing allows the bank to monitor transactions as they occur. If some type of misuse occurs, the time between the misuse and discovery is greatly reduced. If additional controls are needed, they can be deployed in a shortened time frame. Five continuous audit techniques commonly exist, as described in Table 6-6.

Table 6-6   Continuous Audit Techniques

Technique	Description	Issues and Concerns
Systems control audit review file and embedded audit modules (SCARF/ EAM)	The application must contain embedded audit software to act as a monitoring agent.	Cannot be used to interrupt regular processing
Integrated test facilities	Live and dummy data is fed into the system. The results of the dummy data are compared with precalculated results.	Should not be used with test data

Technique	Description	Issues and Concerns
Continuous and intermittent simulation (CIS)	CIS simulates the transaction run. If data meets certain criteria, the simulator logs the transaction; otherwise, processing continues.	Requires examination of transactions that meet specific criteria
Snapshots	This technique tags transactions and then takes snapshots as the data is moved from input to output.	Requires an audit trail
Audit hooks	This technique uses embedded hooks that act as red flags if certain conditions are met.	Detects items that meet specific criteria

NOTE Businesses are often nervous about adding interfaces to live production data because they fear system disruptions. Many audit departments work using extracts of production data to reduce such risks.

Auditing application controls is a big part of auditing system infrastructure. Table 6-7 describes the five major phases and activities performed during each phase of application auditing.

Table 6-7 Auditing Applications

Phase	Activity
Understanding the application	Validation of every input to the system against the applicable criteria
	Review of logical access control and authorization controls
	Evaluation of exception handling and logging
	Examination of data flow to find control weaknesses
Observation and testing	Review Separation of duties
	Test Input authorization
	Review Balancing controls
	Evaluate Report distribution
	Test Error correction and control
	Assess Access control and authorization

Phase	Activity
Data integrity controls	Test Referential integrity
	Evaluate Relational integrity
	Evaluate Entity integrity
Application system testing	Obtain Snapshots
	Review Mapping
	Evaluate Tracing and tagging
	Evaluate Use of test data
	Assess Base case system evaluation
	Examine Parallel operation
	Assess Integrated test facility
	Evaluate Parallel simulation
	Review Transaction selection
Continuous online auditing	Implement Systems control audit review file and embedded audit modules (SCARF/EAM)
	Monitor Integrated test facilities
	Assess Continuous and intermittent simulation (CIS)
	Obtain Snapshots
	Review Audit hooks

Auditing Systems Development, Acquisition, and Maintenance

Today's systems are complex, and systems might be used by different branches located in different areas of the world or accessed by users through the Internet. Many legal regulations and requirements, such as various privacy laws, must be satisfied. This means that coding must be performed by teams of programmers with the help of architects, analysts, testers, auditors, and end users, who must all work together. To manage such a large endeavor, the system development life cycle (SDLC) was created.

The auditor's role in the SDLC process is to work with the development team to ensure that the development, acquisition, and maintenance processes yield a final product that meets user requirements while possessing adequate controls. Throughout the system development life cycle, an auditor should work with the development team to minimize risks and exposures. The following are the general steps an auditor should follow during the development process:

1. Determine the objectives and user requirements of the project.

2. Perform a risk assessment that identifies threats, risks, and exposures.

3. Assess existing controls to determine whether they will adequately reduce risk to acceptable levels. Discuss any needed changes with the development team.

4. Monitor the development process and evaluate controls as they are designed and created.

5. Evaluate the system during rollout and review audit mechanisms to ensure that they function as designed.

6. Take part in any post-implementation reviews.

7. Verify system maintenance procedures.

8. Review production library control to ensure the needed level of security.

Project Management

Implementing good application controls is just part of the task. Organizations must also use good project management techniques. An auditor should ensure that the overall process is sound and meets industry standards. The involvement of an auditor in a project will vary depending on risk. An auditor will most likely not be involved in every project. Auditors' involvement at a project level is typically reserved for large projects with significant impact to the organization. Auditors place reliance on their assessment of the overall process to control risks of smaller projects in which they cannot be personally engaged. An auditor must be comfortable that the end result will be to minimize risk and ensure that adequate controls are in place.

An auditor must evaluate the level of oversight that a project committee has over the process. Other issues, such as reporting, change control, and stakeholder involvement, are also important. Table 6-8 lists additional checks that the auditor should perform. Although this is not a complete list, it should give you an overall idea of how important it is for the auditor to play a proactive role in the process.

Table 6-8   Audit Controls and Quality Assurance Checks

Phase	Items to Review
Feasibility	Examine proposal and documentation.
	Assess the criticality of the user's needs.
	Evaluate how effectively the chosen solution meets the users' needs.
	Investigate the possibility of an alternate or existing solution.
Requirements definition	Assess the total cost of the project and verify that the project sponsors have approved.
	Examine the conceptual design and verify that it meets user demands.
	Evaluate the possibility of embedded audit routines.
	Examine the proposed user acceptance plans.
Software acquisition process	Examine the RFP to ensure that it is complete.
	Examine vendor contracts.
	Verify that the legal department has approved the vendor contract.
Design and development	Study system flowcharts.
	Evaluate input, process, and output controls.
	Examine proposed audit trails and determine the usefulness.
	Review how the system will handle erroneous input and data.
Testing	Examine proposed test plans.
	Verify audit trails, error processing, and error reports.
	Evaluate user documentation and manuals.
	Review test results.
	Examine system security.
Implementation	Examine system documentation.
	Examine system parameters.
	Examine any data conversion activities to verify correctness.

Phase	Items to Review
Post-implementation	Review requirements and user needs to verify that the systems meet user needs.
	Examine user satisfaction and cost–benefit analysis.
	Examine the change-request process.
	Examine error logs.
System change procedures	Determine whether emergency change procedures exist.
	Evaluate the separation of production code from test code and access security controls.
	Interview end users to determine their satisfaction with the turnaround of the change process.

NOTE   A CISA candidate needs to understand what activities occur at each stage of the project management process. For example, user acceptance test plans are reviewed at the requirements definition stage.

Business Application Systems

A business application is any program that is used to run a business. As discussed previously, not all applications have the same importance. A risked-based audit approach looks at the business applications that represent the greatest risk to the business. This means that auditors must understand the business and technical context of an application that is being reviewed.

One good place to start is reviewing application system flowcharts. Business applications can be categorized according to where they are used or by their functionality. Business application programs are used for accounting, payroll, inventory, sales, and so on. These systems can be used in e-commerce systems, for web-based applications, in electronic banking, and even for electronic payment systems. This section discusses a number of different business application systems an auditor will encounter.

NOTE   Flowcharts are one of the first things an auditor should examine to get an understanding of an application or business function. It's not uncommon for flowcharts and application specifications to become outdated. The maintenance of this material may be an audit concern that is raised with management.

E-commerce

Electronic commerce (e-commerce) is about the buying, selling, and servicing of goods via the Internet. The process usually begins with a company advertising its goods on a website. When a buyer finds the goods he or she is looking for, the buyer adds them to a shopping cart. Upon checkout, the buyer is redirected to a secure web page so that credit card and shipping information can be entered.

E-commerce saw tremendous growth in the late 1990s with the wide adoption of the Internet. This created an opportunity for businesses to offer goods and services without the traditional overhead and at better prices than in brick-and-mortar stores. Although a pure Internet model has somewhat held, many companies have a bricks-and-clicks model that supports both online and offline presences.

The following are the different types of e-commerce transactions:

- **Business to business (B-to-B):** Transactions between two or more businesses, such as a business and its suppliers.

- **Business to consumer (B-to-C):** Transactions between businesses and consumers. This area is one of the greatest growth areas for e-commerce. For companies that don't sell products directly to their customer, there are brokers that can sell products for them.

- **Business to government (B-to-G):** Transactions between businesses and governments, such as the online filing of legal documents and reports.

- **Business to employee (B-to-E):** Transactions between businesses and employees. This model can be seen when organizations set up internal websites and portals for employee services such as health care, job benefits, and payroll.

E-commerce adds an additional level of challenge to an organization because data and applications must protect availability, integrity, and confidentiality 24 hours a day, 7 days a week. Companies must also be careful in handling customers' personal information and payment information, such as credit cards. Authentication and non-repudiation are important aspects of this because customers need to know that they are really dealing with the company, not an impostor.

Cloud computing has both simplified and created a number of significant challenges for auditors. *Cloud computing* involves using a network of remote servers hosted on the Internet to store, manage, and process data. In other words, a business no longer has to host its own servers and computing power. Cloud computing can provide major cost savings as businesses do not have to build and maintain their own data centers. Amazon, Google, Microsoft, IBM, and many other technology companies offer cloud computing services. But moving to a cloud service provider also means giving up control. The major cloud service providers have standardized how servers are configured and managed, and this standardization limits choices and can limit auditor access.

Electronic Data Interchange

Electronic data interchange (EDI) is a technology designed to facilitate the exchange of data between computer systems. It was designed to bridge the gap between dissimilar systems. EDI is used to exchange invoices, shipping notices, inventory updates, and so on in a format that both the sending and receiving systems can understand. *ANSI X12* is the most common of the formats used. EDI offers benefits for organizations: It reduces paperwork and results in fewer errors because all information is transmitted electronically. Traditional EDI consists of the following components:

- **Communications handler:** The handler transmits and receives electronic documents. Much of this activity occurs via the Internet.

- **EDI interface:** The EDI interface handles data as it is being passed between the two organizations' applications. Security controls are usually placed here. The EDI interface is composed of the EDI translator and the application interface.

- **Application system:** The application system is the program responsible for processing documents that have been sent or received. Additional controls are usually not placed here.

Electronic funds transfer (EFT) is an example of EDI used among financial institutions, in which money is transferred from one account to another. Examples of EFT transactions include electronic wire transfers, automatic teller machine (ATM) transactions, and direct deposit of payroll via the Internet.

EDI adds a new level of concern for organizations because documents are processed electronically. One big concern with EDI is authorization. EDI processes should therefore have an additional layer of application control to address the issue of authorization, as well as lost or duplicate transactions and issues of confidentiality and invalid distribution. Some common controls include the following:

- Transmission controls to validate sender and receiver

- Manipulation controls to prevent unauthorized changes to data

- Authorization controls to authenticate communication partners

- Encryption controls to protect the confidentiality of information

Auditors should seek to verify that these common controls have been implemented. Other controls include the deployment of *audit monitors*, which are devices used to capture EDI activity as it is sent or received. An auditor should also review systems that process inbound transactions to make sure each transaction is properly logged, as well as use transaction totals to verify that totals agree with those collected by trading partners.

Email

Virtually every business uses email to communicate with its employees, business partners, and others. Email enables individuals to communicate electronically through the Internet or a data communications network. Although email is the most commonly used Internet application, it raises some security concerns. Specifically, email is usually cleartext, which means anyone can easily read it. Email can be spoofed to mask the true identity of the sender. Email also is a major conduit for spam, phishing, and viruses.

Users need to be made aware of potential problems and risks with email. Email carries a number of legal and regulatory requirements, which continue to grow. Email commonly uses two underlying services: Simple Mail Transfer Protocol (SMTP) and Post Office Protocol (POP). The following steps describe basic email operation:

1. The user opens an email program such as Outlook to create an email message.

2. After the email is created and addressed to the recipient, the user sends the email.

3. The email is forwarded to an SMTP server, which provides a message transfer agent (MTA). Just as the postal service sorts mail using a zip code, email messages are sorted by domain. For example, in an email addressed to training@ thesolutionfirm.com, the domain is thesolutionfirm, and it identifies where the message is to be forwarded.

4. The MTA forwards the email toward its final destination.

5. The email is delivered to the destination mail server, where it waits until the recipient user retrieves it.

6. The email is retrieved using Post Office Protocol version 3 (POP3) and is displayed via Outlook on the recipient's computer.

Users must be educated about the fact that sensitive information (such as Social Security numbers) should not be sent by cleartext email. If an organization has policies that allow email to be used for sensitive information, encryption should be used. This requires an evaluation of the business needs. If only some information is to be encrypted, Pretty Good Privacy (PGP) might be the best option. However, if full-time encryption is needed, the company might want to use link encryption or standards such as Secure Multipurpose Internet Mail Extensions (S/MIME) or Privacy Enhanced Mail (PEM).

Business Intelligence

The objective of business intelligence (BI) is to reduce decision-making time and increase the value of a decision. Business intelligence is much like a crystal ball because the organization can use it to make better decisions in a shorter period of time. An organization can use BI to compare itself to its competitors. Business intelligence is also useful in helping understand customer needs as well as the capabilities of the firm. In addition, business intelligence is useful in risk management; it can help a business spot unusual trends, odd transactions, and statistics on loss and exposure. To properly implement an infrastructure to support business intelligence, the business must design and develop a data architecture.

These layers encompass the data architecture:

- **Data sources:** The actual data sources reside here. For example, a grocery store might have customer reward card scanners at each checkout so that customers using the reward card have each item recorded on their account.

- **Data access:** This layer is responsible for connecting the data sources with the data staging layer. For example, the grocery store might process sales to customers with reward cards to a local database.

- **Data staging:** This layer is responsible for copying and formatting data into a standard format for the data warehouse layer.

- **Data warehouse:** Data is captured by many databases and organized into subject-oriented usable groupings. For example, the grocery store collects all the data from various stores across the country into this one centralized database. It is then possible to drill up or drill down and obtain information by region or by item.

- **Data mining:** Large volumes of data are searched for specific patterns. For example, if a grocery store examines paper plate sales, does it see that the same customers who purchase paper plates also purchase plastic cutlery?

- **Data mart:** At this layer resides some type of relational database that enables the user to move the data around to extract specific components. At this point, the user can extract data about data.

- **Presentation layer:** This is the top of the model, the point at which users interact with the system. This layer can include such applications as Microsoft Access and Excel.

Together these components provide the structure for a business intelligence system. Once developed, a BI system can be used in different ways, such as for scorecards, customer relationship management systems, decision support systems, document warehouses, data mining, and supply chain management.

> **NOTE**   Several terms are used to describe large data stores that are used by BI tools. These are two common terms:
>
> - **Data warehouse:** A large store of data obtained from multiple sources that is generally used to guide management decisions.
>
> - **Data lake:** A large store of raw data stored in its native format until it is needed.
>
> Whereas a data warehouse stores processed data in structured files formats, a data lake generally uses a flat architecture to store raw, unprocessed data.

Decision Support Systems

A decision support system (DSS) helps managers solve problems. A DSS uses models and mathematical techniques and usually is designed with fourth-generation programming (4GL) tools. DSS models share these common characteristics:

- Used for decision making
- Used for goal seeking
- Perform simulation
- Linkable
- Perform "what if" modeling
- Provide time series analysis

The true value of a DSS is its capability to help the user make a better decision. These systems must be flexible and adaptable, but they are not always as efficient as lower-level programming tools might be. DSS models include the following:

- **Model-driven DSS:** Uses models based on statistics, finance, or simulation. These are designed to help users make a decision.

- **Communication-driven DSS:** Designed to facilitate sharing so that more than one person can work on a task.

- **Data-driven DSS:** Can access a variety of internal and external data to analyze outcomes. Companies such as Oracle, IBM, and Microsoft build products that support data warehousing and are some of the leaders in this field.

- **Document-driven DSS:** Manipulates and manages unstructured information. eRoom is an example of a document-driven DSS.

- **Knowledge-driven DSS:** Based on rules, facts, and knowledge. It is used for problem-solving and to provide answers.

Artificial Intelligence and Expert Systems

Auditors should understand artificial intelligence and expert systems, and they need to know that these systems are used to solve complex problems. An expert system is a computer program that contains the knowledge base and set of rules needed to extrapolate new facts from existing knowledge and inputted data. The Prolog and LISP programming languages, used most in developing such systems, are both considered 5GL languages. At the heart of these systems is the knowledge base.

> **NOTE** The difference between 4GL and 5GL can be best understood by how the code is developed.
>
> *4GL programming languages* create code by defining algorithms and code logic under which the application processes data.
>
> *5GL programming languages* create code by defining business constraints. The underlying code logic and algorithms are generated by the 5GL language. In some cases, a programmer is not needed to code these business language constraints.

An emerging field in the industry is artificial intelligence (AI), which extends expert systems through self-learning and cognitive processes. In other words, AI systems attempt to think like humans but with the speed of computers. While the definition of AI continues to evolve, and it's questionable how close to human thoughts it will evolve, AI has made major breakthroughs in recent years. Consider IBM Watson, which today has medical applications. IBM Watson can read tens of thousands of medical journal articles daily and compare its understanding against a patient's diagnosis. The ability to read and understand a medical journal article is a major AI breakthrough.

The challenges with these systems include ensuring that accurate data is entered into the system, that access controls are in place, that the proper level of expertise was used in developing the system, and that the knowledge base is secure.

Customer Relationship Management

Customer relationship management (CRM) refers to the tools, techniques, and software companies use to manage their relationships with customers. CRM solutions are designed to track and record everything you need to know about your customers. This includes items such as buying history, budget, timeline, areas of interest, and future planned purchases. Products designed as CRM solutions range from simple off-the-shelf contact management applications to high-end interactive systems that combine marketing, sales, and executive information. CRM typically involves three areas:

- **Sales automation:** Automation of sales force management tasks

- **Customer service:** Automation of customer service processes, such as requests, comments, complaints, and returns

- **Enterprise marketing:** Automation of business enterprise information, such as trends, forecasts, business environment, and competition

Supply Chain Management

Supply chain management (SCM) is the science of matching buyers to sellers to improve the way businesses can acquire the raw materials they need for the products or services they sell to customers. SCM begins with raw materials and ends with finished goods that have been delivered to the customer. SCM involves five basic components:

- **Plan:** Definition of the strategy used for managing resources and monitoring the supply chain

- **Source:** The process of choosing suppliers

- **Make:** The manufacturing process

- **Deliver:** The logistics of moving goods and services to the customer

- **Return:** The systems developed to return noncompliant products to the manufacturer

SCM has become more popular as companies have been moving to a global economy with increased competition. The opportunities SCM offers focus on key items in the supply chain process. First is the focus on keeping transportation costs as low as possible while also keeping enough raw material on hand—but no more than needed. With these two items handled properly, production improves as parts and raw materials are available as needed. This helps ensure that products are available to meet customer demand, thereby preventing loss of sales due to product shortages. The key to the SCM process is cooperation between companies in the supply chain and the business. Applying these principles can reduce inventory, increase transaction speed by causing data to be exchanged in real time, and produce higher revenue.

Social Media

Social media has become increasingly important to organizations. The value of an organization's products and services is not just judged on what's deliverable but also on what is said. Increasingly, an organization's reputation is tied to what is said in social media (via Facebook, for example).

Social media departments are commonplace in large organizations. These teams drive value by doing the following:

- Increasing brand awareness
- Improving brand loyalty
- Attempting to convert new customers
- Enriching the customer experience
- Performing damage control when negative events occur.

Auditing social media is challenging because what appears on social media is not under the direct control of an organization. Consequently, an auditor needs to keep social media assessments focused on the organization's social media strategy, how it communicates expected behavior of its employees on social media, and what mechanisms it puts in place to react to social media events. An auditor should be looking for a well-thought-out and well-defined social media approach. Once the social media approach is understood, the auditor can focus on the effectiveness of execution against the strategy. Some key areas of a social media examination include the following:

1. Business social media strategy
2. Execution metrics against strategy such as conversion rates over social media
3. Employee policies and training on expected behavior
4. Capability to monitor social media for references to the organization
5. Response strategy when negative or false social media stories emerge

Chapter Summary

An auditor needs to know how to audit applications, systems, and related processes. This requires a broad understanding of business and convergence of technology to drive value and deliver business objectives.

This chapter explores a risk-based approach through the definition of an audit universe. It discusses how flowcharts help us learn the process and the functionality of an application. This chapter also discusses in detail application input, process, and output controls. The chapter reviews how to test and validate these controls in a variety of ways, including using snapshots, mapping, and tracing and tagging.

This chapter also considers e-commerce and social media risks to the business. It looks broadly at a number of common business applications to help you better understand how technology supports the business, including supply chain management (SCM), customer relationship management (CRM), decision support systems (DSSs), and business intelligence (BI). Collectively, these applications and tools provide a business with the ability to define how data is handled, access limits placed on the data, and understand how data is transformed into useful business information.

Exam Preparation Tasks

As mentioned in the section "How to Use This Book" in the Introduction, you have a couple choices for exam preparation: the exercises here; Chapter 10, "Final Preparation;" and the exam simulation questions on the book's companion web page (www.informit.com/title/9780789758446).

Review All the Key Topics

Review the most important topics in this chapter, noted with the Key Topic icon in the outer margin of the page. Table 6-9 lists these key topics and the page number on which each is found.

Table 6-9   Key Topics for Chapter 6

Key Topic Element	Description	Page Number
List	Criteria for assessing the risk to functions and processes	236
Table 6-2	Business process control examples	237
Table 6-3	Processing edit control examples	239
Table 6-4	Processing control techniques	240
List	Data category types	241
Table 6-5	Observation and testing	244
List	ACID test descriptions	245
Table 6-6	Continuous audit techniques	247

Key Topic Element	Description	Page Number
Table 6-7	Auditing applications	248
List	Steps an auditor should follow during the development process	250
Table 6-8	Audit controls and quality assurance checks	251
List	Basic email operation	255

Define Key Terms

Define the following key terms from this chapter and check your answers against the glossary:

ACID test, application controls, artificial intelligence (AI), audit universe, automated controls, balance data, batch control, data lake, data warehouse, e-commerce, entity integrity, flowchart, general controls, hash total, long-term business goals, manual controls, short-term business goals, static data, system control parameters, transaction files

Exercises

6-1 Software Application Audit

Estimated time: 60 minutes

In this exercise, you perform a basic audit of a sample of source code.

1. Pick an open source software application on which to perform a security audit. You can use standard Linux utilities or download a simple C program from www.cis.temple.edu/~ingargio/cis71/code/. After you choose a program, download it and save the source code on your local computer.

2. Determine the lines of source code. Count the lines of code manually and record your result here:

   _____

3. Next, use a tool that automatically counts the lines of code for you. For instance, you can cut and paste the code into Excel and look at the last row number and enter the value here:

   _____

   Do the numbers entered here agree with those you calculated in step 2?

4. Spend some time looking at the source code you downloaded. Look for anything that might be a problem or that you do not understand. Document any findings here:

_____

_____

_____

5. Although a manual audit of a small program is possible, the task becomes much more difficult on larger programs. To ease that task, some programs automatically look at the code. One such tool is Codebrag tool, which you can download from http://codebrag.com. After you download the program, install it on your computer.

6. Codebrag is an open source scanning tool that enables an auditor to search for program trouble spots and can suggest remedies. Although it might not find every problem, it can detect potential buffer overflows, race conditions, and other common problems. Run Codebrag (or another tool) against the open source software application in step 1.

7. Did Codebrag (or another tool that you used) find any security holes or potential vulnerabilities? If so, describe them here:

_____

_____

_____

This exercise demonstrates how manual methods of auditing, such as counting lines of code or examining code for potential errors, can be supplemented by automated tools that aid in the process.

Review Questions

1. Of the following options, which process is not an application system testing methodology?

   a. Snapshots

   b. Entity integrity

   c. Mapping

   d. Base case system evaluation

2. Which of the following is a continuous auditing technique that detects items that meet specific criteria?

   a. Audit hooks

   b. Snapshots

   c. Integrated test facilities

   d. Continuous and intermittent simulation

3. A decision support system should be used appropriately. A DSS is designed to do which of the following?

   a. Use structured models to solve complex problems

   b. Support nontraditional support activities

   c. Answer rigidly structured problems

   d. Answer less structured problems

4. You have been asked to recommend a control that can detect exceptions to the following: "An order is normally for no more than 20 items, yet this order is for 2,000." Which control works best to detect this type of exception?

   a. Validity check

   b. Range check

   c. Reasonableness check

   d. Limit check

5. What type of programming language are decision support systems most commonly developed with?

   a. 2GL

   b. 3GL

   c. 4GL

   d. 5GL

6. What is the best way to describe the difference between a data warehouse and a data lake?

   a. Data warehouses always contain customer information

   b. Data warehouses always contain raw data, while data lakes always contain structure and highly processed data.

   c. Data lakes always contain raw data, while data warehouses always contain structure and highly processed data.

   d. There is no difference between a data warehouse and a data lake.

7. When referring to electronic data interchange (EDI), which of the following statements would be most accurate?

   a. EDI has no impact on internal or external controls.

   b. EDI reduces internal controls.

   c. EDI increases internal controls.

   d. EDI has no impact on internal controls.

8. What control is specifically used after data has been entered into a system but before it has been processed?

   a. Editing

   b. Sequence check

   c. Balancing

   d. Input authorization

9. You have been asked to recommend a continuous audit technique. Which of the following techniques is considered the least complex?

   a. Audit hooks

   b. Systems control audit review file and embedded audit modules

   c. Snapshots

   d. Continuous and intermittent simulation

10. All the following are required activities during the project management process in the design and development phase except for which one?

    a. Studying system flowcharts

    b. Examining proposed test plans

    c. Evaluating output controls

    d. Examining proposed audit trails

Suggested Readings and Resources

- **Auditing the software development life cycle:** www.isaca.org/chapters3/ Atlanta/AboutOurChapter/Documents/GW2014/Auditing%20SDLC%20 _%20Van%20Stone%20Kamara.pdf

- **ACID compliance:** www.fredosaurus.com/notes-db/transactions/acid.html

- **Continuous auditing:** www.iia.org.uk/media/1042659/gtag03-continuous-auditing-2nd-edition.pdf

- **Project management basics:** www.managementhelp.org/plan_dec/project/ project.htm

- **Data mining case studies:** www.dataminingcasestudies.com

- **Supply Chain Management Review:** www.scmr.com

- **SQL Server database security audit:** http://isaca-denver.org/Chapter-Resources/ISACA201601SQLServerSecurityAudit.pdf

- **IT audits of cloud and SaaS:** www.isaca.org/Journal/archives/2010/Volume-3/ Pages/IT-Audits-of-Cloud-and-Saas.aspx

The following exam domain is partially covered in this chapter:

Domain 4—Information Systems Operations, Maintenance and Service Management

This chapter covers the following topics:

- **Service Management Frameworks:** All organizations must function with some type of framework and policies.

- **Fundamental Technologies:** While auditors are not expected to be IT experts, they must have an understanding of operating systems and databases.

- **Network Infrastructure:** IT auditing requires a basic understanding of IT infrastructure and the TCP/IP protocol suite.

- **Capacity Planning and Systems Performance Monitoring:** Understanding bottlenecks and system performance is another skill that auditors should possess.

CHAPTER 7

Systems Maintenance and Service Management

This chapter introduces frameworks and fundamental networking technology. Not all networks are created equal. Different protocols are used on local area networks (LANs), metropolitan area networks (MANs), and wide area networks (WANs). Some of these protocols, such as Transmission Control Protocol/Internet Protocol (TCP/IP), might be familiar to you; others, such as Multiprotocol Label Switching (MPLS), might not. A CISA exam candidate must understand these protocols and the equipment that interconnects a network including switches, routers, and firewalls. The design of the network and the type of equipment used can have a big impact on the level of security provided. An IS auditor must be aware of these issues and also must be able to examine the level of services provided by the network. In addition, an auditor must be able to determine the capacity constraints of the network. Just as every modern freeway has a maximum level of capacity, so does a network. It is important to know the current demand and expected future demand requirements. This knowledge provides for the proper planning and budgeting of current and future control requirements. This chapter begins by examining service management frameworks.

"Do I Know This Already?" Quiz

The "Do I Know This Already?" quiz allows you to assess whether you should read this entire chapter thoroughly or jump to the "Exam Preparation Tasks" section. If you are in doubt about your answers to these questions or your own assessment of your knowledge of the topics, read the entire chapter. Table 7-1 lists the major headings in this chapter and their corresponding "Do I Know This Already?" quiz questions. You can find the answers at the bottom of the page following the quiz and in Appendix A, "Answers to the 'Do I Know This Already?' Quizzes and Review Questions."

Table 7-1   "Do I Know This Already?" Section-to-Question Mapping

Foundation Topics Section	Questions
Service Management Frameworks	1–2
Fundamental Technologies	3–5
Network Infrastructure	6–8
Capacity Planning and Systems Performance Monitoring	9–10

CAUTION   The goal of self-assessment is to gauge your mastery of the topics in this chapter. If you do not know the answer to a question or are only partially sure of the answer, you should mark that question as incorrect for purposes of the self-assessment. Giving yourself credit for an answer you correctly guess skews your self-assessment results and might provide you with a false sense of security.

1. The COBIT 5 processes are split into how many areas?

    a. 1

    b. 2

    c. 3

    d. 4

2. Which of the following does not offer a certification for conformance?

    a. CMM

    b. COBIT

    c. ISO 20000

    d. FitSM

3. Which of the following is the combining of several low-sensitivity items to produce a high-sensitivity data item?

    a. Inference

    b. Aggregation

    c. Tuple

    d. Data mining

4. Which of the following stores passwords in the shadow file?

   a. Fedora Linux 9.0

   b. Windows 7

   c. Windows 10

   d. Windows Server 2016

5. The ACID test most closely pertains to which of the following?

   a. Utility software

   b. Audit software

   c. Database software

   d. Operating system software

6. When auditing infrastructure, what would be a concern related to finding a managed switch with the default username and password?

   a. Access to the switch.

   b. The ability to access a SPAN port.

   c. The ability to examine the CAM table.

   d. It is not an issue.

7. At which layer of the OSI model is UDP found?

   a. Presentation

   b. Network

   c. Session

   d. Transport

8. At which layer of the OSI model is IP found?

   a. Presentation

   b. Network

   c. Session

   d. Transport

9. Which of the following tools would allow an auditor to examine network traffic statistics?

   a. Wireshark

   b. Tripwire

   c. Snort

   d. NMAP

10. Before beginning an audit of a cloud-based system, the most important item to reference is which of the following?

   a. Cloud best practices

   b. COBIT

   c. SAS-70

   d. The contract

Foundation Topics

Service Management Frameworks

Organizations can use service management frameworks to align the delivery of IT services with the needs of the company, with the goal of making business processes efficient and reducing costs. These enterprise architectures (EAs) can be used to help determine how an organization can most effectively achieve its current and future objectives. These frameworks can include COBIT, ITIL, FitSM, ISO 20000, and eTOM.

IT Infrastructure Library (ITIL) is one well-known example of a service management framework. ITIL helps everybody operate more efficiently and is a globally recognized set of best practices and standards that support IT service management (ITSM).

Table 7-2 lists some examples of frameworks and best practices, which are described in more detail in the following sections.

Table 7-2   Frameworks and Best Practices

Name	Overview
ITIL	A leading service management standard
FitSM	A lightweight service management standard
ISO 20000	One of the first service management standards
eTOM	Designed for the telecommunications market

NOTE   Regardless of which framework is used, an auditor should consider conducting periodic reviews to determine whether the choosen framework continues to meet compliance and complies with the organization's objectives and enterprise architecture.

COBIT

COBIT (Control Objectives for Information and Related Technologies) is a good-practice framework created by international professional association ISACA for information technology (IT) management and IT governance. COBIT provides an implementable set of controls over IT and organizes them around a logical framework of IT-related processes and enablers. COBIT is divided into governance and management areas. These 2 areas contain a total of 5 domains and 37 processes. These are listed here:

- Governance of enterprise IT
  - Evaluate, Direct and Monitor (EDM)—5 processes
- Management of enterprise IT
  - Align, Plan and Organize (APO)—13 processes
  - Build, Acquire and Implement (BAI)—10 processes
  - Deliver, Service and Support (DSS)—6 processes
  - Monitor, Evaluate and Assess (MEA)—3 processes

FitSM

FitSM is a family of standards designed for service management in IT service provision. It is designed as a free, lightweight set of guidelines. While it is an option for organizations and can be audited, there is no certification for conformance. Therefore, a company cannot be "FitSM certified." FitSM is divided into the following areas:

- **FitSM-0:** Overview and vocabulary
- **FitSM-1:** Requirements
- **FitSM-2:** Objectives and activities
- **FitSM-3:** Role model
- **FitSM-4:** Templates and samples
- **FitSM-5:** Guides
- **FitSM-6:** Maturity assessment

ISO 20000

ISO/IEC 20000 is the first international standard for IT service management. It grew out of the British Standards (BS) 15000 and is used by organizations seeking to demonstrate best practice and excellence in IT management. The standard is used to help validate and provide benchmarks for continuously

Answers to the "Do I Know This Already?" Quiz:

1. B; 2. D; 3. B; 4. A; 5. C; 6. B; 7. D; 8. B; 9. A; 10. D

improving the delivery of IT services. ISO 20000 has 12 parts, including the design, transition, delivery, and improvement of services that fulfill service requirements and provide value for both the customer and the service provider.

eTOM

Enhanced Telecom Operations Map (eTOM) is a widely used set of standards created and designed for the world communications market. eTOM focuses on current telecommunications technologies such as Internet telephony, broadband, and DSL. It is updated on a regular basis to keep up with Internet standards/specifications and hardware updates. eTOM is currently in version 14. The model consists of processes at five levels. The architecture follows customer-centric processes, such as the initial sale, customer support, billing, marketing, follow-up customer support, and after-service support.

Fundamental Technologies

An auditor needs to have an understanding of an organization's IT environment. This includes items such as operating systems, software, storage, databases, and any licensing agreements. These topics are discussed in the following sections.

Operating Systems

An operating system (OS) is key to computer operation because it is the computer program that controls software resources and interacts with system hardware. The OS performs everything from low-level tasks to higher-level interaction with the user. The OS is responsible for managing resources such as the processor, memory, disk space, RAM, and so on. The OS also provides a stable, defined platform that applications can use. This allows the application to deal with the OS and not have to directly address the hardware. The OS is responsible for managing the following key resources (see Figure 7-1):

- **Input devices:** Keyboard, mouse, microphone, webcam, and so on
- **Output devices:** Monitor, printer, soundcard, and so on
- **Memory:** RAM, ROM, CMOS, virtual memory, and so on
- **CPU usage:** Available time, processing order
- **Network communication:** Modems, network interface card (NIC), Bluetooth, wireless, and so on
- **External storage:** DVD drive, CD-ROM drive, hard drive, USB drives, and so on

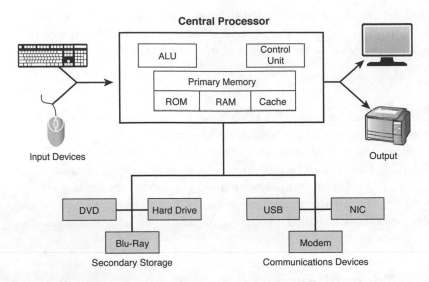

Figure 7-1 Operating System Management Duties

An OS has the capability to interact with the CPU in different ways so that there are different levels of control. In user mode, the operator has limited ability to perform privileged functions. In supervisory mode, the user has total access to the security kernel and has complete access to all memory, devices, and instructions. Some system utilities and other processes run in supervisory mode and, therefore, must be closely controlled because they could be used to bypass normal security mechanisms. Some types of malware, such as rootkits, have the capability to run in supervisory or kernel mode. This means they can corrupt the kernel and do basically anything they want, including lie to the user about their presence, thereby avoiding detection. An auditor will most likely have to deal with multiple operating systems, including the following:

- **Microsoft:** Windows 7, 8, 10, Server 2012, and Server 2016

- **Apple:** OS X and iOS

- **Linux:** Fedora, Ubuntu, and Kali

- **UNIX:** Free BSD, SCO UnixWare, and Solaris

These operating systems can be configured in many different ways. For example, Windows computers store local passwords in the Security Accounts Manager (SAM) for local accounts and in Active Directory (AD) for domain accounts. These accounts are locked with SYSKEY. Linux stores passwords in the etc/shadow file, which is readable only by the root account.

> **TIP**   CISA candidates should know that any user allowed to run programs in kernel mode can bypass any type of security mechanism and gain complete control of the system. Many system utilities run in supervisory mode and should be under strict control.

Secondary Storage

In addition to using long-term storage of information and programs, an OS can use secondary storage. A modern OS can also use secondary storage for *virtual memory*—the combination of the computer's primary memory, RAM, and secondary storage, the hard drive. By combining these two technologies, the OS can make the CPU believe that it has much more memory than it actually has. If the OS is running short on RAM, it can instruct the CPU to use the hard drive as storage. Virtual memory uses the hard drive to save data in pages that can be swapped back and forth between the hard drive and RAM, as needed.

Although memory plays an important part in the world of storage, other long-term types of storage are also needed. One of these is sequential storage. Anyone who is old enough to remember the Commodore 64 knows about sequential storage; these early computers used a cassette tape recorder to store programs. Tape drives are a type of sequential storage that must be read sequentially from beginning to end. Indexed sequential storage is similar to sequential storage, except that it logically orders data according to a key and then accesses the data based on the key. Finally, the direct access method does not require a sequential read; the system can identify the location of the information and go directly to that location to read the data.

Utility Software

Utility software is any software program or application designed to help analyze, configure, optimize, or maintain a computer. A utility software program performs a very specific task, usually related to managing system resources. One good example is antivirus/anti-malware software. While some might argue that anti-malware software will not detect everything, it is a line of defense. From an auditing perspective, anti-malware should be seen as a must on servers and workstations. After all, these devices are connected to a network and maintain the ability to spread viruses, worms, and other forms of malware through the network. To consider its importance, look no further than the WannaCry ransomware that is believed to have infected more than 230,000 computers in one day.

Operating systems have a number of utilities for managing disk drives, printers, and other devices, including disk defragmenting tools, printer software, and network-attached storage (NAS) software.

Database-Management Systems

Databases provide a convenient method by which to catalog, index, and retrieve information. A database consists of a collection of related records, such as name, address, phone number, and date of birth. The structured description of the objects of these databases and their relationships is known as a *schema*. Databases are widely used. For example, if you go online to search for flight times from Houston to Las Vegas, the information is pulled from a database. When you pay for a flight, your stored credit card number that was previously provided to the airline is also pulled from a database. As a CISA candidate, you need to know these database-related terms:

- **Aggregation:** The process of combining several low-sensitivity items to produce a high-sensitivity data item.

- **Attribute:** An attribute of a component of a database, such as a table, field, or column.

- **Field:** The smallest unit of data within a database.

- **Foreign key:** An attribute in one table whose value matches the primary key in another table.

- **Granularity:** Control over someone's view of a database. Highly granular databases have the capability to restrict certain fields or rows from unauthorized individuals.

- **Relation:** Data that is represented by a collection of tables.

The data elements required to define a database are known as *metadata*—or data about data. For example, the number 310 has no meaning, but when described with other data, it may be understood as information that represents the telephone area code used for Beverly Hills and Malibu residents.

Organizations treasure data and the relationships that can be deduced between the individual data elements. That's *data mining*, the process of analyzing data to find and understand patterns and relationships between the data. The patterns discovered in data can help companies understand their competitors and understand usage patterns of their customers so they can carry out targeted marketing.

For example, in most convenience stores, the diapers are located near the refrigerated section of the store, where beer and sodas are kept. The store owners have placed these items close to each other because data mining has revealed that men are usually the ones who buy diapers in convenience stores, and they are also the primary demographic to purchase beer. By placing the diapers close by, both items increase in total sales. Although many of us might not naturally think of these types of relationships, data mining can uncover how seemingly unrelated items might actually be connected.

Data mining operations require the collection of large amounts of data. All this data can be stored in a *data warehouse*, a database that contains data from many different databases. These warehouses have been combined, integrated, and structured so that they can provide trend analysis and be used to make business decisions.

Many companies use knowledge-management systems to tie together all of an organization's information databases, document management, business processes, and information systems into one knowledge repository. This is referred to as *customer relationship management (CRM)*. It's how businesses determine how to interact with their customers. A knowledge-management system can interpret the data derived from a CRM system and automate the knowledge extraction. This knowledge-discovery process takes the form of data mining, in which patterns are discovered through artificial intelligence techniques.

Database Structure

Databases can be centralized or distributed, depending on the database-management system (DBMS) that is implemented. A DBMS enables a database administrator to control all aspects of the database, including design, functionality, and security. Per ISACA, three primary types of database structures exist:

- Hierarchical database-management systems (HDMS)
- Network database-management systems (NDMS)
- Relational database-management systems (RDMS)

With an HDMS, the database has a parent–child structure. These are considered 1:N (one-to-many) mappings. Each record can have only one owner; because of this restriction, a hierarchical database often cannot be used to relate to structures in the real world. However, it is easy to implement, modify, and search. Figure 7-2 shows an example of an HDMS.

An NDMS is based on mathematical set theory. This type of database was developed (in 1971) to be more flexible than a hierarchical database. The network database model is considered a lattice structure because each record can have multiple parent and child records. Although this design can work well in stable environments, it can be extremely complex. Figure 7-3 shows an example of an NDMS.

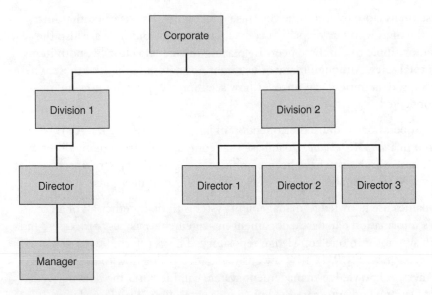

Figure 7-2   Hierarchical Database

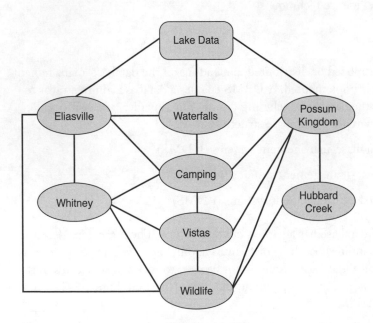

Figure 7-3   Network Database

An RDMS database is a collection of tables that are linked by their primary keys. This type of database is based on set theory and relational calculations. Many organizations use software based on the relational database design, which uses a structure in which the data and the relationship between the data are organized in tables known as *tuples*. Most relational databases use SQL as their query language. Figure 7-4 shows an example of an RDMS.

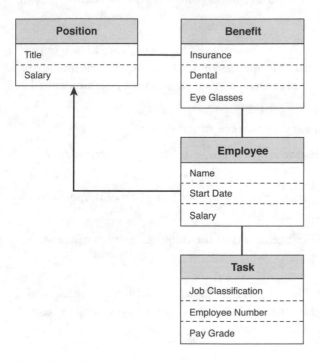

Figure 7-4 Relational Database

TIP Knowledge of databases is important because an auditor might be asked to evaluate database management practices to determine the confidentiality, integrity, and availability of databases, as well as whether they are optimized.

All databases need controls that protect the integrity of the data. Databases should be reviewed periodically to verify that the data quality is adequate and that any changes are made in a controlled fashion so they continue to meet the organization's objectives. Database transactions are protected through the use of controls. Integrity must be protected during storage and transactions. Controls to protect the integrity of the data during storage include the following:

- Enforcing security so that access to the database is restricted

- Defining levels of access for those who must have access to the database

- Establishing controls to verify the accuracy, completeness, and consistency of the data

Controls can be put into place during transactions. The controls are known as the ACID test. The ACID test is a set of properties of database transactions intended to guarantee validity in the event of errors, power failures, etc. These are defined as follows:

- **Atomicity:** The results of a transaction are either all or nothing.

- **Consistency:** Transactions are processed only if they meet system-defined integrity constraints.

- **Isolation:** The results of a transaction are invisible to all other transactions until the original transaction is complete.

- **Durability:** After completion, the results of the transaction are permanent.

TIP   You might be asked in the CISA exam about database management and how to tell if it is adequate for handling transactions. Adequate systems have atomicity, consistency, isolation, and durability. This is described as the ACID test.

Software Licensing Issues

Have you ever stopped to read an end-user license agreement (EULA)? (For example, take a look at the 14-page EULA for Windows 10, at https://www.microsoft.com/en-us/Useterms/Retail/Windows/10/UseTerms_Retail_Windows_10_English.htm.) Many users never read the EULAs they accept all the time. An EULA is a type of contract between the software manufacturer and the end user. It specifies the terms of the conditions under which the end user can use the computer program or software. EULAs and software licensing are issues of concern for a CISA because companies have a legal and moral obligation to use software only in an approved manner. Companies caught using illegal software can be subjected to fines, legal fees, and bad press; they may be identified as companies that use illegal software. The Business Software Alliance pursues companies for using illegal software. According to its website (www.bsa.org), in one case, the defendant received a prison term of more than seven years. IS auditors should review policies and procedures to verify that the company has rules in place that prohibit the use of illegal software. Some companies have employees sign an agreement stating that they will not install or copy software illegally. An auditor should also look at random samples of users' computers to verify that they are loaded only with programs that appear on the company's list of approved programs.

Other software licensing controls include the following:

- Disabling the local installation of software

- Installing application metering

- Using thin clients

- Performing regular compliance scans from the network

TIP   The CISA exam might ask you about ways to reduce illegal use of software. One useful control to prevent unlawful duplication of software on multiple computers at a company's site is to purchase site licensing. This allows the software to be loaded on as many computers as needed at the organization.

Digital Rights Management

Digital rights management (DRM) is a big concern and will become bigger in the coming years. There is a good chance you may be reading a digital version of this book right now. Most likely the music you listen to is in some digital form, not a cassette or a record album, and the movies you watch are streamed from a service provider. For the providers of these services, control of this information and proper licensing are more difficult than ever before. This is why DRM is more important than ever before.

DRM is a structured approach to copyright protection for all forms of digital media. The idea is to restrict and prevent unauthorized redistribution of digital media and to block consumers from copying content in any forms that are not explicitly allowed.

Network Infrastructure

The network infrastructure encompasses all the protocols, hardware, and systems used to provide network services. Networks can be local or distant. Local networks must use an agreed-upon set of protocols and a standardized cabling method.

This might be coaxial cable, twisted-pair cable, or even a wireless system. Distant networks must also have an agreed-upon way to communicate with other distant systems. They, too, need cabling and protocols to operate. Without agreed-upon standards, the Internet would not be possible. TCP/IP is one of these common protocols. The equipment to connect all these systems must also be capable of interacting with the various protocols and communication schemes. Routers are one such piece of equipment. Routers form the backbone of the Internet.

Network Types

Throughout time, there has always been a need to share information. Years ago, that might have been by paper, fax, or phone. Today the computer network has taken over as the primary way to share information. The development of the desktop computer in the 1980s caused a paradigm shift. Much of this change would not have been possible without the capability to link desktops, laptops, tablets, and smartphones together. Some of that work had been done decades earlier. In 1975, the Digital, Intel, and Xerox (DIX) group released the first official Ethernet product.

Ethernet is the standard for *local area networks* (LANs). The computers and other devices in a LAN communicate over a small geographic area, such as the following:

- A section of a one-story building
- The whole floor of a small building
- Several buildings on a small campus
- A work office or home network of computers

Although it is nice to have computers and other networked devices communicate locally, many times the need exists to communicate on a larger scale. For devices that need to communicate on a citywide level, the *metropolitan area network* (*MAN*) was created. A MAN is a network that interconnects a region larger than what's covered by a LAN. A MAN can include a city, geographic region, or other large area.

If you work for a company that owns several buildings located in different states or countries, it's part of a *wide area network* (*WAN*). A WAN spans geographic distances that are too large for LANs and MANs. WANs are connected by routers. When two LANs are connected over a distance, they form a WAN.

A *personal area network* (*PAN*) allows a variety of personal and handheld electronic devices to communicate over a short range. A subset of the PAN is a *wireless PAN* (*WPAN*). There are also *global area networks* (*GANs*). A GAN is a network composed of different interconnected networks that cover an unlimited geographic area.

Another network term worth reviewing is a *storage area network* (*SAN*), which is used to connect multiple servers to a centralized pool of disk storage. SANs improve system administration by allowing the centralization of storage instead of requiring management of hundreds of servers, each with its own disks.

During an audit, network drawings and physical diagrams should be reviewed to verify that they are complete and current. These documents can serve as a starting point for any assessment.

TIP   CISA candidates need to know that good network documentation proves an excellent starting point for an audit.

Network Standards and Protocols

Communication systems need some type of model for devices to communicate and understand what other devices need. Over the years, various standards have been developed to make this possible. These standards and protocols set up rules of operation, or *protocols*. Protocols describe how requests, messages, and other signals are formatted and transmitted over a network. A network will function as long as all computers are consistent in following the same set of rules for communication. Protocols, such as TCP/IP, and standards, such as those included in the Open Systems Interconnection (OSI) reference model, are examples of network rules and standards. They have helped build the Internet and the worldwide data networks we have today. The goal of any set of network standards is to provide the following:

- Interoperability

- Availability

- Flexibility

- Maintainability

Many groups have been working toward meeting this challenge, including the following:

- International Organization for Standardization (ISO)

- Institute of Electrical and Electronics Engineers (IEEE)

- Internet Engineering Task Force (IETF)

- International Telecommunications Union–Telecommunications Sector (ITU-T)

The next section discusses a model created by one of these organizations, the ISO, in greater detail.

The OSI Reference Model

The ISO set the worldwide standards for its work in developing a common approach to networking and is recognized for its development of the Open Systems Interconnection (OSI) reference model. ISO's goal was for all vendors to adopt its standard networking architecture for all hardware and software products, thereby enabling all network users to communicate with each other regardless of the computer products owned or used. The OSI model, developed in 1984, defines networking as a seven-layer process. Within the OSI model, the data is passed down from layer to layer. It begins at the application layer and ends at the physical layer, as shown in Figure 7-5. The data is then transmitted over the medium toward the target device. The seven layers of the OSI model are application, presentation, session, transport, network, data link, and physical.

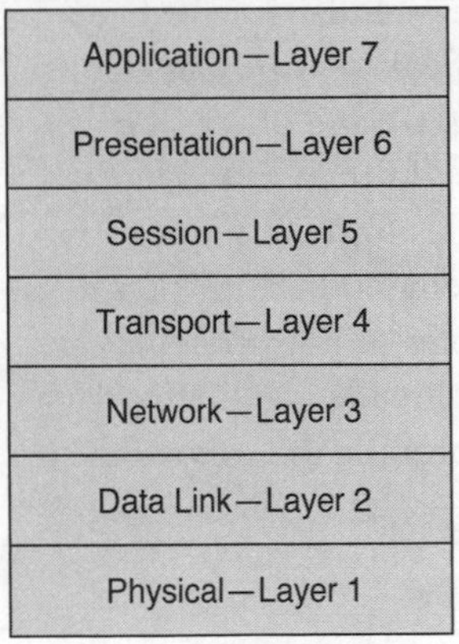

Application—Layer 7
Presentation—Layer 6
Session—Layer 5
Transport—Layer 4
Network—Layer 3
Data Link—Layer 2
Physical—Layer 1

Figure 7-5   The OSI Model

Most people remember the OSI model by one of the many acronyms that have been thought of over the years. One way to remember it is to use the following mnemonic device:

All (application—Layer 7)

People (presentation—Layer 6)

Seem (session—Layer 5)

To (transport—Layer 4)

Need (network—Layer 3)

Data (data link—Layer 2)

Processing (physical—Layer 1)

The following sections describe and examine how each layer of the OSI model is designed to operate. Let's get started by reviewing the application layer and then work our way down the stack.

> **TIP**   CISA candidates need to know the seven layers of the OSI model (from Layer 1 to Layer 7): physical, data link, network, transport, session, presentation, and application layer.

The Application Layer

Layer 7 is known as the application layer. Recognized as the top layer of the OSI model, this layer serves as the window for application services. This is the layer that users are most knowledgeable of. The application layer serves as the interface for applications, such as email programs and web browsers. Without the application layer, email and the web would not exist, and our computers would be unable to interpret and sort the data transmitted by other computers. Layer 7 is not the application itself but rather the channel through which applications communicate. If you think of this in terms of preparing to send a present to a friend, the application layer would be equivalent to buying the gift.

The Presentation Layer

Layer 6 is known as the presentation layer. Consider the gift analogy from the preceding section. At Layer 6, this is when you are now ready to take the gift to the post office. It will require packaging. Although some might be content placing the gift in a paper package, the post office requires a specific type of box if you want to send the gift by priority mail. The presentation layer is concerned about presentation. Data must be formatted so the application layer can understand and interpret the data. The presentation layer is skilled in translation; its duties include encrypting data, changing or converting the character set, and performing protocol conversion. Items such as ASCII would be found at this layer. Data compression is also performed at the presentation layer.

The Session Layer

Layer 5 is known as the session layer. Its purpose is to allow two applications on different computers to establish and coordinate a session. A *session* is a connection between two computers. Ports are defined at the session layer; they are used to identify the application being used. For example, port 22 is used for the Secure Shell (SSH) protocol, and port 443 is used for Hypertext Transfer Protocol Secure (HTTPS). When a data transfer is completed, the session layer is responsible for tearing down the session.

The Transport Layer

Layer 4 is known as the transport layer. Whereas the network layer routes your information to its destination, the transport layer ensures completeness by handling end-to-end error recovery and flow control. Without the transport layer, the network would be unreliable. There are two main transport layer protocols:

- **Transmission Control Protocol (TCP):** TCP is a connection-oriented protocol that provides reliable communication through the use of handshakes, acknowledgments, error detection handling, and session teardown.

- **User Datagram Protocol (UDP):** UDP is a protocol without a connection that offers speed and low overhead as its primary advantages.

For example, when you take your package to the post office, you must decide how to ship it. Should you send it return receipt with delivery confirmation (TCP), or should you just pay for parcel post (UDP) and hope it gets there?

The Network Layer

Layer 3, the network layer, is concerned with routers and routing. The network layer is responsible for the movement of data from network A to network B. The network layer is the home of the *Internet Protocol* (*IP*). IP acts as the postal service, determining the best route from the source to the target network. Like the postal service, IP does not examine the contents of the packet (letter or package); it simply makes a best effort at delivery. Network-layer components include the following:

- Routers
- Routing protocols
- Packet filters

The Data Link Layer

Layer 2, the data link layer, is responsible for formatting and organizing data before sending it to the physical layer. It is also responsible for error handling. The data link layer must frame up packets and deal with the local delivery of traffic within a single LAN. A *frame* is a logical structure in which data can be placed. When a frame reaches the target device, the data link layer is responsible for stripping off the data frame and passing the data packet up to the network layer. Data link layer components include the following:

- Switches

- Network interface cards (NICs)

- Media access control (MAC) addresses

The Physical Layer

Layer 1 is known as the physical layer. Bit-level communication occurs here. The bits have no defined meaning on the wire, but the physical layer defines how long each bit lasts and how it is transmitted and received. All the electrical, mechanical, and functional requirements of the network are specified at this level. The physical layer even establishes parameters to define whether a data bit is a one or zero. Returning to our previous example, the physical layer is equivalent to the mail carrier's truck, where your package and many others are all loaded and bound for delivery. Physical-layer components include the following:

- Copper cabling

- Fiber cabling

- Wireless system components

- Wall jacks and connectors

- Ethernet hubs

TIP   Before taking the CISA exam, make sure you understand what types of functions occur at each layer of the OSI model. For example, the transport layer is home to both TCP and UDP.

At the bottom of the OSI model or stack, the data is broken into electrical signals and transmitted on the fiber, wire, or wireless system used. When the targeted system receives it, the information is pushed back up the stack until it arrives at the application layer and is passed to the appropriate service. Figure 7-6 illustrates this process.

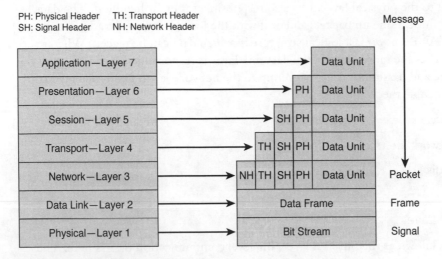

Figure 7-6   Processing Data with the OSI Model

Network Services and Applications

Networks can provide a wide array of applications and enable users to share common services such as file sharing. Networks give users the capability to share files and folders with other users. Users can have read, write, or full control. A common means of sharing files remotely is *File Transfer Protocol* (*FTP*), which enables movement of files from one computer to another. FTP operates on ports 20 and 21. The IETF developed Remote Network Monitoring (RMON) MIB to support monitoring and protocol analysis on data traffic found at OSI Layer 1 and Layer 2. traceroute is another network diagnostic tool; it is used to track the pathway taken by a packet on an IP network from source to destination. ping is a basic Internet program that allows a user to verify that a particular IP address exists and can accept requests. ping functions by sending Internet Control Message Protocol (ICMP) echo requests and waiting for echo replies to be sent from devices that have successfully processed the command.

Email service is another common network service and one of the most widely used network services. Email uses two protocols—one to send email and one to receive email. *Simple Mail Transfer Protocol* (*SMTP*) is used to send email. It is designed for the exchange of electronic mail between network systems. All types of computers can exchange messages with SMTP, which operates on port 25. When you receive email, a second protocol is needed. Historically, this was *Post Office Protocol* version

3 (*POP3*), which provides a simple, standardized way for users to access mail and download messages from a mail server to their own computer. POP3 operates on port 110. Today, however, most email services use *Internet Message Access Protocol* (*IMAP*), which has advantages over POP3 because the email messages are not downloaded to the end user's computer. IMAP leaves the messages on the server so they can be used and manipulated by any number of devices, such as smartphones, tablets, and laptops. IMAP is defined in RFC 3501 and uses port 143.

NOTE   An auditor should understand that many of the original protocols designed for TCP/IP—such as FTP, HTTP, Telnet, TFTP, POP, and SMTP—were designed for usability and not security. An auditor should ensure that secure replacements are used instead and that whenever that is not possible, sufficient controls are deployed to reduce risk to an acceptable level.

Print services are another well-used network service. Print services enable users to use network printers to manage and print documents to remote network printers. *Terminal-emulation software* (*TES*) is a category of network service that enables users to access remote hosts, which then appear as local devices. Historically, an example of TES is *Telnet*, which allows a client at one site to establish a session with a host at another site. The program passes the information typed at the client's keyboard to the host computer system. Telnet, which operates on port 23, sends passwords and other information in cleartext and is not secure. As an auditor, you should look for *Secure Shell* (SSH) to be used instead of Telnet. Other examples of terminal emulation include Remote Desktop Protocol (RDP) and Remote Desktop Services (RDS).

A network-management service is used to control and maintain a network. IT does so by monitoring the status of devices and reporting this information to a management console. Network-management services allow the effective use of the network and help alert staff to problems before they become critical. *Simple Network Management Protocol* (*SNMP*) is the protocol commonly used for network management. SNMP was designed to be an efficient and inexpensive protocol for monitoring networks. SNMP allows agents to gather network statistics and report that information back to its management station. Most corporations use some type of SNMP management. SNMP operates on port 161. It's important for an auditor to understand that SNMP has gone through several changes. Versions 1 and 2 send data and community strings via cleartext. Version 3 uses encryption.

Directory services are the means by which network services are identified and mapped. Directory services perform services similar to that of a phone book as they correlate addresses to names. An example of directory services is *Domain Name Service* (*DNS*), which performs address translation. DNS converts *fully qualified domain names (FQDNs)* into numeric IP addresses—and vice versa. An example of an FQDN is www.thesolutionfirm.com. DNS can resolve this name to its proper IP address, 112.10.8.5. DNS operates on port 53.

No discussion on network services would be complete without mentioning the Internet and *Hypertext Transfer Protocol (HTTP)*. HTTP has helped make the Web the popular tool it is today. The HTTP connection model is known as a *stateless connection*. HTTP is a request/response protocol, in which a client sends a request and a server sends a response. HTTP operates on port 80 and sends data via cleartext. HTTP is not secure. HTTPS, which uses port 443, should be used to protect sensitive information.

Comparing the OSI Model to the TCP/IP Model

Although the OSI model was great in theory, it was never fully implemented. Instead, The TCP/IP model was implemented in its place. TCP/IP is the foundation of computer communications. Its development can be traced back to the U.S. Department of Defense (DoD). The TCP/IP model is similar to the OSI model but consists of only four layers instead of seven, as illustrated in Figure 7-7.

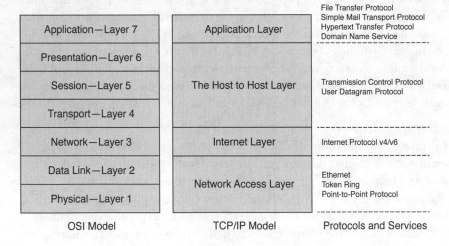

Figure 7-7   TCP/IP Model, OSI Model, and Related Services

The Network Access Layer

The network access layer corresponds to Layers 1 and 2 of the OSI model. The network access layer is responsible for physical delivery of IP packets via frames. The most common frame type is *Ethernet*, a CSMA/CD *(carrier-sense multiple access with collision detection)* technology that places data into frames. Frames contain the source and destination addresses and are referred to as *Media Access Control* (*MAC*) addresses. A MAC address is 6 bytes long. Most tools such as analyzers display MAC addresses in hexadecimal, which look something like this: 00 00 0C 12 34 67. The information found in the Ethernet header and trailer is 18 bytes in total. Ethernet frames can carry between 46 and 1,500 bytes of data.

Ethernet is a collision-detection protocol, whereas *Token Ring*, an older LAN protocol, is a collision-avoidance protocol. For example, consider going to a noisy party with your friends. Everyone's talking, and the only way to be heard is to wait for a brief period of silence to occur and then jump into the conversation. That's how Ethernet works; it's contention based. Ethernet is quite different from Token Ring. A collision-avoidance protocol such as Token Ring is like a very reserved dinner party with your CEO and senior management. Everyone is very reserved, and as long as one person is talking, everyone else stays silent and waits for a turn to speak. This type of protocol is deterministic as the only one that can speak is the one with the token.

Point-to-Point Tunneling Protocol (*PPTP*) is also found at the network access layer. PPTP is used to tunnel private information over the public Internet and is widely used in *virtual private network* (*VPN*) products.

TIP   CISA exam candidates should be aware that the network access layer is primarily responsible for physical addressing. Ethernet MAC addresses are an example of the addresses found at the network access layer.

The Internet Layer

The Internet layer maps to OSI Layer 3. This layer contains the information needed to make sure data can be routed through an IP network. Whereas a MAC address is considered a physical address, an IP address is considered a logical address. IP divides networks into logical groups known as *subnetworks* (subnets). IPv4, an older version of IP that is still in use, uses 32-bit addresses. These addresses are laid out in dotted-decimal notation. The IPv4 address format is four decimal numbers separated by decimal points. Each of these decimal numbers is 1 byte in length, which allows numbers to range from 0 to 255. Three primary ranges of logical addresses are used:

- **Class A networks:** Class A networks consist of up to 16,777,214 client devices; their address range can extend from 1 to 127.

- **Class B networks:** Class B networks host up to 65,534 client devices; their address range can extend from 128 to 191.

- **Class C networks:** Class C networks can have a total of 254 devices; their address range can extend from 192 to 223.

> **NOTE**   While you will still see a lot about IPv4 in books, the current version is IPv6. Besides offering better security, IPv6 also features 128-bit addressing, which allows for the growing need for IP addresses for many years.

If the Internet layer deals with logical addresses and the network access layer deals with physical addresses, how do the two layers communicate? These two layers communicate by using *Address Resolution Protocol* (*ARP*). The purpose of ARP is to map known IP addresses to unknown MAC addresses. This two-step process is performed by first sending a message to all devices on the LAN, requesting the receiver's physical address. If a device recognizes the address as its own, it issues an ARP reply to the sender of the ARP request. A good way to correlate the difference between physical and logical addresses is to think of the postal service. If you were to send a postcard to your mom, you would need to place her physical address on the postcard, such as 1313 Mockingbird Lane. You would also need a logical address to place on the postcard, such as Ms. Smith. Together the logical address and the physical address enable delivery to the end address. Networks provide the capability to send information to more than one device at a time. Actually, there are three different ways to send data packets:

- **Unicast:** A packet is transmitted from the sender to one receiver
- **Multicast:** A packet is transmitted from the sender to a group of receivers
- **Broadcast:** A packet is transmitted from the sender to all other devices on the network

IPv6 has three types of addresses, which can be categorized by type and scope:

- **Unicast addresses:** A packet is delivered to one interface.
- **Multicast addresses:** A packet is delivered to multiple interfaces.
- **Anycast addresses:** A packet is delivered to the nearest of multiple interfaces (in terms of routing distance).

The Internet layer is also where some *routing protocols* reside. Routing protocols direct packets toward their intended destination. Routing protocols are based on distance or link state.

Distance-vector protocols make a decision on the best route to the destination by determining the shortest path, calculated by counting hops. Each router counts as one hop. *Routing Information Protocol* (*RIP*) is one of the most well-known distance-vector protocols. A major shortcoming of a distance-vector protocol is that the path with the lowest number of hops might not be the optimum route; the path with the lower hop count might have considerably less bandwidth than the one with the higher hop count.

Link-state routing protocols are the second type of routing. Link-state protocols determine the best path based on metrics, such as delay or bandwidth. Link-state routing is considered more robust than distance-vector routing. *Open Shortest Path First* (*OSPF*) is probably the most common link-state routing protocol and is often used as a replacement for RIP.

> **TIP**   CISA exam candidates should be aware that the Internet layer is primarily responsible for routing and logical addressing. Protocols such as IP and OSPF can be found at the Internet layer.

The Host-to-Host/Transport Layer

The host-to-host, or transport, layer corresponds to OSI Layers 4, 5, and 6. The host-to-host layer provides end-to-end delivery. This is accomplished by either *Transmission Control Protocol* (*TCP*) or *User Datagram Protocol* (*UDP*).

TCP is a reliable protocol that provides for confirmed delivery of data. TCP is reliable because it performs a three-step handshake before data is sent, uses acknowledgments, and performs a four-step shutdown at the conclusion of communication, as illustrated in Figure 7-8.

UDP provides unconfirmed delivery and offers none of the handshaking process that is performed with TCP. Although this lowers reliability, it increases speed. UDP offers no guarantee of delivery and is used for applications and services that require speed. An example of a UDP application is *Voice over IP* (*VoIP*). UDP communication does not require a reply and is one way in nature, as illustrated in Figure 7-9.

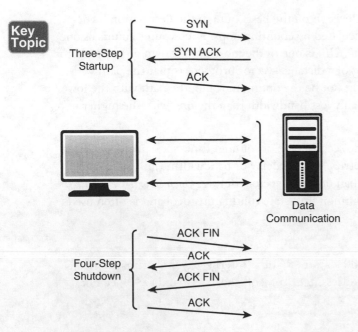

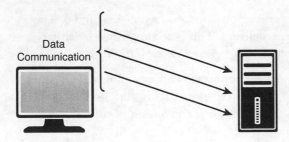

Figure 7-8   TCP Setup, Data Flow, and Shutdown

Figure 7-9   UDP Communication Flow

UDP or TCP can be chosen depending on the completeness, accuracy, and integrity needs of the data transmission.

The Application Layer

The application layer maps to OSI Layers 6 and 7. The application layer is responsible for application support. Applications are typically mapped not by name but by their corresponding port. Ports are placed into TCP and UDP packets so the correct application can be passed to the required protocols below.

Although a particular service might have an assigned port, nothing specifies that services cannot listen on another port. For example, HTTP is assigned to port 80. Your company might decide to run it on another port, such as 8080. As long as your web browser knows on what port to find the application, the change will not present a problem. Standard ports are used primarily to make sure that services can be easily found. Table 7-3 lists some common ports.

Table 7-3   Common Port Numbers

Port	Service	Protocol
20/21	FTP	TCP
22	SSH	TCP
23	Telnet	TCP
25	SMTP	TCP
53	DNS	TCP/UDP
67/68	DHCP	UDP
80	HTTP	TCP
110	POP3	TCP
143	IMAP	TCP
161	SNMP	UDP

Network Services

Common network services include *Domain Name Service* (*DNS*) and *Dynamic Host Configuration Protocol* (*DHCP*). DNS performs address translation by resolving known *fully qualified domain names* (*FQDNs*) to IP addresses. DNS uses UDP for DNS queries (resolutions) and TCP for zone transfers.

An improvement over DNS is DNS Security Extensions (DNSSEC), which is designed to mitigate the vulnerabilities in DNS and protect it from online threats such as spoofing and man-in-the-middle attacks.

DHCP is used to provide IP addresses automatically. DHCP also provides the DNS server, gateway IP address, and subnet mask to a local system upon startup if it is configured to use DHCP.

As previously discussed, email service historically used POP3. A newer mail protocol is Internet Message Access Protocol (IMAP), which is considered an improvement over POP. Where POP moves mail from the mail server to the client to be read,

IMAP leaves the mail on the mail server, which allows the end user to view and manipulate the messages as though they were stored locally on the end user's computing devices. This works well in the modern environment where a user may be checking mail on many different devices, such as a laptop, desktop, smartphone, or tablet.

NOTE   While networks will always be a concern, an auditor needs to also look closely at operational risk and controls related to end-user computing.

Wireless Technologies

An auditor's role has evolved over time to include wireless networks and technologies. The auditor must understand the basics of these technologies to provide assurance that adequate controls are in place to protect the confidentiality, integrity, and availability (CIA) of network resources and shares. An auditor needs to check for common problems, such as unauthorized implementations (for example, rogue wireless access).

Bluetooth

Bluetooth is a technology that makes use of WPANs. There are four classifications of Bluetooth:

- **Bluetooth Class 1:** Up to 100 meters of range and 100 mW of power
- **Bluetooth Class 2:** Up to 20 meters of range and 2.5 mW of power
- **Bluetooth Class 3:** Up to 1 meter of range and 1 mW of power
- **Bluetooth Class 4:** Up to .5 meters of range and 0.5 mW of power

Bluetooth is similar to many other technologies in that it can be configured to be somewhat secure or unsecure. An auditor should look to see if Bluetooth is even needed. If not, it should be turned off. If it is needed, Bluetooth devices should be set in undiscoverable mode. A strong PIN should also be used (not 1234 or 0000, for instance). The PIN should be something that should not be easily guessed or inferred. Without the proper controls, Bluetooth can be vulnerable to attack from a number of issues, such as viruses, worms, Bluebugging, Bluesnarfing, and denial of service. NIST even has a standard for Bluetooth security (see http://nvlpubs.nist. gov/nistpubs/SpecialPublications/NIST.SP.800-121r2.pdf).

NOTE   One example of Bluetooth being exploited is with the Flame cyber espionage malware. This malware hit many systems in the Middle East and beyond, targeting vulnerable computers. Flame had the ability to turn on Bluetooth on infected devices and attempt to extract data (phone numbers, names, and so on) from any accessible Bluetooth device in close proximity.

802.11 Wireless

Today more wireless devices are available than ever before, from wireless LAN (WLAN) to HiperLAN and HomeRF. One of the most popular wireless standard families of specifications is the *802.11* standards, which the IEEE developed. Wireless system components include the following:

- **Service set IDs (SSIDs):** For a computer to communicate or use the WLAN, it must be configured to use the correct service set ID (SSID). The SSID distinguishes one wireless network from another.

- **Wireless access points:** A wireless access point is a centralized wireless device that controls the traffic in the wireless medium and can be used to connect wireless devices to a wired network.

- **Wireless networking cards:** These are used much like wired networking cards, but they connect devices to the wireless network.

- **Encryption:** 802.11 encryption standards include the aging *Wired Equivalent Privacy* (*WEP*) protocol, which was designed to provide the same privacy a user would have on a wired network. WEP is based on the RC4 symmetric encryption standard. WEP is no longer secure, and the standard today is WPA2 with AES encryption. *Wi-Fi Protected Access* (*WPA*) was a stop-gap solution until WPA2 was released.

Implementations of 802.11 include 802.11b, 802.11a, 802.11i, 802.11g, 802.11n, and 802.11ac. Table 7-4 provides details for each.

Table 7-4   WLAN Standards and Details

IEEE WLAN Standard	Rated Speeds	Frequencies
802.11b	11Mbps	2.4000–2.2835GHz
802.11a	54Mbps	5.725–5.825GHz
802.11i	54Mbps	2.4000–2.2835GHz
802.11g	54Mbps	2.4000–2.2835GHz

IEEE WLAN Standard	Rated Speeds	Frequencies
802.11n	540Mbps	2.4000–2.2835GHz
802.11ac	433Mbps minimum	5.825GHz

Wireless devices can use a range of techniques to broadcast. The three most common techniques are as follows:

- **Orthogonal frequency-division multiplexing (OFDM):** OFDM splits a signal into smaller subsignals that use a frequency-division multiplexing technique to send different pieces of the data to the receiver on different frequencies simultaneously.

- **Direct-sequence spread spectrum (DSSS):** DSSS is a spread-spectrum technology that uses a wide range of radio frequencies. Small pieces of data are mapped to a pattern of ratios called a *spreading code*. The higher the spreading code, the more resistant the signal is to interference, but with less available bandwidth. For example, the Federal Communication Commission (FCC) requires at least 75 frequencies per transmission channel. The transmitter and the receiver must be synchronized to the same spreading code.

- **Frequency-hopping spread spectrum (FHSS):** FHSS works somewhat differently from the other techniques, dividing a broad slice of the bandwidth spectrum into smaller subchannels of about 1MHz each. The transmitter then hops between subchannels. Each subchannel is used to send out short bursts of data for a short period of time, known as the *dwell time*. For devices to communicate, each must know the proper dwell time and must be synchronized to the proper hopping pattern.

Table 7-5 summarizes the primary wireless standards.

Table 7-5 WLAN Standards and Details

Standard	Frequency	Max Speed	Transmission Scheme	Security Feature
802.11a	5GHz	54Mbps	OFDM	WEP
802.11b	2.4GHz	11Mbps	DSSS	WEP
802.11g	2.4GHz	54Mbps	OFDM/DSSS	WPA
802.11i	2.4GHz	54Mbps	DSSS	WPA, TKIP, WPA2 AES, RADIUS
802.11ac	5GHz	433Mbps minimum	DSSS/OFDM/MIMO	WPA, TKIP, WPA2 AES, RADIUS

Standard	Frequency	Max Speed	Transmission Scheme	Security Feature
Bluetooth	2.45GHz	2Mbps	FHSS	PPTP, SSL, or VPN
HomeRF	2.4GHz	10Mbps	FHSS	Shared Wireless Access Protocol (SWAP)

802.11ac, one of the newest standards, is a supercharged version of 802.11n. 802.11ac offers speeds ranging from 433Mbps (megabits per second) up to several gigabits per second. It is able to achieve this speed by operating in up to eight spatial streams (MIMO) and by using beamforming. It sends signals directly to client devices.

MIMO (multiple input, multiple output) is a wireless antenna technology that utilizes multiple antennas at both the source and the destination. Multi-user MIMO (MU-MIMO) is a variation in which a set of users that each have one or more antennas communicate with each other.

Wi-Fi devices must agree on several parameters before they can communicate with each other, such as frequency, operating mode (for example, managed, station/ client, ad hoc), network name (SSID), and security features (for example, WPA, WPA2, EAP). Wi-Fi devices send and receive on the same channel, which is known as half-duplex.

The frequency bands are divided into channels:

- 2.4GHz has 14 overlapping channels of 22MHz each.

- 5.8GHz has 5 non-overlapping channels of 20MHz each.

Auditors must examine wireless systems closely and verify that the systems being used are configured per security policy. Some general concerns arise with these systems. One big concern is that wireless networks don't end at the organization's outer walls; the signal can extend far beyond. This raises the issue of confidentiality because unauthorized individuals may be able to intercept the signal.

Another concern is that most wireless systems can have security disabled, or weak security mechanisms such as WEP may be used. WEP is insecure and should not be used; it can be broken in less than five minutes. Even if stronger encryption mechanisms are being used, it's important that the encryption key be periodically changed. Long-term use of static keys is a big security concern. An auditor should also review what defense-in-depth controls have been put in place. 802.1x is an IEEE standard for Port-Based Network Access Control (PNAC). It offers the ability to have both user authentication and port authentication, which helps build defense-in-depth by forcing an authentication mechanism to any device wishing to attach to a wireless LAN or wired LAN.

Smartphones, Tablets, and Hotspots

Smaller wireless devices are a big concern for an auditor. Many organizations have adopted a bring-your-own-device (BYOD) policy. Some of the reasons companies have adopted a BYOD policy is that it helps reduce upfront costs to the organization, allows the employees to use their existing devices, and may offer greater functionality for users. However, there are some real concerns, such as unmanaged devices containing your organization's data, personal and organizational data comingling, and the issue of eDiscovery. eDiscovery is simply the process by which electronic data is searched for, located, and secured with the intent of using it as evidence. This could be for a civil or criminal legal case. Any portable device such as a smartphone or tablet can allow users to take photos in otherwise secure areas. Smartphones and tablets are also easily lost or stolen.

Unfortunately, these devices usually lack the level of security of desktop systems and servers. Organizations need to implement policies and procedures to address the following issues with these devices:

- **Identification and authentication:** Handheld devices should use passwords or have some other type of authentication controls. After a preset number of password attempts, the device should lock or disable itself. One common method used for centralized authentication is RADIUS, and another is DIAMETER.

- **Applications and programs:** Controls should be used to limit what types of programs can be loaded on handheld devices. An organization's security policy should define what users can install or what is allowed.

- **Storage cards and memory:** Most handheld devices have memory slots for additional storage. Using storage cards is an easy way to expand memory, but they can also be removed, lost, or stolen. Because of these concerns, an organization should consider implementing a security policy requiring all such data to be protected by use of encryption.

- **Data transfer:** Handheld devices offer the capability to store, copy, or send large amounts of information via email. Company policy should specify who is allowed to use these devices and what usage is acceptable.

- **Backup and restore:** Handheld devices can be lost, stolen, or transferred to other employees. Company policy should specify how information is to be backed up, restored, or wiped.

- **Lost or stolen devices:** Easily one of the most pressing security issues of handheld devices is loss or theft of the devices. Depending on how the previous issues are addressed, a lost device can be anything from a nuisance to a high-level security threat. This requires that issues such as cell phone tracking and remote wiping have been addressed before the device is ever authorized.

An auditor should ask questions such as the following:

- Who owns these devices—the organization or employees?

- Who is responsible for managing and securing the devices?

- What are the incident response procedures?

- Is antivirus/anti-malware software being used?

- Who is responsible for paying for devices and service plans? Does the answer to this question change responsibilities, and is this covered by existing policy?

- What are the legal and regulatory requirements for your organization and the jurisdictions in which it operates?

NOTE   One important item for an auditor to review is onboarding of BYOD devices. There should be a secure portal for BYOD users to enroll and provision their devices.

Network Equipment

This section presents some basic terms to ensure that you understand common issues related to network equipment. As discussed previously, the most widely used LAN protocol is Ethernet. Because it is a baseband technology, only one device can transmit at a time. *Collisions* occur when more than one device in the same collision domain attempts to transmit at the same time. Therefore, a collision occurs when two devices attempt to transmit at the same time. *Collision domains* are defined by the devices that share the same physical medium. A broadcast domain is a group of devices that can receive other devices' broadcast messages. Routers usually serve as the demarcation line for broadcast domains.

Let's work up the stack and discuss some of the various types of networking equipment. First up for review is the *repeater*, which is an amplifier that can be used to extend the range of a physical network. A repeater receives the signal, regenerates the signal, and forwards it. Not far up the food chain above repeaters are *hubs*. Hubs are rare today, but they are the most basic example of multiport repeaters that provide physical connectivity by allowing all the connected devices to communicate with one another. A hub is basically a common wire to which all computers have shared access. Hubs are rarely seen today because of their low maximum throughput and their security vulnerabilities. Collisions are a big problem with hubs; any time utilization approaches 20 percent or more, the number of collisions skyrockets, and the overall average throughput decreases. Hubs have been replaced with switches.

A layer 2 switch performs in much the same way as a hub, with the exception that switches segment traffic. They operate at the data link layer of the OSI model. Because of this design, each port on a switch is a separate collision domain. On an Ethernet LAN, switches segment traffic by observing the source and destination MAC address of each data frame. These MAC addresses are stored in a *random access memory (RAM)* lookup table, which can then be used to determine which port traffic should be forwarded to. The frame is forwarded to only that switch port; therefore, other ports never see the traffic. A switch provides higher throughput than a hub and can function in full duplex. Not all switches are made the same. Switch manufacturers have developed various ways to handle incoming frames, such as store-and-forward and cut-through. Store-and-forward waits for the frame to be completely inputted into the switch before forwarding. A cut-through design is faster because the frame is quickly forwarded to the targeted device. Switches range in price and functionality. A basic switch is considered unmanaged in that you simply plug it in, and it works. A managed switch has an IP address assigned and allows you to manage various options, such as assignment of ports, port controls, and mirroring. For example, a managed switch allows port security controls so that specific ports can be turned on or off or even assigned to a specific MAC address. You might also want to configure a specific port for an intrusion detection system (IDS). In that situation, port mirroring can be used. This simply means all traffic from all other ports is forwarded to the mirrored port.

Managed switches can also be used to create virtual LANs (VLANs). VLANs are based on logical instead of physical connections, and they are extremely flexible. They eliminate the need for the router in the sense that broadcast domains can be restricted. For example, one switch could be configured into several different VLANs. Network administrators can use identifier tags to group hosts together into VLANs even if the hosts are not on the same network switch. These tags are simply information that is inserted into a packet header to allow the identification of which VLAN the packet is associated with. Switches use VLAN IDs to determine where to send a packet to. One common tag format is the IEEE 802.1Q standard. This is the standard set by the IEEE for identifying Ethernet frames and used in handling such frames.

NOTE   Although traditionally switches are seen as Layer 2 devices, switches can be found at Layer 3 and work up to Layer 7. Higher-layer switches are known as *content switches*, *content services switches*, or *application switches*.

Routers reside at Layer 3 of the OSI model and are used to bridge dissimilar networks, join distant networks, and separate broadcast domains. Routers forward packets from one network to another based on network-layer information. For most networks, this information is an IP address. The IP address identifies the targeted host device. The router uses routing protocols to identify the best path from the source router to the destination device.

Closely related to routers are *gateways*. A *gateway* is a network device that is equipped for interfacing with another network that uses different protocols. In other words, gateways provide protocol conversion and, according to ISACA, can be found at Layer 4 and higher.

Modems are another piece of networking equipment. The word *modem* is short for *modulate/demodulate*. Modems are not very common today but continue to be used in some specialized situations. In addition, the term is used for devices that don't actually convert analog to digital (for example, cable modems, DSL modems).

The final piece of network equipment for review is the *wireless access point* (*wireless AP*). Wireless APs enable users to connect wireless devices to form a wireless network. Wireless APs are usually connected to a wired network and can relay data between wired and wireless devices. Most mobile devices used today offer only wireless connectivity. Table 7-6 provides an overview of the primary types of network equipment.

Table 7-6 Network Equipment

Equipment	OSI Layer	Description
Gateway	OSI Layer 4 or higher	Gateways operate at the transport layer and above. Gateways translate each source-layer protocol into the appropriate destination-layer protocol. For example, an application-layer gateway is found at Layer 7.
Router	OSI Layer 3	Routers are used to connect distant sites connected by a WAN, improve performance by limiting physical broadcast domains, and ease network management by segmenting devices into smaller subnets rather than one large network.
Switch	OSI Layer 2	Switches are hardware based and provide logical segmentation by observing the source and destination physical address of each data frame. Networking VLANs is one function that many switches can provide. VLANs separate various ports on a switch, therefore segmenting traffic much as a Layer 3 router function would.
802.11 wireless access points	OSI Layer 2	Wireless access points can be found at OSI Layer 2. Devices that have wireless and can route would be found at OSI Layer 3.
Hub	OSI Layer 1	Hubs connect individual devices and provide physical connectivity so that devices can share data. Hubs amplify and regenerate the electrical signals. They are similar to repeaters except that hubs have multiple ports.

TIP   CISA exam candidates should understand what each piece of networking equipment does and where it fits into the OSI model. You need to know where devices operate.

Edge Devices

Think of an edge device as anything that acts as an entry or exit point to a network. In the physical world, gates are an example of an edge device. In the logical world, this role is usually filled by a router or firewall.

DMZ

Have you ever been in a facility that has a mantrap? It's a two-door system in which you enter one door and then, after it closes, you authenticate and the inner door opens. The area between the two doors could be considered similar to a demilitarized zone (DMZ). A DMZ is an area where outsiders are allowed access but that is not fully inside a corporate network. This perimeter between the untrusted outside Internet and trusted internal network is the location where services such as web, email, or DNS can be placed. Sometimes a honeypot may be placed in the DMZ. A *honeypot* is a fake system used to distract and trap an attacker to ensure that the attacker leaves the real systems alone.

An organization should take special care with devices placed in the DMZ to ensure that they are hardened against attack. A *bastion host* is any device specifically designed and configured to withstand attacks. Bastion hosts typically have all unused service removed. The idea is to remove all other services that are not specifically needed to reduce the threat to the computer. A common location for a bastion device is in a DMZ. The following are some of the resources that can be used to harden a device:

- NSA Security Configuration Guidelines

- CIS Benchmarks

- Defense Information Systems Agency (DISA) Security Technical Implementation Guides (STIGs)

Firewalls

The term *firewall* has been used since the 1990s to describe a device or software that guards the entrance to a private network. Firewalls were developed to keep out unauthorized traffic. Firewalls have undergone generations of improvements so that today several different types of firewalls exist, including packet filters, application proxies, circuit proxies, and stateful inspection.

Packet filter firewalls operate at Layer 3 of the OSI model. A packet filter looks at a packet's header to determine whether to block or pass traffic. Packet filters can be thought of as the first generation of firewalls. They inspect the TCP/IP headers and make a decision based on a set of predefined rules. Packet filters simply drop packets that do not conform to the predefined rule set. These rules can include the following:

- Source IP address

- Destination IP address

- TCP/UDP source port

- TCP/UDP destination port

- TCP flags (SYN, FIN, ACK, and so on)

Packet filters are considered stateless. This means they store no information about the state of the session, which, in turn, means that packet filters are simple and fast but are vulnerable to attack. Spoofing is an example of a packet filter vulnerability.

One advancement in the firewall was the development of the proxy. By definition, the word *proxy* means "stand-in" or "substitute." Therefore, a proxy is a hardware or software device that can perform address translation and communicate with the Internet on behalf of the network. The real IP address of the user remains hidden behind the proxy server. The host running the proxy service is known as an *application gateway*. Application proxies provide a higher level of security.

Application proxies offer increased security because they don't allow untrusted systems to have a direct connection to internal computers. Application proxies accept packets from the external network, copy the packets, inspect them for irregularities, change the addresses to the correct internal device, and then put them back on the wire to the destination device. An application proxy operates at Layer 7 of the OSI model. For an application proxy to work correctly, it must understand the protocols and applications with which it is working.

Somewhere below an application proxy is a circuit-level proxy, which operates at Layer 5 of the OSI model. A circuit-level proxy closely resembles a packet-filtering device because it makes decisions on addresses, ports, and protocols. It does not provide the depth of security that an application-level proxy does because it does not inspect higher-layer applications. Its advantage is that it works with a wider range of protocols. Application proxies and circuit-level proxies do have something in common because both have the capability to maintain state. Stateful inspection firewalls have the capability to keep track of every communication channel by using a state table. Because of this, they are considered an intelligent type of firewall.

Packet filters do not have this capability. Firewalls continue to change and adapt. For example, a web application firewall (WAF) can be thought of as an advancement form of a regular stateful firewall in that a WAF is able to filter specific web applications, while regular firewalls serve as a safety gate between servers. A WAF filters, monitors, and blocks malicious HTTP traffic that is being sent or received from a web application.

> **TIP**   It is important to note that an application proxy provides the greatest level of protection because it inspects at all levels of the OSI model.

Firewall Configuration

Firewall configurations include *packet filtering, dual-homed gateway, screened host,* and *screened subnet*. A single-tier packet filter design has one packet-filtering router installed between the trusted and untrusted networks—usually the Internet and the corporation's network. The problems with this design become amplified as the network grows larger and because the *packet filter* has limited capabilities. Figure 7-10 illustrates this design.

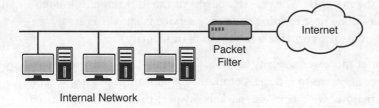

Figure 7-10   Packet Filtering

A *dual-homed gateway* is an improvement over a basic packet-filtering router. A dual-homed gateway consists of a bastion host that has two network interfaces. One important item is that IP forwarding is disabled on the host. Additional protection can be provided by adding a packet-filtering router in front of the dual-homed host. Figure 7-11 illustrates this design.

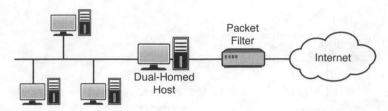

Figure 7-11   Dual-Homed Gateway

NOTE   The term *bastion host* has come to define the servers located in a DMZ or an untrusted area. These servers are designed much differently than those found in an internal network. Bastion hosts are typically hardened so that nonessential services are removed. Bastion hosts commonly perform web, email, and DNS tasks.

A *screened host firewall* adds a router and screened host. The router is typically configured to see only one host computer on the intranet network. Users on the intranet have to connect to the Internet through this host computer, and external users cannot directly access other computers on the intranet. Figure 7-12 illustrates this design.

The *screened subnet* sets up a type of *DMZ*, a term that comes from the demilitarized zone (or no-man's land) that was set up between North and South Korea following the Korean War in the 1950s. DMZs are typically set up to give external users access to services within the DMZ. Basically, shared services such as the Internet, email, and DNS can be placed within a DMZ; the DMZ provides no other access to services located within the internal network. Screened subnets and DMZs are the basis for most modern network designs. Figure 7-13 illustrates this firewall design.

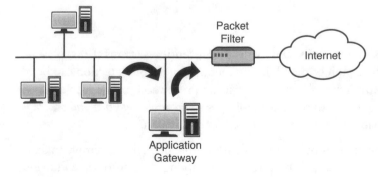

Figure 7-12   Screened Host

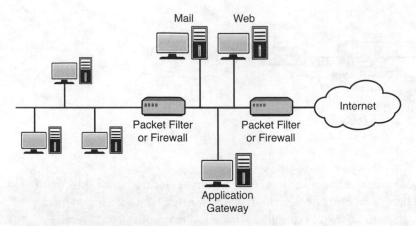

Figure 7-13   Screened Subnet

> **TIP**   A DMZ offers the highest level of protection because defenses have been layered, and shared services are placed in an area that prevents outsiders from fully entering the internal network.

All this talk of DMZs and screened subnets brings up one final issue: network address translation (NAT). NAT allows a single device, such as a router or firewall, to act as an agent between the Internet and a local network. NAT, which is addressed in RFC 1631, was originally designed to deal with the shortage of IPv4 addresses. Besides conserving public IP addresses, NAT provides security by providing address translation. This means that only a single, unique IP address is all that is needed to support an entire group of computers.

IDS/IPS

Intrusion detection systems (IDSs) and intrusion prevention systems (IPSs) play a critical role in the protection of the IT infrastructure. Intrusion detection can be thought of as a detective control, whereas intrusion prevention can be seen as a preventive control. NIST refers to these technologies as *intrusion detection and prevention (IDP)* because many modern solutions are blended in nature.

Intrusion detection involves monitoring network traffic, detecting attempts to gain unauthorized access to a system or resource, and notifying the appropriate individuals so that counteractions can be taken.

IDS can be divided into two broad categories: network-based intrusion-detection systems (NIDSs) and host-based intrusion-detection systems (HIDSs). Both NIDSs and HIDSs can be configured to scan for attacks, track a hacker's movements, or alert an administrator about ongoing attacks. IDSs are composed of the following parts:

- **Network sensors:** Detect and send data to the system

- **Central monitoring system:** Processes and analyzes data sent from sensors

- **Report analysis:** Offers information about how to counteract a specific event

- **Database and storage components:** Perform trend analysis and store the IP address and information about the attacker

- **Response box:** Inputs information from the previously listed components and forms an appropriate response

Figure 7-14 provides some examples of basic IDS types.

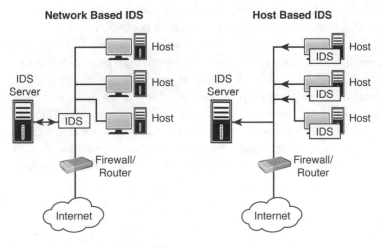

Figure 7-14   IDS Types

An auditor should be concerned about where the IDS sensors are placed. Placement determines what the IDS will see (for example, if the sensor in the DMZ will work well at detecting issues in the DMZ but will prove useless for attackers who are inside the network). Another important concern is tuning. An IDS must be tuned to detect specific events. It must be configured to detect suspicious activity. The primary categories of intrusion detection include pattern matching (signature), protocol decoding, and anomaly detection. Each type takes slightly different approaches to detecting intrusions.

Pattern-matching IDSs rely on a database of known attacks. These known attacks are loaded into the system as signatures. As soon as the signatures are loaded into the IDS, the IDS can begin to guard the network. Each signature is usually given a number or name so that the administrator can easily identify an attack when it sets off an alert. Alerts can be triggered for fragmented IP packets, streams of SYN packets (denial of service [DoS]), or malformed Internet Control Message Protocol (ICMP) packets. An alert might be configured to change to the firewall configuration, set off an alarm, or even page the administrator. The biggest disadvantage to the pattern-matching system is that the IDS can only trigger on signatures that have been loaded. A new or obfuscated (that is, disguised) attack might go undetected.

Anomaly detection is a much different approach in that an administrator must make use of profiles of authorized activities or place the IDS into a learning mode so that it can learn what constitutes normal activity. It can take some time to ensure that the IDS produces few false negatives. If an attacker can slowly change his activity over time, the IDS might actually be fooled into thinking that the new behavior is acceptable.

Somewhere in the middle of the spectrum of intrusion detection is protocol decoding. *Protocol decoding* IDSs have the capability to reassemble packets and look at higher-layer activity. In this type of detection, models are built on the TCP/IP protocols, using their specifications. If an IDS knows the normal activity of a protocol, it can pick out abnormal activity. Protocol decoding intrusion detection requires the IDS to maintain state information. For example, let's look at Domain Name Service (DNS). DNS is a two-step process. Therefore, a protocol matching IDS can detect that when a number of DNS responses occur without a DNS request, a cache poisoning attack might be happening. To effectively detect these intrusions, an IDS must re-implement a wide variety of application-layer protocols to detect suspicious or invalid behavior.

Wide Area Networks

Wide area networks (WANs) are very different from LANs. Whereas almost all companies own their LAN infrastructure, very few own their WAN infrastructure. Running a cable along the side of the interstate from Los Angeles to New York is usually not feasible. WANs and LANs also use very different protocols. WAN protocols are designed for the long-haul transmission of data. CISA candidates must understand WAN protocols and should focus on issues such as redundancy and fault tolerance. WAN protocols can be placed into two broad categories: *packet switching* and *circuit switching*.

Packet Switching

Packet-switched networks share bandwidth with other devices. They are considered more resilient and work well for on-demand connections with bursty traffic.

Packet-switched protocols packetize data in much the same manner as Ethernet would: The data is placed into a frame structure. Let's look at some different types of packet-switching protocols and services:

- **X.25:** X.25 is one of the original packet-switching technologies. It was developed in 1976 and operates at the physical, data link, and network layers of the OSI model. Once used extensively, X.25 is no longer widely used.

- **Frame Relay:** Think of this technology as the son of X.25. Frame Relay improved upon X.25 and relies more on the upper layers of the OSI model for error handling. Frame Relay controls bandwidth usage by use of a *committed information rate* (*CIR*). The CIR specifies the maximum guaranteed bandwidth that the customer is guaranteed. Although higher rates might be possible, the CIR represents the level the service provider is committed to providing. If additional bandwidth is available, the data will pass; if no additional bandwidth is available, the data is marked with discard eligibility and discarded.

- **Asynchronous Transfer Mode (ATM):** This cell-switching technology operates at the data link layer of the OSI model. ATM is an asynchronous protocol that supports classes of service. ATM provides high bandwidth for bursty traffic and works well for time-sensitive applications. Because the switching process occurs in hardware, delays are minimized. ATM can be used on LANs or WANs.

- **Multiprotocol Label Switching (MPLS):** MPLS is a framework that provides for the efficient switching of traffic flows through IP, ATM, and Frame Relay networks. Addresses are read just once as a packet enters the cloud, thereby providing more efficient routing. MPLS features class-of-service so that packets can be prioritized.

NOTE   Although it is not a packet-switching protocol, VoIP is carried on packet-switched networks in IP packets. Networks that have been configured to carry VoIP treat voice communications as just another form of data. Auditors should be aware of VoIP because of its security issues, such as eavesdropping and the potential for denial of service, and also because loss of the data network can disable VoIP.

Circuit Switching

Circuit switching is the second type of WAN technology up for discussion. Telecommunication providers have used circuit switching since 1891, when a

Kansas City undertaker patented the first one. The following are some types of circuit switching:

- **Plain old telephone service (POTS):** This humble voice-grade analog telephone service is used for voice calls and for connecting to the Internet and other locations via modem. Modem speeds can vary from 9,600bps to 56Kbps. Although the POTS service is relatively inexpensive, very reliable, and widely available, it offers only low data speeds.

- **Integrated Services Digital Network (ISDN):** This circuit-switched technology has worldwide usage and is similar to POTS, except that the signal is entirely digital. ISDN uses separate frequencies called *channels* on a special digital connection. It consists of B channels used for voice, data, video, and fax services, as well as a D channel used for signaling by the service provider and user equipment. The D channel operates at a low 16Kbps, and the B channels operate at a speed up to 64Kbps. By binding the B channels together, ISDN can achieve higher speeds. ISDN is available in two levels, *basic rate interface* (BRI) and *primary rate interface* (PRI). ISDN BRI features two 64 B channels and one 16Kbps D channel; ISDN PRI features 23 64 B channels and 1 16Kbps D channel.

- **T-carriers:** This service is used for leased lines assigned to specific locations. Users pay a fixed fee for this service. An example of a T-carrier is T1, which uses time-division multiplexing and has a composite data rate of 1.544Mbps. T3s have a composite data rate of 45Mbps.

- **Digital subscriber line (DSL):** This circuit-switched technology provides high bandwidth and works over existing telephone lines. Most DSL services are asymmetric, which means the download speed is much faster than the upload speed. DSL is considered an "always on" circuit-switched technology.

NOTE   While you might normally think of change management as something related only to software, it's not. There should be change management in place for hardware and items such as firewall configurations. An auditor should review change management practices and verify that they are controlled and documented.

Capacity Planning and Systems Performance Monitoring

Capacity planning is the act of estimating the resources that will be needed over some future period of time and to determine whether they are controlled effectively and continue to support the organization's objectives. The goal of capacity planning is to add new capacity as needed but not so early that the resources go unused for a long period. In large part, capacity planning has to do with the design of the network infrastructure.

How much bandwidth is enough? That common question is hard to answer as there always seems to be the need for more. More devices on the network, interactive websites, streaming content, live feeds, and VoIP all add to the need for additional bandwidth. While no one has a crystal ball, an organization should do its best to ensure adequate capacity planning for its network. Networks must be managed and monitored to ensure they operate at maximum efficiency. Utilization reports can be used to review the status of the network.

An auditor typically uses utilization reports to verify that systems are running correctly. If you use a Windows computer, you can check out system performance with Windows Performance Monitor, which provides feedback on how programs you run affect your computer's performance, both in real time and by collecting log data for later analysis. Windows Performance Monitor uses performance counters, event trace data, and configuration information, which can be combined into Data Collector Sets.

Sometimes you need to monitor more than a single system. You can review the performance of the network with tools such as Simple Network Management Protocol (SNMP). SNMP is used to manage and monitor network elements. Most network elements, such as servers, workstations, printers, and switches, come with bundled SNMP agents. These agents have to be enabled and configured to communicate with the network-management system (NMS). While SNMP is useful, it is important to remember that not all versions are the same. Only version 3 offers encryption. Versions 1 and 2 send data in the clear, with default community strings of public and private.

Another option is *flow analysis*, which provides a different perspective on traffic movement in networks. It provides visibility into how often an event occurred according to a given metric. For example, how often was traffic containing encrypted .zip files leaving the network and destined for Asia between midnight and 4 a.m. on weekends? With flow analysis tools, auditors can view this type of user activity in near real time.

Network Analyzers

Another popular tool for network analysis is an analyzer. Network analyzers are hardware or software devices that allow you to capture and analyze network traffic. Network analyzers can do the following:

- Provide detailed statistics for current and recent activity on a network
- Detect unusual levels of network traffic
- Detect unusual packet characteristics
- Identify packet sources or destinations
- Search for specific data strings in packets.
- Monitor bandwidth utilization as a function of time
- Display all statistics on a user-friendly control panel

One of the most popular network analyzers is Wireshark. Wireshark can display three main views of captured traffic:

- **Summary:** The uppermost window shows the summary display. It is a one-line-per-packet format.
- **Detail:** The middle section shows the captured traffic in an English-like breakdown.
- **Hex:** The bottom section shows the hex value of each portion of the headers and the data.

Figure 7-15 shows data captured with Wireshark and displays some statistics about that data. It's possible for an auditor to use Wireshark to see who is the top talker, what IPs are communicating, and what protocols are being used.

All network analyzers require access to network traffic. Therefore, programs such as Wireshark place the hosting system's network card into promiscuous mode. A network card in promiscuous mode can receive all the data it can see, not just packets addressed to it.

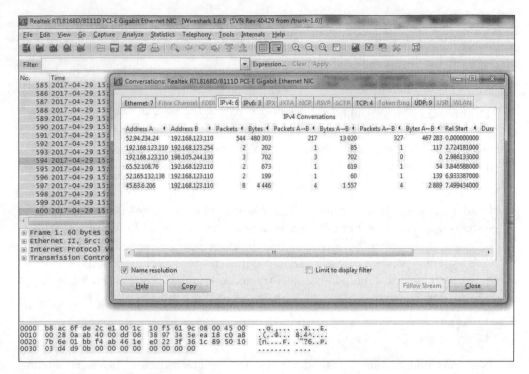

Figure 7-15 Wireshark Conversations

When analysis is performed on a switched network, it is not possible to monitor all the traffic simply by attaching a promiscuous mode device to a single port. To get around this limitation, port mirroring or switch mirroring is used. *Port mirroring* allows an analyzer to see not just its traffic but all the traffic being forwarded by the switch. This feature allows the switch to be configured so that when data is forwarded to any port on the switch, it is also forwarded to the SPAN port. This functionality is a great feature when using a sniffer or a tool such as Snort. Snort is an open source IDS that is signature based. (If you are interested in learning more about this technology, see RFC 2613, which specifies standard methods for managing and configuring SPAN ports.)

System Utilization and Load Balancing

How do you know that an upgrade is needed? One way is by reviewing system utilization reports. A utilization report shows the extent to which network resources are being used. It gives information to organizations on how, where, and how much of their resources are being used.

One way to even out utilization is to use a load balancer to increase capacity and reliability of applications. One common technique is round robin. Round robin can be used with DNS to ensure that DNS requests are not sent to a single IP address but to a list of IP addresses that host identical services. The idea is to balance the load across many different servers.

The order in which IP addresses from the list are returned is the basis for the term *round robin*. With each DNS response, the IP address sequence in the list is permuted. Usually, basic IP clients attempt connections with the first address returned from a DNS query so that on different connection attempts, clients receive service from different providers, thus distributing the overall load among servers.

Load balancing is an important technique that can help manage loads and keep systems from crashing. For example, Pokémon servers crashed from overutilization because the developers didn't realize that the game would be such a massive hit. (See www.independent.co.uk/life-style/gadgets-and-tech/gaming/pokemon-go-down-servers-crash-nintendo-millions-try-access-game-a7140691.html for more information.)

Third Parties and Cloud Providers

Not everything an auditor may want to monitor will be in-house. Third-party monitoring may also be needed for items that are hosted by other organizations or that are in the cloud. Before a contract is signed, it should be reviewed to verify that it meets all required service agreements and regulatory requirements. The contract is your only true fallback mechanism if you have issues with the vendor. The contract should specify issues such as monitoring and overages. Costs for items that exceed normal usage can be expensive. Therefore, auditors should review contracts closely.

Other items of concern include guarantees on service levels. These are typically specified via service level agreements (SLAs). Auditors should include in contracts provisions that allow for periodic review.

Network Design

Networks can use a variety of topologies. The *topology* is the physical design of the network. Topologies include bus, star, ring, and mesh. Table 7-7 provides an overview of the common topologies.

Table 7-7 Network Topologies

Topology	Description	Advantage	Disadvantage
Bus	A single length of cable is used.	The design is simple.	The design is hard to expand. One cable break can disable the entire segment.
Star	Devices all connect to a central wiring point.	Expansion does not disrupt other systems. A cable failure affects only one device.	More cable is required. A hub or switch is required.
Ring	Devices are connected in a loop.	The design is easy to troubleshoot and fault tolerant if dual rings are used.	Network expansion creates a disruption.
Mesh	All points have redundant connections.	Multiple links provide greater fault tolerance. Expansion requires little or no disruption.	The design is expensive to implement.

A *bus topology* consists of a single cable in which all computers are linked. The cable is terminated on each end. Older LAN technologies, such as 10BASE-5 and 10BASE-2, used a bus topology. Bus designs suffer problems ranging from low speeds to network outages because a single cable break can bring down the entire network.

A *star topology* links each device via a hub or switch. Wires radiate outward from the switch in a star-like pattern. Although this design uses the most cable, a single break in a cable affects only one device. This is one of the most widely used LAN topologies.

The *ring topology* is characterized by the fact that no endpoints or terminators exist. The layout of a ring network is a continuous loop of cable to which all networked computers are attached. Ring networks can span great distances and offer high performance. Token Ring and FDDI networks are two examples of protocols that use a ring topology.

The *mesh topology* connects all devices with many redundant connections. This type of design offers the greatest amount of redundancy. The Internet is an example of a mesh network. Figure 7-16 illustrates each of these designs.

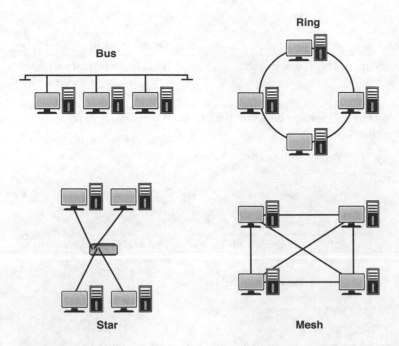

Figure 7-16   Common Network Designs

> **NOTE**   Full-mesh networks provide the most protection against network failure. If each device has a separate link to each other device, the network will provide the greatest amount of fault tolerance.

Network Cabling

Network topology and network cabling are closely associated, and both are part of network architecture. Cabling choices can include wire, fiber, and wireless systems. Although each approach has specific advantages, they all share some common disadvantages. One disadvantage is *attenuation*, which is the reduction of signal. As the signal travels farther away from the transmitting device, the signal becomes weaker in intensity and strength. Therefore, all signals need periodic reamplification and regeneration.

Signals can be transmitted between devices in one of two basic methods:

- **Baseband:** These transmissions use a single channel to communicate. For example, Ethernet uses a baseband transmission scheme. Baseband allows only one signal to be transmitted at any one time. 802.3 is a standard specification for Ethernet.

- **Broadband:** These transmissions use many channels or frequencies. For example, cable television is a broadband technology, as is a *digital subscriber line* *(DSL)*. DSL broadband enables the user to make a phone call and surf the Internet at the same time on the same wire.

Baseband and broadband systems need a transmission medium. If the choice is copper cable, the choices include *coaxial* and *twisted-pair cables*. Coaxial cable, widely used in the early days of networking, consists of a single solid copper wire core that uses a braided shield for the second conductor. Both conductors are covered with a plastic or insulative coating. Coaxial cable standards include 10BASE-5 (which operates over a maximum range of 500 meters) and 10BASE-2 (185 meters).

Twisted-pair cable (100 meters) is a more popular cabling choice than coax. You can look in almost every wiring closet in any organization and find this type of cabling. Twisted-pair cable comes in many different speeds and is rated in categories. Category (Cat) 3 is 10Mbps, and Cat 5 is 100Mbps. Cat 6 is made with 23-gauge conductor wire as opposed to the slightly smaller wire used for Cat 5 and is suitable for Gigabit Ethernet. Cat 6a has reduced crosstalk characteristics. Cat 7 is designed to support speeds of 10Gbps at lengths of up to 100 meters. Cat 8 is the newest standard and supports 1.6GHz minimum and up to 2GHz. The most common connector used is the RJ-45. Twisted-pair cable can be purchased in a shielded or unshielded version. Unshielded, which is known as UTP, is cheaper, but shielded cable, known as STP, does a better job at preventing interference. Plenum-grade cabling has low-smoke and low-flame characteristics. It is generally used to reduce the amount of noxious smoke that people may breath during a fire evacuation.

TIP Guarding the health and safety of employees is always a concern. Plenum-grade cable is designed for use under raised floors or in the plenum space of a building. Plenum-grade cable is coated with a fire-retardant coating and is designed to not give off toxic gasses and smoke as it burns.

Another cabling option is *fiber-optic* cable. Whereas twisted-pair and coaxial cable use copper wire, fiber uses strands of glass that carry light waves representing the data being transmitted. Fiber-optic cable can be multimode or single mode. Multimode fiber-optic cable usually is found in LANs and is powered by LEDs. Single-mode fiber-optic cable is powered by laser light and is used in WANs. Common fiber-optic standards include 10BASE-F, which is rated for 10Mbps,

100BASE-FX, which is rated for 100Mbps and 1000BASE-LX which is rated for 1000Mbps. 802.3ae is the standard that specifies 10 Gigabit Ethernet over fiber.

TIP Fiber offers advantages over copper cable because it does not radiate signals and is harder to tap than copper cabling.

The final transmission method for discussion is wireless communication. Wireless systems can include wireless LAN protocols, such as 802.11b, 802.11g, 802.11n, and 802.11ac. Each of these is designed for LANs and can transmit at speeds from 11Mbps to greater than 10Gbps. Advantages of these systems are that they can be set up easily and do not require a cable plant. Long-range wireless systems include radio systems, microwave radio systems, and satellite systems. Satellite systems have the capability to allow communications to span the globe, but they can introduce delay because it takes about 300 ms to transmit up to the satellite and back down to earth. Table 7-8 discusses each cabling option in more detail.

Table 7-8 Cabling Options

Type	Use	Topology	Maximum Length or Distance	Access Standard
Copper cable	10BASE-T, 10Mbps	Star	100 meters.	Ethernet
	100BASE-TX, 100Mbps		100 meters.	CSMA/CD
	1000BASE-TX, 10Gbps		100 meters.	
Coaxial cable	10BASE5, 10Mbps	Bus	500 meters.	802.3
	10BASE2, 10Mbps		185 meters.	
Fiber-optic cable	10BASE-F, 10Mbps	Bus, star, or mesh	Long distances. For example, 10BASE-F can range up to 2,000 m.	802.3 and 802.3ae
	100BASE-FX, 100Mbps			
	1000BASE-LX, 1000Mbps			
Wireless LAN	In the 2.4GHz bandwidth	Wireless	Varies, depending on the standard.	802.11

Choosing the right topology is important. Services such as VoIP and *streaming video* can place high demands on a network. To make sure the right infrastructure is deployed, the following questions should be answered:

- **What applications will be used on the network?** Demanding applications require high performance. *Ten Gigabit Ethernet*, *Gigabit Ethernet*, and *802.11ac wireless* are three possible choices.

- **What amount of bandwidth is needed?** Modern LANs demand increasing amounts of bandwidth. Virtual machines and increased Internet traffic raise the demand for bandwidth. Whereas 10Mbps connectivity with hubs was once sufficient, 1000Mbps switched connectivity is now seen as the minimum.

- **How much money does the company have to spend?** The price of network equipment has been declining for several years. However, the cost to re-cable a facility is high. This has led many companies to consider wireless as a viable alternative.

NOTE Wireless can be considered problematic when it comes to security. Issues such as social engineering, MITM attacks, free Wi-Fi that is not encrypted, and so on must be considered before making the move to wireless networking.

- **Is remote management required?** Depending on the equipment purchased, it might or might not have the capability for remote management. The need for remote management must be balanced against the budget.

Chapter Summary

This chapter reviews the systems used in modern networks. To better understand these systems, this chapter discusses concepts such as the OSI model, a seven-layer model that defines networking in a layered fashion. Although the OSI model is widely used for teaching, the system most associated with networking today is TCP/IP, a four-layer model that combines some of the layers in the OSI model. The TCP/IP model is based on protocols such as IP, a routable protocol used to carry high-layer headers and data. IP commonly carries TCP or UDP. TCP is a connection-oriented protocol used for reliability. UDP is a connectionless protocol used for speed. TCP carries applications such as HTTP and FTP. UDP carries applications such as DHCP, TFTP, and DNS queries.

An IS auditor is expected to understand all these networking technologies and know how the various pieces of networking equipment work. A CISA candidate should look closely at the technology the organization uses and examine its controls and potential vulnerabilities. Technology is a great benefit, but without proper controls, it can present many dangers.

Exam Preparation Tasks

As mentioned in the section "How to Use This Book" in the Introduction, you have a couple choices for exam preparation: the exercises here; Chapter 10, "Final Preparation;" and the exam simulation questions on the book's companion web page (www.informit.com/title/9780789758446).

Review All the Key Topics

Review the most important topics in this chapter, noted with the Key Topic icon in the outer margin of the page. Table 7-9 lists these key topics and the page number on which each is found.

Table 7-9 Key Topics in Chapter 7

Key Topic Element	Description	Page Number
Table 7-2	Frameworks and best practices	273
List	OSI model layers	286
Figure 7-8	TCP setup, data flow, and shutdown	296
Table 7-3	Common port numbers	297
Table 7-8	Cabling options	322

Define Key Terms

Define the following key terms from this chapter and check your answers against the glossary:

802.11 standard; Address Resolution Protocol (ARP); AES; carrier-sense multiple access with collision detection (CSMA/CD); defense-in-depth; demilitarized zone (DMZ); direct-sequence spread spectrum (DSSS); DNSSEC; Domain Name Service (DNS); Ethernet; fiber-optic cable; frequency-hopping spread spectrum (FHSS); honeypot; hub; Integrated Services Digital Network (ISDN); Internet; Internet Control Message Protocol (ICMP); Internet Protocol (IP); local area network (LAN); multiple input, multiple output (MIMO); Multiprotocol Label Switching (MPLS); MU-MIMO; network address translation (NAT); packet; packet switching; personal area network (PAN); port; Post Office Protocol (POP); protocol; proxy server; Remote Authentication Dial-In User Service (RADIUS); repeater;

service set ID (SSID); Simple Mail Transfer Protocol (SMTP); Simple Network Management Protocol (SNMP); Temporal Key Integrity Protocol (TKIP); Transmission Control Protocol (TCP); Transmission Control Protocol/Internet Protocol (TCP/IP); universal serial bus (USB); User Datagram Protocol (UDP); virtual LAN (VLAN); virtual private network (VPN); Voice over IP (VoIP); wide area network (WAN); Wi-Fi Protected Access (WPA); Wired Equivalent Privacy (WEP); WPA2

Exercises

7.1 Organizing Network Components

Estimated time: 10 minutes

1. Place each of the following items into the proper layer of the OSI model: MAC addresses, ASCII, TCP, IP, and HTTP.

   _____ Application

   _____ Presentation

   _____ Session

   _____ Transport

   _____ Network

   _____ Data link

   _____ Physical

2. Place each of the following pieces of equipment into the proper layer of the OSI model: fiber, routers, hubs, switches, bridges, packet filters, and application proxy firewall.

   _____ Application

   _____ Presentation

   _____ Session

   _____ Transport

   _____ Network

   _____ Data link

   _____ Physical

Answers to questions 1 and 2 are as follows:

Application—HTTP, application proxy firewall

Presentation—ASCII

Session—not applicable

Transport—TCP

Network—IP, routers, packet filters

Data link—MAC addresses, switches, bridges

Physical—Fiber, hubs

3. Review the items shown in Table 7-10. The layers are out of order and scrambled. Write in the correct layer number for each layer along with the layer name, equipment, and protocol found at each layer.

Table 7-10 OSI Equipment and Protocols

Layer	Layer Name	Equipment	Protocol or Service
	Network	Hubs	IP
	Physical	Routers	UDP
	Application	Switches	TCP
	Data link	Gateways	Telnet
	Transport	Copper cable	HTTP
	Presentation	Repeaters	Ethernet
	Session	Bridges	Token Ring

4. Place the layers listed in Table 7-10 in their proper order in Table 7-11. Some items may be used more than once.

Table 7-11   Blank OSI Challenge Table

Layer	Layer Name	Equipment	Protocol or Service

5. Compare the answers you wrote in Table 7-11 to the completed Table 7-11.

Table 7-11   Completed OSI Challenge Table

Layer	Layer Name	Equipment	Protocol or Service
1	Physical	Copper cable Hubs Repeaters	—
2	Data link	Switches Bridges	Ethernet Token Ring
3	Network	Routers	IP
4	Transport	Gateways	TCP UDP
5	Session	Gateways	—
6	Presentation	Gateways	—
7	Application	Gateways	HTTP Telnet

Review Questions

1. Which of the following is the best example of a method to measure latency?

   a. SNMP management tool

   b. ping command

   c. traceroute

   d. RMON

2. Which of the following is the proper order for the OSI model layers, from the bottom up?

   a. Data link, media access, network, transport, session, presentation, application

   b. Physical, data link, network, transport, session, presentation, application

   c. Physical, data link, network, transport, presentation, session, application

   d. Data link, physical link, network, transport, presentation, session, application

3. Which of the following is an example of data transmission to a group of devices on a LAN?

   a. Unicast

   b. Multicast

   c. Anycast

   d. Broadcast

4. Which of the following is the best explanation of ARP?

   a. ARP resolves known domain names to unknown IP addresses.

   b. ARP resolves known IP addresses to unknown MAC addresses.

   c. ARP resolves known IP addresses to unknown domain names.

   d. ARP resolves known MAC addresses to unknown IP addresses.

5. Which of the following best matches the description of a packet-switching technology with a committed information rate?

   a. T1

   b. ATM

   c. X.25

   d. Frame Relay

6. Which of the following is a fiber-optic cable standard?

   a. 1000BASE-TX

   b. 1000BASE-LX

   c. 10BASE-T

   d. 100BASE-TX

7. An auditor has been asked to perform a network audit. Which of the following is the best place for the auditor to start?

   a. Review help-desk report

   b. Review database architecture

   c. Interview users

   d. Review network diagrams

8. Which of the following network designs offers the highest level of redundancy?

   a. Bus

   b. Star

   c. Ring

   d. Mesh

9. Which of the following devices would best be suited for reducing the number of collisions on a LAN?

   a. Switch

   b. Hub

   c. Bridge

   d. Router

10. Which of the following statements best describes packet switching?

    a. Packet switching allows the customer to determine the best path.

    b. Packet switching takes a dedicated path established by the vendor.

    c. Packet switching allows the vendor to determine the best path.

    d. Packet switching takes a dedicated path established by the client.

11. Which of the following could be considered an issue with SNMP?

    a. Hard to configure

    b. Cleartext transfer

    c. Considered outdated

    d. Only useful with printers

12. Which of the following must be performed on a device running Wireshark for it to see all traffic at the network interface?

    a. The switch port must be mirrored.

    b. The device must be placed in promiscuous mode.

    c. The NIC must be modified.

    d. All traffic is accessible by default.

13. Which of the following must be performed on the switch for a device running Wireshark for it to see all network traffic?

    a. The switch port must be mirrored.

    b. The switch must be placed in promiscuous mode.

    c. The NIC must be modified.

    d. All traffic is accessible by default.

14. Which wireless standard operates at speeds of 150/200/600Mbps?

    a. 802.11a

    b. 802.11ac

    c. 802.11i

    d. 802.11g

15. Which of the following was the first to add TKIP?

    a. RADIUS

    b. WEP

    c. WPA2

    d. WPA

Suggested Readings and Resources

- **COBIT 5 framework:** www.isaca.org/cobit/pages/cobit-5-framework-product-page.aspx

- **Auditing operating systems:** https://m.isaca.org/Knowledge-Center/Research/ResearchDeliverables/Pages/UNIX-LINUX-Operating-System-Security-Audit-Assurance-Program.aspx

- **Digital rights management:** http://searchsecurity.techtarget.com/feature/Digital-rights-management-protection-The-next-level-of-data-security

- **Software licensing auditing:** http://emerset.com/insights-and-resources/microsoft-audit-readiness/microsoft-software-licensing-audit-looking/

- **Firewall auditing:** www.algosec.com/firewall-auditing-compliance/

- **Audit and IDS:** https://people.redhat.com/sgrubb/audit/audit-ids.pdf

- **Ransomware:** https://globalvoices.org/2017/05/16/why-is-china-home-to-half-of-the-computers-infected-with-wannacry-ransomware/ for more details.)

- **Privacy impact assessments:** www.dhs.gov/xlibrary/assets/privacy/privacy_pia_template.pdf

- **Auditing network performance:** www.tecmint.com/audit-network-performance-security-and-troubleshooting-in-linux/

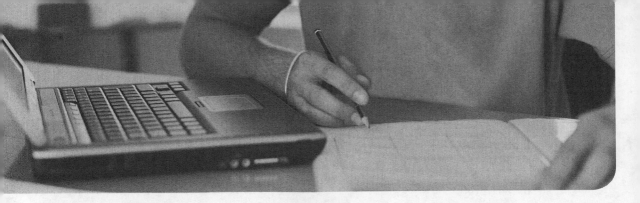

The following exam domain is partially covered in this chapter:

Domain 5—Protection of Information Assets

This chapter covers the following topics:

- **Access Control:** Controlling who has access and how that access occurs is one of the first lines of defense in protecting an organization's assets.

- **Security Controls for Hardware and Software:** Security controls are used to protect critical asserts and can deter, delay, prevent, and detect unauthorized access attempts.

- **Protection of Information Assets:** One of the keys to protecting assets is by means of encryption.

- **Data Leakage and Attacks:** Regardless of the types of controls that are used, data leaks will occur. Auditors should understand the types of data leaks that can occur and the threat of exposure.

CHAPTER 8

Protection of Assets

The protection of assets is one of the key concerns of an auditor. The first step in protecting assets is typically access control—protecting the point at which authorized users are allowed access and unauthorized users are denied access. Another key area is the placement of controls to protect assets. These controls are typically designed to deter, delay, prevent, and detect issues. A large portion of this chapter deals with encryption. Encryption is one of the primary controls used to protect data at rest and data in motion. The chapter concludes by examining the ways security can be breached and assets may be exposed.

"Do I Know This Already?" Quiz

The "Do I Know This Already?" quiz allows you to assess whether you should read this entire chapter thoroughly or jump to the "Exam Preparation Tasks" section. If you are in doubt about your answers to these questions or your own assessment of your knowledge of the topics, read the entire chapter. Table 8-1 lists the major headings in this chapter and their corresponding "Do I Know This Already?" quiz questions. You can find the answers at the bottom of the page following the quiz and in Appendix A, "Answers to the 'Do I Know This Already?' Quizzes and Review Questions."

Table 8-1   "Do I Know This Already?" Section-to-Question Mapping

Foundation Topics Section	Questions Covered in This Section
Access Control	1–4
Security Controls for Hardware and Software	5– 8
Protection of Information Assets	9
Data Leakage and Attacks	10

CAUTION   The goal of self-assessment is to gauge your mastery of the topics in this chapter. If you do not know the answer to a question or are only partially sure of the answer, you should mark that question as incorrect for purposes of the self-assessment. Giving yourself credit for an answer you correctly guess skews your self-assessment results and might provide you with a false sense of security.

1. Which of the following is seen as the weakest form of authentication?

   a. Something you know

   b. Something you have

   c. Something you are

   d. Somewhere you are

2. Which of the following best describes the equal error rate?

   a. This measurement indicates the point at which FRR does not equal FAR.

   b. This measurement indicates the point at which FRR is lower than FAR.

   c. This measurement indicates the point at which FRR is higher than FAR.

   d. This measurement indicates the point at which FRR equals FAR.

3. Which of the following is the best example of SSO?

   a. RADIUS

   b. Diameter

   c. TACACS

   d. Kerberos

4. If Cathy uses the same credentials to obtain access to Company A and Company B, this is best described as which of the following?

   a. RADIUS

   b. Federation

   c. SSO

   d. Two-factor authentication

5. An audit found that controls were needed for the integrity of data. Which of the following algorithms is used for integrity?

   a. RSA

   b. DES

   c. MD5

   d. SSH

6. Which of the following is a symmetric algorithm?

   a. RSA

   b. DES

   c. MD5

   d. ECC

7. Which of the following is an asymmetric algorithm?

   a. RSA

   b. DES

   c. MD5

   d. AES

8. Which of the following can be used for the protection of email?

   a. SMIME

   b. 3DES

   c. Twofish

   d. SAFER

9. Which of the following is the highest business level classification?

   a. Confidential

   b. Top secret

   c. Private

   d. Restricted

10. Which of the following attack techniques requires the hacker to have both the plaintext and the ciphertext of one or more messages?

   a. Ciphertext only

   b. Known ciphertext

   c. Known plaintext

   d. Man-in-the-middle

Foundation Topics

Access Control

Access control is one of the most important topics in this chapter. Controls on information are put into place to protect against unauthorized access by both insiders and outsiders.

This section examines both logical and physical access controls. For logical access controls, user identification and authentication (verifying that users are who they say they are) are considered the first steps of the process. Auditors should verify that users are restricted to only authorized functions and data.

Identification and Authentication (I&A)

The first step of granting logical access to a user is the process of identification. Identification asserts the user's identity and is considered a *one-to-many search process* because the system must match the user to a unique identity. Identity is needed because it provides accountability and holds users responsible for their actions. The most common way for users to identify themselves is by presenting user identification (user ID), such as a username, account number, or personal identification number (PIN).

Authentication is the second step in the I&A process. It is commonly referred to as a *one-to-one process* because it is a comparative process; no search is involved. Three authentication methods exist:

- **Authentication by knowledge:** What a user knows
- **Authentication by ownership:** What a user has
- **Authentication by characteristic:** What a person is and does

Authentication by Knowledge

Of the three types, what a user knows is the most widely used method of authentication. Passwords are a good example of this type of authentication. Good passwords should be easy to remember but difficult for an attacker to guess. Passwords should initially be set by network administrators or generated by a system. Upon initial user

Answers to the "Do I Know This Already?" Quiz:

1. A; 2. D; 3. D; 4. B; 5. C; 6. B; 7. A; 8. A; 9. A; 10. C

logon, the password should be changed. Passwords should have a lockout threshold established. For example, if a user enters the wrong password three times in a row, the account should be disabled or locked for a predetermined length of time. If passwords need to be reset, the process should ensure that the user's identity is verified and that passwords are not passed in any insecure or open format. User identity can be verified by having the user answer several cognitive questions, such as high school attended, first pet's name, or first best friend; or by requiring the user to retrieve the new password in person or by transmitting the password securely to the employee's supervisor.

Passwords are perishable; they grow stale and need to be changed on a regular basis. Most of us lack the cognitive ability to create several complex, unique, and unrelated passwords on a daily or weekly basis. Imagine the following situation: You have just started a new job, and your boss has asked that you create several login passwords. Do you invent hard-to-remember, complex passwords; do you use something that you can easily remember when you return the next day; or do you write down the password? Most individuals will choose an easy password or write it down rather than risk forgetting the password and creating a bad impression.

One of the responsibilities of an auditor is to verify password policies and ensure that they are strong enough to protect the confidentiality, integrity, and availability (CIA) of information and assets. Good password policies should offer the following guidelines regarding password characteristics:

- Do not use personal information.

- Do not use common words or names.

- Ensure that passwords are complex and use upper- and lowercase letters, numbers, and characters (such as !@#$%^&).

- Require that passwords be changed regularly.

- Have session timeouts.

- Limit logon attempts to a small number of times, such as three successive attempts.

NOTE Some organizations use geofencing to control access. Geofencing uses GPS or RFID technology to specify a geographic boundary so that items may or may not be accessible, depending on where you are.

Authentication by Ownership

This type of authentication, what a user has, can include various types of *tokens*, such as badge systems, smart cards, USB keys, and SecurID devices. Tokens are widely used in *two-factor authentication* schemes because they require something you have (the token) and something you know (a personal identification number). The system uses this general process:

1. The server sends the user a value.

2. The value is entered into the token device.

3. The token performs a hashing process on the entered value.

4. The new, computed value is displayed on the LCD screen of the token device.

5. The user enters the displayed value into the computer for authentication.

TIP   Two-factor authentication requires two of these three methods: something you know, something you have, something you are. A bank card and PIN is an example of two-factor authentication; a password and a PIN is not (because it is two things you know).

Authentication by Characteristic

Authentication by characteristic—what a person is or does—is known as *biometrics*. Biometric systems verify identity by either a physiological trait, such as a fingerprint or retina scan, or behavioral characteristic, such as a keystroke or signature pattern. Some common biometric types include the following:

- Fingerprint
- Hand geometry
- Palm scan
- Voice pattern
- Retina pattern/scan
- Iris pattern/recognition
- Signature dynamics
- Facial recognition
- Keystroke dynamics

Important concerns for an auditor when examining biometric systems include the following:

- **Accuracy:** Accuracy demonstrates how well the system can separate authentic users from imposters.

- **User acceptance:** Will users accept the system? The chosen biometric system must fit the environment.

- **Misuse:** Some users may look for ways to bypass or cheat the system. With the right tools (some kind of putty or gel imprint), ingenuity, and a morally ambivalent coworker, an employee can "clock in" without even being there.

- **Processing speed:** Tied closely to user acceptance, processing speed indicates how quickly the decision to accept or deny is made. Slow systems tend to frustrate users and, thus, result in lower acceptance.

- **False reject rate (FRR):** The FRR is the percentage of legitimate users who are denied access. This is also known as a Type I error.

- **False accept rate (FAR):** This measurement is the percentage of users who are allowed access but who are not authorized users. It is also known as a Type II error.

- **Equal error rate (EER):** This measurement indicates the point at which FRR equals FAR. Low numbers indicate that the system has greater accuracy. Figure 8-1 shows an example.

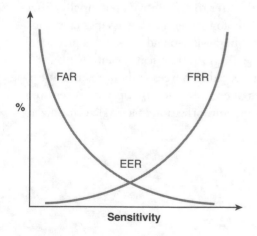

Figure 8-1   Equal Error Rate

TIP   CISA exam candidates must understand the value of biometric data and must ensure that any biometric data stored has adequate mechanisms in place to protect it from attack or disclosure.

No matter which of the three primary types of authentication methods is used, the user most likely will have to log on many times onto many different systems throughout the work day.

NOTE   Some sources list *somewhere you are* as a valid forth type of authentication. This authentication type looks at user location as a factor of authentication.

Somewhere you are systems are beginning to be used in some businesses and government agencies that require extremely high security. An example could be the GPS location of a phone that is used to allow or block access based on the physical location of the device.

Single Sign-on

Many users grow weary of having to log on to many different systems throughout the day to complete their required tasks. Single sign-on (SSO) is an attempt to address this problem. If an organization is using passwords and single sign-on is not being used, each separate system requires the user to remember a potentially different username and password combination. Employees tend to bypass mental strain by writing down passwords and usernames. Single sign-on addresses this problem by permitting users to authenticate once to a single authentication authority, and then they are allowed access to all other protected resources without reauthenticating. Single sign-on can be seen as a process of consolidation that places the entire organization's functions of authentication and authorization in a single centralized location. SSO can include the following:

- Distributed systems
- Mainframe systems
- Local users
- Remote users
- Network security mechanisms

Implementing single sign-on is challenging because most logical networks are heterogeneous. Networks, operating systems, mainframes, distributed systems, and databases must all be integrated to work together. Advantages to single sign-on include the following:

- Efficient logon process

- Stronger passwords created by users

- No need for multiple passwords

- Enforcement of timeout and attempt thresholds across the entire platform

- Centralized administration

Single sign-on does have some drawbacks: It is expensive, and if attackers gain entry, they have access to everything. Including unique platforms also can be challenging. Examples of popular single sign-on systems are Kerberos and SESAME.

Massachusetts Institute of Technology (MIT) created Kerberos, which provides several key services:

- **Security:** Kerberos protects authentication traffic so that a network eavesdropper cannot easily impersonate a user.

- **Reliability:** The service is available to users when needed.

- **Transparency:** For the end user, the process is transparent.

- **Scalability:** Kerberos supports everything from a small number of users to a large number of clients and servers.

Kerberos consists of three parts: the client, the server, and a trusted third-party key distribution center (KDC) that mediates between them. The KDC is composed of two systems:

- **Authentication service:** The authentication service issues ticket-granting tickets (TGTs) that are good for admission to the ticket-granting service (TGS). Before network clients can obtain tickets for services, they must obtain a TGT from the authentication service.

- **Ticket-granting service:** Clients receive tickets to specific target services through this service.

Kerberos follows a structured approach to authentication (see Figure 8-2):

Kerberos Ticket Exchange

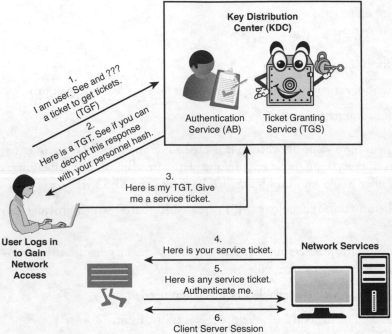

Figure 8-2 Kerberos Authentication

1. The client asks the KDC for a ticket, making use of the authentication service (AS).

2. The client receives the encrypted ticket and the session key.

3. The client sends the encrypted TGT to the TGS and requests a ticket for access to the application server.

4. The TGS decrypts the TGT by using its own private key and returns the ticket to the client, which allows it to access the application server.

5. The client sends this ticket along with an authenticator to the application server.

6. The application server sends confirmation of its identity to the client.

Federation

When managing user access to multiple sites, federation is a useful service. Federation is an access control technique for managing identity across multiple platforms and entities. As organizations have become more tightly tied together, they have developed a greater need to share information and services. The first step in this process is to establish trust. Therefore, many organizations are searching for methods to share common authentication information. You can see an example of a federated identity any time you go to an airline website. After booking a flight, you are asked whether you also need a hotel room. Clicking Yes might take you to a major hotel chain website to which your identity and travel information have already been passed. This process saves the process of logging in a second time (to the hotel website). Such systems are already in use. For example, you can use Facebook or Google credentials to log in to the Digg website (see Figure 8-3).

Figure 8-3 Federation

> **NOTE** *Federation* is an arrangement between two or more organizations that lets users use the same credentials to obtain access to the enterprises in the group.

Today's systems are much more distributed than in the past and have a much greater reliance on the Internet. At the same time, there has been a move toward service-enabled delivery of services. There has also been a move to create web services that have a more abstract architectural style. This style, known as service-oriented architecture (SOA), attempts to bind together disjointed pieces of software. A CISA candidate should have some knowledge of several components in this realm, such as the following:

- **Web Services Security (WS Security):** WS Security is an extension to Simple Object Access Protocol (SOAP) that is designed to add security to web services.

- **Extensible Markup Language (XML):** Years ago, Hypertext Markup Language (HTML) dominated the web. Today, XML is the standard framework. XML is a standard that allows for a common expression of metadata. XML typically follows the SOAP standard.

- **Service Provisioning Markup Language (SPML):** SPML is an XML-based framework that can be used to exchange access control information between organizations so that a user logged into one entity can have the access rights passed to the other.

- **Security Assertion Markup Language (SAML):** SAML is an example of a new protocol designed for cross-web service authentication and authorization. Over time, this protocol holds promise to improve new generations of web services. SAML is an XML-based open standard designed for authentication and authorization between security domains. The protocol was created by the Organization for the Advancement of Structured Information Standards (OASIS), a nonprofit consortium that develops and adopts open standards for the global information society. One product of the group's work is SAML. SAML allows business entities to make assertions regarding the identity, attributes, and entitlements of a subject. At the core of SAML is the XML schema that defines the representation of security data; this can be used to pass the security context between applications. SAML assertions are communicated by a web browser through cookies or URL strings.

- **OpenID:** OpenID is an open standard that is used as an authentication scheme. OpenID allows users to log on to many different websites using the same identity on each of the websites. For example, you may log in to a news site with your Facebook username and password. OpenID, which was developed by the OpenID Foundation, works as a set of standards that includes OpenID Authentication, Attribute Exchange, Simple Registration Extension, and Provider Authentication Policy Exchange.

- **Shibboleth:** Shibboleth is a distributed web resource access control system. Shibboleth enhances federation by allowing the sharing of web-based resources. When using Shibboleth, the target website trusts the source site to authenticate its users and manage their attributes correctly. The disadvantage of this model is that there is no differentiation between authentication authorities and attribute authorities.

- **Where Are You From (WAYF):** WAYF is a single sign-on methodology which allows the use of one single login to access several web-based services. When a claimant submits a request to access a remote website to which the claimant has not authenticated, the remote website forwards the claimant's login request to a WAYF service. The WAYF service creates connections between the login systems at the connected institutions and external web-based services.

Remote Access

Technology has changed the workplace. Email, cell phones, and the Internet have changed when and how employees can work and how they can connect to the organization's assets. Many employees don't even go into the workplace now. The International Telework Association and Council reports that approximately 32 million people work at home at least part-time for an employer. These telecommuters pose a special challenge to security. Clients, consultants, vendors, customer representatives, and business partners might also require remote access to the organization. All these users will expect the same level of access they would have if they were to connect locally. A well-designed architecture is required to provide this level of service. A CISA candidate must understand these issues and common connectivity methods.

TIP When reviewing network access, an auditor should always find all points of access. This is a critical step and is required for a complete and thorough examination.

The following are some common methods for centralized authentication:

- Remote Access Dial-In User Service (RADIUS)
- Diameter
- Terminal Access Control Access Control System (TACACS)

RADIUS

RADIUS uses a modem pool for connecting users to the organization's network. The RADIUS server contains usernames, passwords, and other information used to validate the user. Many systems use a callback system for added security control. When used, the callback system calls the user back at a predefined phone number.

RADIUS is a client–server protocol used to authenticate dial-in users and authorize access.

Diameter

You can never say the creators of Diameter didn't have a sense of humor. Diameter's name is a pun because the "diameter is twice the RADIUS." Actually, Diameter is enhanced RADIUS in that it was designed to do much more than provide services to dialup users. Diameter is detailed in RFC 3588 and can use TCP, UDP, or Stream Control Transmission Protocol (SCTP). The primary advantage of Diameter is that it supports protocols and devices not even envisioned when RADIUS and TACACS were created, such as VoIP (Voice over IP), Ethernet over PPP, and mobile IP. VoIP is the routing of voice communication over data networks, and mobile IP is the ability of a user to keep the same IP. Consider the example of taking your IP-based phone from your provider's network to an overseas location. In such a situation, you need a home IP address and also a care-of address. Although you may be a T-Mobile customer, your data needs to be routed to you while in Jamaica and using the Digicel network. Diameter provides this capability and is considered a very secure solution because cryptographic support of IPsec or TLS is mandatory.

Diameter is designed to use two items. The first is the base protocol that is designed to provide secure communication between Diameter devices and enables various types of information to be transmitted, such as headers, security options, commands, and attribute/value pairs (AVPs). The second item is the extensions. Extensions are built on top of the base protocol to allow various technologies to use Diameter for authentication. This component is what interacts with other services, such as VoIP, wireless, and cell phone authentication. Finally, Diameter offers an upgrade path from RADIUS, but RADIUS components cannot talk to Diameter components.

TACACS

TACACS is a less popular approach and another remote access protocol that provides authentication, authorization, and accountability. TACACS is very similar to RADIUS. TACACS+, an upgrade to TACACS, was introduced in 1990 and offers extended two-factor authentication.

Additional Remote Access Options

The Internet's popularity has made it an option for remote connectivity. That idea has matured into the concept of virtual private networks (VPNs). The Internet Engineering Task Force (IETF) defines a VPN as "an emulation of a private Wide

Area Network (WAN) using shared or public IP facilities, such as the Internet or private IP backbones." The advantage of a VPN is that it is cheaper than a dedicated line. VPNs provide the same capabilities as a private network but at a much lower cost. The biggest concern when using a VPN is privacy; after all, you're sending your company's traffic over the public Internet. Therefore, the traffic must be encrypted before being sent. All remote access methods have a certain degree of risk:

- Denial of service

- Loss of physical control of the client's system

- Possibility that the client system will be hacked to gain remote access capability

- Possibility that the remote access system will be hacked to gain access

These risks can best be addressed by good policies and procedures that specify using strong controls. Strong authentication should also be used to ensure that intruders cannot easily guess passwords or compromise remote access systems. Encryption should also be a key component of any remote access system; encryption is the best control that can be used to prevent the interception of information.

TIP Encryption is the number-one control that can be used to protect information while being transmitted to and from a remote network to the organization's network.

SSH

Not all remote connectivity protocols are designed the same. Years ago Telnet was the standard. Telnet sends all data via cleartext, along with the username and password. A more secure alternative is Secure Shell (SSH), a cryptographic network protocol for operating network services securely over an unsecured network. SSH was designed as a replacement for Telnet and the Berkeley R utilities. For anyone needing to connect to a system remotely, SSH provides for confidentiality and integrity of data.

From an auditing standpoint, it is important to keep in mind that not all versions are the same. The original version has been replaced, and SSH is now at version 2.x. Also, just because someone is allowed to have remote access to a computer does not mean that person always needs root or administrative access. Allowing root login over SSH is considered a poor security practice and should be restricted.

VPNs

While VPNs and SSH tunnels can both securely tunnel network traffic over an encrypted connection, they are not the same. Imagine having 50 SSH connections to a server. The overhead would be unmanageable in many ways. SSH is simply a way to remotely connect to a terminal on another machine. A VPN creates a new network-level connection on a machine. VPNs are generally divided into two categories:

- **Remote access VPN:** Used to connect a user to a private network and access its services and resources remotely.

- **Site-to-site VPN:** Typically used in corporations. Site-to-site VPNs connect the network of one corporate location to the network at another office location. With this VPN type, one router acts as a VPN client, and the other router acts as a VPN server. Communication between these two devices starts only after authentication is validated between the two parties.

Examples of VPN tunneling protocols include the following:

- **Point-to-Point Tunneling Protocol (PPTP):** PPTP was developed by a group of vendors. It consists of two components: the transport, which maintains the virtual connection, and the encryption, which ensures confidentiality. It can operate at 40 bits or 128 bits.

- **Layer 2 Tunneling Protocol (L2TP):** L2TP was created by Cisco and Microsoft to replace Layer 2 Forwarding (L2F) and Point-to-Point Tunneling Protocol (PPTP.) L2TP merged the capabilities of L2F and PPTP into one tunneling protocol. By itself, it provides no encryption; but it is deployed with IPsec as a VPN solution.

- **Secure Sockets Layer (SSL):** SSL was developed by Netscape for transmitting private documents over the Internet. Unlike S-HTTP, SSL is application independent. One of the advantages of SSL is its cryptographic independence. The protocol is merely a framework for communicating certificates, encrypted keys, and data. The most robust version of SSL is SSLv3, which provides for mutual authentication and compression.

- **Transport Layer Security (TLS):** TLS encrypts the communication between a host and a client. TLS typically makes use of an X.509 digital certificate for server authentication. This mechanism provides strong authentication of the server to the client, so the client can trust that it is connected to the correct remote system. TLS consists of two protocols: TLS Record Protocol and the TLS Handshake Protocol.

- **IP Security (IPsec):** Widely used for VPNs, IPsec can provide Encapsulating Security Payload (ESP) and/or an authentication header (AH). ESP provides confidentiality by encrypting the data packet. AH provides integrity and authentication.

Physical and Environmental Access Controls

The first line in the defense-in-depth model is the design and placement of exterior controls. Auditors should have an understanding of how these controls are used for the protection of information assets. As an auditor, you may be asked to be a part of a team to review the design of a new facility, and you might have the ability to ensure that many of these controls are added during design. That's not always the case, however; often you are tasked with examining an existing facility. In both new and old facilities, the goal should be to look for controls that have been designed so that the breach of any one defensive layer will not compromise the physical security of the organization. Perimeter security controls can be any physical barrier, such as a wall, card-controlled entry, or a staffed reception desk. The same types of authentication systems that are used for logical access are also needed for physical access control. This can include badges, smart cards, biometrics, and so on. Perimeter security requires examination of the following:

- Natural boundaries at the location
- Fences or walls around the site
- Physical access control
- Gates, access doors, the delivery dock, and entry points
- The design of the outer walls of a building
- Lighting and exterior design of the complex

Fences, Gates, and Bollards

Fences are one of the simplest levels of physical defense and one of the key components of perimeter security. When it is of the proper design and height, fencing can delay an intruder and also work as a psychological barrier. Just think about the Berlin Wall. This monument to the Cold War was quite effective in preventing East Germans from escaping to the west. Before its fall in 1989, most individuals that escaped to the west did so by hiding in trunks of cars or by bribing guards. The wall worked as a strong physical as well as psychological barrier. Does the height or gauge of wire used in the fence matter? Yes. Taller fences with thicker gauge wire work better at deterring determined intruders, as outlined in Table 8-2 and Table 8-3.

Table 8-2   Fence Mesh and Gauge

Type	Security	Mesh	Gauge
A	Extremely high	3/8 inch	11 gauge
B	Very high	1 inch	9 gauge
C	High	1 inch	11 gauge
D	Greater	2 inch	6 gauge
E	Normal	2 inch	9 gauge

Table 8-3   Fence Height and Purpose

Height	Security	Description
3–4 feet	Very little	Will deter only casual trespassers.
6–7 feet	Moderate	Too tall to easily climb.
8 feet or greater	High	Of sufficient height to deter determined intruders. Topping with three strands of razor wire gives the fence even greater security.

Organizations that require very high security might consider using a perimeter intrusion and detection and assessment system (PIDAS). This special fencing system works somewhat like an intrusion detection system in that it has sensors to detect someone climbing or cutting the fence.

Although fences are a good start, more physical controls, such as proper gates, can help. Gates act as chokepoints to control the ingress and egress of employees and visitors into and out of the facility. Just as with fences, standards govern the strength of gates and the security of their design, as detailed in UL Standard 325.

In addition to people, vehicles must also be restricted and otherwise controlled on the grounds of a facility. One method of controlling vehicles is to use *bollards*. Made of concrete or steel, bollards are used to block vehicular traffic. You might have noticed them in front of the doors of a facility or at a shopping mall; sometimes they even look like large flower pots. Regardless of their shape, they are designed for one purpose: to prevent cars and trucks from ramming into a building and smashing doors. Recently designed bollards have electronic sensors to detect collisions and notify building inhabitants that someone has rammed the facility. Although fences are considered the first line of defense, bollards are a close second because they further protect employees and the facility from common smash-and-grab techniques and terrorist car bombings.

TIP   CISA exam candidates must understand that some physical controls cannot be tested. For example, you most likely will not set off a fire extinguisher, but you can make sure that the fire extinguisher has been serviced regularly and refilled as regulations recommend. Auditing physical controls requires mainly observation. While touring a facility, visually observe the safeguards discussed throughout this chapter and note their presence or absence.

Other Physical and Environmental Controls

A few other exterior controls can further secure the facility:

- **Using dogs for guard duty:** Breeds such as German Shepherds and Chow Chows have been used for centuries to guard facilities and assets. Dogs can be trained and are loyal, obedient, and steadfast, yet they are sometimes unpredictable and could bite or harm the wrong person. Because of these factors, dogs are usually restricted to exterior premises control and should be used with caution.

- **Adopting a low-key design:** The last thing an organization that handles sensitive information or high-value assets wants to do is to advertise its presence to attackers or others that might target the facility. A building or department should be discreetly identified. Server rooms, computer rooms, and other sensitive areas should not be easily visible and should contain no windows.

- **Controlling points of entrance:** Just as gates are used to control how individuals can enter and leave the property, doors should be used to control access into the building. All unnecessary entry points to the grounds and the facility should be eliminated.

- **Using adequate lighting:** Lighting provides great perimeter protection. Far too much criminal activity happens at night or in poorly lit areas. Outside lighting discourages prowlers and thieves. Failure to adequately light parking lots and other high-traffic areas also could lead to lawsuits if an employee or a visitor is attacked in a poorly lit area. Effective lighting means that the system is designed to put the light where it is needed in the proper wattage. More light isn't necessarily better: Too much light causes overlighting and glare.

During an audit of physical security, the auditor will need to look for a number of controls that present. These controls should include warning signs or notices posted to deter trespassing and also, any item that might allow an attacker to bypass physical security. This includes securing any opening that is 96 square inches or larger within 18 feet of the ground, such as manholes and tunnels, gates leading to the basement, elevator shafts, ventilation openings, and skylights. Even the roof, basement, and walls of a building might contain vulnerable points of potential entry and should, therefore, be assessed. When these activities have been completed, the auditor can move on to analyzing interior controls.

Using Guards to Restrict Access

Guards are a very basic type of protection. Guards have one very basic skill that sets them apart from computerized gear: discernment. Guards have the ability to make a judgment call, to look at something and know that it is just not right. Computerized premises-control equipment has actually increased the need for guards because someone must manage all these systems. Guards also can play a dual role by answering the phone, taking on the role of receptionist and escorting visitors while in the facility. If guards are being used at a facility you are visiting, look closely to see how they are used because the principle of defense-in-depth can also be applied here. Guards are most useful with locked doors used in conjunction with closed-circuit TV (CCTV) systems. The CCTV systems can be actively monitored or recorded and watched later. CCTV systems don't prevent security breaches; they just alert the guard to a potential problem as it is occurring or afterward.

Guards do have some disadvantages—after all, they are human. Guards are capable of poor judgment and can make mistakes. Therefore, if an organization hires guards from an external vendor, they should be bonded to protect the agency from loss.

Whether or not a guard is in place, the movement of visitors throughout a facility should be controlled. Anyone entering the building, including friends, visitors, vendors, contractors, and even maintenance personnel, should be escorted. A mantrap, also called a deadman door, can control access into or out of the facility; these usually are found at the entryways of high-security areas and require the outer door to be closed before authentication can take place and the inner door is opened. This is really just a system of doors that are arranged so that when one opens, the other remains locked. Some organizations also use turnstiles to control the ingress and egress of employees and visitors.

> **NOTE** Maintenance procedures of security controls should not be overlooked. An auditor should review who is authorized to work on the controls, how they have been vetted, and what level of access they have. Each of these factors is important.

Locks

Mechanical locks are one of the most effective and widely used forms of access control. Nothing provides as great of a level of protection for so little cost. Locks have been used for at least 4,000 years. The Egyptians used locks made of wood. Lock design improved during the 1700s, when *warded* and *tumbler* locks began to be used. These are the two most common types of locks used today.

The *warded lock*, the most basically designed mechanical lock still in use, uses a series of wards that a key must match up to. This is the cheapest type of mechanical lock and also the easiest to pick. You can find these at any local hardware store, but they should not be used to protect a valuable asset.

Tumbler locks are considered more advanced because they contain more parts and are harder to pick. Linus Yale patented the modern tumbler lock in 1848. When the right key is inserted into the cylinder of a tumbler lock, the pins are lifted to the right height so that the device can open or close. The correct key has the proper number of notches and raised areas that allow the pins to be shifted into the proper position. The pins are spring-loaded so that when the key is removed, the pins return to the locked position. Figure 8-4 shows an example of a tumbler lock.

Another common form of lock is a *tubular* lock. Tubular locks, also known as Ace locks, are considered very secure because they are harder to pick. A tubular lock requires a round key, as the lock itself has the pins arranged in a circular pattern. These are used for computers, vending machines, and other high-security devices.

When examining locks, remember that you get what you pay for: More expensive locks are usually better made. The quality of a lock is determined by its grade. Table 8-4 describes the three grades of locks.

A common type of pin tumbler lock,
of the euro cylinder type.

Figure 8-4   Tumbler Lock

Table 8-4   Lock Grades

Quality	Description
Grade 3	Consumer locks of the weakest design
Grade 2	Light-duty commercial locks or heavy-duty residential locks
Grade 1	Commercial locks of the highest security

Different types of locks provide different levels of protection. The American National Standards Institute (ANSI) defines the strength and durability of locks. For example, Grade 3 locks are designed to function for 200,000 cycles, a Grade 2 lock must function for 400,000 cycles, and a Grade 1 lock must function for 800,000 cycles. Higher-grade locks are designed to withstand much more usage, are less likely to fail sooner, or wear so that they can be easily bypassed. Thus, it's important to select the appropriate lock to obtain the required level of security.

One way to bypass a lock is to pick it. This is usually not a criminal's preferred method. Breaking a window, prying a doorframe, or even knocking a hole in sheetrock might all be faster methods to gain access. Individuals who pick locks do so because it is a stealthy way to bypass security controls and might make it harder for victims to figure out that they have been compromised. These basic components are used to pick locks:

- **Tension wrenches:** These are not much more than a small angled flathead screwdriver. They come in various thicknesses and sizes.

- **Picks:** As the name implies, these are similar to a dentist pick. Picks are small, angled, and pointed.

Together, these tools can be used to pick a lock. One of the easiest techniques to learn is *scrubbing*, which is accomplished by applying tension to the lock with a tension wrench and then quickly scraping the pins. Some of the pins are placed in a mechanical bind and stuck in the unlocked position.

NOTE   Company keys should be stamped "Do Not Duplicate."

Lighting

Lighting is a common type of perimeter protection. Terms used for the measurement of light include lumen, lux, and foot-candle. One lux is one lumen per square meter, and one foot-candle is one lumen per square foot. Some common types of exterior lights include

- Floodlights
- Streetlights
- Searchlights

Take a moment to look at how the lights are configured the next time you do a physical walk-through or audit of a facility. Outside the company, you will most likely see rows of lights placed evenly around the facility. That is an example of continuous lighting. Areas such as exits, stairways, and building evacuation routes should be equipped with standby lighting. Standby lighting activates only in the event of power outages or during emergencies. Security checkpoints are another location where you will see careful design of the illumination. Here, lights are aimed away from the guard post so that anyone approaching the checkpoint can easily be seen and guards are not exposed in the light. This is an example of glare protection. Glare and overlighting can cause problems by creating very dark areas just outside the range of the lighted area. Exterior lighting involves a balance between too little light and too much light. Each exterior light should each cover its own zone but still allow for some overlap between zones.

CCTV

CCTV can be used as a preventive or detective control. Before the first camera is installed, several important questions must be answered. If the CCTV system is to be used in a real time, preventive environment, a guard or another individual is needed to watch as events occur. If the CCTV system is being used after the fact, it is functioning as a detective control. Different environments require different systems.

If a CCTV system is to be used outside, the amount of illumination is important. Illumination is controlled by an iris that regulates the amount of light that enters the CCTV camera. An automatic iris is designed to be used outside, where the amount of light varies between night and day, whereas a manual iris is used for cameras to be used indoors. CCTV cameras can even be equipped with built-in LEDs or configured for infrared recording.

The depth of field is controlled by the focal length of the lens. Although some systems have fixed focal lengths, others offer the capability to pan, tilt, and zoom (PTZ), allowing the operator to zoom in or adjust the camera as needed. Older CCTV cameras are analog, whereas most modern cameras capture enhanced detail quickly by the use of charge-coupled devices (CCDs). A CCD is similar to the technology found in a fax machine or a photocopier.

A CCTV system can be wired or wireless and comprises many components, including cameras, transmitters, receivers, recorders, monitors, and controllers. CCTV systems provide effective surveillance of entrances and critical access points. If employees are not available to monitor in real time, activity can be recorded and reviewed later. If you are auditing CCTV systems, also consider the rights of workers to privacy or notification of the absence of privacy and consider the existence of potential blind spots.

Heating, Ventilation, and Air Conditioning (HVAC)

Do you know what can be hotter than Houston in the summer? A room full of computers without proper HVAC. Plan for adequate power for the right locations. Rooms that have servers or banks of computers and other IT gear need adequate cooling to protect the equipment. Electronic equipment is quite sensitive; temperatures above 110°F to 115°F can damage circuits. Most data centers are kept around 70°F. Just keep in mind that data center temperature guidelines are only recommendations, and the actual temperature can vary widely from company to company.

High humidity can be a problem because it causes rust and corrosion. Low humidity increases the risk of static electricity, which could damage equipment. The ideal humidity for a data center is 35 to 45 percent.

Ventilation is another important concern. Facilities should maintain positive pressurization and ventilation to control contamination by pushing air outside. This is especially important in case of fire because it ensures that smoke will be pushed out of the facility instead of being pulled in.

The final issue with HVAC is access control. Control of who has access to the system and how they can be contacted is an import issue. These systems must be controlled to protect organizations and their occupants from the threat of chemical and biological threats.

Security Controls for Hardware and Software

The purpose of security controls is to provide reasonable assurance that the hardware and software used by an organization operates as intended, the data is reliable, and the organization is in compliance with applicable laws and regulations. While physical controls can include locks, lighting, and guards, one of the primary controls for software and data is encryption.

Securing Voice Communications

Securing voice communication is a critical concern of an auditor. Long ago, that would have meant protecting analog phone lines. Long before modern-day hacking, *phreakers* were practicing their trade. Phreaking is the art of hacking phone systems. This might sound like a rather complicated affair, but back in the early 1970s, John Draper discovered how to make free phone calls by using a Captain Crunch Whistle. The 2600Hz tone it produced is the same as what is required for bypassing the normal billing process. Phreakers might target insecure private branch exchange (PBX) systems. By selling time on the victim's PBX phone network, the phreaker might run up thousands of dollars in phone charges before the company is aware it is happening. These types of hacks use other companies' PBX systems to sell fake auto insurance policies, cruise ship scams, and other types of social engineering attacks. PBX systems might not be their only target; Voice over IP (VoIP) is another potential target.

Auditors must plan for enough time and resources to examine PBX systems and their features. Common features such as direct inward dial (DID) can be a problematic; an external party can use DID to request a dial tone and then call anywhere in the world for free. Most PBX systems also have the capability to do call logging and auditing, which should be enabled to better track telecommunication activity. Finally, all fax machines and modems connected to the PBX should be identified and recorded with the proper documentation.

VoIP offers organizations a low-cost alternative to traditional long-distance services and analog PBX systems. VoIP functions by placing the voice data into packets and sending them over a packet-switched network. With so much going for it, you might wonder what the disadvantage is. There are actually several. As VoIP is being transmitted over the data network, any break can cripple both the data network and the voice network. If the organization is using the Internet to route calls, none of the protection mechanisms of the public switched telephone network (PSTN) exist. Five hops, six hops, or even more intermediate systems might stand between the sender and the receiver. Any one of them could be used to intercept the call, listen to the call, or forward the call to a malicious third party. Although countermeasures are available, VoIP communication is vulnerable to many attacks, including spoofing, eavesdropping, and denial of service. (For VoIP best practices, security tools, and in-depth information, check out the VoIP Security Alliance website, at http://voipsa.org.)

Encryption's Role as a Security Control

Encryption involves obscuring information and rendering it unreadable to those without special knowledge. A CISA candidate should have knowledge of encryption-related techniques and their uses. Encryption has been used for many centuries by many cultures. Caesar had an encryption standard known as Caesar's cipher, and the ancient Hebrews had one called Atbash. Almost as long as there has been encryption, others have been trying to break encrypted messages. Breaking encrypted messages is known as *cryptanalysis*. In the ninth century, Abu al-Kindi published what is considered to be the first paper to discuss how to break cryptographic systems, titled "A Manuscript on Deciphering Cryptographic Messages." People have long been trying to protect sensitive information, and others have at the same time been trying to reveal it.

Although encryption cannot prevent the loss of data or protect against denial of service, it is a valuable tool to protect the assets of an organization. Encryption can be used to provide confidentiality, integrity, authenticity, and nonrepudiation. Before covering the nuts and bolts of encryption, you need to know a few basic terms to better understand encryption and its components:

- **Algorithm:** The rules or mathematical formula used to encrypt and decrypt data.

- **Cryptography:** The study of secret messages, derived from the Greek terms *kryptos*, which means "hidden," and *grafein*, which means "to write."

- **Ciphertext:** Data that is scrambled and unreadable.

- **Cryptographic key:** The value used to control a cryptographic process.

- **Plaintext:** Cleartext that is readable.

- **Encryption:** The process of transforming data into an unreadable format.

- **Symmetric encryption:** An encryption method that uses the same key to encode and decode data.

- **Asymmetric encryption:** An encryption method that uses one key for encryption and a different key for decryption. Each participant is assigned a pair of keys, consisting of an encryption key and a corresponding decryption key.

Encryption systems must be strong to serve their required purpose. The strength of the encryption system is based on several factors:

- **Algorithm:** Remember that this is the set of instructions used with the cryptographic key to encrypt plaintext data. Not all algorithms are of the same strength. For example, Caesar might have thought his system of encryption was quite strong, but it is seen as relativity insecure today.

- **Cryptographic key:** A user needs the correct key to encrypt or decrypt the information. For example, when my brother was a teenager, my parents took the key to his car for violating curfew. Without the key, he had no way to use the car. Had he made a copy, access would have still been possible.

- **Key length:** Weak keys are easily subverted, whereas stronger keys are hard to break. How strong a key needs to be depends on the value of the data.

High-value data requires more protection than data that has little value. More valuable information needs longer key lengths and more frequent key exchange to protect against attacks.

Modern encryption systems use either symmetric or asymmetric encryption. Each method has unique abilities and specific disadvantages. Symmetric encryption uses a single shared key to encrypt and decrypt data. Asymmetric encryption uses two different keys for encryption and decryption. Each user must maintain a pair of keys. The following sections discuss each of these methods in much more detail; however, first take a quick look at the advantages and disadvantages of each method, as shown in Table 8-5.

Table 8-5   Attributes of Symmetric and Asymmetric Encryption

Type of Encryption	Advantages	Disadvantages
Symmetric	Faster than asymmetric encryption	Key distribution
		Provides only confidentiality
Asymmetric	Easy key exchange	Slower than symmetric encryption
	Can provide confidentiality and authentication	

TIP   Symmetric encryption is faster than asymmetric encryption, but it provides only confidentiality. Asymmetric encryption provides confidentiality and authentication, but it is slower than symmetric algorithms.

Private Key Encryption

Symmetric encryption uses a single shared secret key for encryption and decryption. Symmetric algorithms include the following:

- **Data Encryption Standard (DES):** One of the most well-known symmetric algorithm and the first national standard. DES has been replaced by 3DES and AES.

- **Triple Data Encryption Standard (3DES):** A short term replacement for DES designed to apply the DES cipher three times to each block of data. This stopgap solution was designed to be used until a long term replacement for DES was approved. 3DES was replaced by AES.

- **Blowfish:** A general-purpose symmetric algorithm intended as a replacement for the DES, replaced by Advanced Encryption Standard (AES) and Twofish.

- **Rijndael:** A block cipher that the U.S. government adopted as AES to replace DES.

- **Rivest Cipher 4 (RC4):** A stream-based cipher.

- **Rivest Cipher 5 (RC5):** A block-based cipher.

- **Secure and Fast Encryption Routine (SAFER):** A block-based cipher.

All symmetric algorithms are based on the single shared secret key concept, illustrated in Figure 8-5.

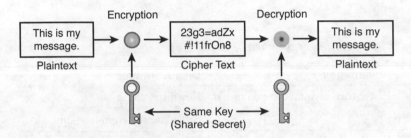

Figure 8-5 Symmetric (Secret Key) Encryption

The strength of symmetric encryption depends on how well the private key is protected. One key is used to both encrypt and decrypt. The dual use of keys makes this system simple and also causes its weakness. Symmetric encryption is fast and can encrypt and decrypt very quickly; it also is considered strong. Symmetric encryption is very hard to break if a large key is used. Even though symmetric encryption has strengths, it also has disadvantages.

One disadvantage of symmetric encryption is key distribution. For symmetric encryption to be effective, there must be a secure method for transferring keys, and it must be done by some type of out-of-band method. For example, if Bob wants to send Alice a secret message but is afraid that a third party can monitor their communication, how can he send the message? If the key is sent in cleartext, the third party can intercept it. Bob could deliver the key in person, mail it, or even send a courier. None of these methods is practical in the world of electronic communication.

Another disadvantage of symmetric encryption is key management. For example, a user who needs to communicate with 10 people would need many unique keys. To calculate the numbers of keys needed in symmetric encryption, use this formula:

$N(N-1)/2$

So, in this example, a user who needs to communicate with 10 people would need this many keys:

10 (10 – 1)/2 = 45 keys

You can see that as the number of users increases, so does the problem of key management.

Another problem with symmetric encryption is that it provides only confidentiality. If other services are needed, such as integrity or nonrepudiation, asymmetric encryption must be considered.

Data Encryption Standard (DES)

The National Bureau of Standards (NBS) published DES as a standard in 1977. NBS is now known as the National Institute of Standards and Technology (NIST). DES is considered a *block cipher* algorithm. The other type of symmetric algorithm is a *stream cipher*. Block and stream ciphers are defined as follows:

- **Block ciphers:** These ciphers divide a message into blocks for processing.

- **Stream ciphers:** These ciphers divide a message into bits for processing.

Because DES is a block cipher, it divides the input data into nice even blocks. If one block is short, padding is added to make sure all the blocks are the same size. DES processes 64-bit blocks of plain text and outputs 64-bit blocks of ciphertext. DES uses a 56-bit key; therefore, the remaining 8 bits are used for parity. DES works by means of permutation. This is a method of scrambling the input. DES performs 16 rounds of scrambling on each 64-bit block. DES has different modes of operation, such as Electronic Code Book (ECB) and Cipher Block Chaining (CBC).

Although DES provided years of useful service, nothing lasts forever; the same is true of DES, which became the victim of increased computing power. Just as Moore's law predicted, processing power has doubled about every 18 to 24 months. As a result, an encryption standard that it might have taken years to brute-force crack in 1977 takes much less time to crack in 2017. The final demise of DES came in 1998 when the Electronic Frontier Foundation (EFF) was able to crack DES in about 23 hours. (Although this sounds easy, the actual attack used distributed computing and required more than 100,000 computers.) This demonstrated the need for stronger algorithms. The short-term fix for the problem was to implement 3DES, which can use two or three keys to encrypt data and performs *multiple encryption*. 3DES has a 168-bit key length. Even this was seen as just a stopgap measure. Therefore, NIST began looking for a new system to replace DES. This new standard was to be referred to as Advanced Encryption Standard (AES).

Advanced Encryption Standard (AES)

NIST provided the guidelines for AES so that vendors could submit their algorithm for review. At the conclusion of this process, NIST chose Rijndael (pronounced *rain doll*) as the choice for the AES standard. Rijndael is a block cipher that supports variable key and block lengths of 128, 192, or 256 bits. It is considered a fast, simple, robust encryption mechanism. Rijndael is also known to be very secure. Even if attackers used distributed computing and invested millions of dollars in computing power, Rijndael should be resistant to attacks for many years to come. Therefore, it is the symmetric algorithm of choice when high security is needed.

Public Key Encryption

Public key encryption is a type of encryption method that was designed to overcome the weaknesses of symmetric encryption and facilitate e-commerce. It's a rather new discovery: Dr. W. Diffie and Dr. M. E. Hellman developed the first public key exchange protocol in 1976. Public key encryption differs from symmetric encryption in that it requires two keys: one to encrypt data and one key to decrypt data. These keys are referred to as *public* and *private keys*. The public key can be published and given to anyone, whereas the user keeps the private key secret.

Public key cryptography is made possible by factoring large prime numbers or using discrete logarithms. Both make it possible to set up one-way functions. This is also called a *trap door function*. For example, given the prime numbers 387 and 283, it is easy to multiply them and get 109,521. However, if you are given the number 109,521, it's quite difficult to extract the two prime numbers 387 and 283. The CISA exam does not expect you to calculate these numbers or perform advanced math. However, you do need to know that anyone who has trap door values can encrypt and decrypt, but anyone who lacks them can perform the function only in one direction. This means that anyone with the public key can perform encryption and signature verification, while anyone with the private key can perform decryption and signature generation.

Diffie-Hellman, RSA, and ECC are all popular asymmetric algorithms. Figure 8-6 illustrates public key encryption.

TIP   While CISA exam candidates are not expected to understand the inner workings of a specific algorithm they should understand what specific algorithms are used for and what is their proper application. As an example, symmetric encryption works well at bulk encryption whereas asymmetric encryption excels at key exchange and key management.

> **TIP** With asymmetric encryption, the sender encrypts the information with the receiver's public key. The receiver decrypts the information with his or her own private key.

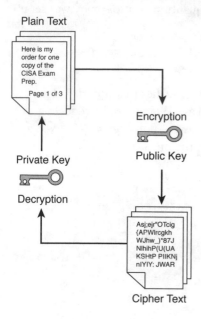

Figure 8-6 Asymmetric (Public Key) Encryption

RSA Encryption

Ron Rivest, Adi Shamir, and Len Adleman developed RSA, which is strong even though it is not as fast as symmetric encryption. The RSA cryptosystem is found in many products, including Microsoft Internet Explorer and Mozilla Firefox. RSA supports a key size up to 2,048 bits. RSA is used for both encryption and digital signatures. Because asymmetric encryption is not as fast as symmetric encryption, the two are often used together, thereby coupling the strengths of both systems. The asymmetric protocol is used to exchange the private key, and the actual communication is performed with symmetric encryption.

Elliptic Curve Cryptography (ECC)

ECC is another asymmetric algorithm. It requires less processing power than some of the algorithms previously discussed. It's useful in hardware devices such as cell phones and tablets.

Quantum Cryptography

Quantum cryptography is seen as the next big step in encryption. Unlike traditional encryption, which is based on mathematics, quantum cryptography is based on the random polarization of photon light pulses. Any third-party attempt to intercept the photons will disturb the photons' quantum state and raise an alarm. This technology holds much promise. The first implementation of quantum cryptography was set up in 2004 in Cambridge, Massachusetts.

Hashing and Digital Signatures

Hashing is used to produce a message digest. Hashing verifies the integrity of data and messages. A well-designed message digest such as MD5 and SHA reduces a large amount of data to a small fixed size hash, as illustrated in Figure 8-7. Even a small change to the data produces a large change in the message hash.

- **MD5:** Provides 128-bit output

- **SHA:** Provides 160-, 256-, or 512-bit output

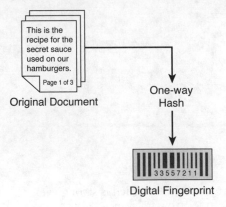

Figure 8-7 The Digital Signature Process

NOTE One reason that hashing algorithms have moved to longer output strings, such as 512-bit strings, is that this makes collision less likely. Collisions occur when two different values result in the same output. This is because hash functions have infinite input length and a fixed output length, so there is a possibility that two different inputs can produce the same output hash.

TIP While hashing is used for integrity, it can be targeted for attack. A hash collision attack is used to attempt to find two input strings of a hash function that produce the same hash result. While not particularly easy, collisions are possible.

Now let's turn our attention to how hashing and asymmetric algorithms are used for authentication. The application of asymmetric encryption for authentication is known as a *digital signature*. Digital signatures are much like signatures in real life because they validate the integrity of the document and the sender. Algorithms used for digital signatures include MD4, MD5, SHA, and HAVAL. Here's how the digital signature process works:

1. Bob produces a message digest by passing a message through a hashing algorithm.

2. The message digest is encrypted using Bob's private key.

3. The message is forwarded to the recipient, Alice.

4. Alice creates a message digest from the message with the same hashing algorithm that Bob used. Alice then decrypts Bob's signature digest by using Bob's public key.

5. Alice compares the two message digests, the one originally created by Bob and the other that she created. If the two values match, Alice can be confident that the message is unaltered.

TIP Digital signatures are created by encrypting a hash of the message with the sender's private key. Digital signatures provide both integrity and authentication.

Public Key Infrastructure (PKI)

Per ISACA requirements, CISA candidates should have a basic understanding of *public key infrastructure* (*PKI*). PKI is a framework that consists of hardware, software, and policies to manage, create, store, and distribute keys and digital certificates. In face-to-face transactions, it's easy to know who you are dealing with. When dealing with companies over the Internet, it's hard to establish the same level of trust. The primary goal of PKI is to provide trust. It works much like a state driver's license bureau. For example, to enter most airports, you must show proof of identification. In most cases, this is done with a driver's license. Airport employees trust driver's licenses because they have confidence in the state that issued them. Companies such as Verisign fill a similar role in providing a level of trust between two unknown parties. PKI is built on public key encryption. The components of the PKI framework include the following:

- **Certificate authority (CA):** A person or group that issues certificates to authorized users. The CA creates and signs the certificate. The CA is the one that guarantees the authenticity of the certificate.

- **Certificate revocation list (CRL):** The CA maintains the CRL. The list is signed to verify its accuracy and is used to report problems with certificates. When requesting a digital certificate, anyone can check the CRL to verify the certificate's integrity.

- **Registration authority (RA):** The RA reduces the load on the CA. The RA cannot generate a certificate, but it can accept requests, verify an owner's identity, and pass along the information to the CA for certificate generation.

- **Certificate server:** The certificate server maintains the database of stored certificates.

- **X.509 standard:** This is the accepted standard for digital certificates.

When a user goes to a website that uses PKI, the certificate is presented to the user when he or she initiates a transaction. The user's system then checks the certificate by querying the CA's database. If the certificate is valid, the transaction continues. Figure 8-8 shows a valid digital certificate. If there is a problem with the certificate, the user is notified, as shown in Figure 8-9.

Figure 8-8 A Digital Certificate

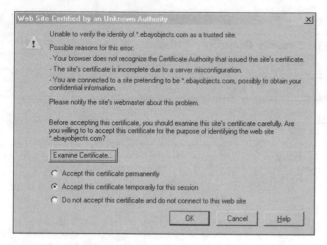

Web Site Certified by an Unknown Authority   ⊠

⚠   Unable to verify the identity of *.ebayobjects.com as a trusted site.

Possible reasons for this error:

- Your browser does not recognize the Certificate Authority that issued the site's certificate.
- The site's certificate is incomplete due to a server misconfiguration.
- You are connected to a site pretending to be *.ebayobjects.com, possibly to obtain your confidential information.

Please notify the site's webmaster about this problem.

Before accepting this certificate, you should examine this site's certificate carefully. Are you willing to to accept this certificate for the purpose of identifying the web site *.ebayobjects.com?

[Examine Certificate...]

○ Accept this certificate permanently

◉ Accept this certificate temporarily for this session

○ Do not accept this certificate and do not connect to this web site

[OK]   [Cancel]   [Help]

Figure 8-9   A Certificate Error

TIP   A digital certificate must always contain the owner's public key, the expiration date, and the owner's information.

Using Cryptography to Secure Assets

Although you need to know how encryption mechanisms work for the CISA exam, what is even more important to know is how the systems are used to provide real-world solutions. To better understand that concept, let us start by quickly reviewing the Open Systems Interconnection (OSI) reference model. The OSI reference model defines seven layers in which services, applications, and protocols are divided. Real-world cryptographic solutions can be found at many of these layers. It is generally agreed that cryptographic solutions exist at all except the physical layer. With so many choices of where to place a cryptographic solution, how do you know which is the right layer for implementation? That depends. Cryptographic solutions at the application layer are somewhat intrusive but offer the most flexibility because they can be designed to blend into the application and build a more seamless solution. Further down the stack, at the transport and network layers, encryption is more transparent yet more costly and can be complex because different systems and applications might need to communicate. Toward the bottom of the stack is the data link layer. Encryption added here is primarily for the LAN because different frame formats are designed according to different standards.

Table 8-6 provides an overview of some of these cryptographic solutions in relation to the OSI model. Some of the options shown are discussed shortly.

Table 8-6 Attributes of Symmetric and Asymmetric Encryption and the OSI Reference Model

TCP/IP	OSI Layer (ISO 7498-1)	Security Control	Security Model (ISO 7498-2)
Application	Application	SSH, PGP, SET	Authentication
	Presentation	SSL and TLS	Access control
	Session		Nonrepudiation
Transport	Transport		Data integrity
Network	Network	IPsec	Confidentiality
Physical	Data link	PPTP, L2TP, WPA2	Assurance
	Physical		Notarization

An organization could decide to use encryption that simply encrypts the data payload, known as *end-to-end encryption*. Or an organization might determine that everything needs to be encrypted, including the data and the header. That is known as *link-state encryption*. End-to-end encryption encrypts the message and the data packet, but the header, IP addresses, and routing information are left in cleartext. The advantage of this type of encryption is speed. The disadvantage is that some information, such as addresses, are left in the clear. Link encryption encrypts everything, including the header, addresses, and routing information. Its advantage is that no one can determine the original source or the final destination. The disadvantage is that all intermediate devices, such as routers, must have the necessary keys, software, and algorithms to encrypt and decrypt the encrypted packets. This adds time and complexity.

With so many ways to encrypt data, you might think that these solutions could be used to build perfect security, but unfortunately, that's not true. Attacks also can be launched against encryption systems, as discussed next.

Internet Security Protocols

Now let's quickly review some of the better-known cryptographic systems that can be applied for confidentiality, integrity, and/or nonrepudiation:

- **Secure Shell (SSH):** An application-layer program that provides secure remote access. It is considered a replacement for Telnet.

- **Secure Electronic Transaction (SET):** An application-layer program developed by Visa and MasterCard to secure credit card transactions. SET uses a combination of digital certificates and digital signatures among the buyer, merchant, and bank to ensure privacy and confidentiality.

- **Secure/Multipurpose Internet Mail Extensions (S/MIME):** A program that adds security to email and uses both digital signatures and public key encryption. Support also is provided for X.509 digital certificates.

- **Pretty Good Privacy (PGP):** An application-layer secure mail solution that adds encryption and builds a web of trust. PGP requires users to sign and issue their own keys.

TIP CISA exam candidates should have a high-level understanding of the configuration, implementation, and operation of network security controls such as encryption.

Protection of Information Assets

Security auditors have many duties and responsibilities, but one of the primary ones is to secure the network and protect the organization from both external and internal threats. This level of protection must be present from cradle to grave.

Information Life Cycle

Data life cycle control is a policy-based approach to managing the flow of an information system's data throughout its life cycle from the point of creation to the point at which it is out of date and is destroyed or archived. The following steps for data classification are used to manage the information life cycle:

- Define the classification level
- Specify the criteria for classification
- Classify data
- Determine the responsibility of the data owner
- Identify the data custodian
- Indicate security controls
- Document any exceptions
- Review methods to transfer ownership
- Create a review policy
- Define termination procedures for declassification
- Perform security awareness training

Access Restriction

Having a data life cycle policy is just a start. Restriction of users to authorized facilities and hardware must also be considered. These restrictions can include the following:

- **Physical controls:** These controls can include locks, gates, fences, bollards, guards, lighting, and so on.

- **Technical controls:** These controls can include encryption, firewalls, NAC, SIEM, IDS, IPS, and so on.

> **NOTE** Packet filters, proxy firewalls, web application firewalls, stateful inspection firewalls, intrusion detection systems, and security incident event management are all examples of technical controls that can be used to help build defense-in-depth.

- **Administrative controls:** These controls can include separation of duties, dual control, mandatory vacations, security awareness training, and so on.

Laws Related to the Protection of Information

Some controls may not be optional. A CISA candidate should have knowledge of privacy principles and security controls to protect sensitive information. Some organizations may have specific rules such as how information is stored, handled, or processed. Some examples are shown in Table 8-7.

Table 8-7 Compliance Laws

Law/Mandate	Applicability
The Federal Information Security Management Act (FISMA)	Federal agencies
Health Insurance Portability and Accountability Act (HIPAA)	Any company handling medical data
The Gramm-Leach-Bliley Act (GLBA)	Banks, brokerage companies, and insurance companies
The Family Educational Rights and Privacy Act (FERPA)	Educational institutions
The Children's Internet Protection Act (CIPA)	Schools' and libraries' Internet protections
The Payment Card Industry Data Security Standard (PCI DSS)	Credit card data

NOTE PCI-DSS is a global standard, not a law. PCI-DSS requires protection of credit card data with proper security controls.

NOTE What security controls does your organization use to protect sensitive data? CISA exam candidates should know that there should be a mix of administrative, technical, and physical controls.

Maintaining Compliance

Failure to maintain compliance can occur for many reasons, including the following:

- Lack of alignment to the business objectives and applicable external requirements
- General misunderstanding about the rationale for IT compliance
- Funding shortfalls
- Continued support from top management
- Misconception of what IT compliance will do for the organization

The following are some tactics that can be used to maintain compliance:

- Regular assessment of security risks and controls
- Configuration and control of management processes
- Monitoring of security controls on an ongoing basis
- Annual audit of the security environment
- Change management

Monitoring is a process whereby the effectiveness of internal controls is assessed on a periodic or continuing basis. Monitoring can be achieved through periodic review, examination of log files, or even by means of keystroke logging.

Keyloggers, which can be hardware or software, are used by an employer to track the activity of users on company devices for purposes such as IT security and regulatory compliance. Employees must generally be aware of such activity and understand that they may be monitored. Informing employees that they are being monitored is required by employee privacy regulations in most countries.

Monitoring can be used for periodic audit activities and to help track what has occurred when something goes wrong. It this scenario, think of the log files as a type of insurance policy in that after an event or system outage, a log file can be used to determine what someone has done to determine if the problem was caused by hackers or insiders or was simply a technical problem.

Protection of Privacy

Control should be placed on sensitive information to prevent it from ending up in the hands of the wrong individual. Privacy of personal information is a very important issue. Companies need to address this concern early by developing a company-wide policy based on a *privacy impact analysis* (*PIA*). PIA should determine the risks and effects of collecting, maintaining, and distributing personal information in electronic-based systems. PIA should be used to evaluate privacy risks and ensure that appropriate privacy controls exist. Existing controls should be examined to verify that accountability is present and that compliance is built in every time new projects or processes are planned to come online. The auditor can use the PIA to review how information is handled or to help build a case for stronger controls.

The PIA is tied to three items:

- **Technology:** Any time new systems are added or modifications are made, reviews are needed.

- **Processes:** Business processes change, and, even though a company might have a good change policy, the change-management system might overlook personal information privacy.

- **People:** Companies change employees and others with whom they do business. Any time business partners, vendors, or service providers change, the impact of the change on privacy needs to be reexamined.

Privacy controls tend to be overlooked for the same reason that many security controls are overlooked. Management might have a preconceived idea that security controls will reduce the efficiency or speed of business processes. To overcome these types of barriers, senior management must make a strong commitment to security and demonstrate support. A key component of the process is security awareness and training. Most managers and users do not instinctively know about good security practices; they require education. Part of the educational process involves increasing awareness of the costs involved in sensitive information being lost. Risk-assessment activities aid in the process by informing employees of the actual costs for the loss of security. Knowing this information helps justify the controls needed to protect sensitive information. One of the controls is system access, our next topic of discussion.

Using Data Classification to Secure Critical Resources

Not all the assets you identify will have the same value. For example, a bank may place a much greater value on customer Social Security numbers than a list that contains branch locations and phone numbers. The best way to classify information is to place it into categories based on the value of the information. When the value is known, it becomes much easier to decide on the level of resources that should be used to protect the data. It wouldn't make sense to spend more on protecting something of lesser value or worth.

Each level of classification that's established should have specific requirements. Luckily for us, others have done much of this work, and two widely used schemes already exist to manage and control information: military and commercial (see Table 8-8).

Table 8-8 Data Classification Types

Commercial Business Classifications	Military Classifications
Confidential	Top secret
Private	Secret
Sensitive	Confidential
Public	Sensitive
	Unclassified

TIP For the exam, you need to know that information can be classified by a military (confidentiality-based) system or a commercial (integrity-based) system. You should also know the labels used for both.

Regardless of which model is used, answering the following questions helps determine the proper placement of the information:

- Who owns the asset?
- Who controls access rights and privileges?
- Who approves access rights and privileges?
- What level of access is granted to the asset?
- Who currently has access to the asset?

Other questions the organization must address to determine the proper placement of the information include these:

- How old is the information?

- What laws govern the protection of the information?

- What regulations pertain to the information's disclosure?

- What regulations or laws govern data retention?

- What is the replacement cost if the information is lost or corrupted?

Data Leakage and Attacks

Regardless of the controls that have been implemented, it's just a matter of time before there is a data breach or exposure. According to the Verizon Data Breach report, around 60 percent of all data breaches are logical, and about 40 percent of them are caused by physical security breaches. See http://www.verizonenterprise.com/verizon-insights-lab/dbir/2017/.

Attacks Against Encryption

Attacks on cryptographic systems are nothing new. If malicious individuals believe that information has enough value, they will try to obtain it. Cryptographic attacks can use many methods to attempt to bypass the encryption someone is using. An attack might focus on a weakness in the code, cipher, or protocol, or it might be aimed at key management. Even if they cannot decrypt the data, attackers might be able to gain valuable information just from monitoring the flow of traffic. E-commerce has increased the potential bounty for malicious users. Attackers typically target transactional databases in an attempt to steal names, Social Security numbers, credit card numbers, and so on. Common types of cryptographic attacks include the following:

- **Known plaintext attack:** This type of attack requires the hacker to have both the plaintext and the ciphertext of one or more messages. For example, if a WinZip file is encrypted and the hacker can find one of the files in its unencrypted state, the two then provide the attacker with both plaintext and ciphertext. Together these two items can extract the cryptographic key and recover the remaining encrypted, zipped files.

- **Ciphertext-only attack:** This attack requires a hacker to obtain messages that have been encrypted using the same encryption algorithm. The attacker then looks for repetitions or patterns.

- **Man-in-the-middle attack:** This form of attack is based on hackers' ability to place themselves in the middle of the communications flow. Once there, they exchange bogus certificates and spoof each user.

Key size plays a large role in the strength of an algorithm. Although 56-bit DES was cracked by the Electronic Frontier Foundation, it took many computers and cost more than \$125,000. Larger key sizes equate to greater security. Increasing the key size by a factor of one doubles the work factor. Although (2^4) is just 16, (2^5) jumps to 32, and by incrementing only up to (2^{25}), you increase to a number large enough to approximate the number of seconds in a year. More often than not, encryption is cracked because users use weak keys or allow keys to become disclosed or compromised in some other way.

Threats from Unsecured Devices

It's sad but true that an attack can come from any angle. One item of concern to an auditor is unsecured devices. First there's the ubiquitous thumb drive. Everyone has them, and most people have more than one. Thumb drives may be a booby trapped thumb or loaded with malware. Thumb drives are also easily lost or misplaced and may be used to store sensitive information that requires strong protection. There arc cvcn thumb drives that have been designed to destroy a computer. The USB Killer requires nothing more than to be inserted into a computer to destroy its electronics (see Figure 8-10).

Figure 8-10 USB Killer

Another thumb drive threat is USB Rubber Ducky, a keystroke injection tool disguised as a generic flash drive. Computers recognize this device as a keyboard and accept potentially malicious code it is designed to run. Figure 8-11 shows some of the tools this thumb drive supports.

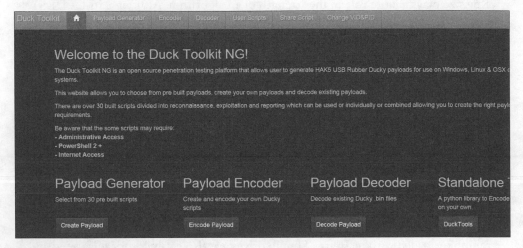

Figure 8-11   USB Rubber Ducky

TIP   CISA candidates should understand that unrestricted USB ports are a prime source of data leakage and data exfiltration.

Pineapples are another threat—not the kind you eat but the kind that are used to set up evil twin Wi-Fi hotspots. These evil twin hotspots look just like real access points (APs) but can be used to lure a victim into connecting to it. Once a victim is connected, the attacker can use a built-in set of wireless penetration testing tools for reconnaissance, man-in-the-middle attacks, tracking, logging, and reporting. Figure 8-12 shows an example of a pineapple.

Another threat, pod slurping, involves using a portable data storage device such as an iPod to illicitly download large quantities of confidential data by directly plugging it into a computer where the data resides.

WIFI PINEAPPLE

$99.99

WiFi Pineapple

| NANO BASIC | NANO TACTICAL | TETRA BASIC |

| TETRA TACTICAL | NANO TACTICAL ELITE |

Quantity

1   ADD TO CART

NANO Basic Edition: WiFi Pineapple NANO, (2x) Antennas, USB Y-Cable and Quick Start Guide.

NANO Tactical Edition: Basics, plus EDC Case, Anker PowerCore Slim 5000 battery, USB adapter & morale patch.

NANO Tactical Elite: NANO Tactical, plus RaLink RT5370 (tertiary radio) & 90° in-case 500 mW antenna upgrade.

TETRA Basic Edition: WiFi Pineapple TETRA, (4x) Antennas, USB Y-Cable, AC Adapter and Quick Start Guide.

Figure 8-12   Wi-Fi Pineapple

An auditor should also be aware of the following concerns:

- **Uncontrolled USB ports:** Not just thumb drives but also the ports they plug into should be locked to prevent unauthorized access. USB ports should be turned off. A variety of software tools can be used to control USB ports, block unauthorized devices, and enforce encryption.

- **Open Wi-Fi:** While an open Wi-Fi access point may look tempting, it might be an evil twin. If it's the corporate Wi-Fi that's been left open, it can be an open door to the rest of the business infrastructure or used to exfiltrate corporate data.

- **Enabled Bluetooth:** Any device that uses Bluetooth should be disabled if it's not being used. If required, a strong PIN should be used and the device should be placed in nondiscoverable mode.

- **Unmanaged smartphones:** All corporate phones should have, at a minimum, a PIN/password enabled, encryption, and remote wipe enabled.

- **Uncontrolled employee devices:** If the organization supports a bring-your-own-device (BYOD) policy, it should dictate when and how such devices can be used and should address the following:

  - Enforcing strong passcodes on all devices

  - Antivirus protection and data loss prevention (DLP)

- Full-disk encryption for disk, removable media, and cloud storage

- Device tracking to locate missing or stolen equipment

- Mobile device management (MDM) to wipe sensitive data when devices are lost or stolen

Threats from Improper Destruction

Data leakage can occur due to improper destruction of data. Auditors should understand the processes that are used for information that is no longer needed. For paper documents, there should be shredders for use by employees or trash bins that are specifically for sensitive information. An auditor should review the process by which this information is collected and destroyed. Many companies use third parties to collect and destroy paper documents. This process should be overseen by a company representative.

Most companies also have many types of electronic information that reach their end of life. While formatting is not an acceptable option, a seven-pass drive wipe can be used, as can degaussing. Just keep in mind when these methods are used, there could be some data remanence. Physical destruction—acid baths, hard drive shredding, or hard drive crushing—is the best way to ensure that no information remains.

Threats to the Infrastructure

Some of the threats that can exploit the infrastructure include the following:

- **Cleartext protocols:** Many protocols, such as FTP, HTTP, and Telnet, send data via cleartext and should be replaced with a secure option.

- **Insecure code or unpatched systems:** All code is vulnerable, so systems must be continually patched and upgraded. Tools such as the National Vulnerability Database (NVD) and Common Vulnerabilities and Exposures (CVE) can help with this process (see Figure 8-13).

- **Weak encryption:** Encryption is a big part of this chapter because it's important for an auditor to understand that all forms of encryption are not the same. Wired Equivalent Privacy (WEP) is much weaker than Wi-Fi Protected Access (WPA2), just as DES is much weaker than AES.

- **Weak passwords:** Passwords remain one of the main forms of authentication. Control on passwords should be used such that password length, complexity, and change requirements are enforced.

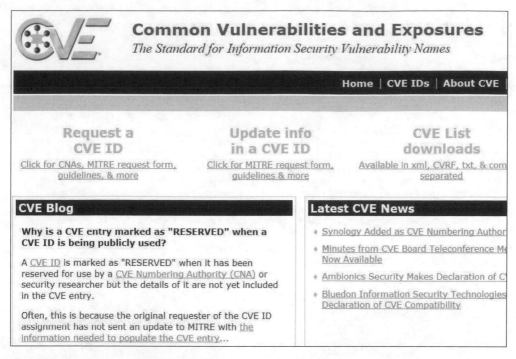

Figure 8-13   Common Vulnerabilities and Exposures.

- **No password clipping level:** Password complexity is just one concern. Another is that there is a limit on how many times an end user can attempt passwords before the account is locked or disabled. Three attempts is a common account lockout threshold.

TIP   Clipping levels are one example of a control related to end-user computing. CISA exam candidates should know that users should not be able to enter incorrect passwords an unlimited number of times.

- **Malicious software:** Attackers can use many tools and software distributions to target an enterprise. Kali Linux is a good example of a Linux distribution that contains many tools that can be used by penetration testers and hackers alike (see Figure 8-14).

Figure 8-14   Kali Linux

NOTE   Keeping the infrastructure secure requires constant patching, updating, and testing.

Chapter Summary

In this chapter, you have learned about mechanisms to protect information assets. This is an area of extreme importance to an auditor. These controls, including information classification, authentication, authorization, and accountability, can help protect the company's vital assets. An Auditor needs to know how these controls are implemented and how they are monitored. You could have the best firewall or intrusion detection system in the world, but if it is not properly set up, configured, and monitored, its value is insignificant. All this clearly points to the value of monitoring and control, in which an auditor plays an important role.

Encryption is another key defense. Encryption can provide confidentiality, integrity, authentication, and nonrepudiation. It's an amazing thing that one item has the potential to make such a huge difference. Consider a lost laptop or exposed hard drive: If encryption is being used, there is an effective barrier that must be compromised before information can be gathered from the device. Also, consider the value of cryptographic solutions that use PKI. With PKI, it is possible to perform commercial transactions with users all around the world with a high level of confidence. You can rest assured that the X.509 certificate you are presented with when you go to your bank's web page does, in fact, validate that you are truly dealing with your bank.

Without sufficient controls and without a defense-in-depth design, the many threats that endanger an organization could be realized. Each of these threats presents a real danger to the organization.

Exam Preparation Tasks

As mentioned in the section "How to Use This Book" in the Introduction, you have a couple choices for exam preparation: the exercises here; Chapter 10, "Final Preparation;" and the exam simulation questions on the book's companion web page (www.informit.com/title/9780789758446).

Review All the Key Topics

Review the most important topics in this chapter, noted with the Key Topic icon in the outer margin of the page. Table 8-9 lists these key topics and the page number on which each is found.

Table 8-9   Key Topics in Chapter 8

Key Topic Element	Description	Page Number
List	Kerberos key services	341
Section	Federation	343
Table 8-5	Attributes of symmetric and asymmetric encryption	359
Table 8-6	Attributes of symmetric and asymmetric encryption and the OSI reference model	368
Table 8-8	Data classification types	373

Complete Tables from Memory

Print a copy of Appendix B, "Memory Tables" (found on the companion web page), or at least the section for this chapter, and complete the tables from memory. Appendix C, "Memory Tables Answer Key," also on the companion web page, includes completed tables you can use to check your work.

Define Key Terms

Define the following key terms from this chapter and check your answers against the glossary:

algorithm, asymmetric algorithm, asymmetric encryption, authentication, biometrics, Blowfish, bring-your-own-device (BYOD), chain of custody, decryption, DIAMETER, digital certificate, digital signature, encryption, encryption key, equal error rate (EER), false acceptance rate (FAR), false rejection rate (FRR), firewall security, hash, hashing algorithm, intrusion detection system (IDS), Kerberos, mantrap, Moore's law, nonrepudiation, password cracking, public key encryption, Public Key Infrastructure (PKI), registration authority (RA), Remote Authentication Dial-In User Service (RADIUS), Rijndael, SHA, symmetric algorithm, symmetric encryption, turnstile, VoIP

Review Questions

1. A new website is being designed to host free application downloads. One requirement is that there must be a method to verify the integrity of these files and that they have not been tampered with. Which of the following would you recommend?

    a. DES

    b. AES

    c. MD5

    d. RSA

2. You have been asked to write a report detailing a new software-management system that uses AES. Which term best describes the advantage of a symmetric algorithm such as AES?

    a. It enables key exchange.

    b. It enables key management.

    c. It provides integrity.

    d. It is fast.

3. A business-to-consumer e-commerce website is worried about security and has had talks about encryption. Specifically, the company would like to set up a system that can monitor, detect, and alert on hacking activity. Which of the following would best meet the required needs?

   a. Packet filtering

   b. Intrusion detection

   c. Stateful inspection

   d. Asymmetric cryptography

4. You have been asked to join an audit team that will review Internet controls at a local college. Which of the following is required for schools and libraries using an Internet connection?

   a. FERPA

   b. FISMA

   c. PCI-DSS

   d. CIPA

5. Which of the following about PKI and the registration authority (RA) is correct?

   a. The RA cannot reduce the load on the CA.

   b. The RA cannot accept requests.

   c. The RA cannot generate a certificate.

   d. The RA cannot verify an owner's identity.

6. Which of the following is the highest priority for an Auditor?

   a. Designing and implementing security controls

   b. Reviewing new policies and procedures

   c. Controlling and monitoring data security and policies

   d. Controlling and monitoring IDS and firewall activity

7. As the result of a recent audit, you have been asked to serve on a team that will look at recommendations to strengthen authentication. Which of the following would you recommend if single sign-on were a requirement?

   a. Kerberos

   b. Diameter

   c. RADIUS

   d. TACACS

8. Which of the following data classification standards is the lowest level of the military classification?

   a. Public

   b. Unclassified

   c. Sensitive

   d. Available

9. During a recent physical security audit, you found several major problems. One was that the data center had one uncontrolled single-door entrance with weak access control. What double-door system would be a good recommendation in this case?

   a. Honeypot

   b. Mantrap

   c. Turnstile

   d. DMZ

10. Several coworkers are using public key encryption and have asked about the advantage of asymmetric encryption. Which of the following is correct?

   a. It is very efficient.

   b. It can be used as part of hashing algorithms.

   c. It can be used for bulk data.

   d. It enables easy key exchange.

Suggested Reading and Resources

- **PCI-DSS standards:** www.pcisecuritystandards.org/document_library

- **Encryption and access control comparison:** https://security.stackexchange. com/questions/89325/encryption-vs-access-control-comparison

- **Protecting data from cradle to grave:** www.computerworld.com.au/ article/40700/protecting_data_from_cradle_grave/

- **Data life cycle management (DLM):** http://searchstorage.techtarget.com/ definition/data-life-cycle-management

- **Difference between hashing and encryption:** www.securityinnovationeurope. com/blog/page/whats-the-difference-between-hashing-and-encrypting

- **Physical security audit checklist:** www.locknet.com/lockbytes/excerpts/ physical-security-audit-checklist/

The following exam domain is partially covered in this chapter:

Domain 5—Protection of Information Assets

This chapter covers the following topics:

- **Security Controls:** These controls play a key role in preventing attackers from successfully attacking an organization.

- **Attack Methods and Techniques:** Auditors should understand the techniques and methods used by attackers.

- **Prevention and Detection Tools and Techniques:** Implementing basic controls such as logging, auditing, and security information and event management (SIEM) can help prevent and detect common attack patterns.

- **Problem and Incident Management Practices:** It is not a matter of if but when a security breach will occur. Incident response and forensics should be documented and tested.

CHAPTER 9

Asset Threats, Response, and Management

It is a sad fact that things will go wrong and that an organization must be prepared to deal with problems. While the first step is to obviously have security controls in place to address issues, it's just as important to think like an attacker to understand how various attacks can occur. If an auditor understands common attack vectors, it's easier to understand what types of controls can be used to prevent these attacks. Luckily, a host of tools are available for detecting common attack patterns by using intrusion detection systems or reviewing of the logs.

The final component of being prepared is to have a plan in place to deal with problems, incidents, and breaches. Plans must be tested. When a breach occurs, you must know how to protect evidence. Before an incident ever occurs, it should be clear who is responsible for specific activities and what must occur from a forensic standpoint to make sure that evidence will be admissible in court.

"Do I Know This Already?" Quiz

The "Do I Know This Already?" quiz allows you to assess whether you should read this entire chapter thoroughly or jump to the "Exam Preparation Tasks" section. If you are in doubt about your answers to these questions or your own assessment of your knowledge of the topics, read the entire chapter. Table 9-1 lists the major headings in this chapter and their corresponding "Do I Know This Already?" quiz questions. You can find the answers at the bottom of the page following the quiz and in Appendix A, "Answers to the 'Do I Know This Already?' Quizzes and Review Questions."

Table 9-1 "Do I Know This Already?" Section-to-Question Mapping

Foundation Topics Section	Questions Covered in This Section
Security Controls	1–2
Attack Methods and Techniques	3–8
Prevention and Detection Tools and Techniques	9
Problem and Incident Management Practices	10

CAUTION   The goal of self-assessment is to gauge your mastery of the topics in this chapter. If you do not know the answer to a question or are only partially sure of the answer, you should mark that question as incorrect for purposes of the self-assessment. Giving yourself credit for an answer you correctly guess skews your self-assessment results and might provide you with a false sense of security.

1. Which of the following is similar to SIEM except that it focuses specifically on database access and activity?

   a. NAC

   b. NetFlow

   c. DAM

   d. SNMP

2. Which of the following is not a concern when hosting data in the cloud?

   a. Regulatory issues related to data type

   b. Encryption

   c. Disaster recovery plan of the cloud provider

   d. Reduction in workforce

3. Which of the following terms is used to describe obtaining personal information about an individual under false pretenses?

   a. Pretexting

   b. Smishing

   c. Whaling

   d. Phishing

4. Which of the following attacks best describes the removal of small amounts of money over a long period of time?

   a. Man-in-the-middle

   b. Salami attack

   c. Integer overflow

   d. TOCTOU

5. Which attack is also known as a race condition?

    a. Man-in-the-middle

    b. Salami attack

    c. Integer overflow

    d. TOCTOU

6. Which of the following is a social engineering attack that is used to target a specific group of people?

    a. Phishing

    b. Spear phishing

    c. Whaling

    d. Integer overflow

7. What attack technique does not provide the attacker access but blocks others?

    a. Session hijacking

    b. Password cracking

    c. Hijacking

    d. DoS

8. Which of the following presents itself as one thing but in reality does something else?

    a. Trojan

    b. Virus

    c. Worm

    d. TOCTOU

9. Which of the following are used to scan for deviations to normal trends?

    a. Audit-reduction tools

    b. Trend- or variance-detection tools

    c. Attack-detection tools

    d. IDSs

10. What type of forensic analysis allows a malicious program to execute in a sandbox?

   a. Dynamic analysis

   b. Static analysis

   c. Reverse engineering

   d. Passive analysis

Security Controls

Security controls are safeguards or countermeasures that are used to avoid, detect, or minimize security risks to an enterprise. NIST speaks of three categories of security controls: technical, administrative, and physical. Each category of control can be broken down by functionality (for example, preventive, detective, corrective, deterrent, recovery, compensating). The idea is to use controls to restrict access to only authorized users and for only authorized data. Chapter 8, "Protection of Assets," discusses physical controls, and the following sections describe technical and administrative controls.

Technical Controls

Technical controls include various technical measures, such as firewalls, identification/authentication systems, intrusion detection systems, and file encryption, among others. Controls are an important concept, and auditors typically review and test controls to verify that they are providing adequate protection for the enterprise.

Cloud Computing

One area of concern is the technical controls used to protect data in the cloud. An auditor may be tasked with providing stakeholders with an assessment of the effectiveness of a cloud computing service provider's internal controls and security. As part of this, the auditor needs to identify internal control deficiencies within the customer organization. For example, is encryption being used? If so, what is its strength? Is the data encrypted at rest or also while in transit? An auditor should also consider how data is stored. Is the data on a private server, or is it in the cloud shared with other organizations?

Operating Systems

For data not stored in the cloud, there is still more work to be done. End user workstations and operating systems are under constant threat of attack. Just take a moment to think of your own computer system. You have many services turned on and have multiple applications (for example, iTunes, Microsoft Office, Java, Adobe Flash, QuickTime) present. This makes for a large attack surface.

An important part of implementing technical controls is hardening the OS. This process is accomplished by turning off, removing, and deleting unused components. An auditor should verify that controls have been implemented to protect operating systems. Figure 9-1 shows an example of Bastille Linux, which can be used to harden Linux systems. The following are some of the guidelines for OS hardening:

- **NSA security configuration guidance:** www.iad.gov/iad/library/ia-guidance/security-configuration/

- **Center for Internet Security benchmarks:** www.cisecurity.org/cis-benchmarks/

- **Security Technical Implementation Guides (STIGs):** http://iase.disa.mil/stigs/Pages/index.aspx

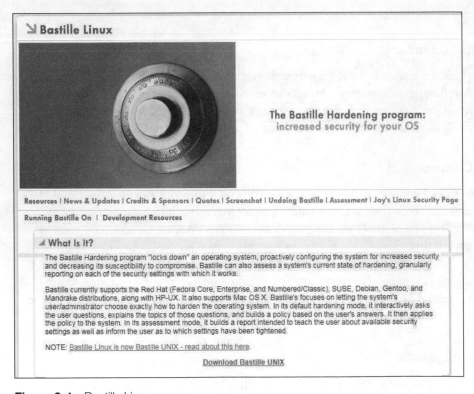

Figure 9-1   Bastille Linux

Answers to the "Do I Know This Already?" Quiz:

1. C; 2. D; 3. A; 4. B; 5. D; 6. B; 7. D; 8. A; 9. B; 10. A

Regardless of what standard or approach you use to harden the OS, the idea is to remove or disable items that are not needed. For example, you would want to turn off the following services and applications unless absolutely necessary: Telnet, FTP, rlogin, TFTP, LPD, CDE, NetBIOS, and even HTTP if it's not used. An auditor should also verify that network resources are secured. Table 9-2 provides some examples of best practices that are based on PCI-DSS standard.

Table 9-2   Best Practices Examples

Item	Recommendation
Logs	Mandatory log monitoring.
Patching	Patching all systems and applications.
Vulnerability assessment	Establish a process to identify newly discovered security vulnerabilities.
Encryption	Enforce encryption for data at rest and data in transit.
User Accounts	Remove inactive user accounts at least every 90 days.
Passwords	Remove default passwords and require unique passwords for all users.

Databases

Databases are high-value assets for most organizations. SQL injection is one common attack vector. It's basically an input problem and typically makes the OWASP top 10 security concerns, as shown in Figure 9-2.

One way to deal with this type of input problem is to use defense-in-depth, which begins by filtering traffic before it ever enters the network. A web application firewall (WAF) can help. A WAF is the next advancement in firewall design. A WAF analyzes web traffic and can be used to filter out SQL injection attacks, malware, cross-site scripting (XSS), and cross-site request forgery (XSRF). (XSS and XSRF are discussed later in the chapter.) WAFs require a high degree of application awareness as they have the ability to analyze web traffic and look for items such as malicious XML constructs and SQL injection commands.

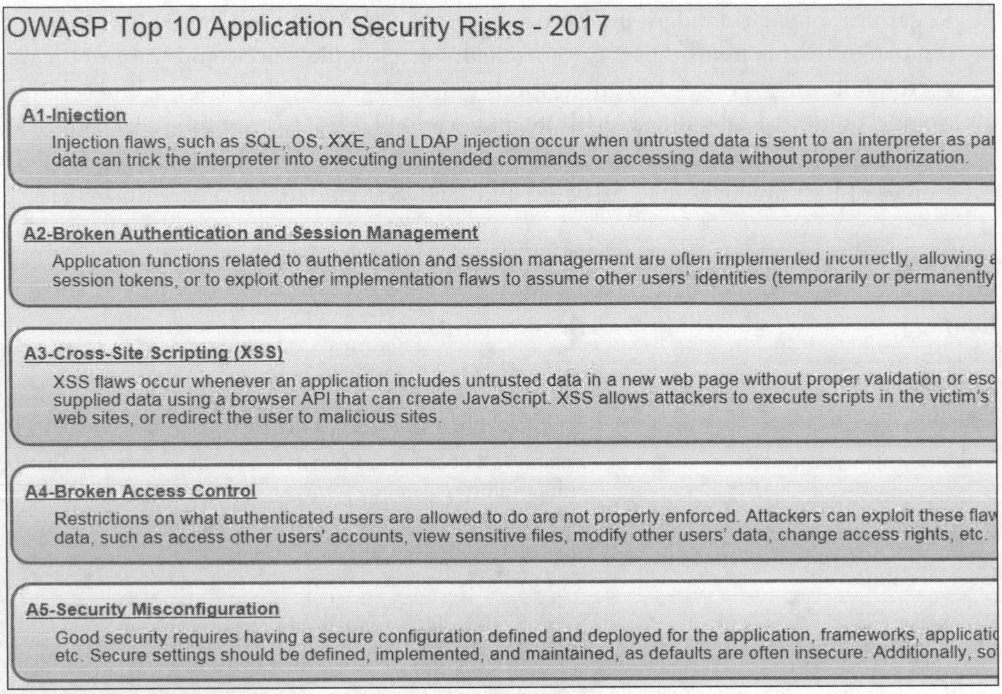

OWASP Top 10 Application Security Risks - 2017

A1-Injection
Injection flaws, such as SQL, OS, XXE, and LDAP injection occur when untrusted data is sent to an interpreter as par data can trick the interpreter into executing unintended commands or accessing data without proper authorization.

A2-Broken Authentication and Session Management
Application functions related to authentication and session management are often implemented incorrectly, allowing a session tokens, or to exploit other implementation flaws to assume other users' identities (temporarily or permanently

A3-Cross-Site Scripting (XSS)
XSS flaws occur whenever an application includes untrusted data in a new web page without proper validation or esc supplied data using a browser API that can create JavaScript. XSS allows attackers to execute scripts in the victim's web sites, or redirect the user to malicious sites.

A4-Broken Access Control
Restrictions on what authenticated users are allowed to do are not properly enforced. Attackers can exploit these flaw data, such as access other users' accounts, view sensitive files, modify other users' data, change access rights, etc.

A5-Security Misconfiguration
Good security requires having a secure configuration defined and deployed for the application, frameworks, applicatio etc. Secure settings should be defined, implemented, and maintained, as defaults are often insecure. Additionally, so

Figure 9-2 OWASP Top 10

Traditional end point solutions such as anti-malware have also advanced as endpoint detection and response (EDR) is now being used by many as an additional defense to protect endpoint systems. This emerging technology describes a category of tools that focus on detecting, investigating, and mitigating suspicious activities and issues on hosts and client systems.

Another item that can be used to help defend against SQL inject attacks is database activity monitoring (DAM). DAM systems emerged as companies began to face more threats, such as SQL injection, than in the past. In addition, they assist with compliance so that companies can track what activity occurs within databases. Laws and regulations such as HIPAA and PCI-DSS have increased this demand. A DAM system basically monitors a database and analyzes the types of activity that are occurring. You can think of DAM as being similar to security information and event management (SIEM) except that an SIEM correlates and analyzes events from multiple sources, whereas DAM focuses specifically on database access and activity.

NOTE CISA exam candidates should have knowledge of security options such as SIEM, DAM, IDSs, and firewalls.

Protecting a database is not just about preventing and detecting problems. Backups are also a concern. Over the past few years, ransomware has grown to be a huge problem, and part of its success is related to the fact that some organizations don't have database backups. That's where database shadowing comes in. A database shadowing system uses two physical disks to write the data to. It creates good redundancy by duplicating the database sets to mirrored servers. Therefore, this is an excellent way to provide fault tolerance and redundancy. Shadowing mirrors changes to the database as they occur.

Virtualization

Virtualized servers have many advantages. One of the biggest is server consolidation. Virtualization allows you to host many virtual machines on one physical server. This reduces deployment time and makes better use of existing resources. Some controls are based on the type of virtualized system being used. A Type 1 hypervisor runs on bare metal and does not have an underlying OS. A Type 2 hypervisor system has an underlying OS. A hypervisor is the computer software or hardware that creates and runs a virtual machine.

Virtualized systems are just as vulnerable to attack as standalone machines. Also, malware has the potential to migrate from one virtual machine to another. This problem, referred to as *VM escape*, means the attacker is able to run malware or code on a virtual machine that allows an operating system running within it to break out and interact directly with the hypervisor. This can be especially problematic when a single platform is hosting multiple companies' virtual machines (VMs) or when VMs of different security levels are used.

Securing virtual servers requires the same focus on defense-in-depth that is used for physical systems. Some basic items to review for securing virtual systems are listed in Table 9-3.

Table 9-3   Common Security Controls for Virtual Systems

Security Control	Comments
Antivirus	Antivirus must be present on the host and all VMs.
Authentication	Use strong access control.
Encryption	Use encryption for sensitive data in storage or transit.
Hardening	All VMs should be hardened so that nonessential services are removed.
Physical controls	Controls should be implemented to limit who has access to the data center.

Security Control	Comments
Remote access services	Remote access services should be restricted when not needed. When required, use encryption.
Resource access	Use administrative accounts only as needed.

Administrative Controls

From an auditing perspective, a big concern is the presence of policies that specify the approved/prohibited activities of employees. For example, years ago it was easy for an organization to control the message of the organization. Today, it's easy for information to spread via instant messaging, message boards, blogs, and social networking. These technologies have the ability to introduce risk to the enterprise.

Although instant messaging (IM) is not as popular as it once was, it is still used and available in many home and corporate settings. IM allows two-way communication in near real time. It enables business users to collaborate, hold informal chat meetings, and share files and information. An auditor should understand that IM programs are not all the same. Some have added encryption, central logging, and user access controls and are aimed at corporate clients, while others operate without such controls. Without adequate controls, IM products are highly vulnerable to malware and can be used for data exfiltration. Sensitive information can be transmitted without the company's knowledge. An auditor should seek answers to the following questions:

- Is the IM solution a critical business requirement?
- What IM product is used? Is it just one, or are multiple applications permitted?
- Is encryption used?
- Is IM just for internal use?
- Is IM used for external clients?
- Is the company subject to regulatory compliance requirements for IM? If so, how is data logged and recorded?
- Are users allowed to transfer files and applications? If so, are any mechanisms in place to control this activity?
- Are virus scanning, file scanning, and content-filtering applications used?
- How many employees are expected to use the system over the next 24 to 36 months?

- Is the IM application available to everyone or only to specific users?

- Does the IM solution use filters on specific words to flag for profanity or inappropriate content?

- Does the organization provide user training for secure use of IM?

Blogs, message boards, and websites can be as concerning as IM. It's relatively easy for an individual to set up a blog or a domain that disparages or slanders an organization or that even leaks sensitive information (see Figure 9-3). Starting in 2015, a new sucks top-level domain was created. It is difficult for an organization to get a damaging blog or website taken down, and often it's up to the courts to determine whether a case involves trademark violation or is protected free speech.

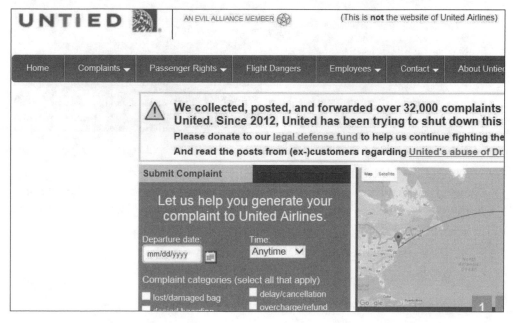

Figure 9-3   Untied Website

Finally, social media has grown immensely in popularity and brought new problems. Workplace social media policies are becoming more common as a growing number of people are sharing, liking, and posting every aspect of their life. Organizations have taken action against employees who post damaging information on social media. For example, Burger King fired a worker who posted pictures of himself standing in bins of lettuce, and Taco Bell fired an employee over a picture posted on Facebook that showed the employee licking a tall stack of taco shells. Figure 9-4 shows an example of a social media page used to show pictures of credit cards people have shared online. Employees can post any number of items on social media. Many of which should clearly not be posted.

Figure 9-4 Twitter Need A Debit Card Page

Companies should have policies that specify what employees should or should not post on their personal social media pages. These policies should address issues such as the following:

- What is considered appropriate online activity

- Whether social media use is allowed while at work

- What is considered confidential information

- The consequences of employees' actions online violating policy

Figure 9-5 shows a site (http://blog.hirerabbit.com) that lists 5 good examples of corporate social media policy.

#1. Adidas:

First let's take a look at how Adidas does things. As you may know, Adidas is one of the market giants in the sports apparel manufacturing industry. Adidas is a world-famous brand with offices and employees situated all around the globe. How exactly do they manage their employees' social media ventures? Adidas takes a very encouraging but strict approach when it comes to their Social Media Guidelines. Here are some highlights from Adidas' Social Media Policy:

1. Employees are allowed to associate themselves with the company when posting but they must clearly brand their online posts as personal and purely their own. The company should not be held liable for any repercussions the employees' content may generate.

2. Content pertaining to sensitive company information (particularly those found within Adidas internal networks) should not be shared to the outside online community. Divulging information like the company's design plans, internal operations and legal matters are prohibited.

3. Proper copyright and reference laws should be observed by employees when posting online.

Figure 9-5   Social Media Policy (REVISED)

Attack Methods and Techniques

Without security measures and controls in place, an enterprise might be subjected to an attack. Some common attack methods are discussed next. These techniques can be social, technical, or physical. Let's look at some examples of social attacks first.

Social Engineering and Nontechnical Attacks

Social engineering predates the computer era. For many years, scams have used the art of manipulation to trick victims into providing private information or improper access. Social-engineering attacks work because they attack a weak link—people.

Social-engineering attacks can be launched in person, on the phone, or via computer. Attacks carried out in person can be as easy as attackers disguising themselves as repair persons or vending machine employees. Attackers may use the phone to call the help desk and ask to have a password reset or seek to gain other privileged information. The low-ranking help desk employee might be bullied, feel scared, or feel coerced into giving out a password or other important information.

Email attacks are also commonly used for social engineering. These typically occur by means of the attacker spoofing a trusted party, such as eBay, Gmail, PayPal, Morgan Stanley, and so on. The attacker sends an official-sounding email, asking the user to verify a password, click a link, or open an attachment. If this type of attack targets a random group of people, it is known as *phishing*. *Spear phishing* is a targeted attack, and *whaling* is the term used for pulling in a big fish. *Pretexting* is a social attack that involves obtaining personal information about an individual under false pretenses. Pretexting is usually done when an individual wants more information about a certain individual to investigate his or her activities, such as to sue that person, to steal his or her assets, or to obtain credit in his or her name. Pretexters use a variety of techniques, but they are all simple variations of social-engineering techniques. A pretexter might, for example, spoof your caller ID and call your cell phone provider to ask for a reprint of a bill. Or a pretexter might call your bank to obtain a replacement for a lost checkbook, or even contact your credit card provider. In most cases, pretexting is illegal, and there are laws against pretending to be someone else to gain personal information. If you have never seen how easily someone can launch this type of attack, check out www.youtube.com/watch?v=PWVN3Rq4gzw.

NOTE   Spoofing can be used with domain names, email addresses, media access control (MAC) addresses, and even IP addresses.

Dumpster diving is another attack that requires no technical skill. Dumpster divers simply dig through the trash, looking for key pieces of information. Sensitive information should be shredded, but this doesn't always happen. Sticky notes and other small pieces of trash can provide critical pieces of information to those seeking to gain sensitive information. As long as no trespassing takes place, dumpster diving is usually not illegal.

Sniffing

A network sniffer, such as Wireshark, is a software tool that captures and displays network traffic. By using a sniffer, an attacker can potentially capture all the information transported by the network. Many sniffers can reassemble packets and create entire messages, including user IDs and passwords. This vulnerability is particularly acute in environments where network connections are easily accessible to outsiders. For example, an attacker could put a laptop or a portable computer in your wiring closet and attach it to your network. Figure 9-6 shows Wireshark running.

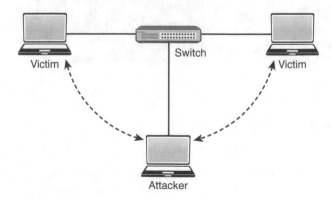

Wireshark capture window showing smtp.pcap with packet list:

No.	Time	Source	Destination	Protocol	Length	Destination	Info
1	2007-07-14 03:31:37.571215	192.168.1.4	217.12.11.66	TCP	62	00:1b:2f:03:9e:c2	3326 > 587 [SYN] Seq=0 Win=6
2	2007-07-14 03:31:37.539876	217.12.11.66	192.168.1.4	TCP	60	08:00:46:db:60:8f	587 > 3326 [SYN, ACK] Seq=0
3	2007-07-14 03:31:37.539938	192.168.1.4	217.12.11.66	TCP	54	00:1b:2f:03:9e:c2	3326 > 587 [ACK] Seq=1 Ack=1
4	2007-07-14 03:31:37.564389	217.12.11.66	192.168.1.4	SMTP	92	08:00:46:db:60:8f	S: 220 smtp001.mail.xxx.xxxx.
5	2007-07-14 03:31:37.564540	192.168.1.4	217.12.11.66	SMTP	69	00:1b:2f:03:9e:c2	C: EHLO Percival
6	2007-07-14 03:31:37.580439	217.12.11.66	192.168.1.4	SMTP	148	08:00:46:db:60:8f	S: 250-smtp001.mail.xxx.xxxx
7	2007-07-14 03:31:37.580553	192.168.1.4	217.12.11.66	SMTP	66	00:1b:2f:03:9e:c2	C: AUTH LOGIN
8	2007-07-14 03:31:37.598353	217.12.11.66	192.168.1.4	SMTP	72	08:00:46:db:60:8f	S: 334 VXNlcm5hbwU6
9	2007-07-14 03:31:37.598452	192.168.1.4	217.12.11.66	SMTP	64	00:1b:2f:03:9e:c2	C: Z2Fsdw50
10	2007-07-14 03:31:37.616320	217.12.11.66	192.168.1.4	SMTP	72	08:00:46:db:60:8f	S: 334 UGFzc3dvcmQ6
11	2007-07-14 03:31:37.616439	192.168.1.4	217.12.11.66	SMTP	68	00:1b:2f:03:9e:c2	C: vjF2MXRyMG4=
12	2007-07-14 03:31:37.733218	217.12.11.66	192.168.1.4	TCP	60	08:00:46:db:60:8f	587 > 3326 [ACK] Seq=169 Ack
13	2007-07-14 03:31:37.802416	217.12.11.66	192.168.1.4	SMTP	81	08:00:46:db:60:8f	S: 235 ok, go ahead (#2.0.0)
14	2007-07-14 03:31:37.802617	192.168.1.4	217.12.11.66	SMTP	87	00:1b:2f:03:9e:c2	C: MAIL FROM: <xxxxxx@xxxxx.
15	2007-07-14 03:31:37.823379	217.12.11.66	192.168.1.4	SMTP	62	08:00:46:db:60:8f	S: 250 ok
16	2007-07-14 03:31:37.823487	192.168.1.4	217.12.11.66	SMTP	85	00:1b:2f:03:9e:c2	C: RCPT TO: <xxxxxx@xxxxx.co

Frame 1: 62 bytes on wire (496 bits), 62 bytes captured (496 bits)
Ethernet II, Src: 08:00:46:db:60:8f (08:00:46:db:60:8f), Dst: 00:1b:2f:03:9e:c2 (00:1b:2f:03:9e:c2)
Internet Protocol Version 4, Src: 192.168.1.4 (192.168.1.4), Dst: 217.12.11.66 (217.12.11.66)
Transmission Control Protocol, Src Port: 3326 (3326), Dst Port: 587 (587), Seq: 0, Len: 0

Figure 9-6   Using Wireshark to Sniff Network Traffic

Man-in-the-Middle Attacks and Hijacking

A technique attackers can use that is similar to sniffing is hijacking. Hijacking occurs when an attacker pretends to be a trusted party. For example, with session hijacking, a legitimate user logs on to a service or an application and then an attacker takes control of the session. The attacker gets an authenticated connection and the ability to masquerade as the victim.

A man-in-the-middle (MITM) attack occurs when an attacker secretly relays and possibly alters the communication between two parties, as shown in Figure 9-7. *Packet replay* is a similar technique that an attacker can use to gain access. For example, the attacker might sniff an authentication session on the network and replay it later to try to gain unauthorized access.

Victim — Switch — Victim

Attacker

Figure 9-7   Man-in-the-Middle Attack

Denial of Service

A denial of service (DoS) attack does not give an attacker access; instead, it blocks legitimate users from using resources they have access to. While DoS attacks are not as prominent as ransomware, point-of-sale attacks, or retail data breaches, they can affect a large number of users. What keeps these attacks popular is that they are easy to launch and difficult to defend against. DoS attacks target availability, and they provide an easy way for an attacker to disrupt services. Denial-of-service attacks consume resources or flood the network to the point that legitimate access is not possible.

Distributed DoS (DDoS) attacks work in much the same manner, except that they are launched from many more devices and add a layer between the attacker and the victim. Anyone can launch a DDoS attack against your company. Figure 9-8 shows the top 10 DDoS attack sites.

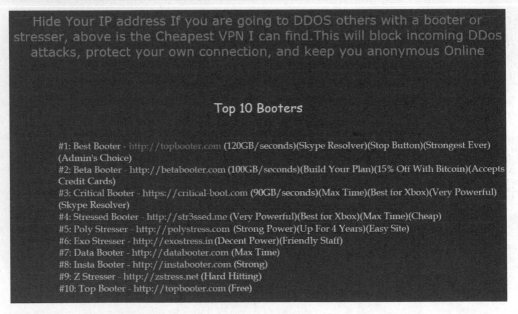

Figure 9-8   Top 10 DDoS Attack Sites

Some DoS/DDoS attack tools and techniques include the following:

- **Ping of death:** A DoS attack that employs an oversized IP packet.

- **Smurf:** A DoS attack that involves sending a message to the broadcast address of a subnet or network so that every node on the network produces one or more response packets.

- **Syn flood:** A DoS attack that manipulates the standard three-way handshake used by TCP.

- **hping:** A tool that is not strictly a DDoS tool but provides a range of functionality by sending large volumes of TCP traffic to a target while spoofing the source IP addresses, making it appear to be random or even to originate from a specific, user-defined source.

- **Slowloris:** A tool that causes a DoS condition for a server by using a very slow HTTP request. Sending HTTP headers to the target site in tiny chunks as slowly as possible forces the server to continue to wait for the headers to arrive.

- **R U Dead Yet? (RUDY):** A DDoS tool that knocks systems offline by using long-form field HTTP POST submissions.

- **Low Orbit Ion Cannon (LOIC):** An open source network stress testing and DoS attack application that is written in C#.

- **High Orbit Ion Cannon (HOIC):** An open source network stress testing and DoS attack tool capable of attacking as many as 256 URLs at the same time.

Botnets

Botnets have in many ways replaced DoS attack tools as they are much more functional. Botnets can be used for DoS but also other activities, such as pump-and-dump financial schemes, extortion, fake/counterfeit software distribution, ransomware, and other malicious activities.

A botnet is a network of compromised computers that can be accessed remotely and used for malicious activity. An attacker infects scores of computers that then just wait until commanded to action by the attacker. These compromised machines can communicate with each other or with a bot herder and can act in a coordinated way, based on commands (see Figure 9-9).

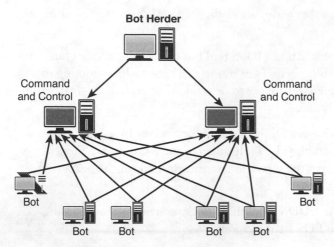

Figure 9-9 Botnet Communication

The hackers who create botnets must make sure that the bots can receive their instructions. If the communication channels can be shut down, the botnet can be disabled. Therefore, actively controlling botnets is of critical importance, as is protecting a botnet from attempts to hijack or shut it down. Botnets generally make use of one of three types of command and control (C&C) structures:

- **Centralized C&C:** This approach relies on a single centralized resource to communicate with all infected systems. Each infected system is issued new instructions directly from the central control point.

- **Decentralized C&C:** The advantage of this approach is that it overcomes the weakness of centralized C&C: its single point of failure. With a decentralized design, each bot acts as both a client and a server. This lack of centralized C&C and the many-to-many communication makes this form of botnet much more difficult to shut down.

- **Hybrid botnets:** Hybrid botnets use a mix of centralized C&C and decentralized C&C.

Malware

Malware comes in a variety of forms. Sometimes malware targets unknown vulnerabilities. These are known as *zero-day attacks* because they are not known by anti-malware vendors and so the software cannot defend against them. There is a growing market in zero-day exploits, and entire websites have been set up to market and sell them to the highest bidder.

A very common type of malware is *viruses*. Viruses require some type of human interaction. One early type of virus was the macro virus, which targets Office documents. Some viruses have the ability to mutate and are known as polymorphic. *Worms* require no interaction and can self-replicate. *Trojans* are yet another type of malware. Think of a Trojan as something you think you want but really do not. A Trojan masks itself as a legitimate program to a user, such as a .pdf, .ppt, .docx, or other file type. Hackers use *droppers* or *wrappers* to combine malware with a legitimate program. An example of a wrapper is shown in Figure 9-10. When a user clicks on or runs a program that has been wrapped, malicious code may be installed.

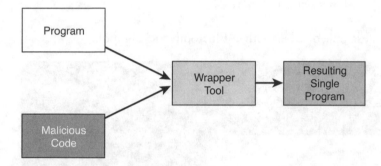

Figure 9-10 Malware Wrapper

Wireless and Bluetooth

An organization's electronic equipment (wireless keyboards, mouse devices, monitors, and so on) transmits a wide range of electronic signals. One such technology is Bluetooth, which is designed as a short-range wireless system used in a personal area network (PAN), or a network of devices close to a single individual. Bluetooth was originally designed to be broadcast about 3 meters. However, attackers can launch attacks from much greater distances if they use long-range antennas.

When Bluetooth devices are first configured, they are placed in Discovery mode so others can identify them. While in Discovery mode, a Bluetooth device broadcasts its physical address and allows other devices to see it and potentially connect. Discovery mode is required for initial paring. During this time, attackers can attempt to pair to a device to gain access. Whenever possible, a device should have Discovery mode turned off.

NOTE Attacks are much easier when Bluetooth devices remain in Discovery mode.

With the right software, an attacker can then launch the following types of attacks:

- **Bluejacking:** This Bluetooth attack is launched by sending unsolicited messages to nearby Bluetooth devices.

- **Bluesnarfing:** This attack is any unauthorized access to or theft of information from a Bluetooth connection. Attackers might target information such as email, contact lists, calendars, and text messages.

- **Bluebugging:** This type of attack allows an attacker to take over a mobile phone. Attackers can potentially eavesdrop on phone conversations, carry out call forwarding, send messages, and more.

Figure 9-11 shows an example of Ubertooth, a Bluetooth hacking tool.

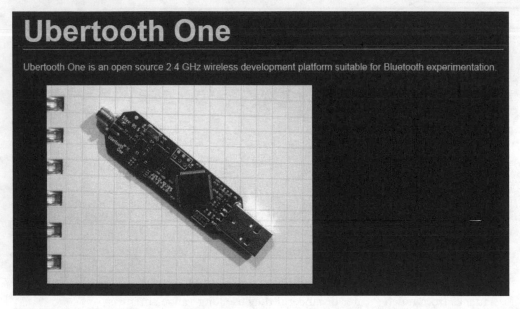

Figure 9-11   Ubertooth One

802.11 wireless connections are also an area of concern. While wireless access points may support one of three wireless encryption standards—Wired Equivalent Privacy (WEP), Wi-Fi Protected Access (WPA), or WPA2—this does not mean encryption will always be used. Many access points have no encryption at all. You can look for unsecured access points by performing a site survey or by using one of multiple websites that list access points and the types of encryption used. Figure 9-12 shows the Wigle website and a map of some identified wireless points. The act of looking for wireless access points is known as war driving, and sites such as Wigle depend on others to war drive and upload their data to the Wigle database.

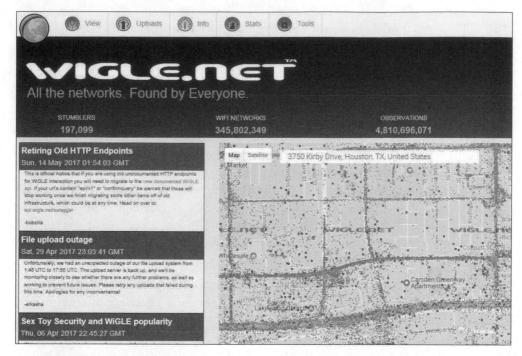

Figure 9-12   Wigle Website

While open access points may have few controls in place to prevent someone from gaining access, access points that use WEP are not much better.

An IV is simply a random number that's used along with a secret key for data encryption. If these random numbers are pulled from a small range of numbers or are not truly random, they repeat over time; it's possible that these values can be easily recovered, guesses, or calculated. WEP suffers from a flaw in the implementation of the RC4 cipher used. The 802.11 standard does not specify how to generate IVs, and cracking WEP typically doesn't require more than a few minutes' work.

WPA, which was designed as a stopgap measure, uses the Temporal Key Integrity Protocol (TKIP) and a 64-bit message integrity check (MIC) to improve security. While more secure than WEP, WPA can be targeted for attack with tools such as Aircrack, which is one of the most popular tools for targeting WEP and WPA.

WPA2 is the newest wireless standard and uses AES to protect data. An auditor should ensure that an organization's wireless technology uses layers of defense—such as WPA2, MAC filtering, wireless IDS, non-broadcast of the service set ID (SSID), and other security measures—to build defense-in-depth.

TIP   CISA exam candidates should understand that wireless access points should be secured to the highest level of encryption possible.

SQL Injection

What if a database is the target of an attack? If a database does not have the proper security controls in place, an attacker can create queries against the database to get it to disclose unauthorized information. This type of attack is generally known as *SQL injection*. A SQL injection attack is carried out when an attacker uses a series of malicious SQL queries to directly manipulate the SQL database. SQL injection is not a database issue as much as an application issue. It occurs because of poor input validation. It's sad but true that there are hundreds if not thousands of websites that are vulnerable to SQL injection and have not been secured.

SQL injection attacks can be launched from the any query field on a webpage, from within application fields, or through queries and searches. There are Internet sites that list websites vulnerable to SQL injection. One example is shown in Figure 9-13.

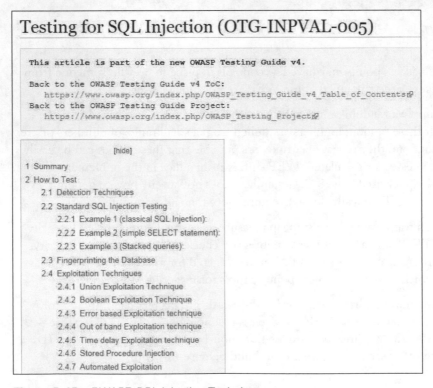

Figure 9-13   OWASP SQL Injection Techniques

Once a SQL injection attack is launched, the attacker typically seeks to enumerate the database and then extract password hashes or steal credit card or other personally identifiable information (PII). Malformed input may cause the database to become unstable or leak information. Attackers use logic such as a single quote (') to test a database for vulnerabilities. Responses such as the one shown in the following code give feedback the attackers need that the database is vulnerable to attack:

```
Microsoft OLE DB Provider for ODBC Drivers error '80040e14'
[Microsoft][ODBC SQL Server Driver][SQL Server]Syntax error converting
                the nvarchar value 'sa_login' to a column of data
                type int. /index.asp, line 5
```

Buffer Overflow

A buffer overflow occurs when a software application somehow writes data beyond the allocated end of a buffer in memory. Buffer overflows are commonly found in programming languages that don't do good bounds testing. If an attacker can launch a buffer overflow attack, there is a possibility the attacker will be able to load malicious code and force the application to run it. This malicious code could do any number of things, such as open a command prompt or pass shell access back to the attacker.

The best defense against buffer overflow attacks is to put controls in code when it is designed. Building secure code is less costly than attempting to secure an application after it has been developed and released. A range of tools can be used to analyze code. One example is Microsoft Attack Surface Analyzer, which is described in Figure 9-14.

Good coding is what is needed to prevent these types of vulnerabilities. Auditors should be included in the design and build process to ensure that the proper testing of controls will be included in the build process. For precompiled applications, and situations where the source code is not available, another approach is black-box testing or fuzzing. An auditor can use fuzzing tools to enter random values into input fields to see if an application will crash or hang, as shown in Figure 9-15.

Microsoft's Free Security Tools – Attack Surface Analyzer

Tim Rains - Director, Security

In this second article in my series focused on Microsoft's free security tools, I'd like to introduce you to the Attack Surface Analyzer version 1.0. Back in January of 2011 the Security Development Lifecycle team released a beta version of the Attack Surface Analyzer and today they announced the release of version 1.0.

Attack Surface Analyzer can help software developers and Independent Software Vendors (ISVs) understand the changes in Windows systems' attack surface resulting from the installation of the applications they develop. It can also help IT Professionals, who are responsible for managing the deployment of applications or the security of desktops and servers, understand how the attack surface of Windows systems change as a result of installing software on the systems they manage. Some use cases include:

- Developers can use the tool to view changes in the attack surface resulting from the introduction of their code on to the Windows platform
- IT Professionals can use the tool to assess the aggregate attack surface change by the installation of an organization's line of business applications
- IT Security Auditors can use the tool to evaluate the risk of a particular piece of software installed on the Windows platform during threat risk reviews
- IT Security Incident Responders can potentially use the Attack Surface Analyzer to gain a better understanding of the state of a system's security during investigations (if a baseline scan was taken of the system during the deployment phase)

Figure 9-14   Attack Surface Analyzer Description

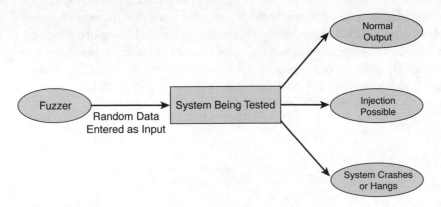

Figure 9-15   Fuzzing

TIP   CISA exam candidates should understand that fuzzing is an automated software testing technique that involves providing invalid, unexpected, or random data as inputs to a computer program to see if the program will crash or hang.

XSS and XSRF

Cross-site scripting (*XSS*) attacks are injection attacks targeted against dynamically generated web pages in which malicious scripts are injected into the otherwise benign and trusted web content. XSS allows an attacker to forcibly load any website when unsuspecting users visit malicious web pages. The attacker can then steal usernames and passwords typed into HTML forms or cookies—or compromise any confidential information on the screen. Situational awareness requires users to use caution when clicking on links in emails or clicking on links at suspicious sites.

Cross-site request forgery (*XSRF*) is a client-side attack that occurs when a malicious website tricks users into unknowingly loading a URL from a site at which they're already authenticated, thus making use of their authenticated status.

Logic Bombs, Rounding Down, and Asynchronous Attacks

Imagine that a company's programmer is able to access and change applications at will. What if this person could change the company's payroll application? The programmer might not destroy the code but might add a few lines to the code to have it checked for his employee number each week before printing checks. If his employee ID is verified, the program prints checks as normal. If his employee ID is not found, each check is printed but is made out to a random dollar amount. This is a *logic bomb*, designed to detonate sometime after the perpetrator leaves. A logic bomb can cause a great deal of damage: Because it is buried deeply in the code, it is unlikely to be detected before it becomes active.

Similar to a logic bomb is a *trap door*, a shortcut created by a programmer during development. It acts as a hidden access point in the software or application and can aid in the testing process. When testing is completed, the trap door should be removed. A trap door that isn't removed can act as a hidden shortcut for attackers.

An *asynchronous attack* is a complex attack that targets timing. These attacks are also known as time-of-check, time-of-use (TOCTOU) attacks, or race conditions, because the attacker is racing to make a change to the object after it has been changed and just before it's used by the system. For example, if a program creates a data file to hold the amount a customer owes, and the attacker can replace the value before the program reads it, the attacker can successfully manipulate the program. An IS auditor is likely to need the help of a programmer or an IT specialist to evaluate this complex attack.

Some attacks are launched for financial reasons. For example, *rounding-down attack* involves skimming off small amounts of money by rounding down the last few digits. For example, the amount $5,239,812.33 might be rounded down to $5,239,812.30. Similar to this attack is the *salami technique*, which slices off small amounts of money so that the last few digits are truncated. For example, $5,239,812.33 might become $5,239,812.00. Both the rounding-down technique and the salami technique work under the assumption that small amounts will not be missed; over a period of time, this can add up to big profits for the attacker. This type of attack can be seen in movies such as *Superman III* and *Office Space*.

Integer Overflow

Integer overflow occurs when a program or an application attempts to store a number in a variable that is larger than that variable's type can handle. Consider the situation where an allocated buffer can hold a value up to 65,535. If the maximum size is exceeded, the value essentially wraps around to 0. The result can cause some unusual behavior if the resulting value is used in a computation. Years ago this type of attack could be exploited in arcade games such as Pac-Man. Pac-Man used an 8-bit counter, and players who were good enough to complete all 255 levels could roll over the counter and crash the game.

Password Attacks

Common attacks against access control are dictionary attacks, hybrid attacks, brute-force attacks, and rainbow tables. Unfortunately, many passwords are based on weak dictionary words. *Dictionary attacks* exploit this fact and use a predefined dictionary to look for a match between a hashed password and a hashed value in the dictionary. Many dictionary files are available online. Although passwords are commonly stored in a hashed format, password-cracking programs use a technique called *comparative analysis*. Each potential password found in a dictionary list is encrypted and compared to the encrypted password. If a match is obtained, the password has been discovered. If it's not obtained, the program continues on to the next word, computes its hashed value, and compares it to the hashed password.

Another type of password cracking method is the *hybrid attack*, used to target individuals who use variations of a common word. For example, consider the word *password*. Hybrid password cracking would process the word as *Password*, *password*, *PASSWORD*, *PassWord*, *PaSSword*, and so on. Hybrid password cracking also attempts to add common prefixes, suffixes, and extended characters to try to crack the password. For example, the word *password* would also be tried as *123password*, *abcpassword*, *drowssap*, *p@ssword*, *pa55w0rd*, and so on. These various attempts increase the odds of successfully cracking an ordinary word. An example of a password cracking tool is John the Ripper (see www.openwall.com/john/).

Yet another type of password attack is a *brute-force attack*, which attempts to use every possible combination of letters, numbers, and characters. Depending on the length and complexity of the original password, this attack can take hours, days, months, or years.

Finally, a *rainbow table* is a precomputed table for finding password hashes. Tables are usually used in recovering a plaintext password up to a certain length and consisting of a limited set of characters. Instead of computing each hash one at a time and then comparing, a rainbow table is filled with precomputed hashed passwords. This form of time–memory trade-off requires that a rainbow table be generated for all possibilities within a given range, such as 1- to 14-character alphanumeric passwords. Then, if any password is a match that's 14 characters or less, it is found in just a few seconds. Rainbow tables are incorporated into many password cracking programs.

An advancement on rainbow tables is the thunder table. Imagine that you have a 14-character rainbow table and use it against five password hashes. If it is successful against four of the passwords but not the fifth one, the historic approach would have been to brute-force the remaining one. As we have discussed, brute-force attacks take time. Thunder tables can be used to reduce that amount of time. Thunder tables contain additional data that lists all attempts for which rainbow tables failed. Therefore, a thunder table knows which brute-force values to check and which ones it should not spend time trying. Figure 9-16 shows an example of an online password cracking program.

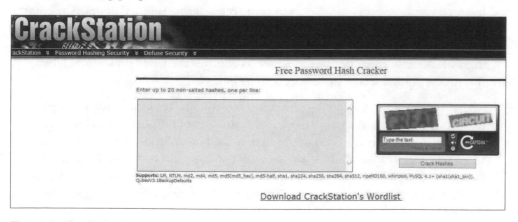

Figure 9-16 Online Password Cracker

Prevention and Detection Tools and Techniques

Part of the internal audit function is a review of prevention and detection controls to ensure normal and efficient functioning of the enterprise's activities. These controls include those that are responsible for logging, monitoring, and real-time analysis of security alerts. Some of these controls can be thought of as administrative. For example, an auditor should verify that each individual's responsibility is clearly defined. Policies should require that employees be trained and aware of proper procedure. Users need to know why logging off before leaving for the day is a requirement, how social engineers con employees out of information or access, and how to practice safe computing. The end user also should be made aware of keystroke logging, email scanning, and Internet acceptable use policies (AUPs). Employees should know they will be held accountable. Auditing is a good way to determine whether repetitive mistakes are being made or if someone is trying to gain unauthorized access. As a detective control, auditing provides a means of uncovering suspicious activity.

Audit and Log Review

From a control standpoint, an IS auditor needs to examine log-retention policies to make sure they comply with local, state, or federal laws. If possible, audit records should be transferred to a centralized location. This makes auditing and analysis easier for the appropriate administrator, and it makes log tampering harder for the malicious user because logs are not kept on the local system. Strong access controls to the logs, encryption, and integrity checks should also be considered. The idea behind integrity checks is to have a means of detecting log tampering. One good approach is for an auditor to periodically check the logs to make sure no one has attempted to exceed access privileges or gain access during unusual hours. Any control or procedure that bypasses normal security measures should be examined closely. For example, *bypass label processing* can be used to bypass the normal process of reading a file security label. Because most access controls are based on security labels, this means normal security control could be bypassed.

Manual analysis of logs is time-consuming and tedious. It's best to use automated tools for log analysis. Although the CISA exam does not expect you to know the names of specific tools, you do need to know the types of tools that can be used when working with log files. *Attack-detection tools* are audit tools that look for known attack signatures. For example, Bob normally is able to log in on the first attempt, but now he has attempted to log in 5,000 times. This type of activity should be flagged for analysis.

Trend- or variance-detection tools are similar to *attack-detecting tools* except that they scan for deviations from normal trends. For example, there could be a problem if

Bob normally logs in at 9 a.m. but now is attempting to log in at 4 a.m. Finally, *audit-reduction tools* reduce the volume of information to be examined to ease manual analysis.

The bottom line on auditing logs is that you need to strike a balance because a system that produces auditing information takes a hit in performance as the number of auditable events increases. One widely used tool is Syslog, a standard Linux service that uses UDP to send log messages within a network. Syslog provides a wide range of system info, which makes it an important part of network monitoring.

One big question is how much should be logged? Reducing auditable events raises performance but reduces the amount of usable information. Even if performance were not a factor and you could audit every conceivable event, there would still be a huge burden on the analysis side. It would be impossible to review so much information. This means that collecting the information in the first place would be of little or no value. The art of auditing is best accomplished by balancing a required number of metrics to log and measure that against the time and effort required to periodically review the logged data. This entire process should be documented and policy driven.

NetFlow is another tool that can be used to collect and analyze network traffic statistics. It uses multiple sources of internal and external information and processes it in real time to detect threats. The key is to use existing network infrastructure that's already inline and available. Two other technologies an auditor should understand are network access control (NAC) and security information and event management (SIEM). NAC is a technology for unifying endpoint security technology that can be used for network security enforcement. SIEM is used for real-time analysis of security alerts generated by network hardware and applications.

Security Testing Techniques

While IT auditing is generally concerned with reviewing policies and procedures that have been implemented to protect confidentiality, integrity, and availability of data, there is also a need to have an understanding of other types of security testing techniques. An organization's policies and procedures should set the tone for good security practices and should assign responsibility for a secure infrastructure. Policies on logical access control should be designed so that least privilege is established and users are granted access to only the minimum level of access needed to perform their assigned tasks. Two techniques for this are vulnerability scanning and penetration testing.

Vulnerability Scanning

Vulnerability scanning typically involves using software tools to scan a network, devices, and applications for vulnerabilities. Some of these tools are commercial and require an annual subscription; others are open source and don't cost anything to acquire initially. These tools can be run against a single computer or against a range of network addresses. Nessus is an example of a well-known vulnerability scanning tool. Nessus is now both an open source and a commercial tool.

Vulnerability scanning tools can be used to run regularly scheduled scans or can be used if a target system or network has been patched or changed due to upgrades. Periodic network assessments should review a list of best practices to make sure security best practices are being followed. Table 9-4 presents a basic checklist of these items.

Table 9-4 Network Assessment Checklist

Item	Finding
Strong authentication used?	Yes/No
Intrusion detection in place and tuned?	Yes/No
Firewalls deployed and properly configured?	Yes/No
Encryption used?	Yes/No
Antivirus present and updated?	Yes/No
Patch management used?	Yes/No
Application controls in place?	Yes/No

Penetration Testing

Penetration testing is more in-depth than vulnerability scanning. Penetration testing is adversarial in nature. It examines what an attacker can see, what the attacker can access, how that information can be leveraged, and whether anyone would notice. Penetration testing is the process of evaluating an organization's security measures by using the same tools and techniques a criminal hacker (cracker) would use. The big difference is that penetration testing is done with the enterprise's permission. This type of security evaluation is also known as a *pen test*, *ethical hacking*, or a *red team activity*. The organization's security team might or might not be made aware of a pending test. In a blind test, the pen test team has no knowledge of the internal network. A double-blind test is similar, but with the added requirement that the internal security employees have no knowledge of the test.

During a pen test, operational control of computers might be the target, or the goal might simply be to plant a flag or download usernames and passwords to prove that vulnerabilities exist. A pen test can also be conducted internally, examining the security of the internal or external network; these attacks seek to gain control from outside the organization's security perimeter. After the test methodology is determined, the pen test team is responsible for determining the weaknesses; technical, administrative, or physical flaws; and vulnerabilities. Recommendations for addressing security shortcomings should be included. Test results should be delivered in a comprehensive report to management.

Several good documents detail ways to conduct penetration testing. The Open Source Security Testing Methodology Manual (OSSTMM) is one. It is a peer-reviewed methodology for performing security tests, and you can find it at www.osstmm.org. Another is NIST-800-42. Table 9-5 lists the different stages of penetration testing, per NIST.

Table 9-5 The NIST Four-Stage Pen Test Methodology

Stage	Description
Planning	At this stage, a signed letter of authorization is obtained. The rules of engagement are established here. The team must have goals, know the time frame, and know the limits and boundaries.
Discovery	This stage is divided into two distinct phases: **Passive:** This phase is concerned with information gathered in a very covert manner. Examples of passive information gathering include surfing the organization's website to mine valuable information and reviewing job openings to gain a better understanding of the technologies and equipment used by the organization. **Active**: This phase of the test is split between network scanning and host scanning. As individual networks are enumerated, they are further probed to discover all hosts, determine their open ports, and attempt to pinpoint the OS. Nmap is a popular scanning program.
Attack	At this stage, the pen testers attempt to gain access, escalate their privilege, browse the system, and expand their influence.
Reporting	In this final stage, documentation is used to compile the final report. This report serves as the basis for corrective action, which can range from nothing more than enforcing existing policies to closing unneeded ports and adding patches and service packs.

NIST 800-115 is another document to review. This is just one of several documents available to help guide you through an assessment. Find out more at http://csrc.nist.gov/publications/PubsSPs.html.

> **NOTE**   To learn more about ethical hacking and pen testing, consider reading *Certified Ethical Hacker (CEH) Version 9 Cert Guide* by one of the authors of this book, Michael Gregg.

Throughout the pen test process, the security team should be in close contact with management to keep them abreast of any findings. The team should never exceed its level of authorization or attempt any type of test that has not been previously approved in writing. There shouldn't be any big surprises at the conclusion of the pen tests. Leading a pen test team is a huge undertaking that requires managerial, technical, and project-management skills.

> **NOTE**   During a pen test, team members try to exploit potential vulnerabilities. If vulnerabilities are discovered that cannot be removed, the team should look for ways to implement compensating controls.

Problem and Incident Management Practices

If one thing is a given in life, it's that things will go wrong. Problem and incident management procedures can be thought of as pre-disaster planning.

Tracking Change

One way to prevent problems before they occur is to have a good change management program. Change management is a structured process whose purpose is to control modifications made to systems and programs. Without effective change-management procedures, unauthorized changes to software could endanger the security of an organization. During an audit, controls to prevent unauthorized changes should be verified. Some common change controls include the following:

- **Separation of duties:** Development, administration, and operation duties should be performed by different individuals.

- **Controlling the development environment:** Software developers should have access restricted to a controlled area used only for code development.

- **Restricting access:** Access to source code should be restricted to only individuals who have a valid need for it.

Fraud Risk Factors

Fraud risk factors are events or conditions that indicate an incentive or pressure to commit fraud or provide an opportunity to commit fraud. Fraud can be caused by insiders or outsiders. When there is no internal audit function, it is unlikely that incorrect or inappropriate transactions will be spotted or corrected.

Insiders

Errors can result from honest mistakes or intentional fraud. One of the basic tests to help identify or eliminate a suspect is *means, opportunity, and motive (MOM)*. Also known as *the crime triangle*, MOM demonstrates why insiders pose a greater threat to security than outsiders. Insiders possess the means and opportunity to launch an attack, whereas outsiders might have only a motive.

Outsiders

The percentage of insider threats compared to outsider threats is the subject of ongoing debate. Regardless of who is responsible for an attack, admitting to falling prey to computer crime can have a negative impact on an organization's image, can make the company appear vulnerable, or can even motivate additional attacks. However, data breaches often must be reported. Some laws and regulations require reporting, including PCI-DSS, HIPAA, SOX, and the EU Privacy Shield. Some of the individuals responsible for computer crimes include the following:

- **Hackers:** Hackers typically try to overcome the technical and physical barriers that restrict their access to information and systems. They may be driven by many factors, such as money, prestige, thrill, or activism.

- **Script kiddies:** A script kiddie is a young or inexperienced attacker who uses only well-known vulnerabilities and scripts to launch attacks. Tool sets such as Kali Linux make it easy for anyone to hack. Script kiddies do not have any serious programming skills or an in-depth understanding of networks or operating systems.

- **Criminal hackers:** These hackers seek to cash in, do damage, or perform other illegal activities. They may be technically proficient or may just download a crimeware kit that's readily available on the dark web.

- **Phreakers:** These hackers of yesterday are interested in breaking into telecommunication and PBX systems. In the past, their motive might have been to exploit systems for free phone calls, for illegal use, or to provide telecommunication access to others for a profit. Phreakers can access telecommunication equipment, reprogram it, and spoof caller ID or send fake text messages, which is known as smishing.

■ **Terrorists:** These individuals might be funded by other countries, covert organizations, or industries. Their goal is to conduct acts of terror, and their activities can range from using social media to gain followers, launch a DoS attack, deface a website, or potentially even compromise critical infrastructure, such as nuclear power plants, electric plants, water plants, gas refineries, and so on. Figure 9-17 shows a Shodan search for automated gas pump controls. Shodan allows anyone to search for industrial control systems or other types of critical infrastructure.

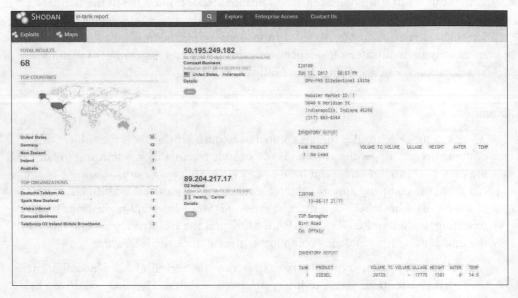

Figure 9-17 Shodan Search for Industrial Control Systems

Incident Response

To be able to respond to security incidents, organizations need to have incident response and incident handling policies in place. These policies should dictate how the organization handles various types of incidents. Most companies set up a Computer Security Incident Response Team (CSIRT). A very early example of incident response occurred, 1988 in response to the Morris worm, which knocked out more than 10 percent of the systems connected to the Internet. Having an incident response team in place, along with the policies needed to function, can give an organization an effective and efficient means of reducing the potential impact of these situations. These procedures should also give management sufficient information to decide on an appropriate course of action. By having these procedures in place, an organization can maintain or restore business continuity, defend against future attacks, and deter attacks by prosecuting violators.

Incident response team members need diverse skill sets. Members should come from various departments throughout the organization, such as the following:

- Information security

- Legal

- Human resources

- Public relations

- Physical security

- Network and system administration

- IS auditing

Being a diverse group better prepares an incident response team to deal with the many types of incidents that can occur. Per ISACA, auditors should ensure that an organization has documented incident response plans in place to deal with these common types of security incidents:

- Malware infections

- Trojans

- Website attacks

- Unauthorized access

- Hardware theft and physical intrusion

- Unauthorized software

- Denial of service

- Slander and media misinformation

- Proper forensic response and investigation practices

Documentation to address common types of potential incidents is critical because investigating computer crime is complex and involved. Missteps can render evidence useless and unusable in a court of law. Team members must therefore be knowledgeable about the proper procedures and have training on how to secure and isolate the scene to prevent contamination. That is the role of computer forensics.

Whatever the motive or reason, the response should always be the same. Security breaches should be investigated in a structured, methodical manner. Most companies would not operate a business without training their employees how to respond to fires, but many companies do not build good incident response and investigation procedures.

> **NOTE** Honeypots can be used to learn more about what hackers do during an attack. A honeypot is a fake system used to jail an attacker and learn more about his or her activities so you are better prepared during a real attack.

The first step is the analysis of the event. An *event* is a noticeable occurrence. For example, say that an IDS alert was tripped. This requires an investigation because it must be determined whether the event was an incident. An *incident* is an adverse event or series of events that violates law, policy, or procedure.

Emergency Incident Response Team

The emergency incident response team, which investigates incidents, needs a variety of skills, including the following:

- Recognition skills and abilities
- Technical skills and abilities
- Investigative and response skills

The individuals in charge of an incident must be able to recognize that something has happened. For example, this could be that an IDS has tripped. Recognition is not enough; those responsible must also have the ability to look at logs and event records and perform incident analysis. Skills are also needed to properly investigate an incident.

There should be a variety of individuals on an incident response team. For example, if an employee is thought to have been hacking, the manager may want to fire the person but will most likely have to consult the legal department and human resources. This means the team needs to include employees from many different parts of the company. While all members of the team may not be involved in every single incident, there will be a need to have contacts in many different departments, and these individuals should understand that they may be called on as needed. This team also must know how to contain damage and determine how to proceed.

Incident Response Process

Incident response requires organizations to define the specific steps that will be carried out when an incident takes place. Good incident response procedures give the organization an effective and efficient means of dealing with an incident in a manner that reduces the potential impact. These procedures should also provide management with sufficient information to decide on an appropriate course of action. By having these procedures in place, the organization can maintain or restore business continuity, defend against future attacks, and deter attacks by prosecuting violators.

The primary goal of incident response is to contain the damage, find out what happened, and prevent it from reoccurring. Crime can be greatly reduced by eliminating any one of the three sides of the crime triangle commonly referred to as means opportunity, and motive. (see Figure 9-18).

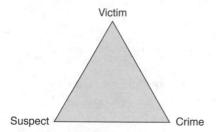

Figure 9-18 Crime Triangle

The steps to emergency response are many and follow a structured approach such as the format shown here:

Step 1. **Planning and preparation**: The organization must establish policies and procedures to address potential security incidents.

Step 2. **Identification and evaluation**: Automated systems should be used to determine whether an event occurred. Was an event real, not a false positive? The tools used for identification include IDSs, IPSs, firewalls, audits, logging, and observation.

Step 3. **Containment and mitigation**: Preplanning, training, and the use of predeveloped procedures are key to this step. The incident response plan should dictate what action is required. The incident response team must have had the required level of training to properly handle response.

Step 4. **Eradication and recovery**: Containing the problem is not enough; it must be removed, and steps must be taken to return to normal business processes.

Step 5. **Investigate and closure**: What happened? When the investigation is complete, a report, either formal or informal, must be prepared. This is needed to evaluate any needed changes to the IR policies.

Step 6.   **Lessons learned**: At this final step, all those involved must review what happened and why. Most importantly, necessary changes must be put in place to prevent future problems. Learning from what happened will help prevent it from happening again.

> **NOTE**   Management needs to make a decision about whether law enforcement should be called in during a security breach. There are reasons both for and against calling in law enforcement.

Incident Response and Results

Incident response procedures must be of such detail that specific types of incidents are documented and advice given about what the proper response would be. Documentation to address each of these potential incidents is critical because investigating computer crime is complex and involved. Missteps can render evidence useless and unusable in a court of law. This means that team members must be knowledgeable about the proper procedures and trained on how to secure and isolate the scene to prevent contamination. Table 9-6 outlines some sample response strategies.

Table 9-6   Sample Escalation and Response Procedures

Incident	Response Procedure
Possible data theft	Contact legal department, make forensic image, secure evidence
External hacker attack	Capture logs, monitor activities, gather evidence, contact management
Unauthorized use of computer resources	Gather evidence, make forensic image, analyze data, review corporate policy

In the end, incident response is about learning. Results of your findings should be fed back into the system to make changes or improve the environment so that the same incident isn't repeated. Tasks you might end up doing as a result of an attack include the following:

- Figuring out how the attack occurred and looking for ways to prevent it from happening again

- Upgrading tools or software in response to finding out what the team lacked that prevented effective response to the incident

- Finding things that went wrong and making changes to the incident response plan to improve operations during the next incident

Although no one ever wants to end up in court or to take incident response to the next level, this is not always how it works out. All incident response must be handled meticulously so you can be prepared for whatever unfolds in an investigation. Sometimes the forensic skill level required mandates that the forensic analysis be handed off to a more skilled forensics lab. The next section discusses what happens in forensic labs.

NOTE   Ultimately, incident response is about learning. An incident response team needs to answer questions such as the following: What happened? How did it happen? Can we prevent it from happening again? How can we better prepare and respond for the next time? and What did we learn?

Forensic Investigation

Forensics and incident response are very closely related except that incident response is most closely associated with getting systems back up and running, while forensics is more closely associated with capturing information in such a way that it is acceptable. *Computer forensics* is the systematic step-by-step examination and analysis of data that is stored, retrieved, or processed on computer systems in a legal, approved way so that the evidence can be used in court, if needed. Computers are a part of just about all crimes today. Consider the following ways that computers may be involved in crimes:

- **Computers used in a crime:** Criminals may use computers as a tool much as they would use a crowbar or gun. For example, whereas in the past a criminal might have used the post office for extortion or fraud, he might now use a computer and email to achieve the same goal.

- **Computers targeted as a crime:** Crimes may be directed at computers. For example, LulzSec targeted MasterCard and Visa in 2010 with an extended DDoS attack.

- **Computers are incidental in a crime:** Sometimes a computer may aid a criminal in some way. For example, a criminal might keep a list of earnings from illegal gambling in an Excel spreadsheet instead of in a spiral notebook.

The chain of custody helps protect the integrity and reliability of evidence by providing an evidence log that shows every access to evidence, from collection to appearance in court. Forensic specialists must know how to record evidence at the scene by taking photographs, documenting their activities in an investigator's notebook, interviewing suspects and witnesses, and knowing the proper procedures for collecting or seizing suspected systems or media. Doing all this correctly protects the chain of custody and the legality of the evidence.

Although law enforcement has been practicing forensics for a long time, the computer forensics field is relatively new to the corporate sector. Many IS auditors are not highly skilled in auditing this important field. An IS auditor must look carefully at the policies and procedures that detail forensic activities during an audit. Such policies might address computers, but other devices could be subject to forensic analysis, including cell phones, tablets, digital cameras, and USB thumb drives. Any existing policy must specify how evidence is to be handled. Mishandling can cost companies millions.

Forensics Steps

Because electronic information can be changed easily, a rigid methodology should be followed in handling electronic evidence:

1. **Identify and acquire:** The information must be identified and retrieved. Once in the custody of an investigator, a copy is usually created. Standard practice dictates making a bit-level copy, which is an exact duplicate of the original data. This enables the investigator to examine the copy while leaving the original copy intact.

2. **Preserve and authenticate:** Preservation is the act of maintaining the evidence in an unchanged state. This process requires that an investigator show that the data is unchanged and has not been tampered with. Authentication can be accomplished through the use of integrity checks and hashes such as MD5 and SHA.

3. **Analyze, record, and present:** An investigator must be careful to examine the data and ensure that any activity is documented. The investigator usually extracts evidence by examining drive slack space, file slack space, hidden files, swap data, Internet cache, and other locations, such as the recycle bin. Specialized tools are available for this activity. All the activities of an investigator must be recorded to ensure that the information will be usable in court, if needed.

Because the collection of electronic information is an important concern, the International Organization on Computer Evidence (IOCE) was appointed to develop international principles for procedures related to digital evidence. The goal was to develop standards and practices that many countries and states would recognize as legal to allow digital evidence collected by one state to be used in the courts of another state. (See https://archives.fbi.gov/archives/about-us/lab/forensic-science-communications/fsc/april2000/swgde.htm.)

- When dealing with digital evidence, all the generally accepted forensic and procedural principles must be applied.

- Upon seizing digital evidence, actions taken should not change that evidence.

- When it is necessary for a person to access original digital evidence, that person should be trained for the purpose.

- All activity related to the seizure, access, storage, or transfer of digital evidence must be fully documented, preserved, and available for review.

- An individual is responsible for all actions taken with respect to digital evidence while the digital evidence is in his or her possession.

- Any agency responsible for seizing, accessing, storing, or transferring digital evidence is responsible for compliance with these principles.

Other Forensic Types

While the discussion so far has been about computer forensics, there are other forensics types, including network forensics and software forensics.

Network forensics involves the examination of network traffic and can be used to examine traffic as it passes over a network. Common tools used for network forensics include Wireshark, RSA NetWitness, and NetworkMiner. Regardless of what tool is used, the idea is to examine network traffic. Network forensics might be used to look for the exfiltration of data, track the activity of botnets, or detect employee Internet misuse.

Software forensics involves the examination of software. Maybe you have found what may be a malicious application or even a Trojan. Software forensics can help analyze the software's purpose and actions. Software forensics can be carried out in one of two ways: dynamic or static forensic analysis.

With dynamic forensic analysis, the idea is to have the software run or execute in a controlled environment or sandbox to learn more about its activity. This is tricky because if the malware gets out of its sandbox, it might infect the entire organization. One approach is to use a virtualized system that has been isolated to perform this task. Another approach is to upload the suspected malware to an online sandbox. ThreatExpert, as shown in Figure 9-19, is an example of such a service.

Figure 9-19 ThreatExpert

Static forensic analysis overcomes the worry of allowing the potential malware to spread because the application is not executed. Static analysis involves disassembling or decompiling the application to examine the inner workings of the code. The creators of malware don't make this activity easy, and there are many things they do, such as using encryption, to make analysis more difficult. An example of a static analysis tool is IDA Pro, shown in Figure 9-20.

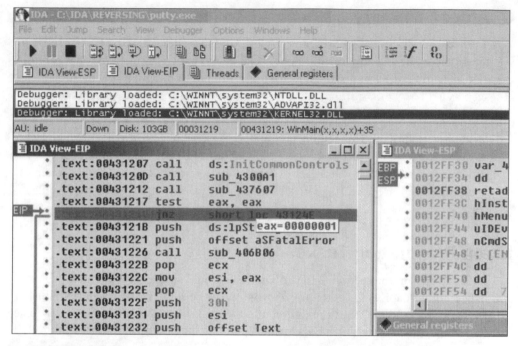

Figure 9-20   IDA Pro

Computer Crime Jurisdiction

The unpleasant truth is that even after conducting incident response and forensics, it is difficult to track and prosecute computer criminals. This is due in part to the international nature of computer crime. Unlike conventional crimes that occur in one location, computer crimes might originate in China, use a compromised computer network located in Singapore, and target a computer network located in the United States. Each country's conflicting views on what constitutes cybercrime and how or even if the hackers should be punished can cause legal nightmares. It is hard to apply national borders to a medium such as the Internet that is essentially borderless.

If computer crime prosecution is possible, the presentation of evidence in court has to meet specific standards. Evidence is every type of proof legally presented at trial used to convince the judge and/or jury of alleged facts. Computer evidence is very volatile, and if it's not handled correctly, it can be considered hearsay. This should drive home the fact that crimes involving computers must be handled in a very specific way so the chain of custody is protected.

Chapter Summary

This chapter discusses asset threat, response, and management. The threats to organizations can be physical, technical, or social. This chapter focuses on the technical and social threats. Organizations face a large number of potential technical threats, such as MITM, DoS, sniffing, XSS, and botnets. Social threats involve people and include phishing, smishing, and other forms of social engineering.

Dealing with these threats requires that policy be developed for incident response as well as forensic response, and these policies must be tested and verified before bad events occur so that when they do, steps such as chain of custody and proper handling of data are performed in such a way that any evidence will be admissible in court.

Exam Preparation Tasks

As mentioned in the section "How to Use This Book" in the Introduction, you have a couple choices for exam preparation: the exercises here; Chapter 10, "Final Preparation;" and the exam simulation questions on the book's companion web page (www.informit.com/title/9780789758446).

Review All the Key Topics

Review the most important topics in this chapter, noted with the Key Topic icon in the outer margin of the page. Table 9-7 lists these key topics and the page number on which each is found.

Table 9-7 Key Topics in Chapter 9

Key Topic Element	Description	Page Number
Table 9-2	Best practices examples	393
Table 9-3	Common security controls for virtual systems	395
Section	Social engineering and nontechnical attacks	399
Section	Wireless and Bluetooth	405
Table 9-5	The NIST four-stage pen test methodology	417

Complete Tables from Memory

Print a copy of Appendix B, "Memory Tables" (found on the companion web page), or at least the section for this chapter, and complete the tables from memory. Appendix C, "Memory Tables Answer Key," also on the companion web page, includes completed tables you can use to check your work.

Define Key Terms

Define the following key terms from this chapter and check your answers against the glossary:

assessment, audit, backdoor, blackbox testing, Bluejacking, Bluesnarfing, botnet, buffer overflow, cracker, cross-site request forgery (XSRF), cross-site scripting (XSS), dictionary attack, dropper, ethical hack, ethical hacker, exploit, file infector, fuzzing, gray box testing, honeypot, Internet packet spoofing (IP spoofing), logic bomb, MAC filtering, macro infector, macro virus, man-in-the-middle (MITM) attack, media access control (MAC), multipartite virus, penetration test, phishing, phreaker, polymorphic virus, rounding down, script kiddie, service set ID (SSID), smurf attack, social engineering, SQL injection, SYN flood attack, virus, virus scanning, war driving, white box testing, Wi-Fi Protected Access (WPA), Wired Equivalent Privacy (WEP), zero-day exploit

Review Questions

1. When responding to a potential computer crime, what should an auditor do first?

    a. Seek to identify the attacker

    b. Remove the device from the network

    c. Ensure that the evidence remains unchanged

    d. Contact the police

2. While reviewing her email, an auditor notices that one email message contains an obscured link. Which of the following is not the appropriate action?

    a. Inform IT

    b. Open the link

    c. Delete the email

    d. Mark the email source as spam

3. When examining change management, an auditor should not be concerned with which of the following?

   a. Restricted access controls.

   b. Separation of duties.

   c. Controls in the development environment.

   d. Access to source code by developers.

4. To aid in the successful completion of the company's first penetration test, an auditor should recommend which of the following?

   a. SOX

   b. NIST 800-42

   c. PCI-DSS

   d. SSAE-16

5. Which of the following activities would an auditor most like to see carried out on a weekly basis?

   a. Penetration testing

   b. Change management

   c. Vulnerability assessment

   d. Rotation of duties

6. Which of the following would an auditor expect to see as the first step in the incident response process?

   a. Recovery

   b. Mitigation

   c. Planning and preparation

   d. Identification

7. As an auditor, how would you describe a penetration test in which the structure of the network is unknown and the test team has no prior knowledge of the infrastructure?

   a. Double-blind

   b. Blind

   c. Zero proof

   d. Unknown

8. You have been invited to a postmortem review of a recent malware attack. The attacker was able to exploit the fact that the victim was connected to a legitimate site and a malicious site at the time the attack was carried out. Which of the following best describes this situation?

   a. XSS

   b. XSRF

   c. Buffer overflow

   d. TOCTOU

9. An auditor has been asked to attend an application acquisition meeting for commercial off-the-shelf (COTS) software. Which of the following would be the best recommendation for testing and evaluating a compiled existing application?

   a. Fuzzing

   b. Code review

   c. Reverse engineering

   d. Decompiling

10. From an audit perspective, which of the following would be the best technique to use to scan for deviations from normal activity?

    a. Bypass label processing

    b. Use attack detection tools

    c. Use trend variance detection tools

    d. Use audit reduction tools

Suggested Reading and Resources

- **The five steps of incident response:** https://digitalguardian.com/blog/five-steps-incident-response

- **Forensic tools for auditors:** http://whitecollarinv.com/wp-content/uploads/2010/03/ForensicToolsTechniquesforIA4-19.ppt

- **Common hacking techniques:** https://fossbytes.com/hacking-techniques/

- **IT security audits:** www.tracesecurity.com/services/it-security-audit

- **Chain of custody:** https://ovc.ncjrs.gov/sartkit/develop/issues-coc.html

- **ITIL incident management:** www.bmc.com/guides/itil-incident-management. html

- **Risk factors that increase employee fraud:** www. facilitiesnet.com/facilitiesmanagement/article/ Three-Risk-Factors-That-Increase-Employee-Fraud--10923

- **Social Media Policy Examples:** http://blog.hirerabbit. com/5-terrific-examples-of-company-social-media-policies/

- **Top 10 DoS attack sites:** http://top10stressers.com/

CHAPTER 10

Final Preparation

The first nine chapters of this book cover the techniques, processes, audit concepts, and considerations required to be prepared to pass the Information Systems Audit and Control Association (ISACA) CISA exam. Those chapters cover the information that is required to pass the exam. However, you should not expect to pass the exam just by reading a book. The CISA exam requires hands-on experience with auditing and audit practices, including general audit concepts as well as technical skills. Exam candidates who have a technical background often struggle with governance and auditing concepts. Exam candidates with audit and accounting backgrounds excel in these areas but struggle with the technical aspects of the exam. This exam requires a balance of skills. Technical knowledge is important, and exam candidates must understand the concepts and core objectives of auditing. Successful exam candidates think like an auditor and realize that the technology is a tool used to accomplish a business goal.

This short chapter has two main sections. The first section lists the exam preparation tools useful at this point in the study process. The second section provides a suggested study plan you can use now that you have completed all the earlier chapters in this book.

Tools for Final Preparation

This section lists some information about the available tools and how to access them.

Pearson Test Prep Practice Test Software and Questions on the Website

Register this book to get access to the Pearson Test Prep software that displays and grades a set of exam-realistic multiple-choice questions. Using the Pearson Test Prep practice test software, you can either study by going through the questions in Study Mode or take a simulated (timed) CISA exam.

The Pearson Test Prep software comes with two full practice exams, which are available to you either online or as an offline Windows application. To access these practice exams, please see the instructions in the card inserted in the sleeve in the back of the book. This card includes a unique access code that enables you to activate your exams in the Pearson Test Prep software.

Accessing the Pearson Test Prep Software Online

The online version of the Pearson Test Prep software can be used on any device that has a browser and connectivity to the Internet, including desktop machines, tablets, and smartphones. To start using your practice exams online, simply follow these steps:

Step 1.   Go to www.PearsonTestPrep.com.

Step 2.   Select **Pearson IT Certification** as your product group.

Step 3.   Enter your email/password for your account. If you don't have an account on PearsonITCertification.com or CiscoPress.com, you need to establish one by going to PearsonITCertification.com/join.

Step 4.   In the **My Products** tab, click the **Activate New Product** button.

Step 5.   Enter the access code printed on the insert card in the back of your book to activate your product.

Step 6.   The product will now be listed in your My Products page. Click the **Exams** button to launch the exam settings screen and start your exam.

Accessing the Pearson Test Prep Software Offline

If you wish to study offline, you can download and install the Windows version of the Pearson Test Prep software. There is a download link for this software on the book's companion website, or you can just enter this link in your browser: www. pearsonitcertification.com/content/downloads/pcpt/engine.zip.

To access the book's companion website and the software, simply follow these steps:

Step 1.   Register your book by going to PearsonITCertification.com/register and entering the ISBN 9780789758446.

Step 2.   Correctly answer the challenge questions.

Step 3.   Go to your account page and select the **Registered Products** tab.

Step 4.   Click the **Access Bonus Content** link under the product listing.

Step 5.   Click the **Install Pearson Test Prep Desktop Version** link under the Practice Exams section of the page to download the software.

Step 6.   When the software finishes downloading, unzip all the files on your computer.

Step 7. Double-click the application file to start the installation and follow the onscreen instructions to complete the registration.

Step 8. When the installation is complete, launch the application and click the **Activate Exam** button on the My Products tab.

Step 9. Click the **Activate a Product** button in the Activate Product Wizard.

Step 10. Enter the unique access code found on the card in the back of your book and click the **Activate** button.

Step 11. Click **Next** and then click **Finish** to download the exam data to your application.

Step 12. You can now start using the practice exams by selecting the product and clicking the **Open Exam** button to open the exam settings screen.

NOTE   The offline and online versions will sync together, so saved exams and grade results recorded on one version will be available to you on the other as well.

Customizing Your Exams

When you are in the exam settings screen, you can choose to take exams in one of three modes:

- **Study Mode:** Study Mode allows you to fully customize your exams and review answers as you are taking the exam. This is typically the mode you use first, to assess your knowledge and identify information gaps.

- **Practice Exam Mode:** Practice Exam Mode locks certain customization options and presents a realistic exam experience. Use this mode when you are preparing to test your exam readiness.

- **Flash Card Mode:** Flash Card Mode strips out the answers and presents you with only the question stem. This mode is great for late-stage preparation, when you really want to challenge yourself to provide answers without the benefit of seeing multiple choice options. This mode will not provide the detailed score reports that the other two modes will, so it should not be used if you are trying to identify knowledge gaps.

In addition to using these three modes, you can select the source of your questions. You can choose to take exams that cover all the chapters, or you can narrow your selection to just a single chapter or the chapters in specific parts of the book. All chapters are selected by default. If you want to narrow your focus to individual chapters, simply deselect all the chapters then select only those on which you wish to focus in the Objectives area.

You can also select the exam banks on which to focus. Each exam bank comes complete with a full exam of questions that cover topics in every chapter. You can have the test engine serve up exams from all four banks or just from one individual bank by selecting the desired banks in the exam bank area.

There are several other customizations you can make to your exam from the exam settings screen, such as the time allowed for the exam, the number of questions served up, whether to randomize questions and answers, or whether to serve up only specific types of questions. You can also create custom test banks by selecting only questions that you have marked or questions for which you have added notes.

Updating Your Exams

If you are using the online version of the Pearson Test Prep software, you should always have access to the latest version of the software as well as the exam data. If you are using the Windows desktop version, every time you launch the software, it will check to see if there are any updates to your exam data and automatically download any changes that have been made since the last time you used the software. You must be connected to the Internet at the time you launch the software.

Sometimes, due to many factors, the exam data may not fully download when you activate your exam. If you find that figures or exhibits are missing, you may need to manually update your exams.

To update a particular exam you have already activated and downloaded, simply select the **Tools** tab and click the **Update Products** button. Again, this is only an issue with the desktop Windows application.

If you wish to check for updates to the Pearson Test Prep exam engine software, Windows desktop version, simply select the **Tools** tab and click the **Update Application** button to ensure that you are running the latest version of the software engine.

Premium Edition

In addition to the free practice exam provided on the website, you can purchase additional exams with expanded functionality directly from Pearson IT Certification. The Premium Edition of this title contains two additional full practice exams and an eBook (in both PDF and ePub formats). In addition, the Premium Edition title also provides remediation for each question to the specific part of the eBook that relates to that question.

Because you have purchased the print version of this title, you can purchase the Premium Edition at a deep discount. There is a coupon code in the book sleeve that contains a one-time-use code and instructions for where you can purchase the Premium Edition.

To view the premium edition product page, go to www.informit.com/title/9780789758446.

Memory Tables

Like most other cert guides from Pearson, this book purposely organizes information into tables and lists for easier study and review. Rereading these tables before the exam can be very helpful. However, it is easy to skim over the tables without paying attention to every detail, especially when you remember having seen the table's contents when reading the chapter.

Instead of just reading the tables in the various chapters, this book's Appendixes B and C give you another review tool. Appendix B lists partially completed versions of many of the tables from the book. You can open Appendix B as a PDF available on the book's website after registering and print the appendix. For review, you can attempt to complete the tables, which can help you focus on the review. This type of review exercises the memory connectors in your brain, and it makes you think about the information without as much prompting, which forces a little more contemplation about the facts.

Appendix C, also a PDF located on the book's website, provides the completed tables so you can check yourself. You can also just refer to the tables as printed in the book.

Chapter-Ending Review Tools

Chapters 2 through 9 each have several features in the "Exam Preparation Tasks" section at the end of the chapter. You might have already worked through them in each chapter. It can also be useful to use these tools again as you make your final preparations for the exam.

Suggested Plan for Final Review/Study

This section lists a suggested study plan from the point at which you finish reading through Chapter 9 until you take the CISA exam. Certainly, you can ignore this plan, use it as is, or pick and choose suggestions from it.

The plan uses five steps:

Step 1. **Review key topics and the "Do I Know This Already?" (DIKTA) quiz questions:** You can use the table that lists the key topics in each chapter or just flip the pages and look for key topics. Also, reviewing the DIKTA questions from the beginning of the chapter can be helpful for review.

Step 2. **Complete the memory tables:** Open Appendix B from the book's website and print the entire thing or print the tables by major part. Then complete the tables and check them against the answer key in Appendix C.

Step 3. **Review the "Review Questions" sections:** Go through the review questions at the end of each chapter to identify areas where you need more study.

Step 4. **Use the Pearson Test Prep practice test software to practice:** The Pearson Test Prep practice test software can be used to study using a bank of unique exam-realistic questions available only with this book.

Summary

The tools and suggestions in this chapter have been designed with one goal in mind: to help you develop the skills required to pass the CISA exam. This book has been developed from the beginning to not just tell you the facts but also to help you learn how to apply the facts. No matter what your experience level leading up to when you take the exams, it is our hope that the broad range of preparation tools and the structure of the book will help you pass the exam with ease. We hope you do well on the exam.

Glossary

802.11 standard   A legacy set of wireless LAN standards developed by Working Group 11 of the IEEE LAN/MAN Standards Committee. 802.11 is known for its use of WEP and RC4.

A

accreditation   Management's formal acceptance of a system or an application.

ACID test   Testing the following: **a**tomicity, to divide work so that the results are either all or nothing; **c**onsistency, to ensure that transactions are processed only if they meet system defined integrity constraints; **i**solation, to ensure that each transaction is isolated from all others until complete; and **d**urability, to ensure that when a transaction is processed, the transaction cannot be rolled back and is accurate.

Address Resolution Protocol (ARP)   A protocol used to map a known IP address to an unknown physical address on the local network. For example, IPv4 uses 32-bit addresses, whereas Ethernet uses 48-bit MAC addresses. The ARP process can use the known IP address that is being passed down the stack to resolve the unknown MAC address by means of a broadcast message. This information is helpful in an ARP cache.

AES   The current symmetric standard and a replacement for DES. AES uses the Rijndael algorithm. Used by WPA2.

agile   An iterative, expedited, and incremental software development methodology.

algorithm   A mathematical procedure used for solving a problem. Commonly used in cryptography.

application controls   Controls related to a specific individual process within an application.

artificial intelligence (AI)   An extension of expert systems that involves self-learning and cognitive processes used to mimic the thinking of humans with the speed of computers.

assessment   An evaluation and/or valuation of IT assets based on predefined measurement or evaluation criteria. An accounting or auditing firm is not typically required to conduct an assessment such as a risk or vulnerability assessment.

asymmetric algorithm   A routine that uses a pair of different but related cryptographic keys to encrypt and decrypt data.

asymmetric encryption   In cryptography, use of an asymmetric key algorithm with a pair of cryptographic keys to encrypt and decrypt. The two keys are related mathematically, and a message encrypted by the algorithm using one key can be decrypted by the same algorithm using the other. In a sense, one key "locks" a lock (encryption), and a different key is required to unlock it (decryption).

audit   An investigation by an accounting or auditing firm that conforms to a specific and formal methodology and definition for how the investigation is to be conducted, with specific reporting elements and metrics being examined (such as a financial audit according to Public Accounting and Auditing Guidelines and Procedures).

audit function   An independent and objective function that provides leadership assurance that the organization complies with regulatory rules and industry norms.

audit universe   The range of audit activities and auditable entities to be covered in an audit.

authentication   A method that enables identification of someone. Authentication verifies the identity and legitimacy of an individual to access a system and its resources. Common authentication methods include passwords, tokens, and biometric systems.

automated controls   Controls that are triggered through automation, such as validation and edit checks, programmed logic functions, and controls.

B

backdoor   A piece of software that allows access to a computer without using the conventional security procedures. Backdoors are also known as Trojans.

balance data   Various values and totals that might be held temporarily during processing.

balanced scorecard (BSC)   A scorecard that brings together in one view an array of key measurements, such as metrics, target values, and key indicators.

baseline   A platform-specific rule that is accepted across the industry as providing the most effective approach to a specific implementation.

batch control   Control that validates a batch of transactions, such as total dollar amounts, total counts, or total document numbers.

biometrics   A method of verifying a person's identify for authentication by analyzing a unique physical attribute of the individual, such as a fingerprint, retinal scan, or palm print.

blackbox testing   A form of testing in which the tester has no knowledge of the target or its network structure.

Blowfish   A form of symmetric block encryption designed in 1993.

Bluejacking   Sending unsolicited messages, pictures, or information to a Bluetooth user.

Bluesnarfing   Stealing information from a wireless device through a Bluetooth connection.

botnet   A collection of robot-controlled workstations.

bring-your-own-device (BYOD)   The practice of allowing users to bring and use their personal devices on a corporate network.

buffer overflow   In computer programming, a problem that occurs when a software application somehow writes data beyond the allocated end of a buffer in memory. Buffer overflow is usually caused by software bugs and improper syntax and programming, and it exposes an application to malicious code injections or other targeted attack commands.

Business continuity planning   A system or methodology to create a plan for how an organization will resume partially or completely interrupted critical functions within a predetermined time after a disaster or disruption occurs. The goal is to keep critical business functions operational.

business impact analysis   A component of the business continuity plan that involves looking at all the components that an organization is reliant upon for continued functionality. It seeks to distinguish which are more crucial than others and requires a greater allocation of funds in the wake of a disaster.

C

capability maturity model (CMM)   A process that scores maturity of processes against industry standards.

carrier-sense multiple access with collision detection (CSMA/CD)   The access method used by local area networking technologies such as Ethernet.

chain of custody   The process and tools used to account for who had access to collected data and to protect it from being tampered with.

CISA certification   A certification which ensures that individuals have the competency to provide leadership with the assurance that their organization complies with regulatory and industry norms.

CISA exam domains   The basis for the CISA exam and the requirements to earn the certification; see *job practice areas, or job domains.*

CISA exam windows   The three times per year when an individual can take the CISA exam. Each exam window is approximately 60 days long.

Code of Professional Ethics   The code that ISACA has presented to guide the professional and personal conduct of members of the association and/or its certification holders. This is one of the three agreements you must sign off on as part of the CISA application.

cold site   A site that contains no computing-related equipment except for environmental support, such as air conditioners and power outlets, and a security system made ready for installing computer equipment.

compliance function   A discipline accountable for certifying compliance with regulatory rules and industry norms.

compliance test   A test used to verify conformity to a specific standard.

computer-assisted audit techniques (CAATs)   Software audit tools used for statistical sampling and data analysis.

computer-based testing (CBT)   A format of testing completed on the computer instead of with paper and pencil.

continuing professional education (CPE)   Continuing education hours that are required to maintain CISA certification. An individual maintains competency by attaining and reporting annual CPE hours.

continuous monitoring   Repeated testing of a control through automation and alerting when a variance or defect is identified.

control function   A discipline accountable for building, implementing, and maintaining technology controls.

Control Objectives for Information and Related Technologies (COBIT)   A framework used to ensure quality, control, and reliability of information systems by establishing IT governance, management structure, and objectives.

control risk   The risk related to a deployed control not working as expected.

control self-assessment (CSA)   A process in which a business participates in a formal self-assessment of risk.

CPE hours   See *continuing professional education (CPE)*.

cracker   A term derived from "criminal hacker," someone who acts in an illegal manner.

Criticality   The quality, state, degree, or measurement of the highest importance.

critical path methodology (CPM)   A methodology that determines what activities are critical and what the dependencies are among the various tasks.

Cross-Site Request Forgery (XSRF)   An attack that occurs when unauthorized commands are transmitted from a user that the web application trusts.

Cross-Site Scripting (XSS)   An attack that enables attackers to inject client-side scripts into web pages viewed by other users.

D

data classification   A method to simplify data handling rules by categorizing data into distinct data classes.

data lake   A large store of raw data stored in its native format until it is needed.

data warehouse   A large store of processed and refined data obtained from multiple sources that is generally used to guide management decisions.

decryption   The process of converting encrypted content into its original form, often the process of converting ciphertext to plaintext. Decryption is the opposite of encryption.

defense-in-depth   Multilayered security that includes administrative, technical, or logical layers.

demilitarized zone (DMZ)   The middle ground between a trusted internal network and an untrusted, external network. Services that internal and external users must use, such as HTTP, are typically placed in the DMZ.

detection risk   The risk of a control defect going undetected, such as when an auditor fails to find a material error or a defect in a control.

Diameter   A centralized authentication system that is seen as a replacement for RADIUS.

dictionary attack   A type of cryptographic attack in which the attacker uses a word list or dictionary list to try to crack an encrypted password. A newer technique is to use a time/memory trade-off, as in rainbow tables.

digital certificate   A certificate usually issued by a trusted third party that contains the name of a user or server, a digital signature, a public key, and other elements used in authentication and encryption. X.509 is the most common type.

digital signature   An electronic signature that can be used to authenticate the identity of the sender of a message. A digital signature is usually created by encrypting the user's private key and is decrypted with the corresponding public key.

direct-sequence spread spectrum (DSSS)   A technique used to scramble the signal of wireless devices.

Disaster   A natural or man-made event that can include fire, flood, storm, and equipment failure that negatively affects an industry or facility.

Disaster recovery   A set of policies, procedures, and methodologies used to address the recovery or continuation of vital technology infrastructure and systems following a disaster.

Domain Name Service (DNS)   A service that translates alphanumeric domain names into IP addresses and vice versa. Because domain names are alphanumeric, it's easier to remember these names than to remember IP addresses.

Domain Name System Security Extensions (DNSSEC)   A secure version of DNS that provides authentication and integrity.

dropper   A program designed to drop a Trojan horse or malware onto the infected computer and then execute it. Also known as a wrapper.

E

e-commerce   The buying, selling, and servicing of goods via the Internet.

encryption   The process of turning plaintext into ciphertext.

encryption key   A sequence of characters used by an encryption algorithm to encrypt plaintext into ciphertext.

enterprise architecture (EA)   A blueprint that defines the business structure and operation of the organization.

enterprise risk management (ERM)   The process of identifying and managing a portfolio of risk to provide key stakeholders with a substantiated and consistent opinion of risk across the enterprise.

entity integrity   Assurance that each database transaction record contains a primary key.

entity relationship diagram (ERD)   A diagram that helps map the requirements and define the relationships between elements.

equal error rate (EER) A comparison measurement for different biometric devices and technologies to measure their accuracy. The EER is the point at which FAR and FRR are equal or cross over. The lower the EER, the more accurate the biometric system.

Ethernet A network protocol that defines a specific implementation of the physical and data link layers in the OSI model (IEEE 802.3). Ethernet LANs provide reliable high-speed communications up to 10Gbps in a limited geographic area (such as an office complex or a university complex).

ethical hack A type of hack done to help a company or an individual identify potential threats on the organization's IT infrastructure or network. Ethical hackers must obey rules of engagement, do no harm, and stay within legal boundaries.

ethical hacker A security professional who legally attempts to break into a computer system or network to find its vulnerabilities.

exploit A vulnerability in software or hardware that can be exploited by a hacker to gain access to a system or service.

F

false acceptance rate (FAR) A type II biometric device error. It is a biometric system measurement that indicates the percentage of individuals who are incorrectly granted access. This is the worst type of error that can occur because it means that unauthorized individuals have been allowed access.

false rejection rate (FRR) A biometric device error that is considered a type I error. It is a biometric system measurement that indicates the percentage of authorized individuals who are incorrectly denied access.

fiber-optic cable A medium for transmission composed of many glass fibers. Light-emitting diodes or lasers send light through the fiber to a detector that converts the light back to an electrical signal for interpretation. Advantages include huge bandwidth, immunity to electromagnetic interference, and the capability to traverse long distances with minimal signal degradation.

fiduciary A duty of an individual (such as an auditor) who holds a position of special legal trust and responsibility.

file infector A type of virus that copies itself into executable programs.

financial audit A review and evaluation of financial statements and processes.

firewall security A system in hardware or software form used to manage and control both network connectivity and network services. Firewalls act as chokepoints for traffic entering and leaving the network and prevent unrestricted access. Firewalls can be stateful or stateless.

flowchart A graphical categorization of inputs and outputs related to a process or code logic.

frequency-hopping spread spectrum (FHSS) One of the basic modulation techniques used in spread-spectrum signal transmission. FHSS makes wireless communication harder to intercept and more resistant to interference.

function point analysis (FPA) An ISO-approved method for estimating the complexity of software.

fuzzing A blackbox testing technique.

G

general controls Controls that apply across all system components, processes, and data.

gray box testing Testing that occurs with only partial knowledge of the network or that is performed to see what internal users have access to.

guidelines A suggested set of behaviors.

H

hash A cryptographic sum that is a one-way value. A hash is considerably shorter than the original text and can be used to uniquely identify it. You might have seen a hash value next to applications available for download on the Internet. By comparing the hash of the application with the one on the application vendor's website, you can make sure the file has not been changed or altered.

hashing algorithm An algorithm that is used to verify the integrity of data and messages. A well-designed hashing algorithm examines every bit of the data while it is being condensed, and even a slight change to the data results in a large change in the message hash. It is considered a one-way process. MD5 and SHA are examples of hashing algorithms.

hash total A calculation generated by choosing a selected number of fields in a series of transactions.

honeypot An Internet-attached server that acts as a decoy, luring in potential hackers in order to study their activities and monitor how they are able to break into a system.

hot site A fully prepared and configured site that is ready for use.

hub An older network device used for physical connectivity in networks. It provides connectivity, amplification, and signal regeneration.

I

information security/cybersecurity   The people, processes, and technology in which technology security risks are assessed and electronic data is protected against unauthorized access.

information systems standards   The standards adopted by ISACA that are a cornerstone of its professional contribution to the audit and assurance community. One of the three agreements you must sign off on as part of the CISA application.

Information Technology Infrastructure Library (ITIL)   A series of documents that define how to execute information technology service management (ITSM) processes.

inherent risk   The risk that exists if no controls are deployed.

integrated audit   An audit that covers all controls, including technology, financial, and operational controls, in determining an effective set of internal controls for the protection of an organization's assets.

Integrated Services Digital Network (ISDN)   A system that provides simultaneous voice and high-speed data transmission through a single channel to the user's premises. ISDN is an international standard for the end-to-end digital transmission of voice, data, and signaling.

Internet   An interconnected system of networks that connects computers around the world via TCP/IP.

Internet Control Message Protocol (ICMP)   Part of TCP/IP that supports diagnostics and error control. ping is a type of ICMP message.

Internet packet spoofing (IP spoofing)   A technique used to gain unauthorized access to computers or conduct denial of service attacks. Newer routers and firewall arrangements can offer protection against IP spoofing.

Internet Protocol (IP)   One of the key protocols of TCP/IP. The IP protocol is found at Layer 3 (network layer) of the OSI model.

intrusion detection system (IDS)   A network monitoring device typically installed at Internet ingress/egress points that is used to inspect inbound and outbound network activity and identify suspicious patterns that might indicate a network or system attack from someone attempting to break into or compromise a system.

IT steering committee   A group that is tasked with ensuring that the IT department's goals are properly aligned with the goals of the business.

J

JBOD   A technique that is somewhat like RAID, in that two or more hard drives are combined into one storage array. However, JBOD offers none of the fault tolerance advantages of RAID.

job practice areas, or job domains   The five domains of the CISA exam:

Domain 1—The Process of Auditing Information Systems

Domain 2—Governance and Management of IT

Domain 3—Information Systems Acquisition, Development and Implementation

Domain 4—Information Systems Operations, Maintenance and Service Management

Domain 5—Protection of Information Assets

K

Kerberos   A single sign-on service that is composed of an authentication service and a ticket-granting service.

key goal indicator (KGI)   A key metric that shows how well a process is performing against a stated goal.

key performance indicator (KPI)   A key metric that shows how well a process is performing.

kilo lines of code (KLOC)   A technique used to determine the cost of software development that is based solely on length of code.

knowledge statements   Questions on the CISA exam that cover hard skills such as how to plan an audit.

L

lagging indicator   An indicator of an event that appears well after the initial event occurs.

leading indicator   An indicator of an event that appears before the initial event occurs.

legal function   A discipline accountable for understanding the core set of commonly accepted rules and principles of the industry in adherence to the law.

local area network (LAN)   A group of wired or wireless computers and associated devices that share a common communications line and typically share the resources of a single processor or server within a small geographic area (for example, within an office building).

logic bomb   A dangerous type of malware that waits for a predetermined event or an amount of time to execute its payload. Typically used by disgruntled employees for insider attacks.

long-term business goals   Goals with a strategic focus on activities planned for the next three to five years.

M

MAC filtering   A method of controlling access on a wired or wireless network by denying access to a device based on the MAC address not matching one that is on a preapproved list.

macro infector   A type of computer virus that uses Microsoft Office products such as Work and Excel. When a user opens a Microsoft document containing a macro, the computer can become infected.

macro virus   A type of computer virus that infects macro files. I Love You and Melissa are examples of macro viruses.

man-in-the-middle (MITM) attack   A type of attack in which the attacker can read, insert, and change information being passed between two parties without either party knowing that the information has been compromised.

mantrap   A system of two doors that allows one person to enter the first door; then, after it is closed, the second door is allowed to open. Mantraps are used to control access and are also known as deadman doors.

manual controls   Controls that staff must manually verify or execute, such as the review of reconciliation reports and exception reports.

massive array of inexpensive disks (MAID)   A backup solution that is designed to remove the biggest obstacle of power consumption to the use of hard disks as archive storage. MAID is only fully powered up when accessed in use and has power removed when not in use.

material   Significant and having a real impact on an organization.

maximum tolerable downtime (MTD)   The maximum period of time that a given business process can be inoperative before the organization's survival is in jeopardy.

media access control (MAC)   The hard-coded address of a physical-layer device that is attached to a network. Every network interface controller must have a hard-coded and unique MAC address. A MAC address is 48 bits long.

metadata   Data about data, which describes the type of data contained in a file.

mindset   An attitude and core principles we need to follow as professionals. The mindset sets the bar on how we should think about the challenges presented to us.

Moore's law   The belief that processing power of computers will double about every 18 months due to the rise in the number of transistors doubling per square inch.

multipartite virus   A virus that attempts to attack both the boot sector and executable files.

multiple input, multiple output (MIMO)   A system used in the implementation of the 802.11n standard that has multiple antennas and multiple radios.

Multiprotocol Label Switching (MPLS)   A method of data-carrying used for long haul of data by high-performance telecommunications networks. MPLS directs traffic by using short path labels rather than long network addresses, thereby speeding up the process.

MU-MIMO   A set of multiple-input and multiple-output technologies for wireless communication that is used by newer wireless access points to allow more devices to communicate simultaneously.

My Certifications (ISACA website)   A web page on the ISACA website where you can manage your ISACA accounts and certifications.

N

network address translation (NAT)   A method of connecting multiple computers to the Internet using one IP address. Many private addresses can be converted to a single public address.

Network Operations Center (NOC)   An organization's help desk or interface to its end users in which trouble calls, questions, and trouble tickets are generated.

nonrepudiation   A system or method put in place to ensure that an individual cannot deny his or her own actions.

nonstatistical sampling   A type of sampling in which an auditor selects the sample size and determines which items to select; also known as judgmental sampling.

O

object breakdown structure (OBS)   A diagram that is used to display organizational relationships and define which users are assigned to work on a specific area of a project.

operational audit   An audit to assess how well business operations are managed. This includes reviewing the organization's policies, key processes, controls, and operating environment.

Operational Risk   Operational risk is the risk of loss or disruptions from inadequate or failed internal processes, controls, people and systems. In context to information systems operational risk, it's the loss or disruptions of technology capability due to failed internal processes, controls, people and systems.

outsourcing   Using an external service provider to deliver services or solutions on an organization's behalf.

P

packet   A block of data sent over a network that transmits the identities of the sending and receiving stations for error control.

packet switching   A data transmission method that involves dividing messages into standard-sized packets for greater efficiency in routing and transporting them through a network.

paper test   A type of disaster-recovery test that involves reviewing the steps of the test without actually performing the steps. This type of disaster-recovery test is usually used to help team members review the proposed plan and become familiar with the test and its objectives.

password cracking   The process of recovering passwords from data that has been secured by various mechanisms such as hashing.

penetration test   A method of evaluating the security of a network or computer system by simulating an attack by a malicious hacker but without doing harm and with the owner's consent.

personal area network (PAN)   A small network used to connect Bluetooth devices.

phishing   The act of misleading or conning an individual into releasing and providing personal and confidential information to an attacker masquerading as a legitimate individual or business.

phreaker   An individual who hacks phone systems or phone-related equipment. Phreakers predate computer hackers.

Plan-Do-Check-Act (PDCA)   An iterative four-step problem-solving model that promotes continuous improvement.

policy   A set of behavior rules mandated by management; the policy environment often includes standards, procedures, and baselines.

polymorphic virus   A virus that is capable of change and self-mutation.

port   A connection used by protocols and applications. Port numbers are divided into three ranges: well-known ports, registered ports, and dynamic and/or private ports. Well-known ports are those from 0 through 1023, registered ports are those ranging from 1024 through 49151, and dynamic and/or private ports are those from 49152 through 65535.

Post Office Protocol (POP)   A commonly implemented method of delivering email from a mail server to a client machine. Other methods include IMAP and Microsoft Exchange.

principle of least privilege   A principle that improves security by limiting access to just the functions consistent with the individual's job function.

procedures   A written set of steps to execute policies through specific, prescribed actions; this is the *how* in relation to a policy. Procedures tend to be more detailed than policies. They identify the method and state in a series of steps exactly how to accomplish an intended task, achieve a desired business or functional outcome, and execute a policy.

protocol   A set of formalized rules that describe how data is transmitted over a network. Low-level protocols define the electrical and physical standard, whereas high-level protocols deal with formatting of data. TCP and IP are examples of high-level LAN protocols.

prototyping   The process of quickly putting together a working model (a prototype) to test various aspects of a design, illustrate ideas or features, and gather early user feedback. Prototyping is often an integral part of the development process, where it is believed to reduce project risk and cost.

proxy server   A type of firewall that is used to improve performance and for added security. A proxy server intercepts all requests to the real server to see whether it can fulfill the requests itself. If not, it forwards the request to the real server.

public key encryption   An encryption scheme that uses two keys. In an email transaction, the public key encrypts the data and a corresponding private key decrypts the data. Because the private key is never transmitted or publicized, the encryption scheme is extremely secure. For digital signatures, the process is reversed: The sender uses the private key to create the digital signature, and anyone who has access to the corresponding public key can read it.

Public Key Infrastructure (PKI)   An infrastructure based on public-key cryptography that is used to facilitate e-commerce and build trust. PKI consists of hardware, software, people, policies, and procedures; it is used to create, manage, store, distribute, and revoke public key certificates.

Q

qualitative risk assessment   A type of assessment that involves ranking the seriousness of risks and threats based primarily on an individual's expertise and opinion.

Quality Assurance (QA)   The processes and techniques involved in monitoring operations and testing outputs to ensure consistent quality by identifying errors and opportunities to improve products and services.

quantitative risk assessment   A type of assessment that involves ranking the seriousness of risks and threats based primarily on data collection and data modelling.

R

rapid application development (RAD)   An alternative to the conventional waterfall model that focuses on speed and uses techniques such as prototyping, iterative development, and time boxing.

recovery point objective (RPO)   The amount of time in which files must be recovered from backup storage for normal operations to resume.

recovery testing   Testing aimed at verifying a system's capability to recover from various degrees of failure.

recovery time objective (RTO)   During the execution of disaster recovery or business continuity plans, the time goal for the reestablishment and recovery of a business function or resource.

redundant array of inexpensive disks (RAID)   A type of fault tolerance and performance improvement for disk drives that employs two or more drives in combination.

registration authority (RA)   An entity responsible for the identification and authentication of a PKI certificate. The RA is not responsible for signing or issuing certificates.

Remote Authentication Dial-In User Service (RADIUS)   A client/server protocol and software that allows remote-access servers to communicate. Used in wireless systems such as 802.1x.

repeater   A network device used to regenerate or replicate a signal. Repeaters are used in transmission systems to regenerate analog or digital signals distorted by transmission loss.

resilience   The ability for a computer system, control, or process to recover quickly after a disruption event such as a data transmission failure, power outage, etc.

return on investment (ROI)   A common profitability ratio that is calculated by dividing net profit by net worth.

reverse engineering   The process of taking a software program apart and analyzing its workings in detail, usually to construct a new device or program that does the same thing without actually copying anything from the original.

right-to-audit clause   A contract term that allows an organization to audit an outsourcing partner's operation.

Rijndael   A symmetric encryption algorithm chosen to be the Advanced Encryption Standard (AES).

risk acceptance   A decision an organization makes when it knows about a risk but makes a conscious decision to accept the risk.

risk avoidance   A situation in which an organization does not perform an activity that allows risk to be present.

risk reduction   A situation in which an organization employs a method of mitigating the chance a risk will occur.

risk transference   A situation in which an organization transfers risk to someone else.

rotation of assignment   A process that involves ensuring that individuals are moved between roles over time.

rounding down   A form of computer fraud that involves rounding down dollar amounts and stealing small amounts of money. For example, the value $1,199.50 might be rounded down to $1,199.00.

S

script kiddie   The lowest form of cracker, who looks for easy targets and well-worn vulnerabilities.

segregation of duties (SoD)   The splitting of functions between roles to ensure that at least two individuals are engaged to perform high-risk functions.

Service level agreements (SLAs)   A contractual agreement between an organization and its service provider. SLAs define and protect the organization with regard to holding the service provider accountable for the requirements as defined in an SLA.

service set ID (SSID)   A sequence of up to 32 letters or numbers that is the ID, or name, of a wireless local area network and is used to differentiate networks.

SHA   A hashing algorithm that uses a 160-, 256-, or 512-bit hash function.

short-term business goals   Goals that address immediate concerns that are no more than 18 months into the future.

Simple Mail Transfer Protocol (SMTP)   An Internet standard for electronic mail (email) transmission defined by RFC 821.

Simple Network Management Protocol (SNMP)   An application-layer protocol that facilitates the exchange of management information between network devices. SNMPv1 uses well-known community strings of public and private. More recent versions, SNMPv2c and SNMPv3, provide improved performance, flexibility, and security.

smurf attack   A DDoS attack in which an attacker transmits large amounts of ICMP echo request (ping) packets to a targeted IP destination device, using the targeted destination's IP source address. This is called spoofing the IP source address. IP routers and other IP devices that respond to broadcasts respond to the targeted IP device with ICMP echo replies, thus multiplying the amount of bogus traffic.

social engineering   The practice of tricking employees into revealing sensitive data about their computer system or infrastructure. This type of attack targets people using the art of human manipulation. Even when systems are physically well protected, social engineering attacks are possible.

source lines of code (SLOC)   A software metric used to measure the size of a computer program by counting the number of lines in the text of the program's source code.

SQL injection   An attack in which malicious code is embedded in a poorly designed application and passed to the SQL database.

standards   Mandatory actions, explicit rules, controls, or configuration settings that are designed to support and conform to a policy.

static data   Data that does not change frequently, such as an individual's Social Security number.

statistical sampling   Sampling based on probability, in which every item of the population has a known chance of selection.

stochastic   Based on random behavior because the occurrence of individual events cannot be predicted, yet measuring the distribution of all observations usually follows a predictable pattern.

storage area network (SAN)   A high-speed subnetwork that interconnects different data storage devices with associated data servers for a large network. SANs support disk mirroring, backup and restore, archival and retrieval of archived data, data migration from one storage device to another, and the sharing of data among different servers in a network.

substantive test   A test used to verify the integrity of a claim by making sure that the controls are working.

symmetric algorithm   An algorithm with which both parties use the same cryptographic key.

symmetric encryption   An encryption standard that requires all parties to have a copy of a shared key. A single key is used for both encryption and decryption.

SYN flood attack   A DDoS attack in which the attacker sends a succession of SYN packets with a spoofed address to a targeted destination IP device but does not send the last ACK packet to acknowledge and confirm receipt. This leaves half-open connections between the client and the server until all resources are absorbed, rendering the server or targeted IP destination device unavailable because of resource allocation to the attack.

system control parameters   Control values that affect how a system processes transactions.

systems development life cycle (SDLC)   A method for developing information systems that has five main stages: analysis, design, development, implementation, and evaluation. Each stage has several components; for example, the development stage includes programming (coding, including internal documentation; debugging; testing; and documenting) and acquiring equipment (selection, acquisition [purchase or lease], and testing).

T

Taguchi model   A statistical approach to optimizing the design of a process and improving the quality of each of its components by identifying the processes affected by outside influences (noise) that have the greatest effects on product variability and then eliminating them.

task statements   Questions on the CISA exam that tests a candidate on how an auditor applies their hard skills, such as how to communicate audit examination results.

telecommunications   Systems that transport information over a distance, sending and receiving audio, video, and data signals through electronic means.

Temporal Key Integrity Protocol (TKIP)   An encryption protocol included as part of the IEEE 802.11i standard for wireless LANs that was created to add more security to WEP.

threat   Any circumstance or event that has the potential to negatively impact an organization.

three lines of defense   The idea of managing risk through three independent layers within the organization to minimize the failure to identify a major risk.

top-down testing   Testing that is used to simulate the behavior of lower-level modules that are not yet integrated.

total cost of ownership (TCO)   A dollar estimate used to help buyers and owners determine the direct and indirect costs of a developed system or application.

transaction   A unique and logical step performed by software to perform a specific task, such as crediting a bank account after making a deposit.

transaction files   Files involved in the transmission of information between two systems or applications.

Transmission Control Protocol (TCP)   One of the main protocols of IP, which is used for reliability and guaranteed delivery of data.

Transmission Control Protocol/Internet Protocol (TCP/IP)   A collection of protocols used to provide the basis for Internet and World Wide Web services.

turnstile   A one-way gate or access control mechanism used to limit traffic and control the flow of people.

U

uninterruptible power supply (UPS)   A device designed to provide a backup power supply during a power failure. Basically, a UPS is a battery backup system with an ultra-fast sensing device.

universal serial bus (USB)   A specification standard for connecting peripherals to a computer. It can connect up to 127 devices to a computer, and USB 3.0 is capable of transferring data at up to 5Gbps (625Mbps).

User Datagram Protocol (UDP)   A connectionless protocol that provides very few error recovery services but offers a quick and direct way to send and receive datagrams.

V

virtual LAN (VLAN)   A group of devices on one or more LANs that are configured to communicate directly when in fact they may be located on a number of different LAN segments.

virtual private network (VPN)   A private network that uses a public network to connect remote sites and users.

virus   A computer program that has the capability to generate copies of itself and thereby spread. Viruses usually require the interaction of an individual and can have rather benign results, such as flashing a message to the screen, or rather malicious results, such as destroying data, systems, integrity, or availability.

virus scanning   One of the most basic ways of scanning for computer viruses, which works by comparing suspect files and programs to signatures of known viruses stored in a database.

Voice over IP (VoIP)   A combination of software and hardware that enables people to use the Internet as the transmission medium for telephone calls by sending voice data in packets via Internet Protocol.

vulnerability   A flaw or weakness in a security system, software, or procedure.

W

waiver program   An ISACA program for individuals who are new in the technology field which allows individuals to substitute up to three years of work experience credit, verified through the employer, when applying for CISA certification.

war driving   The process of driving around a neighborhood or an area to identify wireless access points.

warm site   An alternative computer facility that is partially configured and can be made ready in a few days.

white box testing   A security assessment or penetration test in which all aspects of the network are known.

wide area network (WAN)   A network that spans the distance between buildings, cities, and even countries. WANs are LANs connected using wide area network services from telecommunications carriers; they typically use technologies such as standard phone lines—called plain old telephone service (POTS) or public switched telephone network (PSTN)—Integrated Services Digital Network (ISDN), Frame Relay, Asynchronous Transfer Mode (ATM), and other high-speed services.

Wi-Fi Protected Access (WPA)   A security standard for wireless networks designed to be more secure than WEP. Developed from the draft 802.11i standard.

Wired Equivalent Privacy (WEP)   Encryption based on the RC4 encryption scheme. It was designed to provide the same level of security as a wired LAN. Because of 40-bit encryption and problems with the initialization vector, it was found to be insecure.

work breakdown structure (WBS)   A process that shows what activities need to be completed in a hierarchical manner.

WPA2   The current standard in wireless security. WPA2 uses the AES and the optional Pre-Shared Key (PSK) authentication.

Z

zero-day exploit   An exploit for a vulnerability that has no available vendor patch.

Answers to the "Do I Know This Already" Quizzes and Review Questions

Do I Know This Already? Answers

Chapter 2	Chapter 3	Chapter 4
1. C	1. B	1. D
2. A	2. C	2. B
3. B	3. B	3. A
4. C	4. A	4. C
5. B	5. D	5. A
6. D	6. D	6. A
7. C	7. C	7. D
8. D	8. C	8. C
9. B	9. A	9. B
10. D	10. D	10. C
	11. C	
	12. A	

Chapter 5

1. C
2. A
3. B
4. C
5. B
6. D
7. C
8. D
9. B
10. D

Chapter 6

1. C
2. D
3. B
4. C
5. B
6. A
7. C
8. D
9. B
10. D

Chapter 7

1. B
2. D
3. B
4. A
5. C

6. B
7. D
8. B
9. A
10. D

Chapter 8

1. A
2. D
3. D
4. B
5. C
6. B
7. A
8. A
9. A
10. C

Chapter 9

1. C
2. D
3. A
4. B
5. D
6. B
7. D
8. A
9. B
10. A

Review Questions Answers and Explanations

Chapter 2

1. **D.** A baseline is correct because it is a platform-specific rule related to the security configuration for an Active Directory server. Answers A, B, and C are not platform specific.

2. **B.** Qualified audit opinion is correct here because (1) testing was limited to if the control existed and as stated did not include substantive testing, and (2) the control failure was not pervasive, occurring in 3 of the 1,300 sites, or .0023% of the population. Answer A is incorrect because the lack of a substantive test is a qualifier. Answer C is incorrect because there is no pervasive control weakness. Answer D is incorrect because compliance test–obtained evidence was sufficient to demonstrate instances of control weakness.

3. **B.** Integrated auditing is a methodology that combines the operational audit function, the financial audit function, and the IS audit function. Therefore, Answers C and D are incorrect because they do not list all three types of functions to be integrated. Answer A is incorrect because it describes control self-assessment (CSA), which is used to verify the reliability of internal controls and places internal controls in the hands of management.

4. **D.** The best choice would be a locked cabinet on the department floor with only one key, in the possession of the auditor. With only one key in the auditor's possession, there is clear accountability, and access is limited to one person. Answer A is incorrect because multiple individuals may still have access to the safe. Answer B is incorrect because it would call into question the security of the home and the ability to restrict access to family members. Answer C is incorrect because third-party access cannot be verified in a third-party site, given the way the facts were presented.

5. **D.** A control risk is risk caused by failure of internal controls; it can result in a material error. Answer A is incorrect because residual risk is the amount of risk the organization is willing to accept. Answer B is incorrect because inherent risk is the risk that can occur because of the lack of compensating controls. Combined, inherent risks can create a material risk. Answer C is incorrect because detection risk is the risk if an auditor does not design tests in such a way as to detect a material risk.

6. **A.** Attending board meetings is not one of the best ways to gather evidence during an audit. The best ways to gather evidence include observing employee activity, examining and reviewing procedures and processes, verifying employee security awareness training and knowledge, and examining reporting relationships to verify segregation of duties.

7. B. CSA is not an audit function replacement. Answers A, C, and D are all advantages of CSA.

8. D. A disclaimer is used when an auditor cannot obtain appropriate evidence to base an opinion.

9. A. Internal accounting controls used to safeguard financial records are an example of a general control procedure. Answers B, C, and D all describe information system control procedures.

10. B. The word *material* describes a significant level of risk that the organization is unwilling to accept. Answers A, C, and D do not define the term.

11. B. An integrated test facility is a type of substantive test that uses data represented by fake entities, such as products, items, or departments. Answer A is incorrect because a parallel test compares real results to those generated by the auditor to compare the control function. Answer C is incorrect because embedded audit modules identify and report specific transactions or other information, based on predetermined criteria. Answer D is incorrect because test data uses theoretical transactions to validate program logic and control mechanisms.

12. D. Variable sampling would be the best sampling technique to review an organization's balance sheet for material transactions. It is also known as dollar estimation. Answer A is incorrect because attribute sampling is used to determine the rate of occurrence. Answer B is incorrect because frequency sampling is another name for attribute sampling; both terms describe the same sampling technique. Answer C is incorrect because stop-and-go sampling is used when an auditor believes that only a few errors will be found in a population.

13. A. Task statements describe how to apply knowledge statements. Answers B and D are types of audits, not domain question types. Answer C is incorrect because knowledge statements questions are the facts you are expected to know.

14. D. Regulatory audits are not impacted by a CSA program. Answers A, B, and C are all potential benefits of CSA.

15. C. Regulatory requirements are not optional and must be given priority due to the impact on the organization. Answers A, B, and D are important, but unlike regulatory mandates, they are under the control of the organization in terms of timing and scope of implementation.

Chapter 3

1. **B.** This capability maturity model (CMM) specifies five levels of control for software maturity levels. Answer A is incorrect because ISO 17799 is a comprehensive set of controls designed to gauge best practices in information security. Answer C is incorrect because COSO was designed to help prevent and detect fraud in financial reports. Answer D is incorrect because COBIT was designed to aid in the development of good IT process and policies.

2. **C.** A network administrator should not have programming responsibilities. Answers A, B, and D are all duties that an administrator can hold, and a network administrator might have end-user responsibilities, aid in the system administration, and help in the early phases of design.

3. **C.** Key verification would provide the highest level of confidence. Answer A is incorrect because audit trails would provide details of the entered activities but would not improve accuracy. Answer B is incorrect because separating job roles would be an additional control but would not add any accuracy to the information that was entered incorrectly. Answer D is incorrect because the supervisory review is a detective and compensating control but is not the best answer.

4. **B.** Any time you are inspecting unfamiliar records, you need to understand what type of data is stored. Metadata describes the type of data. Answers A and D are not the best answers because they primarily provide insights but only after you understand the type of data contained in the records. Answer C is incorrect because while it allows you to understand who can access the information, it does not help to understand the data.

5. **D.** Bottom-up policy development addresses the concerns of operational employees because it starts with their input and concerns and examines risk. Answers A, B, and C are incorrect because all these items are tied to top-down policy development. A top-down approach aligns with company policy, is a slow process, and might not fully address the concerns of employees.

6. **C.** A balanced scorecard is used to match the organization's information technology to the strategy of the organization. Answer A is incorrect because it is not used for benchmarking, Answer B is incorrect because it is not used to measure effectiveness, and Answer D is incorrect because it is not used to evaluate help desk employees.

7. **A.** Any time an outsourcing provider will provide a time-sensitive process, such as ISP services, an SLA can be used to obtain a guarantee of the level of service the outsourcing partner is agreeing to provide. The SLA should specify the uptime, response time, and maximum outage time they are agreeing to.

Answer B is incorrect because although physical security is important, it is not the most important in this case. Answers C and D are incorrect because neither would serve as an adequate measure for an independent evaluation of the ISP's service capability.

8. **B.** Custody is related to access to cash, merchandise, or inventories. Answer A is incorrect because authorization describes verifying cash, approving purchases, and approving changes. Answer C is incorrect because record keeping deals with preparing receipts, maintaining records, and posting payments. Answer D is incorrect because reconciliation deals with comparing monetary amounts, counts, reports, and payroll summaries.

9. **D.** Database administrator and systems analyst are two roles that ISACA believes can be combined. Answers A, B, and C are incorrect because none of these positions should be combined. An auditor should understand how the combination of certain roles increases risk. For example, a systems analyst should be discouraged from performing the duties of someone in a quality assurance role. If these roles are combined, quality assurance levels could be compromised if strong compensating controls are not being used.

10. **D.** Before auditors can begin any technical duties, they must understand the environment in which they are working. The best way to do that is to review the business plan, which details the goals of the organization. Only after the business plan has been reviewed should the other items listed be reviewed. Therefore, Answers A, B, and C are incorrect.

Chapter 4

1. **B.** The recovery point objective (RPO) is the earliest point in time at which recovery can occur. If RPO is low, tape backup or another solution is acceptable. Answer A is incorrect because a high RPO would require mirroring or another type of timely recovery method. Answer C is incorrect because a low RTO would mean that little time is available for recovery. Answer D is incorrect because low fault tolerance indicates that little time is available for unavailable services.

2. **D.** Although hot sites are an expensive alternative, they are ready for service. Answer A is incorrect because a hot site cannot be used for long-term processing. Answer B is incorrect because a hot site is a subscription service. Answer C is incorrect because there are additional fees; the organization must pay a variety of fees for use, testing, and access.

3. **A.** JBOD allows users to combine multiple drives into one large drive. JBOD's only advantage is that, in case of drive failure, only the data on the affected drive is lost. Answers B, C, and D are incorrect because JBOD is not superior to disk mirroring, is not faster than RAID, and offers no fault tolerance.

4. **C.** Critical processes that produce revenue are considered a core activity. Answer A is incorrect because discretionary processes are considered nonessential. Answer B is incorrect because supporting processes require only minimum BCP services. Answer D does not specify a process; *critical* is a term used to describe how important the service or process is.

5. **D.** Business continuity planning is an ongoing process that should be revisited each time there is a change to the environment. Therefore, Answers A, B, and C are incorrect.

6. **D.** The most critical concern is keeping the copies of critical information current at an offsite location. Answers A, B, and C are important but are not the *most* important.

7. **B.** BIA is an important part of the BCP process. The purpose of BIA is to document the impact of outages, identify critical systems, prioritize critical systems, analyze outage impact, and determine recovery times needed to keep critical systems running. Answers A, C, and D are incorrect because they do not specify steps performed during BIA.

8. **B.** There is no BCP test known as a structured walk-through. Valid types are listed in Answers A, C, and D: paper test, full operation test, and preparedness test.

9. **C.** Diverse routing is the practice of routing traffic through different cable facilities. Answer A is incorrect because alternate routing is the ability to use another transmission line if the regular line is busy or unavailable. Answer B is incorrect because long-haul diversity is the practice of having different long-distance communication carriers. Answer D is incorrect because last-mile protection provides a second local loop connection.

10. **A.** *Vital* meets the description of functions that are important and can be performed by a manual backup process but not for a long period of time. Answer B is incorrect because it describes tasks that are important but can be performed manually at a reasonable cost. Answer C is incorrect because *critical* refers to extremely important functions. Answer D is incorrect because *demand driven* does not describe a valid functional label.

Chapter 5

1. **C.** Implementation is the stage at which user acceptance is usually performed. Therefore, Answers A, B, and D are incorrect.

2. **B.** The critical path is the sequence of activities that must be completed on time for the project to stay on schedule. Delays of any items on the critical path will slow the entire project. Answers A, C, and D are incorrect because, although the budget, team skills, and individual tasks are all items to consider, the critical path should be examined first because that will affect all other items.

3. **A.** Following implementation, a cost–benefit analysis or ROI calculation should be performed. Answer B is incorrect because the audit trail should be designed during the design phase. Answer C is incorrect because an ERD should be performed during the requirements phase. Answer D is incorrect because final acceptance testing should be performed during the implementation phase.

4. **D.** Sociability testing is performed to confirm that a new or modified system will work in its intended environment. Answer A is incorrect because regression testing verifies that changes have not introduced errors. Answer B is incorrect because function testing verifies that systems meet specifications. Answer C is incorrect because pilot testing is used for limited evaluations.

5. **D.** Extreme programming does not work well for large project teams. Extreme programming requires that teams include business managers, programmers, and end users. These teams are responsible for developing usable applications in short periods of time. Answer A is incorrect because the spiral model is based on the concept that software development is evolutionary. The spiral model begins by creating a series of prototypes to develop a solution. As the project continues, it spirals out, becoming more detailed. Each step passes through planning, requirements, risks, and development phases. Answer B is incorrect because RAD requires well-trained development teams that use integrated power tools for modeling and prototyping. Answer C is incorrect because scrum uses short cycles referred to as sprints and is focused on object-oriented technology.

6. **C.** Fourth-generation languages (4GL) are most commonly used for databases. Examples of 4GLs include FOCUS, Natural, and dBase. Answer A is incorrect because 2GL is assembly language. Answer B is incorrect because 3GL includes languages such as FORTRAN, Pascal, and C. Answer D is incorrect because 5GLs are very high-level languages such as Prolog.

7. **C.** PERT is used to schedule, organize, and coordinate tasks. The PERT weighted average examines the shortest time, average time, and longest time a task is scheduled to be completed. Therefore, Answers A, B, and D are incorrect.

8. **B.** A direct changeover requires the establishment of a cut-off date so that all users must switch to the new system by then. Answer A is incorrect because a pilot scenario is used when an entire new system is used at one location. Answer C is incorrect because a phased changeover is gradual. Answer D is incorrect because a parallel changeover brings the new system online while the old is still in operation.

9. **C.** Entity relationship diagrams are built using two essential components that include entities and relationships. Therefore, Answers A, B, and D are incorrect.

10. **C.** Scrum uses short cycles referred to as sprints and is focused on object-oriented technology. Answer A is incorrect because the spiral model is based on the concept that software development is evolutionary. The spiral model involves creating a series of prototypes to develop a solution. As the project continues, it spirals out, becoming more detailed. Each step passes through planning, requirements, risks, and development phases. Answer B is incorrect because RAD requires well-trained development teams that use integrated power tools for modeling and prototyping. Answer D is incorrect because extreme programming requires that teams include business managers, programmers, and end users. These teams are responsible for developing useable applications in short periods of time.

11. **A.** Dropbox is an example of a public cloud service. A private cloud model is based on the concept that the cloud is owned and operated by a private entity. A community cloud model can be used by several entities. A hybrid cloud model can be a combination of any of the other cloud models. Therefore, Answers B, C, and D are incorrect.

12. **B.** Tokenization randomly generates a value for plain text and stores the corresponding value in a database. Answers A, C, and D are incorrect because random numbers, cookies, and user IDs are not used as a replacement for encryption.

13. **B.** Type 2 hypervisors are those that require an underlying OS. Examples of Type 2 systems include VirtualBox and VMware Workstation. Answers C and D are incorrect as there are no Type 3 or 4 hypervisors. Virtualization systems fall into two categories: Type 1 and Type 2. Answer A is incorrect because a Type 1 hypervisor resides directly on hardware.

14. **D.** The most common implementation of n-tier is the three-tier approach. A three-tier architecture is typically composed of a presentation tier, a domain logic tier, and a data storage tier such as a workstation, server, and database. Answer A is incorrect because a workstation and a server is not the most common implementation of n-tier. Answer B is incorrect because the LAMP stack is Linux, Apache, MySQL, and PHP/Python/Perl. Answer C is incorrect because a workstation and cloud is not considered n-tier.

15. **D.** An SAS 70 report verifies that the outsourcing or business partner has had its control objectives and activities examined by an independent accounting and auditing firm. Answer A is incorrect because privacy shield is used for EU protection of data. Answer B is incorrect because COBIT is a good-practice framework created by international professional association ISACA for information technology (IT) management and IT governance. Answer C is incorrect because ITIL is a set of detailed practices for IT service management that seeks to align IT services with the needs of the business.

Chapter 6

1. **B.** Valid application testing methodologies include snapshots, mapping, tracing and tagging, using test data, and base case system evaluation. Answer B is an example of a data integrity control.

2. **A.** Audit hooks detect items that meet specific criteria. Answer B is incorrect because snapshots require an audit trail. Answer C is incorrect because integrated test facilities should not be used with test data. Answer D is incorrect because continuous and intermittent simulation requires examination of transactions that meet specified criteria.

3. **D.** Decision support systems (DSSs) are software-based applications that help analyze data to answer less structured problems. DSS typically uses knowledge databases, models, and analytical techniques to make decisions. Answer A is incorrect because a DSS does not use structured models to solve complex problems. Answer B is incorrect because a DSS is designed to support traditional decision-making activities. Answer C is incorrect because a DSS is designed to support unstructured problems.

4. **C.** A reasonableness check verifies the reasonableness of the data. Answer A is incorrect because a validity check is usually used with dates. Answer B is incorrect because range checks are typically used to verify that data is within a specified range. Answer D is incorrect because a limit check is used to verify that sales do not exceed a specified limit (for example, limiting one per customer).

5. **C.** Decision support systems are typically developed with 4GL programming languages. Answers A, B, and D are incorrect.

6. **C.** A data lake always contains raw data. A data warehouse stores data in files and database tables that are highly structured and searchable.

7. **B.** The impact of EDI on internal controls is that there are fewer opportunities for review and authorization. Answers A, C, and D are, therefore, incorrect.

8. **B.** An edit control is used with data that has been entered but not yet processed. A sequence check is an example of an edit control. Answers A, C, and D are incorrect because they are all examples of processing controls, which ensure that data remains unchanged until it is processed by an authorized process.

9. **A.** Audit hooks are considered the least complex technique because they use embedded hooks that act as red flags if certain conditions are met. Answer B is incorrect because using systems control audit review files and embedded audit modules requires embedded audit software and is considered one of the most complex techniques. Answer C is incorrect because snapshots are considered moderately complex. Answer D is incorrect because the continuous and intermittent simulation is also considered moderately complex; it simulates the transaction run.

10. **B.** The examination of proposed test plans is part of the testing phase. Items to be addressed during the design and development phase include studying flowcharts; evaluating input, output, and process controls; examining proposed audit trails; and reviewing how the system will deal with erroneous input.

Chapter 7

1. **B.** Latency can be caused because data must travel great distances or because of high volumes of network traffic and inadequate bandwidth. Latency can be measured with the ping command. Answer A is incorrect because SNMP is used for network management. Answer C is incorrect because traceroute is used to determine the path that traffic takes from one network to another. Answer D is incorrect because RMON is another example of a network-management tool.

2. **B.** The proper order for the OSI model layers from the bottom up is physical, data link, network, transport, session, presentation, application. Therefore, Answers A, C, and D are incorrect.

3. **B.** Network traffic on a LAN can be addressed to one device, many devices, or all devices on a network. Sending information to a group is known as multicasting. Answer A describes one device; answer C describes a technique used in IPv6, which is a directed broadcast; and answer D describes the transmission to everyone.

4. **B.** ARP resolves known IP addresses to unknown MAC addresses. This two-step process is performed by first sending a message to all devices on the LAN requesting the receiver's physical address. If a device recognizes the address as its own, it issues an ARP reply to the sender of the ARP request. Answers A, C, and D are incorrect because they do not properly describe the ARP process.

5. **D.** Frame Relay controls bandwidth usage with a *committed information rate* (CIR) that specifies the maximum guaranteed bandwidth that the customer is guaranteed. Although higher rates might be possible, the CIR represents the level the service provider is committed to providing. Answer A, T1, does not use a CIR and is not packet switching. Answer B, ATM, does not use a CIR. Answer C, X.25, does not use a CIR.

6. **B.** Some of the standards for optical fiber cabling include 10BASE-F, 100BASE-FX, and 1000BASE-LX. Answers A, C, and D are all copper cabling standards.

7. **D.** Reviewing network diagrams is usually the best place for an auditor to start. The diagrams give the auditor a foundational understanding of the network. Although Answers A, B, and C are all items that can be performed, they should not be the starting point of an audit.

8. **D.** A mesh offers the highest level of redundancy. Answers A, B, and C are incorrect.

9. **A.** A switch is best suited for reducing the number of collisions on a LAN. Switches segment physical networks. Answer B is incorrect because a hub provides only physical connectivity. Answer C is incorrect because a bridge is inferior to a switch. Bridges are software based and are much slower. Answer D is incorrect because a router is an OSI Layer 3 device.

10. **C.** Packet switching allows a telecommunications vendor to determine the best path. The vendor is free to route the packetized traffic through the network as it sees fit. Answer A is incorrect because the customer does not determine the path. Answer B is incorrect because packet switching does not use a dedicated path. Answer D is incorrect because the client does not set a dedicated path for packet-switched traffic.

11. **B.** One of the biggest drawbacks to SNMP is that Versions 1 and 2 send data via cleartext. Answers A, C, and D are incorrect because SNMP is not hard to configure, is not considered obsolete, and can be used with many types of devices, not just printers.

12. **B.** For Wireshark to see all the traffic that is at the network interface, the device must be placed in promiscuous mode. Therefore, Answers A, C, and D are incorrect.

13. **A.** Network traffic on a LAN is visible only when the switch is configured to forward that traffic to the monitoring port. That activity is referred to as mirroring. Answer B describes the activity that occurs on the device; answer C is incorrect as the NIC is not modified; and answer D is incorrect as switches segment traffic so one port sees only its traffic by default.

14. **B.** 802.11ac operates at 150/200/600Mbps. Answers A, C, and D are incorrect because 802.11a, 802.11i, and 802.11g do not properly operate at the stated speeds in the question.

15. **D.** TKIP was first added to WPA. TKIP was designed to provide more secure encryption than the weak and outdated WEP standard. Answers A, B, and C were not the first to add TKIP and are, therefore, incorrect.

Chapter 8

1. **C.** MD5 is a hashing algorithm. Hashing algorithms are used to verify integrity. Answer A is incorrect because DES is a symmetric algorithm and offers confidentiality, Answer B is incorrect because AES is also a symmetric algorithm that offers confidentiality, and Answer D is incorrect because RSA is an asymmetric algorithm that generally offers confidentiality, authentication, and nonrepudiation.

2. **D.** One of the big advantages of symmetric encryption is that it is fast. Answer A is incorrect because symmetric encryption does not offer easy key exchange and must be done out of band. Answer B is incorrect because as the number of participants grows, so does the number of keys. Answer C is incorrect because symmetric encryption does not provide integrity.

3. **B.** Intrusion detection is the best method of monitoring and detecting break-ins or attempts to attack via the Internet. Answer A is incorrect because packet filtering is a type of stateless inspection and can make a decision on only a set of static rules. Answer C is incorrect because stateful inspection is not specifically designed to detect and report hacking activities. Answer D is incorrect because encryption does not meet any of the company's stated goals.

4. **D.** CIPA requires that schools and libraries use Internet filters and implement other measures to protect children from harmful online content. Answer A is incorrect because FERPA protects the privacy of student education records. Answer B is incorrect because FISMA addresses federal agencies. Answer C is incorrect because PCI-DSS covers the protection of credit card data.

5. **C.** While it is true that the RA cannot generate a certificate, it does play a useful role in PKI. Answer A is incorrect because the RA does reduce the load on the CA. Answer B is incorrect because the RA can accept requests. Answer D is incorrect because the RA can verify an owner's identity.

6. **C.** Data security is one of the primary duties of an auditor. This task is achieved by controlling and monitoring data security policies. Answer A is incorrect because auditors are usually not the individuals responsible for implementing security controls. Answer B is incorrect because an auditor is concerned not just with new policies but with all policies. Answer D is incorrect because the IT security group usually handles day-to-day activities of the IDS and the firewall.

7. **A.** Kerberos is an example of single sign-on. Answers B, C, and D all describe methods of centralized authentication.

8. **B.** The lowest level of the military data classification is unclassified. Answers A, C, and D are incorrect because public, sensitive, and available are not the lowest data classification.

9. **B.** A mantrap is a system of doors that is arranged so that when one opens, the others remain locked. Mantraps are typically used in high-security facilities. Answers A, C, and D are incorrect because a honeypot describes a system used to lure in an attacker, a turnstile is used to control access, and a DMZ is used in networking, not physical security.

10. **D.** Asymmetric encryption offers easy key exchange. Answer A is incorrect because it is not as efficient as symmetric encryption. Answer B is incorrect because it is not a part of a hashing algorithm. Answer C is incorrect because asymmetric encryption is not used for bulk data.

Chapter 9

1. **C.** Ensuring that the evidence remains unchanged is one of the most important goals. Answer A is incorrect because the first priority would not be to identify the attacker. Answer B is incorrect because you may or may not want to remove the device from the Internet. In some cases, the system may be left up and running to avoid alerting the attacker. Answer D is incorrect because you may or may not contact the police, depending on the circumstances.

2. **B.** One thing that should not be done is to click on the link, which could lead to malware. Answers A, C, and D are all activities that would be acceptable when dealing with a malicious link.

3. **D.** Change management should dictate a structured controlled process that has preventive controls built in. For example, developers would typically have access to source code. Answer A is incorrect because access controls would be used to prevent access to items such as the production application. Answer B is incorrect because there would be controls in the development environment. For example, individuals responsible for writing the code would not test the code. Although there may be controls in the development process, these must be reviewed by the auditor to verify they are present and implemented correctly; therefore, Answer C is incorrect.

4. **B.** Penetration testing typically follows a structured approach, such as the stages outlined in NIST 800-42. Answer A is incorrect because SOX deals with financial records. Answer C is incorrect because PCI-DSS covers the protection of credit card data. Answer D is incorrect because SSAE-16 is an auditing standard and is not used for penetration testing.

5. **C.** While it is true that any of these activities could be carried out on a weekly basis, the most likely activity would be vulnerability scanning. Answer A is incorrect because penetration testing might be performed once a year. Answer B is incorrect because change management occurs when change occurs, which can be at any time. Answer D is incorrect because rotation of duties might be performed monthly or yearly.

6. **C.** Planning and preparation is the first step of the incident response process. This task should be accomplished before any incident ever occurs. Answers A, B, and D are incorrect because these are not the first steps of the incident response process.

7. **A.** The question describes a double-blind penetration test. Answers B, C, and D do not describe a double-blind penetration test. Blind would describe the situation where only one party knows, and the other options, zero proof and unknown, are not valid choices.

8. **B.** An XSRF attack can occur when a victim is connected to both a legitimate site and a malicious site at the same time. Answers A, C, and D are incorrect because they do not describe an XSRF attack. XSS does not require a connection to both the legitimate site and the malicious site at the same time. A buffer overflow occurs when too much data is placed in the buffer. A TOCTOU attack exploits the time between when something is read and when it is used.

9. **A.** Answer A is correct because fuzzing is a form of black box testing that is carried out when the source code is not available. Answers A, C, and D are incorrect because a code review is performed when the code is available. Reverse engineering is used to tear apart existing code. A decompiler is used to examine the internal operation of an application.

10. **C.** Trend variance detection tools are best used to scan for deviations from normal activity. All other answers are incorrect because bypass label processing can be used to bypass the normal process of reading a file security label. Attack detection tools look for known attack signatures. Audit reduction tools reduce the volume of information to be reviewed.

Index

D

F

J

K

L

O

U

X

Y-Z